mediterranean
cooking

jacqueline clarke and joanna farrow

mediterranean
cooking

a culinary tour of sun-drenched shores with
over 400 dishes from southern europe

HH
HERMES
HOUSE

This edition is published by Hermes House

Hermes House is an imprint of Anness Publishing Ltd
Hermes House, 88–89 Blackfriars Road, London SE1 8HA
tel. 020 7401 2077; fax 020 7633 9499; info@anness.com

© Anness Publishing Ltd 1999, 2002
Published in the USA by Hermes House, Anness Publishing Inc.
27 West 20th Street, New York, NY 10011; fax 212 807 6813

A CIP catalogue record for this book is available from the British Library.

Publisher: Joanna Lorenz
Managing Editor: Linda Fraser
Editor: Emma Gray
Designer: Nigel Partridge
Proofreader: Richard McGinlay
Illustrator: Anna Koska

The majority of the recipes for this book were provided by Jacqueline Clark and Joanna Farrow; other recipes were
contributed by Angela Boggiano, Jacqueline Clark, Carole Clements, Roz Denny, Christine France, Silvano Franco,
Rebekah Hassan, Christine Ingram, Judy Jackson, Soheila Kimberley, Lesley Mackley, Maggie Mayhew, Anne Sheasby,
Steven Wheeler, Elizabeth Wolf-Cohen, Jeni Wright.

The majority of the photographs in this book were taken by Michelle Garrett, assisted by Dulce Ribiero; other
photographs were taken by William Adams-Lingwood, Karl Adamson, Edward Allwright, John Heseltine, Amanda
Heywood, Janine Hosegood, Patrick McLeavey.

Previously published as *Mediterranean*

1 3 5 7 9 10 8 6 4 2

NOTES

For all recipes, quantities are given in both metric and imperial measures and, where appropriate, measures are also
given in standard cups and spoons. Follow one set, but not a mixture, because they are not interchangeable.

Standard spoon and cup measures are level.
1 tsp = 5ml, 1 tbsp = 15ml, 1 cup = 250ml/8fl oz

Australian standard tablespoons are 20ml. Australian readers should use 3 tsp in place of 1 tbsp for measuring small
quantities of gelatine, cornflour, salt, etc.

CONTENTS

INTRODUCTION

The countries bounded by the Mediterranean sea
produce some of the finest food the world has to
offer — set sail with us on a culinary tour.

Azure skies, even bluer seas, white-gold sands, bright, whitewashed walls, the vibrant reds, greens, yellows, purples and oranges of the flowers, fruit and vegetables on display in the market – these are the paint palette colours of the Mediterranean. These evocative images are familiar to many of us, although, of course, we will not all be thinking of the same country – after all, there are fifteen to consider, surrounding the sea itself. A quick tour will take us from the shores of Spain, to France, Italy, Greece, Turkey, Syria, Lebanon, Israel, and into Africa to Egypt, Libya, Tunisia, Algeria and Morocco. The islands of Malta and Cyprus are truly Mediterranean, encircled by the sea. Nor does it end there – the influence of the Mediterranean stretches far beyond its shores, into the Middle East as far as Iran.

Centuries before Christ, the area surrounding the Mediterranean sea was colonized by the Phoenicians, Greeks and Romans, who shared a basic cultivation of wheat, olives and grapes. These, in turn, became bread,

ABOVE: A grove of old olive trees lit by the afternoon sun in Southern Provence.

oil and wine, three components which are still very important in today's Mediterranean diet. With the building of ships came import and export, and the various countries began a cross-pollination of crops, ingredients and recipes. Spices and flavourings were introduced through North Africa and Arabia, and saffron, cloves, chillies, ginger and allspice continue to be popular all over the Mediterranean, appearing in sweet and savoury dishes alike. Nuts, too, are common to many of the countries, almonds, pistachio and pine nuts proving particularly popular as they are native to the region.

When thinking of Mediterranean food, however, it is the fresh fruit, vegetables and herbs which immediately spring to mind. Open-air markets from Marseilles to Morocco are a feast for the senses. Fabulous arrays of tomatoes, aubergines, courgettes, peaches, figs, garlic and pungent herbs such as basil and thyme are tantaliz-ingly displayed. To add to the experience the hot sun beats down, drawing out the flavours and scents. Mediterranean cooking depends on the freshest of ingre-dients; it is honest, simple and prepared with respect.

Children learn from a young age that food is not mere fuel, but one of life's pleasures, to be savoured and celebrated. Meals tend to be relaxed affairs, often eaten outdoors, where the scents and colours of a sun-drenched garden provide the perfect backdrop for a table spread with food that is as healthy as it is good to eat: fresh fish, often grilled or baked and served simply with just a squeeze of lemon; vitamin-rich vegetables and fruit and complex carbohydrates like pasta. Meat tends to play a minor role, except on special occasions.

ABOVE: *Watermelons and other gourds lie piled in the sun in a Greek market.*

BELOW: Glossy green leaves shade juicy oranges in a grove near Seville.

Recent research has highlighted just how healthy this way of eating is. So much so, that the term Mediterranean diet has become synonymous with sen-sible eating. Olive oil is at the heart of this approach; high in mono-unsaturated fats, it plays a role in lowering cholesterol levels and is credited with being one of the reasons why the incidence of coronary heart disease is relatively low in Mediterranean countries.

Olive oil – like wine – is not a single, uniform ingre-dient, but many; each region boasting its own speciality, from the golden Spanish varieties to the deep greens of some Greek, Provençal and Italian oils. Colour is not really an indication of quality; oils, like wines, need to be tasted, and flavours vary immensely.

The peoples of the Mediterranean have provided us with a vast and wonderful repertoire of recipes, ancient and new, and it is their love and respect for good food that is celebrated in this book. In this wonderful collec-tion you will find traditional dishes such as Gazpacho, Ratatouille, Greek Salad and Provençal Beef and Olive Daube alongside more contemporary creations like Grilled Vegetable Terrine, Pan-fried Red Mullet with Basil and Citrus, Mushroom and Pesto Pizza and Turkish Delight Ice Cream.

You only need travel as far as your kitchen to explore the true taste of the Mediterranean.

INGREDIENTS

Mediterranean markets are sheer delight. Colourful displays of seasonal fruit and vegetables vie for your attention alongside stalls selling hams, cheeses, oils and herbs. Fresh fish is displayed on crushed ice, and culinary advice is freely offered.

VEGETABLES

Vegetables have always played an important role in Mediterranean cooking. They are sometimes served as dishes in their own right, and sometimes as accompaniments. Either way, the range of imaginative vegetable recipes from all over the Mediterranean is infinite.

ARTICHOKES There are two different types of artichoke, the globe and the Jerusalem, neither of which is in any way related to the other. The globe artichoke belongs to the thistle family and is common throughout the Mediterranean. It appears as different varieties, depending on the country, and ranges from tiny purple plants with tapered leaves, which are so tender that they can be eaten raw, to large bright or pale green globes, whose cooked leaves are pulled off one by one by the diner, who strips off the succulent flesh at the base with his or her teeth. The base is also edible. Baby varieties are completely edible and are sometimes eaten raw.

Globe artichokes were once thought to be aphrodisiacs, and women were forbidden to eat them.

They may not win any beauty contests, but Jerusalem artichokes taste delicious.

Globe artichokes are at their best in summer. Whichever variety you are buying, look for tightly packed leaves, as open leaves indicate that they are too mature. Look, too, for a very fresh colour. When an artichoke is old, the tips of the leaves will turn brown. If possible, buy artichokes that are still attached to their stems, as these will stay fresh for longer. Artichokes will keep fresh for several days if you place the stalks in water. If they have no stalks, wrap them in clear film and keep in the vegetable drawer of the fridge for a day or two.

The Jerusalem Artichoke is an entirely different vegetable. It is, in fact, a tuber, belonging to the sunflower family, and has nothing to do with Jerusalem. One explanation is that its name is a corruption of *girasole*, "sunflower", because its yellow flower turns towards the sun. Jerusalem artichokes look rather like knobbly potatoes, and can be treated as such. They have a lovely distinctive flavour and are good in soups. They are also delicious baked, braised, sautéed or puréed.

Buy asparagus spears of uniform thickness, so that they cook evenly.

ASPARAGUS Asparagus has been cultivated in the Mediterranean for hundreds of years and is still highly prized there as a luxury vegetable. It has a short growing season, from spring to early summer, and is really only worth eating during this period. Both green and white asparagus are cultivated. The green variety is grown above ground so that the entire spear is bright green and is harvested when it is about 15cm/6in high. The fat white spears with their pale yellow tips are grown under mounds of soil to protect them from the light, and harvested almost as soon as the tips appear above the soil to retain their pale colour.

Asparagus spears can be boiled, steamed or roasted in olive oil, and served as a first course with butter and freshly grated Parmesan, or with a vinaigrette. When served as an accompaniment, they can be dipped in egg and breadcrumbs and fried. Asparagus tips also make a luxury addition to risotto. Allow about eight medium spears per serving as a first course and always buy spears of uniform thickness.

AUBERGINES Although aubergines originated in Asia, they feature in dishes from every Mediterranean country. The plump purple variety is the most common. Look for firm, taut, shiny-skinned specimens with green stalks.

Some people believe sliced aubergines should be salted for about 30 minutes and drained before cooking, which helps to extract bitter juices. Others maintain that this is unnecessary. Salting does stop the aubergine from absorbing large quantities of oil during cooking, so on balance it seems worth doing.

When buying aubergines, look for specimens that feel quite heavy for their size, as a light aubergine may indicate a dry, spongy inside and could well contain a lot of seeds. Do not buy aubergines with wrinkled or damaged skins. Aubergines will keep in the fridge for up to a week and are very versatile vegetables. They can be grilled, baked, stuffed, stewed and sautéed, either on their own or with other vegetables and since they absorb flavours well, they can be used with most seasonings.

Glossy and good to eat, aubergines are among the most popular Mediterranean vegetables.

Broad beans are at their best when they are small and tender. Young ones can be eaten pods and all.

BROAD OR FAVA BEANS In the spring these beans are often exported from various Mediterranean countries to countries whose growing seasons are later.

The beans are at their best when they are small and tender, with a bittersweet flavour. When young, they can be cooked and eaten, pods and all, or shelled and eaten raw with cheese, as in Italy. When the beans are older, they are shelled, cooked, and sometimes peeled. Cooked broad beans have a milder flavour than raw.

Dried broad beans are popular in the Middle East where they are cooked with spices or added to stews.

COURGETTES These baby marrows have shiny green skin, a sweet delicate flavour and a crisp texture. They are at their best when they are small. They can be sliced or grated and eaten raw, or they can be cooked, combining well with other Mediterranean vegetables.

Courgettes can also be battered and deep-fried, made into fritters or served with a white sauce flavoured with Parmesan or nutmeg. Served cold with a mint-flavoured vinaigrette or tomato sauce, they can be served as part of a first course. They can also be halved and stuffed with a meat or vegetable filling.

The larger courgettes become, the less flavour they have. When buying, choose firm, shiny specimens. Do not buy flabby courgettes, or those with blemished skins. Yellow varieties, sometimes called "banana courgettes" are sometimes available and, although there is no difference in flavour, they make a pretty alternative to the usual green variety.

In Italy and France, the golden courgette flowers are highly prized; they are frequently stuffed and cooked, or deep-fried in batter. Courgettes are available almost all year round, but are at their best in spring and summer. Allow 250g/9oz courgettes per serving. They will keep in the vegetable drawer of the fridge for up to one week.

FENNEL Originally a medicinal remedy for flatulence, fennel has become one of the most important Mediterranean vegetables, especially in Italy.

Bulb or Florence fennel – so called to distinguish it from the feathery green herb, resembles a fat white celery root with overlapping leaves and green, wispy fronds. It has a delicate but distinctive flavour of aniseed and a crisp, refreshing texture. It can be eaten raw, dressed with a vinaigrette or served in a mixed salad. It can also

For the finest flavour and texture, choose young courgettes that are firm, not flabby.

be cooked – either sautéed, baked or braised. When it is cooked, the aniseed flavour becomes more subtle and the texture resembles cooked celery. Braised fennel is particularly good with white fish or chicken, but it is also delicious served as a separate vegetable course, either roasted, or baked with a cheese sauce.

Fennel is available all year round. Choose firm, rounded bulbs, in which the outer layers are crisp and white, not wizened and yellow. Some people claim that the plumper "female" bulbs have the better flavour. If possible, buy fennel bulbs with their topknots of feathery green fronds intact, which you can chop and use for garnishing or as a herb in any dish in which you would use dill.

Whole fennel bulbs will keep in the fridge for up to a week. Once cut, however, they must be used immediately, or the cut surfaces will discolour and the texture will soften. Allow a whole bulb per serving. If using raw, toss the slices in lemon juice to prevent them from discolouring.

Wild mushrooms are still collected in many parts of the Mediterranean. These are oyster mushrooms.

GARLIC Sold in "strings" or as separate bulbs, the main consideration when buying garlic is that the cloves are plump and firm. Garlic is one of the most vital ingredients in Mediterranean cookery and there are few recipes in which its addition would be out of place. Used crushed, sliced or even whole, garlic develops a smooth, gentle flavour with long, slow cooking. Used raw in salads, sauces and mayonnaise, garlic packs a punch.

MUSHROOMS Man has collected and eaten mushrooms for centuries, and people still collect wild mushrooms in many parts of the Mediterranean region. The varieties used in Mediterranean cooking are button, open cup and flat, but regional wild species, such as ceps, chanterelles and oyster mushrooms are to be found in the markets during autumn.

Mushrooms can be finely sliced and eaten raw, dressed with extra virgin olive oil. Or they can be brushed with olive oil and grilled.

Mushrooms should never be washed or they will become waterlogged and mushy. To clean them, cut off the earthy base of the stalk and lightly brush the caps with a soft brush or wipe them clean with a damp cloth.

Never store mushrooms in a plastic bag, as they will sweat and turn slimy and mouldy. Put them in a paper bag and keep in the vegetable drawer of the fridge for one or two days.

Delicious raw or cooked, fennel is a versatile vegetable. It is particularly good braised.

OKRA This unusual vegetable, sometimes known as lady's fingers, is a five-sided green pod with a tapering end. It has a subtle flavour and a gelatinous texture which helps to thicken and enrich certain dishes. Used in Middle Eastern and Greek cookery, its most successful partners are garlic, onion and tomatoes. Choose small, firm pods and use sliced or whole in cooking.

ONIONS The starting point of so many dishes, the onion is invaluable to Mediterranean cooking. There are many varieties, differing in colour, size and strength of flavour, from mild yellow onions to stronger-flavoured white onions. For salads, or when onion is to be used raw, choose red or mild white globes, which have a sweet, mellow flavour. Large Spanish onions have a mild flavour, too, and are a good choice when a large quantity of onion is called for in a recipe. Baby onions are perfect for adding whole to stews, or for serving as a vegetable dish on their own. Large onions can be stuffed with minced meat and herbs or cheese, and baked.

Okra has an unusual texture and is an acquired taste, but is popular in Greek and Middle Eastern cookery.

There are many different types of onions, be sure to choose the appropriate variety for each recipe.

You may be lucky enough to find young fresh onions in markets. These are sold in bunches like large, bulbous spring onions, complete with their leaves. They have a mild flavour and can be used for pickling or in salads. They will keep in the fridge for three or four days, but should be wrapped tightly to prevent their smell pervading everything else.

Older onions have thin, almost papery skins that should be unblemished. The onions should feel firm and should not be sprouting. They quickly deteriorate once cut, so buy assorted sizes, then you can use a small onion when the recipe calls for only a small amount. Stored in a dry, airy place, onions will keep for several weeks.

Some onions are easier to peel than others. The skins of red and yellow onions can be removed without much difficulty, but white onions may need to be plunged into boiling water for 30 seconds to make peeling easier.

For most cooked dishes, onions should be sliced or chopped, but for salads they are sliced into very thin rings.

In Mediterranean cooking, onions are seldom browned, which can give them a slightly bitter taste, but are generally sweated gently in olive oil to add a mellow flavour to a multitude of dishes.

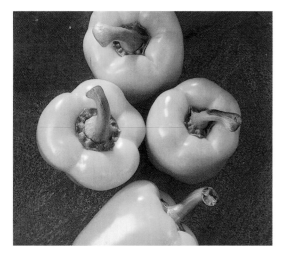

Peppers are a delicious addition to salad, they add a lovely crunch and a wonderful colour, ranging from green to red.

PEPPERS Generically known as capsicums, the shape of these peppers gives them the alternative name of "bell peppers". They come in a range of colours, including green, red, yellow, orange and even a purplish-black – and add colour to markets throughout the Mediterranean region – though they all have much the same sweetish flavour and crunchy texture. They are a very healthy food, being rich in vitamin C and a good source of fibre. Peppers can be used raw or lightly roasted in salads or as an antipasto, and can be cooked in a variety of ways – roasted and dressed with olive oil or vinaigrette dressing and capers, stewed, marinated in olive oil, or stuffed and baked. To make the most of their flavour, grill peppers until charred, then rub off and discard the skins. Peppers have a great affinity with other Mediterranean ingredients, such as olives, capers, aubergines, courgettes, tomatoes and anchovies.

RADICCHIO This red chicory is one of the most popular salad leaves in Mediterranean countries, especially in Italy. There are several varieties, but the most common is the round type which looks like a lettuce. The leaves are crisp and pleasantly bitter and can be eaten raw or cooked.

SPINACH This dark green leafy vegetable is popular in Mediterranean countries. Originally cultivated in Persia in the 6th century, it was brought to Europe by Arab traders some thousand years later. Cooked or raw, it is a particularly good source of vitamins A and C, and is also rich in minerals, especially iron.

Young spinach leaves can be eaten raw and need little preparation, but older leaves should be washed in several changes of water and then picked over and the tough stalks removed.

Spinach is used in Middle Eastern pastries, Spanish tapas, French tarts and many more dishes – eggs and fish, for instance, make good partners. All types of spinach should look very fresh and green, with no signs of wilting. The leaves should be unblemished and the stalks crisp. Spinach leaves wilt down to about half their weight during cooking, so you always need to buy far more than you think you will need – if the spinach is to be cooked, allow 250g/9oz raw weight per person. Using a heavy-pan will aid even cooking.

Mediterranean cooks have a marvellous way with spinach, often using it in pastries.

Buy tomatoes on the vine if possible, as they will have ripened naturally.

TOMATOES Some of the best tomatoes in the world are to be found in Mediterranean markets, so it is hardly surprising that it is impossible to imagine Mediterranean food without them. But these "golden apples" were unknown in the Mediterranean until the 16th century, when they were brought from Mexico. In some countries, they were known as "love-apples" because they resembled the heart. Their popularity soon spread and they were cultivated all over the Mediterranean region and incorporated into the cooking of almost every country.

Sun-ripened and full of flavour, tomatoes come in many varieties – beefsteak tomatoes, plum tomatoes, cherry tomatoes and baby pear-shaped ones. Bright red fruits literally bursting with aroma and flavour, tomatoes are essential ingredients in so many Mediterranean dishes. They are used in so many different ways that it is hard to know where to start. They can be eaten raw, sliced and served with a trickle of extra virgin olive oil and some torn basil leaves. They are the red component in insalata tricolore, partnering white mozzarella and green

basil to make up the colours of the Italian flag. Raw ripe tomatoes can be chopped with herbs and garlic to make a fresh-tasting pasta sauce. Tomatoes are at their best in summer, when they have ripened naturally in the sun.

Choose your tomatoes according to how you wish to prepare them. Salad tomatoes should be firm and easy to slice. The best tomatoes for cooking are plum tomatoes, which have a superb flavour and hold their shape well. Beefsteak tomatoes are the best for stuffing. Tomatoes will only ripen properly if they are left for long enough on the vine, so try to buy "vine-ripened" varieties. As well as fresh tomatoes, canned and sun-dried tomatoes are invaluable store cupboard items.

VINE LEAVES These pretty leaves have been used in cooking for hundreds of years. They can be stuffed with a variety of fillings and also make perfect, and very decorative, wrappers for meat, fish and poultry. Fresh leaves must be young and soft. If using brined vine leaves, soak them in hot water for 20–30 minutes before stuffing or wrapping.

Vine leaves make ideal wrappers for rice, and are famously used to make the Greek dolmades.

FRUIT

DATES Plump and slightly wrinkled fresh dates have a rich honey-like flavour and dense texture. They are delicious stoned and served with Greek yogurt. The dried dates can be used in the same way, but fewer will be needed as the flavour is very concentrated.

FIGS Fresh figs are delicious served on their own, but they have an affinity with nuts such as walnuts, pistachios and almonds. They can be served raw as a first course with Parma ham or salami, or with Greek yogurt and honey or stuffed with raspberry coulis or mascarpone and served as a dessert. Poached in a little water or wine flavoured with cinnamon or nutmeg, they make an excellent accompaniment to duck, game or lamb. Ripe figs are extremely delicate and do not travel well, so it is hard to find imported fruit at a perfect stage of maturity, but they can be ripened at home, by storing them on a high shelf. In season throughout the Mediterranean, you will find delectable local figs that are just ripe for eating. They should be soft and yielding, but not squashy.

There are few fruits more delicious than ripe figs, but treat them with care, as they bruise very easily.

Grapes grow all over the Mediterranean region, and make the perfect finale to a simple meal.

GRAPES Grapes grow all over the Mediterranean. Despite their high calorific value, they are extremely good for you. Fresh grapes are rich in potassium, iron, enzymes and vitamins. Dessert grapes are best eaten on their own or as an accompaniment to cheese, but they can also be used in pastries or as a fruit garnish for cooked quails, guinea fowl or other poultry. The seeds are pressed into grapeseed oil, which has a neutral taste and is high in polyunsaturated fatty acids. Choosing white, black or red grapes is simply a matter of preference. Beneath the skin, the flesh is always pale green and juicy. Buy bunches of grapes with fruit which is of equal size and not too densely packed on the stalk. Check that none is withered or bad. The skins should have a delicate, not heavy bloom, and be firm to the touch. Try to eat one grape from a bunch to see how they taste before buying. Grapes should be washed immediately after purchase, then placed in a bowl and kept in the fridge for up to three days. Keeping them in a plastic bag causes them to become over-ripe very quickly.

Melons that ripen naturally in the sun have a wonderful perfume and flavour.

LEMONS These bright yellow citrus fruits originated in India and Malaysia and were brought by the Assyrians to Greece, which in turn took them to Italy. The Greeks and Romans greatly appreciated their culinary and medicinal qualities. Later seafarers ate them in large quantities to protect against scurvy, and society ladies used them as a beauty treatment to whiten their skin, bleach their hair and redden their lips. They are rich in vitamin C and have an aromatic flavour which enhances almost any dish. Lemons are an extraordinarily versatile fruit. The juice can be squeezed to make a refreshing drink, or it can be added to tea, dressings and sauces. It is an antioxidant, and prevents discolouration when brushed over fruits and vegetables which have a tendency to turn brown when cut. A squeeze of lemon juice makes a difference to bland foods, such as fish, poultry, veal or certain vegetables. Its acidity also helps to bring out the

A bowl of fresh lemons is a common sight in the Mediterranean kitchen.

flavour of other fruits. The zest makes a wonderfully aromatic flavouring for cakes and pastries, and is an essential ingredient in many desserts. Quartered lemons are served with fried fish and other foods fried in batter. Depending on the variety, lemons may have thick indented skins, or be perfectly smooth. Their appearance does not affect the flavour, but they should feel heavy for their size, which indicates plenty of juice. If you intend to use the zest, buy unwaxed lemons. Lemons will keep in the fridge for up to two weeks.

MELONS This fruit comes in many different sizes, shapes and colours – cantaloupe, charentais, galia, honeydew, ogen, orange- and green-fleshed varieties, and the wonderful pink watermelon. Melons can be eaten as a starter, sometimes accompanied by wafer-thin prosciutto or cured meats. In the Mediterranean, melons and watermelons are often served as dessert fruit on their own, but sometimes appear as part of a fruit salad. Ripe melons should yield to gentle pressure from your thumbs at the stalk end and have a fragrant, slightly sweet scent. If they smell highly perfumed and musky, they will probably be over-ripe. A melon should feel heavy for its size and the skin should not be bruised or damaged. Melons will ripen quickly at room temperature and should be eaten within two or three days.

Oranges – and orange rind – are favourite flavourings, used in savoury as well as sweet dishes.

ORANGES Many varieties of the orange are grown all over the Mediterranean, particularly in Spain. Seville oranges, the bitter marmalade variety, have a very short season, just after Christmas. The best of the orange flavour comes from the zest – the outer layer of the skin – this is often included in recipes using oranges. Sweet oranges are used for both sweet and savoury recipes and are a favourite addition to salads. Oranges are available all year round, but are at their best in winter. They should have unblemished shiny skins and feel heavy for their size, which indicates that they contain plenty of juice and that the flesh is not dry. If you intend to candy the rind or to incorporate it into a recipe, choose unwaxed oranges. Oranges will keep at room temperature for a week and for at least two weeks in the fridge. Bring them back to room temperature before eating.

PEACHES AND NECTARINES These are among the most delicious summer fruits. Peaches need plenty of sun to ripen them and grow in France, Spain and Italy. There are yellow-, pink- and white-fleshed varieties, with velvety skin. Look for bruise-free specimens that just give when squeezed gently. Nectarines are smooth-skinned, with all the luscious flavour of peaches. They also come in yellow and white varieties and, like peaches, the white nectarines have a finer flavour. Some people prefer nectarines to peaches as a dessert fruit because they do not require peeling. Peaches and nectarines are interchangeable in cooked dishes. They can both be macerated in fortified wine or spirits or poached in white wine and syrup. They also have a special affinity with almonds. Peaches are also delicious served with raspberries, or made into fruit drinks and ice creams and sorbets. Peaches are in season during the Mediterranean summer. Make sure they are ripe, but not too soft, with unwrinkled and unblemished skins. They should have a sweet, intense scent. Peaches and nectarines bruise very easily, so try to buy those that have been kept in compartmented trays rather than piled into punnets. Do not keep peaches and nectarines for more than a day or two. If they are very ripe, store them in the fridge.

A nectarine or peach makes the perfect dessert, either fresh or baked.

19

The best Parmesan has the words "Parmigiano Reggiano" stamped on the rind.

DAIRY PRODUCE

CHEESE The variety of cheeses from Mediterranean countries is huge and diverse, ranging from fresh mild cheeses such as mozzarella, to soft, blue-veined ones such as Gorgonzola and aged hard types with a strong, mature flavour such as Parmesan and Pecorino. Cheeses are made from cow's, goat's, ewe's and, in the case of Italian mozzarella, buffalo's milk. Cream cheese is also common to many countries, varying a little according to the milk and the method used for preparing it.

Perhaps the best known Mediterranean cheese is Parmesan. There are two types, Parmigiano Reggiano and Grana Padano, but the former is infinitely superior. A really fine Parmesan may be aged for up to seven years, during which time it matures, becoming pale golden with a slightly granular, flaky texture and a nutty, mildly salty flavour. Always buy Parmesan in the piece and grate it yourself.

YOGURT This live product (pasteurized milk combined with two beneficial bacteria) is perhaps most associated with the Middle Eastern countries, where it is used extensively in cooking. Greek yogurt is thick and creamy, and French yogurt is traditionally of the set variety. Yogurt is used as a marinade, a dip and to enrich soups and stews. It can be made from goat's, ewe's or cow's milk.

FISH AND SEAFOOD

RED MULLET Very popular along the coasts of the Mediterranean, the red mullet is a pretty fish. It is usually treated simply by grilling over a wood fire, often with the liver still inside to add flavour.

SALT COD Most salt cod is prepared in Norway, Iceland and Newfoundland and then exported to Mediterranean countries. It looks very unappetizing, and has a pungent smell, but after being soaked for 48 hours and cooked in the Mediterranean style, it is delicious.

SEA BASS This is quite an expensive fish and is usually sold and cooked whole. The flesh is soft and delicate and needs careful attention when cooking. Methods include poaching, steaming, grilling and baking.

SQUID Popular in the Mediterranean region, particularly in Spain, Italy and Portugal, squid vary in size from the tiny specimens that can be eaten whole, to larger varieties, which are good for stuffing, grilling or stewing. The flesh is sweet and, when carefully cooked, tender.

When buying fresh fish, bright eyes, fresh red gills and firmly attached scales are signs to look out for.

SWORDFISH This delicious fish is widely available through-out the Mediterranean. Swordfish steaks can be very large, so do not automatically order one per person. Brush them with oil when grilling.

TUNA An oily fish belonging to the same family as the mackerel. The flesh, which is sold in steaks or large pieces, is dark red and very dense, and has a tendency to dry out when cooked. Marinating before cooking helps to keep the flesh moist, as does basting while cooking. Tuna can be baked, fried, grilled or stewed.

CRAB There are thousands of species of crab around the world. In the Mediterranean countries, brown and spider crabs are the most common. The meat of the crab is divided into two sorts – brown and white. Crabs are often sold cooked and dressed, which means that the crab is ready to eat. Choose cooked crabs which are heavy for their size and therefore meaty.

MUSSELS Available in the Mediterranean through the win-ter, mussels usually need to be scrubbed and have the beard – the hairy tuft attached to the shell – removed. Any open mussels should be discarded if they do not close after a sharp tap, as this indicates that they are old and therefore should not be eaten. Mussels vary in size from very small to quite large, and the shell can be blue-black to dappled brown. They are easy to cook – just steam for a few minutes in a covered pan. Discard any that fail to open after cooking.

PRAWNS These vary enormously in size. The classic Mediterranean prawn is very large, about 20cm/8in long and reddish brown in colour when raw. When prawns are cooked over a fierce heat, such as a barbecue, the shell is often left on to protect the flesh from charring. Prawns can be bought ready-cooked and frozen.

Mediterranean prawns are a treat. Cooked fresh from the sea, with garlic and olive oil, they are delicious.

GRAINS

BULGUR WHEAT Also known as burghul, this cereal has been partially processed, so cooks quickly.

COUSCOUS This semolina product simply needs moisten-ing, then steaming to swell the grains. It is usually served with a spicy meat or vegetable stew.

RICE There are many varieties of this world-wide staple food. In Italy, which produces more and a greater vari-ety of rice than anywhere else in Europe, there are at least four short-grained types used for risotto, and in Spain, Valencia rice is the preferred variety for paella. In the Middle East rice is served with every meal, either plainly boiled or cooked with saffron and other spices to create fragrant pilaffs.

POLENTA This grainy yellow flour is a type of cornmeal. It is cooked into a kind of porridge with a wide variety of uses. Polenta is available ground to various degrees of coarseness to suit different dishes.

Pasta comes in a remarkable range of shapes and sizes, from tiny soup shells to long strands.

PULSES

CHICK-PEAS This pulse looks like a golden hazelnut and has a nutty flavour. In the Middle East they are made into flour, and in Greece they are puréed to produce a dip. Soak them for 5 hours before cooking, and cook for up to 4 hours until tender. Timing will vary, depending on the age of the chick-peas.

HARICOT BEANS These white beans are quite soft when cooked, and are used in casseroles in Spain, Portugal and France. They need to be soaked for 4 hours before being cooked, and are also good in soups and salads. They taste great with a rich tomato sauce.

LENTILS These come in different sizes and can be yellow, red, brown or green. The tiny green Puy lentils are favoured in France and the brown and red ones in the Middle East, where they are cooked with spices to make dhals. They do not need soaking. Red lentils cook quite quickly – in about 20 minutes, but Puy lentils take considerably longer.

One of the most colourful stalls on the market is the one selling pulses.

PASTA

Pasta is simply the Latin word for "paste", the flour-and-egg-based dough from which it is made. Although a staple of Italian cooking, pasta is also widely used throughout the Mediterranean and has much in common with Chinese noodles, which filtered from China via the Middle Eastern trade routes. In Italy today there are countless varieties of pasta, from flat sheets of lasagne and ribbon noodles to pressed and moulded shapes specifically designed to pocket substantial amounts of the sauce with which they are served. Dried pasta, made from hard durum wheat, is a good standby and keeps for weeks in an airtight container. Fresh pasta has a better flavour and texture, but will only keep for a couple of days, although it can be successfully frozen. Fresh pasta is usually made by hand, using plain white flour enriched with eggs. Commercially, made fresh pasta is made with durum wheat flour, water and eggs. The flavour and texture of all fresh pasta is very delicate, so it is best suited to creamier sauces. Pasta is a wonderfully simple and nutritious staple food. Both fresh and dried pasta can be bought flavoured with tomato, olive, spinach or mushroom paste. Black pasta, made with the addition of squid ink, is increasingly popular. Pasta is easy to make at home if time is allowed for chilling the fresh dough. Rolling it can be done effortlessly using a pasta machine.

Browning pine nuts, either under the grill or in a dry frying pan, really brings out their wonderful flavour.

NUTS

ALMONDS Cultivated commercially in Spain, Italy and Portugal, the almond is widely used in the Arab-influenced countries. It is an important ingredient in sweet pastries and is often added to savoury dishes, too. Almonds are sold fresh in their green velvety shells in Mediterranean markets.

HAZELNUTS Used in desserts and sweetmeats, hazelnuts are particularly good in halva.

PINE NUTS These little nuts are used in both sweet and savoury dishes, and are one of the principal ingredients in pesto, the basil sauce from Italy.

PISTACHIO NUTS These colourful nuts originated in the Middle East. They have flesh which ranges from pale to dark green, and a papery, purple-tinged skin. Pistachio nuts have a subtle flavour and are used in a wide range of dishes, from pastries to ice creams and nougat.

WALNUTS These versatile nuts are used in both sweet and savoury dishes. Walnut oil is a popular addition to salad dressings in France. Elsewhere, walnuts are chopped and added to pastries, ground to make sauces, or eaten fresh as "wet" walnuts.

HERBS

BASIL One of the herbs most crucial to Mediterranean cooking, particularly in Italian dishes, basil has a wonderful aroma and flavour. The sweet, tender leaves, sometimes as large as cabbage leaves, have a great affinity with tomatoes, aubergines, peppers, courgettes and cheese. A handful of torn leaves enlivens a green salad and is a great addition to a tomato sandwich. Basil is perhaps best known as the basis of pesto, that glorious green sauce which is so widely used in Italy and beyond. Pesto also includes pine nuts and olive oil, but it is basil that gives it its incomparable flavour. The herb is easy to grow in pots and should be picked just before use, though it will not survive the colder winter months outdoors if the temperature drops. Tear the leaves, rather than chopping them, if possible. Chopping the leaves can reduce them to an unappealing pulp and sometimes leave an unpleasant flavour from the metal on the leaves, a taste that may transfer to the dish you are preparing and spoil it.

Under the Mediterranean sun, basil leaves grow better and bigger than they do in colder climes.

Tied in bunches, chives look as good as they taste.

BAY LEAVES Taken from the bay shrub or tree, these are widely used to flavour slow-cooked recipes like stocks, soups and stews. They are also added to marinades, threaded on to kebab skewers, thrown on the barbecue to invigorate the smoky flavour, or used for decoration. One or two young bay leaves, infused with milk or cream in puddings, add a warm, pungent flavour. They do not soften with cooking, so it is advisable to remove them before serving.

CHERVIL This delicate gentle herb with its lacy leaves, tastes rather like a mild parsley and needs to be used generously to impart sufficient flavour. Widely used in French cooking, it works well in herb butters and with eggs and cheese.

CHIVES Thin stems with a mild onion flavour, chives are one of the easiest herbs to grow. They are cut in short lengths and most often used raw.

BOUQUET GARNI A collection of herbs that classically includes parsley, thyme and bay; although other herbs like rosemary and marjoram can be added, different regions vary the combination of herbs. Bouquet garni is available dried, tied in muslin bundles or in "teabag-like" sachets. Fresh bouquet garni can be tied together with string for easy removal from the dish before serving.

CORIANDER Huge bundles of fresh coriander are a familiar sight in Eastern Mediterranean markets, their warm, pungent aroma rising at the merest touch. The leaves impart a distinctive flavour to soups, stews, sauces and spicy dishes when added towards the end of cooking. They are also used sparingly in salads and yogurt dishes.

Oregano grows wild all over the Mediterranean. Its pungent scent seems to linger in the air.

DILL Feathery dill leaves have a mild aniseed taste, popular in the Eastern Mediterranean, particularly Greece and Turkey. Dill is chopped into fish and chicken dishes, as well as stuffings and rice. Pickled gherkins and cucumbers are often flavoured with dill.

MARJORAM A versatile herb of which there are several varieties. It grows wild and is also cultivated and goes very well with red meats, game and tomato dishes.

MINT One of the oldest and most widely used herbs. In Greece, chopped mint accompanies other herbs to enhance stuffed vegetables and fish dishes, and in Turkey and the Middle East finely chopped mint adds a cooling tang to yogurt dishes as well as teas and iced drinks.

A rosemary bush is a gift to any gardener who likes cooking Mediterranean food.

OREGANO is a wild form of marjoram, with a far more pungent flavour. The name means "joy of the mountains" in Greek, which is appropriate, as the scent makes walking in the mountains pure pleasure. Oregano is a very popular herb, widely used throughout the Mediterranean region.

PARSLEY Flat leaf parsley is far more widely used in Mediterranean cookery than the tightly curled variety. Mixed with garlic and lemon zest, it makes a wonderfully aromatic gremolata, a colourful, refreshing garnish for scattering over tomato and rice dishes.

ROSEMARY Cut from the pretty flowering shrub, rosemary grows well throughout the Mediterranean and is most widely used in meat cookery. Several sprigs, tucked under a roast chicken or lamb with plenty of garlic, impart an inviting warm, sweet flavour.

SAGE Native to the Northern Mediterranean, soft, velvety sage leaves vary in colour from yellow to green to purple and have a strong, distinctive flavour which is used sparingly in meat and game dishes. Sage can be added to stuffings, nut dishes or pan-fried with pigeon and liver.

TARRAGON Long, lank tarragon leaves have a very individual aroma and flavour, most widely appreciated in French cookery. The herb is used generously in chicken and egg dishes, and with salmon and trout. Tarragon-flavoured vinegar makes a delicious ingredient in a good mayonnaise or Hollandaise sauce.

THYME There are many types of thyme, from lemon thyme to plain garden thyme, ranging in colour from yellow to grey-green. A few sprigs will add a warm, earthy flavour to slow-cooked meat and poultry dishes, pâtés, marinades, soups and vegetable dishes.

SPICES

CARDAMOM Usually a spice associated with Indian cookery, the use of cardamom extends as far as the Eastern Mediterranean. The pods should be pounded to release the black seeds, which are bruised to release the flavour.

CHILLIES These are the small fiery relatives of the sweet pepper family. Mediterranean chillies are generally milder in flavour than the unbearably fiery South American ones but should still be used with caution.

CINNAMON Cinnamon sticks, the thin curled bark of the cinnamon tree, has an aromatic, sweet flavour that is used extensively in the Eastern Mediterranean for savoury dishes, and to infuse milk puddings. Ground cinnamon is convenient but lacks the intensity of stick cinnamon.

CORIANDER SEEDS The seeds of the coriander herb have a warm, slightly orangey flavour that is essential to many dishes of the Eastern Mediterranean. Their flavour can be accentuated if they are crushed before use and used in either sweet or savoury dishes.

Nutmeg has a wonderful warm flavour. Buy whole nutmegs and grate them as needed.

CUMIN SEEDS These dark, spindly seeds are frequently married with coriander when making spicy dishes that are typical of North Africa and the Eastern Mediterranean.

MACE This is the thin, lacy covering of nutmeg, available ground to a powder or as thin "blades". It has a gentler flavour than nutmeg.

NUTMEG Nutmeg's beautiful, sweet warm aroma makes a good addition to sweet and savoury dishes, particularly with spinach, cheese and eggs or in terrines and pâtés.

PEPPER There are several different types of peppercorns, all of which are picked from the pepper vine, a plant unrelated to the capsicum family. Black peppercorns have the strongest flavour. Green peppercorns are fresh unripe berries.

SAFFRON The colour and flavour of this exotic spice is indispensable in many Mediterranean dishes, such as French fish stews, Spanish rice dishes and Italian risottos. Crush the strands and soak them in boiling water before use.

PRESERVES, PICKLES AND FLAVOURINGS

CAPERS These are the pickled buds of a shrub native to the Mediterranean region. The best are those preserved in salt rather than brine or vinegar. When capers are roughly chopped, their sharp piquant tang is used to cut the richness of lamb, enliven fish sauces and flavour salads and pastes such as tapenade.

HARISSA A fiery, hot paste used mostly in North African cookery. It is made from a blend of chillies, garlic, cumin, coriander and cayenne and can be bought in small jars.

HONEY An ancient sweetener that depends on the flowers on which the bees have fed for its individual fragrance and flavour. The Turks and Greeks use it in their syrupy pastries and puddings and small quantities are added to some savoury dishes.

PRESERVED LEMONS AND LIMES Lemons or limes preserved in salt develop a rich, mellow flavour. To make preserved

lemons, scrub and quarter the fruits almost through to the base and rub the cut sides with salt. Pack together tightly into a large sterilized jar. Half fill the jar with more salt, adding some bay leaves, peppercorns and cinnamon, and any other spices, if liked. Cover completely with lemon juice. Top with a lid and store for two weeks, shaking the jar daily. Add a little olive oil to seal and use within one to six months, washing off the salt before use.

Preserved lemons give a mellow flavour to Mediterranean dishes.

26

One of the Mediterranean's most important ingredients, olive oil has been called liquid gold.

ROSE WATER This distilled essence of rose petals is used mainly in Eastern Mediterranean desserts, giving a mild rose fragrance and flavour.

TAHINI A smooth, oily paste ground from sesame seeds tahini gives a nutty flavour to Middle Eastern dishes.

TOMATO PUREE A concentrated paste made from fresh tomatoes, perfect for boosting the flavour of bland tomatoes in soups, stews and sauces.

OLIVES The fruit of one of the earliest known trees native to the Mediterranean. There are many varieties, differing in size and taste. Colour depends purely on ripeness – the fruit changes from yellow to green, purple, brown and finally black when fully ripened. Fresh olives are picked at the desired stage, then soaked in water, bruised and immersed in brine to produce the familiar-tasting result. They can be bought whole or pitted, and sometimes stuffed with peppers, anchovies and nuts.

Perfect for antipasto, tapas, salads or savoury dishes of all types, olives have a wonderful flavour.

OLIVE OIL

Unlike other oils, which are extracted from the seeds or dried fruits of plants, olive oil is pressed from the pulp of ripe olives, which give it an inimitable richness and flavour. Besides being polyunsaturated and a natural fat, making it a healthy alternative to many other fats, olive oil is valued for its fine, nutty flavour. Italy, France and Spain produce some of the best, and different regions produce distinctively different olive oils. The production of olive oil is strictly controlled and regulated, rather like wine. The richest and best oil comes from the first cold pressing of the olives, with no further processing, producing a rich green "extra virgin" oil. It must have an acidity level of less than 1 per cent. The distinctive fruity flavour of this oil makes it ideal for salad dressings and using raw. Virgin oil is pressed in the same way, but is usually from a second pressing, but has a higher acidity level and not such a fruity flavour. It, too, can be used as a condiment, but is also suitable for cooking. Unclassified olive oil is refined, often using heat and chemicals to aid extraction, then blended with virgin oil to add flavour. It has an undistinguished taste but is ideal for cooking as it is generally much cheaper than the best olive oil which is decidedly expensive. It is made with slightly under-ripe olives, which give it a luminous green colour. Once opened, keep olive oil in a cool, dark place. Use it within six months of opening.

APPETIZERS

There is a splendid array of appetizers to be
enjoyed throughout the Mediterranean. The
variety of flavours makes them irresistible.

"Tapas", "Apéritifs", "Mezze", "Mezedes" – all these terms describe the inexhaustible and highly flavoured range of appetizers or nibbles that are served with drinks before a meal or as a light snack at almost any time of day. This is one of the most enticing aspects of Mediterranean cookery; the irresistible "tasters" enjoyed in a casual, unhurried atmosphere, offering a culinary glimpse of the good things to follow.

For the cook, the preparation of these savouries can be as simple or as demanding as time and circumstances allow. Whether it is a selection of marinated olives, regional cheeses or fresh seafood or, on a more elaborate scale, delicious baked vegetables, pickles and spicy pastries, this informal style of cooking and enjoying food is quintessentially Mediterranean.

RIGHT: Bent double, Moroccan farm workers bring in the olive harvest.

LEFT: On the mountainous Greek island of Naxos, arable land is precious, and hillsides are extensively terraced.

In Spanish, "tapa" means a lid and it was the custom of bartenders serving glasses of sherry covered with a slice of sausage or ham which evolved into the most fascinating and imaginative selection of "little dishes" served today. Tapas bars, particularly abundant in southern Spain, serve a variety of such dishes. In these bars you can enjoy pre-dinner tasters or thoroughly indulge yourself with a selection of dishes as a main meal. Fried new potatoes, chorizo sausage in olive oil, garlic prawns and empanadillas are tapas classics. Tortilla, an omelette in which fried potatoes are layered in a pan, covered with beaten eggs and baked to a set "cake" is another well-established dish. It is served warm or cold, cut into wedges, washed down with local chilled wines or, like other tapas, with sherry, port or beer.

In the Eastern Mediterranean, in places like Turkey, Greece, Lebanon and North Africa, local and specialized variations of a mezze are popular with both locals and visitors. Arak, raki and ouzo, as well as wine, are drunk with a wonderful selection of appetizers to whet the appetite. These are usually highly spiced and aromatic. In Greece, sheep's and goat's yogurt are hung to produce thickened cheeses that are bottled in spiced olive oil.

ABOVE: Scales at the ready, a Turkish fisherman sets out his catch on his stall.

Spread on to warmed toast, this delicious snack is good enough to enjoy as a complete meal. Dressed tomatoes, fried halloumi or Keflotyri cheese drizzled with lemon juice and pepper and a bowl of garlic-flavoured Greek yogurt complete a mouthwatering spread.

Vegetables, salads and pulses feature highly on a North African or Lebanese mezze. Simple vegetable *crudités* such as carrots, turnips and cucumber are scattered with coarse salt and left to marinate lightly before being moistened with lemon juice or wine vinegar. Miniature versions of national dishes such as *kibbeh* and little filo pastries are also ideal for whetting the appetite.

Sampling a selection of nibbles before a Turkish meal is almost compulsory and the range of dishes is extensive. A rich sauce of chilli tomatoes and a refreshing Cacik provide a stimulating contrast to specialities such as garlic mussels, grilled vegetables and stuffed peppers.

The classic Italian appetizer is the "antipasto", usually an assortment of cured meats such as salami, prosciutto and other such treats, served alongside roasted pepper salads, artichokes in olive oil, dressed green beans, anchovy fillets and breads such as crostini and focaccia.

Tasty dips like Tapenade, Herb Aïoli or a very garlicky French dressing are essential appetizers in France, often accompanied by a selection of raw or roasted *crudités*, herb salads and radishes with salt and butter.

Part of the pleasure of serving appetizers is that they can be as simple or as complicated as you like. Serve several as a light summer's meal, two or three as a simple starter or a varied selection for a larger party. Added interest can be provided, at little extra effort, with bowls of assorted olives, interesting Mediterranean breads and salted or spiced nuts.

Essentially, plenty of time must be allowed so that the selection of nibbles can be enjoyed in the unhurried and relaxed atmosphere that is an integral part of the Mediterranean way of life.

TAPENADE AND HERB AIOLI WITH SUMMER VEGETABLES

A beautiful platter of salad vegetables served with one or two interesting sauces makes a thoroughly appetizing and informal starter. This colourful French appetizer is perfect for entertaining as it can be prepared in advance.

FOR THE TAPENADE
175g/6oz/1½ cups pitted black olives
50g/2oz can anchovy fillets, drained
30ml/2 tbsp capers
120ml/4fl oz/½ cup olive oil
finely grated rind of 1 lemon
15ml/1 tbsp brandy (optional)
ground black pepper

FOR THE HERB AIOLI
2 egg yolks
5ml/1 tsp Dijon mustard
10ml/2 tsp white wine vinegar
250ml/8fl oz/1 cup light olive oil
45ml/3 tbsp chopped mixed
fresh herbs, such as chervil,
parsley or tarragon
30ml/2 tbsp chopped watercress
5 garlic cloves, crushed
salt and ground black pepper

TO SERVE
2 red peppers, seeded and cut into
wide strips
30ml/2 tbsp olive oil
225g/8oz new potatoes
115g/4oz green beans
225g/8oz baby carrots
225g/8oz young asparagus
12 quail's eggs (optional)
fresh herbs, to garnish
coarse salt for sprinkling

SERVES 6

1 To make the tapenade, finely chop the olives, anchovies and capers and beat together with the oil, lemon rind and brandy if using. (Alternatively, you can lightly process the ingredients in a blender or food processor, scraping down the mixture from the sides of the bowl if necessary.)

2 Season with pepper and blend in a little more oil if the mixture is very dry. Transfer to a serving dish.

3 To make the aïoli, beat together the egg yolks, mustard and vinegar. Gradually blend in the oil, a trickle at a time, whisking well after each addition until thick and smooth. Season with salt and pepper to taste, adding a little more vinegar if the aïoli tastes bland.

4 Stir in the mixed herbs, watercress and garlic, then transfer to a serving dish. Cover and chill in the fridge.

5 Put the peppers on a foil-lined grill rack and brush with the oil. Grill under a high heat until just beginning to char.

6 Cook the potatoes in a large pan of boiling, salted water until just tender. Add the beans and carrots and cook for 1 minute. Add the asparagus and cook for a further 30 seconds. Drain the vegetables.

7 Cook the quail's eggs in boiling water for 2 minutes. Drain and remove half of each shell.

8 Arrange all the vegetables, eggs and sauces on a serving platter. Garnish with fresh herbs and serve with coarse salt for sprinkling.

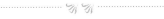

COOK'S TIP
Keep any leftover sauces for serving with salads. The tapenade is also delicious tossed with pasta or spread on to warm toast.

AUBERGINE DIP

—

This is an appetizer to serve with drinks and crisp sticks of raw vegetables. Aubergines are particularly popular in Israel, where they are almost a staple food.

·················· 🌾 🌾 ··················

2 aubergines, about 275g/10oz each
150ml/¼ pint/⅔ cup olive oil
2 onions, chopped
3 garlic cloves, crushed
freshly squeezed juice of 1 lemon
salt and ground black pepper
fresh coriander sprigs, to garnish
black and green olives, to serve

SERVES 4 AS A STARTER OR MORE AS A
DIP WITH PITTA BREAD

·················· 🌾 🌾 ··················

1 Preheat the grill. Cut both the aubergines in half lengthways and put them on a sheet of foil, skin side up. Grill at least 5cm/2in away from the heat for 20 minutes. The skin will start to wrinkle and the flesh will become slightly smoky and soft.

2 Meanwhile, heat about 60ml/ 4 tbsp of the oil and sauté the onions in a frying pan over a medium heat. Then add the garlic and cook both the onions and garlic until they are soft but not brown. Season with plenty of salt and pepper.

3 Scoop the flesh out of all the aubergine halves and put it into a food processor or blender with the onion and garlic. Pour in the freshly squeezed lemon juice.

4 With the blades running, slowly pour in the remaining olive oil to make a smooth mixture. Taste to check the seasoning and add more salt or pepper if needed.

5 Spoon the dip into bowls. Garnish with sprigs of fresh coriander and serve with black and green olives.

CHARRED ARTICHOKES WITH LEMON OIL DIP

This citrus dressing marries particularly well with roasted artichokes. They are usually boiled, but dry-heat cooking also works well.

 2 Drain the artichoke wedges and place in a roasting tin with the garlic. Add half the oil and toss well to coat. Sprinkle with salt and roast for 40 minutes, stirring once or twice, until the artichoke wedges are tender and a little charred.

3 Next, begin to make the dip. Using a small, sharp knife, thinly pare away two strips of rind from the lemon. Lay the strips on a board and carefully scrape away any remaining pith. Place the rind in a small pan with water to cover. Bring to the boil, then simmer for 5 minutes. Drain the rind, refresh it in cold water, then chop it roughly. Set aside.

4 Arrange the cooked artichokes on a serving plate and set aside to cool for 5 minutes. Using the back of a fork, gently flatten the garlic cloves so that the flesh squeezes out of the skins. Transfer the garlic flesh to a bowl, mash to a purée, then add the lemon rind. Squeeze the juice from the lemon and, using the fork, whisk it into the garlic mixture, together with the remaining oil. Serve the artichokes warm with the lemon dip. Garnish with a few sprigs of flat leaf parsley.

15ml/1 tbsp lemon juice or
white wine vinegar
2 globe artichokes, trimmed
12 garlic cloves, unpeeled
90ml/6 tbsp olive oil
1 lemon
sea salt
sprigs of flat leaf parsley, to garnish

SERVES 4

1 Preheat the oven to 200°C/400°F/Gas 6. Add the lemon juice or vinegar to a bowl of cold water. Cut each artichoke into wedges. Pull the hairy choke out from the centre, then drop them into the acidulated water until needed.

BABA GANOUSH WITH LEBANESE FLATBREAD

*Baba Ganoush is a delectable puréed aubergine dip from the Middle East.
Tahini — a sesame seed paste with cumin — is the main flavouring,
giving a subtle yet significant hint of spice.*

2 small aubergines
1 garlic clove, crushed
60ml/4 tbsp tahini paste
25g/1oz/¼ cup ground almonds
juice of ½ lemon
2.5ml/½ tsp ground cumin
30ml/2 tbsp fresh mint leaves
30ml/2 tbsp olive oil
salt and ground black pepper
fresh thyme sprigs, to garnish

FOR THE LEBANESE FLATBREAD
6 pitta breads
3 tbsp toasted sesame seeds
3 tbsp chopped fresh thyme leaves
3 tbsp poppy seeds
150ml/¼ pint/⅔ cup olive oil

SERVES 6

1 Start by making the Lebanese flatbread. Split the pitta breads through the middle and carefully open them out. Mix the sesame seeds, chopped thyme and poppy seeds in a mortar. Crush them lightly with a pestle to release the flavour.

2 Stir in the olive oil. Spread the mixture lightly over the cut sides of the pitta bread. Grill until golden brown and crisp. When cool, break the pitta breads into rough pieces and set aside.

3 Grill the aubergines, turning them frequently, until the skin is blackened and blistered. Remove the peel, chop the flesh roughly and leave to drain in a colander.

4 Squeeze out as much liquid from the aubergines as possible. Place the flesh in a blender or food processor. Add the garlic, tahini, ground almonds, lemon juice and cumin, season to taste and process to a smooth paste. Roughly chop half the mint and stir into the dip.

5 Spoon the dip into a bowl, scatter the remaining leaves on top and drizzle with olive oil. Place the bowl on a platter, surround with the Lebanese flatbread and garnish with the fresh thyme sprigs.

HUMMUS BI TAHINA

Blending chick-peas with garlic and oil makes a surprisingly creamy purée that is delicious as part of a Turkish-style mezze, or as a dip with vegetables. Leftovers make a good sandwich filler.

150g/5oz/¾ cup dried chick-peas
juice of 2 lemons
2 garlic cloves, sliced
30ml/2 tbsp olive oil
pinch of cayenne pepper
150ml/¼ pint/⅔ cup tahini paste
salt and ground black pepper
extra olive oil and cayenne pepper,
for sprinkling
flat leaf parsley, to garnish

SERVES 4–6

1 Put the chick-peas in a bowl with plenty of cold water and leave to soak overnight.

2 Drain the chick-peas and cover with fresh water in a saucepan. Bring to the boil and boil rapidly for 10 minutes. Reduce the heat and simmer gently for about 1½–2 hours, or until soft. Drain.

3 Process the chick-peas in a food processor to a smooth purée. Add the lemon juice, garlic, olive oil, cayenne pepper and tahini and blend until creamy, scraping the mixture down from the sides of the bowl.

4 Season the purée with salt and pepper and transfer to a serving dish. Sprinkle with oil and cayenne pepper and serve garnished with a few parsley sprigs.

COOK'S TIP
For convenience, canned chick-peas can be used instead. Allow two 400g/14oz cans and drain them thoroughly. Tahini paste can now be purchased from most supermarkets or health food shops.

FONDUTA

Fontina is an Italian medium-fat cheese with a rich salty flavour, a little like Gruyère, which makes a good substitute. This delicious cheese dip needs only some warm ciabatta or focaccia, a herby salad and some robust red wine for a thoroughly enjoyable meal.

250g/9oz fontina cheese, diced
250ml/8fl oz/1 cup milk
15g/½oz/1 tbsp butter
2 eggs, lightly beaten
ground black pepper

SERVES 4

1   Put the cheese in a bowl, pour over the milk and leave to soak for 2–3 hours. Transfer to a double boiler or a heatproof bowl set over a pan of simmering water.

2   Add the butter and eggs and cook gently, stirring until the cheese has melted to a smooth sauce with the consistency of custard.

3   Remove from the heat and transfer to a serving dish. Grind over some pepper and serve immediately.

COOK'S TIP
Don't overheat the sauce, or the eggs might curdle. A very gentle heat will produce a lovely smooth sauce.

SPICY MOROCCAN OLIVES

*Green olives, marinated in these two spicy herbal concoctions,
are simple to prepare and absolutely delicious.*

*450g/1lb/2⅔ cups green or tan olives
(unpitted) for each marinade*

FOR THE SPICY HERBAL MARINADE
*45ml/3 tbsp chopped fresh coriander
45ml/3 tbsp chopped fresh flat
leaf parsley
1 garlic clove, finely chopped
good pinch of cayenne pepper
good pinch of ground cumin
30–45ml/2–3 tbsp olive oil, plus extra
if necessary
30–45ml/2–3 tbsp lemon juice, plus
extra if necessary*

FOR THE HOT CHILLI MARINADE
*60ml/4 tbsp chopped fresh coriander
60ml/4 tbsp chopped fresh flat
leaf parsley
1 garlic clove, finely chopped
5ml/1 tsp grated fresh root ginger
1 red chilli, seeded and finely sliced
¼ preserved lemon, cut into thin strips*

SERVES 6–8

1 Crack the olives, hard enough
to break the flesh but taking
care not to crack the stones. Place in
a bowl of cold water and leave
overnight to remove the excess brine.
Drain thoroughly and divide the
olives between two jars.

2 Mix all the ingredients for the
spicy herbal marinade in a jug.
Pour over the olives in one of the jars,
adding more olive oil and lemon juice
to cover, if necessary.

COOK'S TIP
A jar of marinated olives makes the
perfect present for anyone who
appreciates their delectable flavour.
Experiment with different herbs and
spices in the marinade – try oregano
and basil, and substitute lime juice for
the lemon juice, or even use
flavoured vinegars.

3 To make the hot chilli
marinade, mix together all the
ingredients. Pour over the olives in
the second jar. Store both jars in the
fridge for at least 1 week, shaking
them occasionally.

40

TAPAS OF ALMONDS, OLIVES AND CHEESE

These three simple ingredients are lightly flavoured to create a delicious Spanish tapas medley that's perfect for a casual starter or nibbles to serve with pre-dinner drinks.

FOR THE MARINATED OLIVES
2.5ml/½ tsp coriander seeds
2.5ml/½ tsp fennel seeds
5ml/1 tsp chopped fresh rosemary
10ml/2 tsp chopped fresh parsley
2 garlic cloves, crushed
15ml/1 tbsp sherry vinegar
30ml/2 tbsp olive oil
115g/4oz/⅔ cup black olives
115g/4oz/⅔ cup green olives

FOR THE MARINATED CHEESE
150g/5oz goat's cheese, preferably manchego
90ml/6 tbsp olive oil
15ml/1 tbsp white wine vinegar
5ml/1 tsp black peppercorns
1 garlic clove, sliced
3 fresh tarragon or thyme sprigs
tarragon sprigs, to garnish

FOR THE SALTED ALMONDS
1.5ml/¼ tsp cayenne pepper
30ml/2 tbsp sea salt
25g/1oz/2 tbsp butter
60ml/4 tbsp olive oil
200g/7oz/1¾ cups blanched almonds
extra salt for sprinkling (optional)

SERVES 6–8

| 1 | To make the marinated olives, crush the coriander and fennel seeds with a pestle and mortar. Mix together with the rosemary, parsley, garlic, vinegar and oil and pour over the olives in a small bowl. Cover and chill for up to 1 week. |

| 2 | To make the marinated cheese, cut the cheese into bite-size pieces, leaving the rind on. Mix together the oil, vinegar, peppercorns, garlic and herb sprigs and pour over the cheese in a small bowl. Cover and chill for up to 3 days. |

COOK'S TIP
If serving with pre-dinner drinks, provide cocktail sticks for spearing the olives and cheese.

| 3 | To make the salted almonds, mix together the cayenne pepper and salt in a bowl. Melt the butter with the olive oil in a frying pan. Add the almonds to the pan and fry, stirring for about 5 minutes, until the almonds are golden. |

| 4 | Tip the almonds out of the frying pan into the salt mixture and toss together until the almonds are coated. Leave to cool, then store them in a jar or airtight container for up to 1 week. |

| 5 | To serve the tapas, arrange in small, shallow serving dishes. Use fresh sprigs of tarragon to garnish the cheese and scatter the almonds with a little more salt, if liked. |

YOGURT CHEESE IN OLIVE OIL

Sheep's milk is widely used in cheese making in the Eastern Mediterranean, particularly in Greece where sheep's yogurt is hung in muslin to drain off the whey before patting into balls of soft cheese. Here it is bottled in olive oil with chilli and herbs — an appropriate gift for a "foodie" friend.

750g/1¾lb Greek sheep's yogurt
2.5ml/½ tsp salt
10ml/2 tsp crushed dried chillies or
chilli powder
15ml/1 tbsp chopped fresh rosemary
15ml/1 tbsp chopped fresh thyme
or oregano
about 300ml/½ pint/1¼ cups olive oil,
preferably garlic-flavoured

FILLS TWO 450G/1LB JARS

1 | Sterilize a 30cm/12in square of muslin by steeping it in boiling water. Drain and lay over a large plate. Mix the yogurt with the salt and tip on to the centre of the muslin. Bring up the sides of the muslin and tie firmly with string.

2 | Hang the bag on a kitchen cupboard handle or suitable position where the bag can be suspended with a bowl underneath to catch the whey. Leave for 2–3 days until the yogurt stops dripping.

3 | Sterilize two 450g/1lb glass preserving or jam jars by heating them in the oven at 150°C/300°F/Gas 2 for 15 minutes.

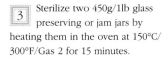

4 | Mix together the chilli and herbs. Take teaspoonfuls of the cheese and roll into balls with your hands. Lower into the jars, sprinkling each layer with the herb mixture.

5   Pour the oil over the cheese until completely covered. Store in the fridge for up to 3 weeks.

6   To serve the cheese, spoon out of the jars with a little of the flavoured olive oil and spread on to lightly toasted bread.

COOK'S TIP
If your kitchen is particularly warm, find a cooler place to suspend the cheese. Alternatively, drain the cheese in the fridge, suspending the bag from one of the shelves.

STUFFED VINE LEAVES WITH GARLIC YOGURT

An old Greek recipe which comes in many guises. This meatless version is highly flavoured with fresh herbs, lemon and a little chilli.

225g/8oz packet preserved vine leaves
1 onion, finely chopped
½ bunch of spring onions, trimmed
and finely chopped
60ml/4 tbsp chopped fresh parsley
10 large mint sprigs, chopped
finely grated rind of 1 lemon
2.5ml/½ tsp crushed dried chillies
7.5ml/1½ tsp fennel seeds, crushed
175g/6oz/scant 1 cup long grain rice
120ml/4fl oz/½ cup olive oil
150ml/¼ pint/⅔ cup thick
natural yogurt
2 garlic cloves, crushed
salt
lemon wedges and mint leaves,
to garnish (optional)

SERVES 6

1 Rinse the vine leaves in plenty of cold water. Put in a bowl, cover with boiling water and leave for 10 minutes. Drain thoroughly.

2 Mix together the onion, spring onions, parsley, mint, grated lemon rind, crushed chillies, fennel seeds, rice and 25ml/1½ tbsp of the olive oil. Mix thoroughly and season lightly with salt.

3 Place a vine leaf, veined side facing upwards, on a work surface and cut off any stalk. Place a heaped teaspoonful of the rice mixture near the stalk end of the leaf.

4 Fold the stalk end of the leaf over the rice filling, then fold over the sides and carefully roll up into a neat cigar shape.

5 Repeat with the remaining filling to make about 28 stuffed leaves. If some of the vine leaves are quite small, use two and patch them together to make parcels of the same size.

6 Place any remaining leaves in the base of a large heavy-based saucepan. Pack the stuffed leaves in a single layer in the pan. Spoon over the remaining oil then add about 300ml/½ pint/1¼ cups boiling water.

COOK'S TIP
To check that the rice is cooked, lift out one stuffed leaf and cut in half. The rice should have expanded and softened to make a firm parcel. If necessary, cook the stuffed leaves a little longer, adding boiling water if the pan is becoming dry.

7 Place a small plate over the leaves to keep them submerged in the water. Cover the pan and cook on a very low heat for 45 minutes.

8 Mix together the yogurt and garlic and put in a small serving dish. Transfer the stuffed leaves to a serving plate and garnish with lemon wedges and mint, if you like. Serve with the garlic yogurt.

GRILLED VEGETABLE TERRINE

A colourful, layered terrine, using all the vegetables associated with the Mediterranean.

2 large red peppers, quartered, cored
and seeded
2 large yellow peppers, quartered,
cored and seeded
1 large aubergine, sliced lengthways
2 large courgettes, sliced lengthways
90ml/6 tbsp olive oil
1 large red onion, thinly sliced
75g/3oz/½ cup raisins
15ml/1 tbsp tomato purée
15ml/1 tbsp red wine vinegar
400ml/14fl oz/1⅔ cups tomato juice
15g/½oz/2 tbsp powdered gelatine
fresh basil leaves, to garnish

FOR THE DRESSING
90ml/6 tbsp extra virgin olive oil
30ml/2 tbsp red wine vinegar
salt and ground black pepper

SERVES 6

2 Arrange the aubergine and courgette slices on separate baking sheets. Brush them with a little oil and cook under the grill, turning occasionally, until tender and golden.

3 Heat the remaining olive oil in a frying pan, and add the sliced onion, raisins, tomato purée and red wine vinegar. Cook gently until soft and syrupy. Leave to cool in the frying pan.

4 Line a 1.75 litre/3 pint/7½ cup terrine with clear film, (it helps to lightly oil the terrine first) leaving a little hanging over the sides.

5 Pour half the tomato juice into a saucepan, and sprinkle with the gelatine. Dissolve gently over a low heat, stirring.

6 Place a layer of red peppers in the bottom of the terrine, and pour in enough of the tomato juice with gelatine to cover. Continue layering the aubergine, courgettes, yellow peppers and onion mixture, finishing with another layer of red peppers. Pour tomato juice over each layer of vegetables.

7 Add the remaining tomato juice to any left in the pan, and pour into the terrine. Give it a sharp tap, to disperse the juice. Cover the terrine and chill until set.

8 To make the dressing, whisk together the oil and vinegar, and season. Turn out the terrine and remove the clear film. Serve in thick slices, drizzled with dressing. Garnish with basil leaves.

1 Place the prepared red and yellow peppers skin side up under a hot grill and cook until the skins are blackened. Transfer to a bowl and cover with a plate. Leave to cool.

MARINATED BABY AUBERGINES WITH RAISINS AND PINE NUTS

Aubergines are popular in all the Mediterranean countries. This is a dish with an Italian influence, using ingredients that have been included in recipes since Renaissance times. Prepare a day in advance, to allow the sour and sweet flavours to develop.

12 baby aubergines, halved
lengthways
250ml/8fl oz/1 cup extra virgin
olive oil
juice of 1 lemon
30ml/2 tbsp balsamic vinegar
3 cloves
25g/1oz/⅓ cup pine nuts
25g/1oz/2 tbsp raisins
15ml/1 tbsp granulated sugar
1 bay leaf
large pinch of dried chilli flakes
salt and ground black pepper

SERVES 4

1 Preheat the grill to high. Place the aubergines, cut side up, in the grill pan and brush with a little of the olive oil. Grill for 10 minutes, until slightly blackened, turning them over half way through cooking.

2 To make the marinade, put the remaining olive oil, the lemon juice, vinegar, cloves, pine nuts, raisins, sugar and bay leaf in a jug. Add the chilli flakes and salt and pepper and mix well.

3 Place the hot aubergines in an earthenware or glass bowl, and pour over the marinade. Leave to cool, turning the aubergines once or twice. Serve cold.

ROASTED PEPPER ANTIPASTO

Jars of Italian mixed peppers in olive oil are now a common sight in many supermarkets. None, however, can compete with this colourful, freshly made version, perfect as a starter on its own, or with some Italian salamis and other cold meats.

3 red peppers
2 yellow or orange peppers
2 green peppers
50g/2oz/½ cup sun-dried tomatoes
in oil, drained
1 garlic clove
30ml/2 tbsp balsamic vinegar
75ml/5 tbsp olive oil
few drops of chilli sauce
4 canned artichoke hearts, drained
and sliced
salt and ground black pepper
basil leaves, to garnish

SERVES 6

1 Preheat the oven to 200°C/
400°F/Gas 6. Lightly oil a foil-lined baking sheet and place the whole peppers on the foil. Bake for about 45 minutes until beginning to char. Cover with a dish towel and leave to cool for 5 minutes.

2 Slice the sun-dried tomatoes into thin strips. Thinly slice the garlic. Set the tomatoes and garlic aside.

3 Beat together the vinegar, oil and chilli sauce, then season with a little salt and pepper.

4 Peel and slice the peppers. Mix with the artichokes, tomatoes and garlic. Pour over the dressing and scatter with the basil leaves.

SHERRIED PIMIENTOS

Pimientos are simply cooked, skinned peppers. You can buy them in cans or jars, but they are much tastier when made at home.

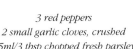

3 red peppers
2 small garlic cloves, crushed
45ml/3 tbsp chopped fresh parsley
15ml/1 tbsp sherry vinegar
30ml/2 tbsp olive oil
salt

SERVES 2–4

3. Using a sharp knife, cut each halved pepper lengthways into 1cm/½in wide strips and place them in a small bowl.

4. Whisk the garlic, parsley, vinegar and oil into the pepper juices. Add salt to taste. Toss with the strips. Serve at room temperature.

1. Preheat the grill to high. Place the red peppers on a baking sheet and grill for 8–12 minutes, turning occasionally, until the skins have blistered and blackened. Remove the peppers from the heat, cover with a clean dish towel and leave to stand for 5 minutes so that the steam softens the skins and makes them easy to peel.

2. Make a small cut in the bottom of each pepper and squeeze out the juice into a jug and reserve for later use. Peel away the skin and cut each pepper in half. Remove and discard the cores and scrape out the seeds. Place the peppers on a cutting board.

LEMON-SOAKED ANCHOVIES

—

Make these at least 1 hour and up to 24 hours in advance. Fresh anchovies are tiny, so be prepared to spend time filleting them — the results will be well worth the effort.

225g/8oz fresh anchovies
juice of 3 lemons
30ml/2 tbsp extra virgin olive oil
2 garlic cloves, finely chopped
15ml/1 tbsp chopped fresh parsley
flaked sea salt

SERVES 4

1 Cut off the heads and tails from the anchovies, then split them open down one side, using a small knife with a short, sharp blade.

2 Open each anchovy out flat and carefully lift out the bone.

3 Arrange the anchovies, skin-side down, in a single layer on a plate. Pour over two-thirds of the lemon juice and sprinkle with sea salt. Cover and leave for 1–24 hours, basting occasionally with the juices, until the flesh is white and opaque.

4 Put the fish on a platter. Drizzle over the oil and the remaining lemon juice. Scatter with the garlic and parsley, cover and chill.

DEEP FRIED NEW POTATOES WITH SAFFRON AIOLI

Aïoli is a Spanish garlic mayonnaise, similar to the French mayonnaise of the same name.
In this recipe saffron adds colour and flavour.

1 large egg yolk
2.5ml/½ tsp Dijon mustard
300ml/½ pint/1¼ cups extra virgin olive oil
15–30ml/1–2 tbsp lemon juice
1 garlic clove, crushed
2.5ml/½ tsp saffron strands
20 baby new potatoes
vegetable oil for frying
salt and ground black pepper

SERVES 4

1 To make the aïoli, put the egg yolk in a bowl with the mustard and a pinch of salt. Beat together with a wooden spoon. Still beating, add the olive oil very slowly, drop by drop to begin with, then, as the aïoli gradually thickens, in a thin stream. Add the lemon juice and salt and pepper to taste, then beat in the crushed garlic.

2 Place the saffron in a small bowl, and add 10ml/2 tsp hot water. Press the saffron with the back of a teaspoon, to extract the colour and flavour, and leave to infuse for 5 minutes. Beat the saffron and the liquid into the mayonnaise.

3 Cook the potatoes in boiling salted water for 5 minutes, then turn off the heat. Cover the pan and leave for 15 minutes. Drain the potatoes, then dry them thoroughly.

4 Heat 1cm/½ in oil in a deep pan. When the oil is very hot, add the potatoes, and fry quickly, turning, until crisp and golden. Drain on kitchen paper, and serve with the saffron aïoli.

DATES STUFFED WITH CHORIZO

A delicious combination from Spain, using fresh dates and spicy chorizo sausage.

50g/2oz chorizo sausage
12 fresh dates, stoned
6 streaky bacon rashers
oil for frying
plain flour for dusting
1 egg, beaten
50g/2oz/1 cup fresh breadcrumbs
cocktail sticks for serving

SERVES 4–6

1 Trim the ends of the chorizo sausage and peel away the skin. Cut into three 2cm/¾in slices. Cut these in half lengthways, then into quarters, giving 12 pieces.

2 Stuff each date with a piece of chorizo, closing the date around it. Stretch the bacon, by running the back of a knife along the rasher. Cut each rasher in half, widthways. Wrap a piece of bacon around each date and secure with a cocktail stick.

3 In a deep pan, heat 1cm/½in of oil. Dust the dates with flour, dip them in the beaten egg, then coat in breadcrumbs. Fry the dates in the hot oil, turning them, until golden. Remove the dates with a slotted spoon, and drain on kitchen paper. Serve immediately.

GARLIC PRAWNS

For this simple Spanish tapas dish, you really need fresh raw prawns which absorb the flavours of the garlic and chilli as they fry. Have everything ready for last-minute cooking so you can take it to the table still sizzling.

350–450g/12oz–1lb large
raw prawns
2 red chillies
75ml/5 tbsp olive oil
3 garlic cloves, crushed
salt and ground black pepper

SERVES 4

1 Remove the heads and shells from the prawns, leaving the tails intact.

2 Halve each chilli lengthways and discard the seeds. Heat the oil in a flameproof pan, suitable for serving. (Alternatively, use a frying pan and have a warmed serving dish ready in the oven.)

3 Add all the prawns, chilli and garlic to the pan and cook over a high heat for about 3 minutes, stirring until the prawns turn pink. Season lightly with salt and pepper and serve immediately.

CHORIZO IN OLIVE OIL

Spanish chorizo sausage has a deliciously pungent taste; its robust seasoning of garlic, chilli and paprika flavours the ingredients it is cooked with. Frying chorizo with onions and olive oil is one of its simplest and most delicious uses.

75ml/5 tbsp extra virgin olive oil
350g/12oz chorizo sausage, sliced
1 large onion, thinly sliced
roughly chopped flat leaf parsley,
to garnish

SERVES 4

VARIATION
Chorizo is usually available in large supermarkets or delicatessens. Other similarly rich, spicy sausages can be used as a substitute.

1 Heat the oil in a frying pan and fry the chorizo sausage over a high heat until beginning to colour. Remove from pan with slotted spoon.

2 Add the onion to the pan and fry until coloured. Return the sausage slices to the pan and heat through for 1 minute.

3 Tip the mixture into a shallow serving dish and scatter with the parsley. Serve with warm bread.

KING PRAWNS IN SHERRY

*These prawns couldn't be simpler, or quicker, to prepare — yet they're deceptively impressive
in terms of flavour and appearance. A winning starter for any special meal.*

*12 raw king prawns or tiger
prawns, peeled
30ml/2 tbsp olive oil
30ml/2 tbsp sherry
a few drops of Tabasco sauce
salt and ground black pepper*

SERVES 4

1 Make a shallow cut down the back of each prawn, then pull out and discard the dark intestinal tract. Leave the tails on the prawns; when they are cooked they will curl and look more decorative.

2 Heat the oil in a frying pan and fry the prawns for 2–3 minutes until pink. Pour over the sherry and season with Tabasco sauce, salt and pepper. Tip the prawns into a dish and serve immediately.

SIZZLING PRAWNS

*This dish works particularly well with tiny shrimps which can be eaten whole, but any type of prawns in
the shell will be fine. Choose a small flameproof dish or frying pan that can be taken to the table for
serving while the prawns are still sizzling.*

*2 garlic cloves, peeled
and halved
25g/1oz/2 tbsp butter
1 small red chilli, seeded and
finely sliced
115g/4oz cooked prawns, in the shell
sea salt and coarsely ground
black pepper
lime wedges, to serve*

SERVES 4

1 Rub the cut surfaces of the garlic cloves over the surface of a frying pan. This will delicately flavour the prawns and make them a little sweet. After use, discard the garlic cloves. Add the butter to the pan and melt over a fairly high heat until it just begins to turn golden brown.

2 Toss in the chilli and prawns. Stir-fry for 1–2 minutes until heated through, then season to taste and serve with lime wedges to squeeze over.

GRILLED SCALLOPS WITH BROWN BUTTER

This is a very striking dish, as the scallops are served on the half-shell, still sizzling from the grill.
Reserve this dish for a special occasion, when you want to impress your guests.

50g/2oz/¼ cup unsalted butter, diced
8 scallops, prepared on the half-shell
15ml/1 tbsp chopped fresh parsley
salt and ground black pepper
4 lemon wedges, to serve

SERVES 4

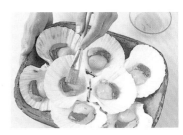

1 Preheat the grill to high. Melt the butter in a small saucepan over a moderate heat until it is pale golden brown. Remove the pan from the heat immediately; the butter must not be allowed to burn.

2 Arrange the scallop shells in a single layer in a flameproof serving dish or a shallow roasting tin. Brush a little of the brown butter over the scallops and grill for 4 minutes – it will not be necessary to turn the scallops in the shells.

3 Brush the remaining brown butter over, then sprinkle with a little salt and pepper, together with the parsley. Serve the grilled scallops at once, with lemon wedges.

FRIED SQUID

The squid is simply dusted in flour and dipped in egg before being fried, so that the coating is light,
and does not mask the flavour.

115g/4oz squid
rings
30ml/2 tbsp seasoned flour
1 egg
30ml/2 tbsp milk
olive oil, for frying
sea salt
lemon wedges, to serve

SERVES 4

1 Toss the squid rings in the seasoned flour in a bowl or strong plastic bag. Beat together the egg and milk in a shallow bowl. Heat the oil in a heavy-based frying pan.

2 Dip the floured squid rings one at a time into the egg mixture, shaking off any excess liquid. Add to the hot oil, in batches if necessary, and fry for 2–3 minutes on each side until golden.

3 Drain the fried squid on kitchen paper, then sprinkle with salt. Transfer to a small, warm bowl and serve with the lemon wedges. Offer finger bowls and napkins.

COOK'S TIP
For a crispier coating, dust the rings in flour, then dip them in batter.

FRIED WHITEBAIT WITH TOMATO SALSA

Fresh, crispy whitebait is served with a slightly spicy tomato salsa for a sensational combination of flavours and textures.

225g/8oz whitebait, thawed if frozen
30ml/2 tbsp seasoned flour
60ml/4 tbsp olive oil
60ml/4 tbsp vegetable oil

FOR THE SALSA
1 shallot, finely chopped
2 garlic cloves, finely chopped
4 ripe tomatoes, roughly chopped
1 small red chilli, seeded and
finely chopped
30ml/2 tbsp olive oil
60ml/4 tbsp sweet sherry
30–45ml/2–3 tbsp chopped fresh herbs
25g/1oz/½ cup fresh white
breadcrumbs
salt and ground black pepper

SERVES 4

1 To make the salsa, place the shallot, garlic, tomatoes, chilli and oil in a pan. Cover with a lid and cook gently for 10 minutes.

2 Pour in the sherry and add salt and pepper to taste. Stir in the herbs – basil, parsley or coriander could be used – then add the breadcrumbs. Stir to mix, then cover and keep hot while the whitebait is being prepared.

3 Wash the whitebait, drain, then dust in the seasoned flour. Heat both oils together in a frying pan and cook the fish in batches until crisp and golden. Drain on kitchen paper and keep warm in a low oven.

4 Spoon the whitebait into a bowl. Stir the tomato salsa, spoon it into a separate bowl and serve at once, with the whitebait.

CRISPY FISH BALLS

You can use any white fish to make these crispy balls. Cod, haddock and monkfish fillets all work well.

1 egg
a pinch of saffron threads
2 garlic cloves, roughly chopped
45ml/3 tbsp fresh parsley leaves
225g/8oz white fish, skinned, boned
and cubed
75g/3oz white bread, crusts removed
60ml/4 tbsp seasoned flour
vegetable oil, for frying
salt and ground black pepper
lemon wedges, to serve

SERVES 4

1 Beat together the egg and saffron threads in a cup, then set aside for 5 minutes.

2 In a food processor, whizz together the garlic and parsley until finely chopped. Add the fish and bread and whizz until well blended. Scrape the fish mixture into a bowl and stir in the egg and saffron. Season with plenty of salt and pepper.

3 Shape the mixture into 24 small balls. Spread out the seasoned flour in a shallow dish and add the balls. Shiver the bowl to coat the fish balls on all sides.

4 Heat the oil in a deep frying pan. Fry the fish balls, in batches if necessary, until crisp and golden, shaking the pan to keep them moving. Drain on kitchen paper and serve immediately with lemon wedges. Offer a small bowl of plain or garlic-flavoured mayonnaise for dipping, if you like, and cocktail sticks for spearing.

SARDINES IN ESCABECHE

This spicy marinade is widely used in Spain and Portugal as a traditional means of preserving fish, poultry or game. It is particularly good with fried fish.

16 sardines
450g/1lb seasoned flour
30ml/2 tbsp olive oil
roasted red onion, green pepper and
tomatoes, to garnish

FOR THE MARINADE
90ml/6 tbsp olive oil
1 onion, sliced
1 garlic clove, crushed
3–4 bay leaves
2 cloves
1 dried red chilli
5ml/1 tsp paprika
120ml/4fl oz/½ cup wine or
sherry vinegar
120ml/4fl oz/½ cup white wine
salt and ground black pepper

SERVES 8

2 Close the sardines up again and dust them with seasoned flour. Heat the olive oil in a deep pan and fry the sardines for 2–3 minutes on each side. Remove the fish from the pan and allow to cool, then place in a single layer in a large shallow dish.

3 To make the marinade, add the olive oil to the oil remaining in the pan. Fry the sliced onion and garlic gently for 5–10 minutes until soft. Add the bay leaves, cloves, chilli and paprika, with pepper to taste. Fry, stirring, for another 1–2 minutes.

4 Stir in the vinegar, wine and a little salt. Allow to bubble up, then pour over the sardines. When cool, cover and chill overnight or for up to 3 days. Serve on individual plates, garnished with roasted red onion, pepper and tomatoes. Offer bread for mopping up the marinade.

1 Cut the heads off the sardines and split each of them along the belly. Clean them, if necessary, then turn them over so that the backbone is uppermost. Press down along the backbone to loosen it, then carefully lift out the backbone and as many other bones as possible.

SAUTEED MUSSELS WITH GARLIC AND HERBS

These mussels are served without their shells, in a delicious paprika-flavoured sauce.
Eat them with cocktail sticks.

900g/2lb fresh mussels
1 lemon slice
90ml/6 tbsp olive oil
2 shallots, finely chopped
1 garlic clove, finely chopped
15ml/1 tbsp chopped fresh parsley
2.5ml/½ tsp sweet paprika
1.5ml/¼ tsp dried chilli flakes
parsley sprigs, to garnish

SERVES 4

1 Scrub the mussels, discarding any damaged ones that do not close when tapped with a knife. Put the mussels in a large pan with 250ml/8fl oz/1 cup water and the slice of lemon. Bring to the boil for 3–4 minutes and remove the mussels as they open. Discard any that remain closed. Take the mussels out of the shells and drain on kitchen paper.

2 Heat the oil in a sauté pan, add the mussels (left) and cook, stirring, for a minute. Remove from the pan. Add the shallots and garlic and cook, covered, over a low heat, for about 5 minutes, until soft. Stir in the parsley, paprika and chilli, then add the mussels with any juices. Cook briefly. Remove the pan from the heat, cover and leave for 1–2 minutes to let the flavours mingle. Serve, garnished with parsley.

SUPPLI AL TELEFONO

These are risotto fritters with nuggets of mozzarella inside. When they are bitten into, the cheese is drawn out in thin strings, like telephone wires — hence the name.

*45ml/3 tbsp finely chopped
fresh parsley
675g/1½lb/6 cups risotto
200g/7oz mozzarella cheese,
cut into 20 cubes
2 eggs, beaten
150g/5oz/1¼ cups natural-coloured
dried breadcrumbs
corn or vegetable oil, for deep-frying
fresh herbs, to garnish*

MAKES 20

1 Stir the parsley into the risotto, cool, then chill until firm. Divide into 20 portions and shape each into a ball. Press a cube of cheese into each ball and reshape neatly. Coat the rice balls in the beaten egg, then the breadcrumbs, and chill again for 30 minutes to set the coating.

2 Heat the oil for deep-frying to 180°C/350°F. Cook about five fritters at a time for 3–5 minutes until golden brown and crisp. Drain the fritters on kitchen paper and keep warm on an uncovered plate so that the coating remains crisp. Serve, garnished with fresh herbs.

MOZZARELLA IN CAROZZA WITH FRESH TOMATO SALSA

The name of this delectable Italian snack translates as cheese "in a carriage". It contains mozzarella and is dipped in beaten egg and fried like French toast.

200g/7oz mozzarella cheese,
finely sliced
8 thin slices of bread, crusts removed
a little dried oregano
30ml/2 tbsp freshly grated
Parmesan cheese
3 eggs, beaten
olive oil, for frying
salt and freshly ground black pepper
fresh herbs, to garnish

FOR THE SALSA
4 ripe plum tomatoes, peeled, seeded
and finely chopped
15ml/1 tbsp chopped fresh parsley
5ml/1 tsp balsamic vinegar
15ml/1 tbsp extra virgin olive oil
salt and freshly ground black pepper

SERVES 4

1 Arrange the mozzarella on 4 slices of the bread. Season with salt and pepper and sprinkle with a little dried oregano and the Parmesan. Top with the other bread slices and press them firmly together.

2 Pour the beaten eggs into a large shallow dish and season with salt and pepper.

3 Add the cheese sandwiches, two at a time, pressing them into the egg with a spatula until they are well coated. Repeat with the remaining sandwiches, then leave them to stand for 10 minutes.

4 To make the salsa, put the chopped tomatoes in a bowl and add the parsley. Stir in the vinegar and the extra virgin olive oil. Season well with salt and pepper and set aside.

5 Heat oil for frying to a depth of 5mm/¼in in a large frying pan. Carefully add the sandwiches in batches and cook for about 2 minutes on each side until golden and crisp. Drain well. Cut in half, garnish with herbs and serve with the salsa.

ARTICHOKE RICE CAKES WITH MELTING MANCHEGO

For really impressive tapas, serve these rice cakes with a tangy garlic mayonnaise.

1 globe artichoke
50g/2oz/¼ cup butter
1 small onion, finely chopped
1 garlic clove, finely chopped
115g/4oz/⅔ cup risotto rice
450ml/¾ pint/scant 2 cups hot
chicken stock
50g/2oz/⅔ cup freshly grated
Parmesan cheese
150g/5oz Manchego cheese,
finely diced
45–60ml/3–4 tbsp fine cornmeal
olive oil, for frying
salt and ground black pepper
flat leaf parsley, to garnish

SERVES 6

1 Remove the stalk, leaves and choke from the artichoke, leaving the heart; finely chop this. Melt the butter in a saucepan and gently fry the chopped artichoke heart, onion and garlic for 5 minutes until softened. Stir in the risotto rice and cook for about 1 minute.

2 Keeping the heat fairly high, gradually add the stock, stirring constantly for about 20 minutes, until all the liquid has been absorbed and the rice is cooked. Season well, then stir in the Parmesan. Transfer to a bowl. Leave to cool, then cover and chill for at least 2 hours.

3 Spoon about 15ml/1 tbsp of the mixture into the palm of one hand, flatten slightly, and place a few pieces of diced Manchego cheese in the centre. Shape the rice around the cheese to make a small ball. Flatten slightly, then roll it in the cornmeal. Repeat with the remaining mixture to make about 12 cakes in all.

4 Heat the oil and shallow-fry the rice cakes, in batches of three or four if necessary, for 4–5 minutes until they are crisp and golden brown. Drain on kitchen paper and serve hot, garnished with flat leaf parsley.

CHEESE CHOUX

Deliciously light, these cheese puffs are perfect for parties.

50g/2oz/¼ cup butter, cubed
1.5ml/¼ tsp salt
250ml/8fl oz/1 cup water
115g/4oz/1 cup plain flour
2 whole eggs, plus 1 yolk
2.5ml/½ tsp dry mustard
2.5ml/½ tsp cayenne pepper
50g/2oz/½ cup finely grated well-
flavoured cheese, such as
Manchego or Gruyère

SERVES 4

1 Preheat the oven to 220°C/ 425°F/Gas 7. Bring the butter, salt and water to the boil in a pan. Sift the flour on to a sheet of greaseproof paper, then tip the flour into the boiling liquid and stir it in very quickly.

2 Beat the mixture with a wooden spoon to form a thick paste that leaves the sides of the pan clean. Remove the pan from the heat.

3 Beat in the eggs and yolk, one at a time, then add the mustard, cayenne pepper and grated cheese.

4 Place teaspoonfuls of the mixture on to a non-stick baking sheet and bake for 10 minutes. Lower the oven temperature to 180°C/350°F/Gas 4 and cook for a further 15 minutes until well browned. Serve hot or cold.

SPICY MEATBALLS WITH CHILLI SAUCE

These meatballs are delicious served piping hot, with chilli sauce on the side so guests can add as much heat as they like.

115g/4oz fresh spicy sausages
115g/4oz minced beef
2 shallots, finely chopped
2 garlic cloves, finely chopped
75g/3oz/1½ cups fresh white
breadcrumbs
1 egg, beaten
30ml/2 tbsp chopped fresh parsley,
plus extra to garnish
15ml/1 tbsp olive oil
salt and ground black pepper
Tabasco sauce or other hot chilli
sauce, to serve

SERVES 6

 Heat the olive oil in a large frying pan and cook the meatballs, in batches if necessary, for about 15–20 minutes, stirring regularly until browned and cooked through.

 Transfer the meatballs to a warmed plate and sprinkle with the extra chopped parsley. Serve with chilli sauce on the side, and offer cocktail sticks for spearing.

1 With a sharp knife, nick the skin of each sausage to create a small split and carefully peel off the skin. Repeat until all the sausages have been skinned. Place the sausage meat in a small mixing bowl.

2 Add the minced beef, shallots, garlic, breadcrumbs, beaten egg and parsley, with plenty of salt and pepper to the sausage meat. Mix the ingredients well, then shape into 18 small balls.

SWEET CRUST LAMB

These little noisettes are just big enough for two mouthfuls and so are ideal for tapas. If you would prefer something a little more substantial, small lamb cutlets or chops can be prepared in the same way.

2 Remove the grill pan from the heat. Turn over the lamb rounds and spread with the mustard.

3 Sprinkle the sugar evenly over the lamb rounds, then return the grill pan to the heat.

4 Cook the lamb for 2–3 minutes more, until the sugar has melted, but the lamb is still pink in the centre. Serve with cocktail sticks for spearing.

175g/6oz tender lamb fillet, sliced into
1cm/½ in rounds
5ml/1 tsp mild mustard
30ml/2 tbsp light muscovado sugar
salt and ground black pepper

SERVES 8

1 Preheat the grill to high. Sprinkle the lamb with salt and pepper, and grill on one side for 2 minutes until well browned.

PRAWN BRIOUATES

In Morocco, briouates are made using a special pastry called ouarka. Like filo, it is very thin but it is tricky to make and requires a great deal of practice. Filo makes a good substitute.

175g/6oz filo pastry
40g/1½ oz/3 tbsp butter, melted
sunflower oil, for frying
spring onions and coriander leaves,
to garnish
ground cinnamon and icing sugar,
to serve (optional)

For the prawn filling
15ml/1 tbsp olive oil
15g/½ oz/1 tbsp butter
2–3 spring onions, finely chopped
15g/½ oz/2 tbsp plain flour
300ml/½ pint/1¼ cups milk
2.5ml/½ tsp paprika
350g/12oz cooked peeled
prawns, chopped
salt and ground black pepper

Makes about 24

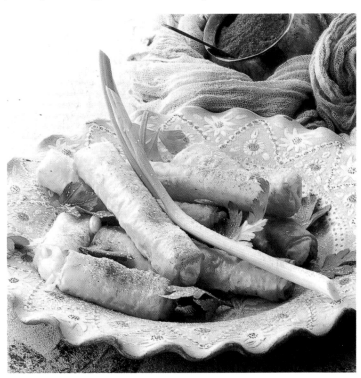

1 First make the filling. Heat the olive oil and butter in a saucepan and fry the spring onions over a gentle heat for 2–3 minutes until soft. Stir in the flour, and then slowly add the milk to make a thick, smooth sauce. Season the filling with paprika, salt and pepper, and stir in the prawns.

2 Take a sheet of filo pastry and cut it in half widthways, to make a rectangle measuring about 18 × 14cm/7 × 5½in. Cover all the remaining pastry with a damp dish towel to prevent it from drying out while you make the first briouate.

3 Brush the pastry with melted butter and then place a heaped teaspoon of filling along one edge. Roll up the pastry like a cigar, tucking in the sides as you go. Continue in this way until you have used all the filling.

4 Heat about 1cm/½ in oil in a heavy-based pan and fry the briouates, in batches if necessary, for 2–3 minutes until golden, turning occasionally. Drain on kitchen paper, then serve garnished with a spring onions and coriander leaves, and sprinkled with cinnamon and icing sugar, if you like.

MEAT BRIOUATES

The Moroccans, who enjoy mixing sweet and savoury tastes, traditionally sprinkle these little pastry snacks with ground cinnamon and icing sugar. It is an unusual but delicious combination.

175g/6oz filo pastry
40g/1½ oz/3 tbsp butter, melted
sunflower oil, for frying
fresh flat leaf parsley, to garnish
ground cinnamon and icing sugar,
to serve (optional)

FOR THE MEAT FILLING
30ml/2 tbsp sunflower oil
1 onion, finely chopped
1 small bunch fresh
coriander, chopped
1 small bunch fresh parsley, chopped
375g/12oz lean minced beef or lamb
2.5ml/½ tsp paprika
5ml/1 tsp ground coriander
good pinch of ground ginger
2 eggs, beaten

MAKES ABOUT 24

1 First make the filling. Heat the oil in a frying pan and fry the onion and herbs over a gentle heat for about 4 minutes until the onion is softened. Add the meat and cook for about 5 minutes, stirring frequently, until the meat is evenly browned and most of the moisture has evaporated.

2 Drain away any excess fat and stir in the spices. Cook for 1 minute, remove the pan from the heat and stir in the beaten eggs. Stir until they begin to set and resemble lightly scrambled eggs. Set aside.

3 Take a sheet of filo pastry and cut into 8.5cm/3½in strips. Cover the remaining pastry with damp dish towels to prevent it from drying out. Brush the strip with melted butter, then place a heaped teaspoon of the meat filling at one end of the strip, about 1cm/½in from the end. Fold one corner over the filling to make a triangular shape.

4 Fold the "triangle" over itself and then continue to fold, keeping the triangle shape, until you reach the end of the strip. Continue in this way until all the mixture has been used up. Make about 23 more in the same way.

5 Heat about 1cm/½ in oil in a heavy-based pan and fry the *briouates* in batches for 2–3 minutes until golden, turning once. Drain on kitchen paper and arrange on a serving plate. Serve garnished with fresh parsley and sprinkled with ground cinnamon and icing sugar, if you like the combination.

PASTRY-WRAPPED CHORIZO PUFFS

These flaky pastry puffs, filled with spicy chorizo sausage and grated cheese, make a perfect accompaniment to a glass of cold sherry or beer. You can use any type of hard cheese for the puffs, but for the best results choose a mild variety, as the chorizo has plenty of flavour.

225g/8oz puff pastry
115g/4oz chorizo sausage, chopped
50g/2oz/½ cup grated cheese
1 small egg, beaten
5ml/1 tsp paprika, to dust

MAKES 16

1 Roll out the pastry thinly on a floured surface. Using a 7.5cm/3in cutter, stamp out as many rounds as possible, then re-roll the trimmings, if necessary, and stamp out more rounds to make 16 in all.

COOK'S TIP
You can prepare the chorizo puffs a day or two ahead. Chill them without the glaze, wrapped in a plastic bag, until ready to bake, then allow them to come back to room temperature while you preheat the oven. Glaze before baking.

2 Preheat the oven to 220°C/450°F/Gas 7. Put the chopped chorizo sausage and grated cheese in a bowl and toss together lightly until well mixed.

3 Lay one of the pastry rounds on the palm of your hand and place a little of the chorizo mixture across the centre.

4 Using your other hand, pinch the edges of the pastry together along the top to seal, as when making a miniature pastie. Repeat the process with the remaining rounds.

5 Place the pastries on a non-stick baking sheet and brush lightly with the beaten egg. Using a small sieve or tea strainer, dust the tops lightly with a little of the paprika.

6 Bake the pastries for 10–12 minutes, until puffed and golden brown. Transfer the pastries to a wire rack and leave to cool for 5 minutes. Transfer to a plate and serve warm, dusted with the rest of the paprika.

VARIATION
Try cutting the pastry in different shapes such as stars and hearts. They are ideal nibbles for children's parties.

SPINACH EMPANADILLAS

These are little pastry turnovers, filled with pine nuts and raisins — ingredients that have a strong Moorish influence.

25g/1oz/2 tbsp raisins
25ml/1½ tbsp olive oil
450g/1lb fresh spinach, washed
and chopped
6 drained canned anchovies, chopped
2 garlic cloves, finely chopped
25g/1oz/⅓ cup pine nuts, chopped
1 egg, beaten
350g/12oz puff pastry
salt and ground black pepper

MAKES 20

1 To make the filling, soak the raisins in a little warm water for 10 minutes. Drain, then chop roughly. Heat the oil in a large sauté pan or wok, add the spinach, stir, then cover and cook over a low heat for about 2 minutes. Uncover, turn up the heat and let any liquid evaporate. Add the anchovies, garlic and seasoning. Cook, stirring, for a further minute. Remove from the heat, add the raisins and pine nuts, and cool.

2 Preheat the oven to 180°C/ 350°F/Gas 4. Roll out the pastry to a 3mm/⅛in thickness.

3 Using a 7.5cm/3in pastry cutter, cut out 20 rounds, re-rolling the dough if necessary. Place about two teaspoons of the filling in the middle of each round, then brush the edges with a little water. Bring up the sides of the pastry and seal well (*left*). Press the edges together with the back of a fork. Brush with egg. Place the turnovers on a lightly greased baking sheet and bake for about 15 minutes, until golden. Serve warm.

FALAFEL

*In North Africa these spicy fritters are made using dried broad beans, but chick-peas are much easier
to buy. They are lovely served as a snack with garlicky yogurt or stuffed into warmed pitta bread.*

150g/5oz/¾ cup dried chick-peas
1 large onion, roughly chopped
2 garlic cloves, roughly chopped
60ml/4 tbsp roughly chopped parsley
5ml/1 tsp cumin seeds, crushed
5ml/1 tsp coriander seeds, crushed
2.5ml/½ tsp baking powder
salt and ground black pepper
oil for deep frying
pitta bread, salad and yogurt, to serve

SERVES 4

1 Put the chick-peas in a bowl with plenty of cold water. Leave to soak overnight.

2 Drain the chick-peas and cover with water in a pan. Bring to the boil. Boil rapidly for 10 minutes. Reduce the heat and simmer for about 1½–2 hours until soft. Drain.

3 Place in a food processor with the onion, garlic, parsley, cumin, coriander and baking powder. Add salt and pepper to taste. Process until the mixture forms a firm paste.

4 Shape the mixture into walnut-size balls and flatten them slightly. In a deep pan, heat 5cm/2in oil until a little of the mixture sizzles when added. Fry the falafel in batches until golden. Drain on kitchen paper and keep hot while frying the remainder. Serve warm in pitta bread, with salad and yogurt.

CROSTINI

These are Italian canapés, consisting of toasted slices of bread, spread with various toppings.
The following recipes are for a chicken liver pâté and a prawn butter.

FOR THE CHICKEN LIVER PATE
150g/5oz/⅔ cup butter
1 small onion, finely chopped
1 garlic clove, crushed
225g/8oz chicken livers
4 sage leaves, chopped
salt and ground black pepper

FOR THE PRAWN BUTTER
225g/8oz cooked, peeled prawns
2 drained canned anchovies
115g/4oz/½ cup butter, softened
15ml/1 tbsp lemon juice
15ml/1 tbsp chopped fresh parsley
salt and ground black pepper

FOR THE CROSTINI
12 slices crusty Italian or
French pain de campagne bread, cut
1cm/½ in thick
75g/3oz/6 tbsp butter, melted

FOR THE GARNISH
sage leaves
flat leaf parsley

SERVES 6

 To make the chicken liver pâté, melt half the butter in a frying pan, add the onion and garlic, and fry gently until soft. Add the chicken livers and sage and sauté for about 8 minutes, until the livers are brown and firm. Season with salt and pepper and process in a blender or food processor with the remaining butter.

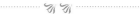 To make the prawn butter, chop the prawns and anchovies finely. Place in a bowl with the butter and beat together until well blended. Add the lemon juice and parsley and season with salt and pepper. Preheat the oven to 200°C/400°F/Gas 6. Place the bread slices on one or two baking sheets and brush with the butter.

 Bake for 8–10 minutes, until pale golden. Spread half the hot crostini with the pâté and the rest with the prawn butter, garnishing with sage and parsley, respectively. Serve the crostini at once.

COOK'S TIP
Both the chicken liver pâté and the prawn butter can be made ahead, but should be used within two days. Let the chicken liver pâté cool, then cover both toppings closely and store them in the fridge.

GOAT'S CHEESE AND CROSTINI WITH FRUIT

A sherry marinade accentuates the flavour of the goat's cheese and contrasts beautifully with the fruity tomato, orange and basil salsa.

8 slices of goat's cheese
15ml/1 tbsp sherry
30ml/2 tbsp walnut oil
30ml/2 tbsp olive oil
4 slices of Italian or French bread
1 garlic clove, halved
2 spring onions, sliced
6 shelled walnut halves,
roughly broken
15ml/1 tbsp chopped fresh parsley
salt and ground black pepper
tomatoes and mixed salad leaves,
to serve

FOR THE SALSA
5 tomatoes, peeled, seeded
and chopped
2 oranges, peeled and segmented
15ml/1 tbsp chopped fresh basil
30ml/2 tbsp olive oil
pinch of soft light brown sugar
fresh basil sprig, to garnish

SERVES 4

1 Put the goat's cheese slices into a shallow bowl, pour over the sherry, walnut oil and olive oil, then marinate in a cool place for 1 hour.

2 In a bowl, mix together all the ingredients for the salsa. Season to taste. Garnish with the basil.

3 Toast the slices of bread on one side, then turn them over and rub the untoasted surfaces with the cut sides of the garlic. Brush with the marinade, then sprinkle the sliced spring onions on top. Arrange two of the marinated slices of cheese on each slice of bread.

4 Pour over any remaining marinade, sprinkle with pepper and cook the crostini under a hot grill until the cheese has browned. Scatter the walnuts and parsley on top. Serve with the tomatoes, salad leaves and the bowl of salsa.

COOK'S TIP
French goat's milk cheese or chèvre is often cylindrical in shape, which makes it perfect for this dish.

TOMATO AND GARLIC BREAD

A basket of warm, crusty, garlic-flavoured bread is always welcome when appetizers are being served.

4 large ripe tomatoes,
roughly chopped
2 garlic cloves, roughly chopped
1.5ml/¼ tsp sea salt
grated rind and juice of ½ lemon
5ml/1 tsp soft light brown sugar
1 flat loaf of bread, such as ciabatta
30ml/2 tbsp olive oil
ground black pepper

SERVES 4–6

1 Preheat the oven to 200°C/ 400°F/Gas 6. Place the tomatoes, garlic, salt, lemon rind and brown sugar in a small pan. Cover and cook gently for 5 minutes until the tomatoes have released their juices.

2 Split the loaf in half horizontally, then cut each half widthways into 2–3 pieces. Bake on a baking sheet for 5–8 minutes until hot, crisp and golden brown.

3 While the bread is baking, stir the lemon juice and olive oil into the tomato mixture. Cook uncovered for 8 minutes more, until the mixture is thick and pulpy.

4 Spread the tomato mixture on the hot bread, sprinkle with pepper and serve at once, in a basket or on a platter.

OLIVE AND ANCHOVY BITES

These melt-in-the-mouth morsels store very well; freeze them for up to 3 months or keep in an airtight container for 2–3 days before serving.

115g/4oz/1 cup plain flour
115g/4oz/½ cup chilled butter
115g/4oz/1 cup finely grated cheese,
such as Manchego or Gruyère
50g/2oz can anchovy fillets in oil,
drained and roughly chopped
50g/2oz/½ cup pitted black olives,
roughly chopped
2.5ml/½ tsp cayenne pepper
sea salt

MAKES 40–45

1 Place the flour, butter, cheese, anchovies, olives and cayenne in a food processor and pulse until the mixture forms a firm dough.

2 Wrap the dough loosely in clear film. Chill for 20 minutes.

3 Preheat the oven to 200°C/ 400°F/Gas 6. Roll out the dough thinly on a lightly floured surface.

4 Cut the dough into 5cm/2in-wide strips, then cut across each strip diagonally, in alternate directions, to make triangles. Place on baking sheets. Bake for 8–10 minutes until golden. Cool on a wire rack. Sprinkle with sea salt and serve.

BLACK PUDDING CANAPES

Black pudding (morcilla) is a very popular tapas dish. In Spain the sausage is often home-made.

15ml/1 tbsp olive oil
1 onion, thinly sliced
2 garlic cloves, thinly sliced
5ml/1 tsp dried oregano or marjoram
5ml/1 tsp paprika
225g/8oz black pudding, cut in
12 thick slices
1 small French stick, sliced into
12 rounds
30ml/2 tbsp dry sherry
sugar, to taste
salt and ground black pepper
chopped fresh oregano, to garnish

SERVES 4

2 Add the slices of black pudding, raise the heat and cook for 3 minutes on each side until crisp.

3 Arrange the rounds of bread on a large serving plate and top each with a slice of black pudding. Stir the sherry into the mixture remaining in the frying pan, with sugar to taste. Heat, stirring, until the mixture bubbles, then season.

1 Heat the oil in a large frying pan and fry the onion, garlic, oregano and paprika for 7–8 minutes until the onion is soft and golden.

COOK'S TIP
If you find real *morcilla*, fry slices in olive oil and top bread rounds.

4 Spoon a little of the onion mixture on top of each slice of black pudding. Scatter over the oregano and serve immediately.

GRILLED PEPPER TARTLETS

*These individual little tarts, topped with red and yellow peppers,
are as colourful as they are scrumptious.*

175g/6oz/1½ cups plain flour,
plus extra for rolling
a pinch of salt
75g/3oz/6 tbsp chilled butter, diced
30–45ml/2–3 tbsp water
1 red pepper, seeded and quartered
1 yellow pepper, seeded and quartered
60ml/4 tbsp double cream
1 egg
15ml/1 tbsp freshly grated Parmesan
salt and ground black pepper

MAKES 12

1 Sift the flour and salt into a bowl. Add the butter and rub it in with your fingertips until the mixture resembles fine breadcrumbs. Stir in enough of the water to make a firm, but not sticky, dough.

2 Preheat the oven to 200°C/400°F/Gas 6. Roll out the dough thinly on a lightly floured surface and line 12 individual moulds or a 12-hole tartlet tin. Prick the pastry bases with a fork and cover them with crumpled foil. Bake blind for 10 minutes.

3 Meanwhile, place the peppers, skin side up, on a baking sheet and grill for 10 minutes until the skin is blistered and blackened. Cover with a dish towel and leave for 5 minutes, then peel away the skin.

4 Cut each piece of pepper lengthways into very thin strips. Remove the foil from the pastry bases and divide the pepper strips among them.

5 Whisk the cream and egg in a bowl. Add plenty of salt and pepper and pour over the peppers in the pastry bases. Sprinkle the Parmesan over each filled tartlet and bake for 15–20 minutes until firm and golden brown. Cool for 2 minutes before removing from the moulds and transferring to wire racks; serve the tartlets warm or cold.

SOUPS

❦ ❦

Soups are a vital part of the culinary heritage of the Mediterranean. From winter warmers to summer coolers, there's a soup for every season.

LEFT: In Morocco the nights can be bitterly cold, and a bowl of hot, spicy soup is very welcome.

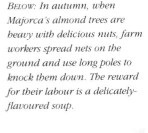

BELOW: In autumn, when Majorca's almond trees are heavy with delicious nuts, farm workers spread nets on the ground and use long poles to knock them down. The reward for their labour is a delicately-flavoured soup.

Soups were, and still are, an important part of the Mediterranean diet. In the past, when a lot of the countries were poverty-stricken, soup constituted a meal for many. These broths were made with beans, lentils and other pulses, particularly during the cold winter months. Eaten with plenty of bread or other starchy food, they were filling and provided nourishment. Fresh vegetables were added in season, and sometimes eggs. Many of these soups, therefore, were extremely simple. Some of the recipes that exist today have been passed down through the generations, only to be given new life, and new status, with the rising popularity of "peasant food" in restaurants and cookbooks. These are unfussy recipes, which rely for their success on the quality of the ingredients. Take garlic soup, for example, which is made in various ways throughout Spain and France. In its simplest form, it is nothing but garlic, water and seasoning, but with the best garlic, these basic ingredients are transformed into a delicious and fragrant liquor. This basic method is applied to many vegetables, with the water sometimes replaced with a meat or vegetable stock, and the mixture sometimes passed through a sieve, to produce a smooth soup.

Pumpkins, Jerusalem artichokes, tomatoes, peppers, asparagus and spinach are just a few of the many varieties of vegetables used to make soup.

Soups containing meat are usually hearty, combined as they are with pulses such as lentils, chick-peas, or potatoes, rice or pasta. In the Middle East, beef and lamb are used, and soups are seasoned with spices and herbs. There are special feast day soups, and soups to eat after sunset during the fast of Ramadan. However, the more

ABOVE: Dawn in Corfu, and a fisherman prepares to head out to sea.

typical Mediterranean soup is based on vegetables, pulses, and, of course, fish and seafood. Wonderful fish soups come in numerous different guises; the now famous, and often poorly imitated *bouillabaisse* is a "stew" of various varieties of fish and seafood native to the coast of the south of France, and the port of Marseilles, where the dish originated. Again, these soups serve as complete meals, sometimes with the broth strained off from the fish and served separately, and accompanied by bread or toasted croûtes.

Every country and coastal region has its own speciality, and often the soup will never be quite the same, the ingredients depending on the fishermen's catch that day. Many of the recipes were originated by the fishermen themselves, who cooked them on the boats, using the fish which they couldn't sell in the market, because it had no commercial value. Today, with a wide choice of fish available in fishmongers and supermarkets, it is easy to recreate many of these wonderful dishes at home.

Chilled soups come from the south of Spain, where *gazpacho* is extremely popular – this is a delicious and refreshing mixture of raw tomatoes, peppers and cucumbers which makes the perfect lunch for a hot summer day. Again, there are variations on this classic recipe, with such diverse ingredients as almonds and grapes. Cold soups also feature in the Middle East – usually yogurt-based, and mixed with cucumber, garlic and mint.

Tourists who travel to the Mediterranean seldom sample more than a few of the many soups on offer, but it is worth investigating that delicious smell wafting from a restaurant kitchen, or asking the name of that delectable-looking soup that is being enjoyed at the next table.

Changing at the whim of the cook, or to take best advantage of the finest market produce, Mediterranean soups are certainly a cause for celebration.

BOUILLABAISSE

—

Perhaps the most famous of all Mediterranean fish soups, this recipe originated from Marseilles in the south of France. It is a rich and colourful mixture of fish and shellfish, flavoured with tomatoes, saffron and orange.

························ 🐟 🐟 ························

1.5kg/3–3½lb mixed fish and raw shellfish, such as red mullet, John Dory, monkfish, red snapper, whiting, large prawns and clams
225g/8oz well-flavoured tomatoes
pinch of saffron strands
90ml/6 tbsp olive oil
1 onion, sliced
1 leek, sliced
1 celery stick, sliced
2 garlic cloves, crushed
1 bouquet garni
1 strip pared orange rind
2.5ml/½ tsp fennel seeds
15ml/1 tbsp tomato purée
10ml/2 tsp Pernod
4–6 thick slices French bread
45ml/3 tbsp chopped fresh parsley
salt and ground black pepper

SERVES 4–6

························ 🐟 🐟 ························

1 Remove the heads, tails and fins from the fish and put them in a large pan, with 1.2 litres/2 pints/ 5 cups water. Bring to the boil, and simmer for 15 minutes. Strain, and reserve the liquid.

2 Cut the fish into large chunks. Leave the shellfish in their shells. Scald the tomatoes, then drain and refresh in cold water. Peel and roughly chop them. Soak the saffron in 15–30ml/1–2 tbsp hot water.

3 Heat the oil in a large pan, add the onion, leek and celery and cook until softened. Add the garlic, bouquet garni, orange rind, fennel seeds and tomatoes, then stir in the saffron and liquid and the fish stock. Season with salt and pepper, then bring to the boil and simmer for 30–40 minutes.

4 Add the shellfish and boil for about 6 minutes. Add the fish and cook for a further 6–8 minutes, until it flakes easily.

5 Using a slotted spoon, transfer the fish to a warmed serving platter. Keep the liquid boiling, to allow the oil to emulsify with the broth. Add the tomato purée and Pernod, then check the seasoning. To serve, place a slice of French bread in each soup bowl, pour the broth over the top and serve the fish separately, sprinkled with the parsley.

SAFFRON MUSSEL SOUP

This is one of France's most delicious seafood soups. Serve it with plenty of French bread to mop up all the delectable juices.

40g/1½ oz/3 tbsp unsalted butter
8 shallots, finely chopped
1 bouquet garni
5ml/1 tsp black peppercorns
350ml/12fl oz/1½ cups dry white wine
1kg/2¼ lb fresh mussels, scrubbed
and bearded
2 medium leeks, trimmed and
finely chopped
1 fennel bulb, finely chopped
1 carrot, finely chopped
several saffron strands
1 litre/1¾ pints/4 cups fish or
chicken stock
30–45ml/2–3 tbsp cornflour, blended
with 45ml/3 tbsp cold water
120ml/4fl oz/½ cup whipping cream
1 medium tomato, peeled, seeded and
finely chopped
30ml/2 tbsp Pernod (optional)
salt and ground black pepper

SERVES 4–6

1 In a large heavy pan, melt half the butter over a medium-high heat. Add half the shallots and cook for 1–2 minutes until softened but not coloured. Add the bouquet garni, peppercorns and white wine and bring to the boil. Add the mussels, cover tightly and cook over a high heat for 3–5 minutes, shaking the pan occasionally, until the mussels have opened.

2 With a slotted spoon, transfer the mussels to a bowl. Strain the cooking liquid through a muslin-lined sieve and reserve.

3 When the mussels are cool enough to handle, discard any that are closed. Pull open and remove the flesh from the rest Add any juices to the reserved liquid.

4 Rinse the saucepan and melt the remaining butter over a medium heat. Add the remaining shallots and cook for 1–2 minutes. Add the leeks, fennel, carrot and saffron and cook for 3–5 minutes.

5 Stir in the reserved cooking liquid, bring to the boil and cook for 5 minutes until the vegetables are tender and the liquid is slightly reduced. Add the stock and bring to the boil, skimming any foam that rises to the surface. Season with salt, if needed, and black pepper. Cook for a further 5 minutes.

6 Stir the blended cornflour into the soup. Simmer for 2–3 minutes until the soup is slightly thickened, then add the cream, mussels and chopped tomato. Stir in the Pernod, if using, and cook for 1–2 minutes until hot, then serve.

PRAWN BISQUE

The classic French way to make a bisque requires you to push the shellfish through a tamis, or drum sieve. This is a much simpler method and the result is just as smooth.

675g/1½ lb small or medium cooked
prawns in their shells
25ml/1½ tbsp vegetable oil
2 onions, halved and sliced
1 large carrot, sliced
2 celery sticks, sliced
2 litres/3½ pints/8 cups water
a few drops of lemon juice
30ml/2 tbsp tomato purée
bouquet garni
50g/2oz/¼ cup butter
50g/2oz/½ cup plain flour
45–60ml/3–4 tbsp brandy
150ml/¼ pint/⅔ cup whipping cream
salt and white pepper

SERVES 6–8

1 Remove the heads from the prawns and peel away the shells, reserving the heads and shells for the stock. Chill the peeled prawns.

2 Heat the oil in a large pan, add the prawn heads and shells and cook over a high heat, stirring, until they start to brown. Reduce the heat, add the onions, carrot and celery, and fry gently for about 5 minutes.

3 Add the water, some lemon juice, tomato purée and bouquet garni. Bring the stock to the boil, then reduce the heat, cover and simmer gently for 25 minutes. Strain the stock through a sieve.

4 Melt the butter in a heavy saucepan over a medium heat. Stir in the flour and cook until just golden, stirring occasionally. Add the brandy and gradually pour in about half of the prawn stock, whisking vigorously until smooth, then whisk in the remaining liquid. Season with salt, if necessary, and white pepper. Reduce the heat, cover and simmer for 5 minutes, stirring frequently.

5 Strain the soup into a clean saucepan. Add the cream and a little extra lemon juice to taste, then stir in most of the reserved prawns and cook over a medium heat, stirring frequently, until hot. Serve at once, garnished with the remaining reserved prawns. Add a sprig of flat leaf parsley to each portion, if you like.

SEAFOOD SOUP WITH ROUILLE

This is a really chunky, aromatic mixed fish soup from France, flavoured with plenty of saffron and herbs. Rouille, a fiery hot paste, is served separately for everyone to swirl into their soup to flavour.

3 gurnard or red mullet, scaled
and gutted
12 large prawns
675g/1½lb white fish, such as cod,
haddock, halibut or monkfish
225g/8oz fresh mussels
1 onion, quartered
5ml/1 tsp saffron strands
75ml/5 tbsp olive oil
1 fennel bulb, roughly chopped
4 garlic cloves, crushed
3 strips pared orange rind
4 thyme sprigs
675g/1½lb tomatoes or 400g/14oz can
chopped tomatoes
30ml/2 tbsp sun-dried tomato paste
3 bay leaves
salt and ground black pepper

FOR THE ROUILLE
1 red pepper, seeded and
roughly chopped
1 red chilli, seeded and sliced
2 garlic cloves, chopped
75ml/5 tbsp olive oil
15g/½oz/¼ cup fresh breadcrumbs

SERVES 6

1 To make the rouille, process the pepper, chilli, garlic, oil and breadcrumbs in a blender or food processor until smooth. Transfer to a serving dish and chill.

2 Fillet the gurnard or mullet by cutting away the flesh from either side of the backbone, reserving the heads and bones. Cut the fillets into small chunks. Shell half the prawns and reserve the trimmings to make the stock. Skin the white fish, discarding any bones, and cut into large chunks. Scrub the mussels well, discarding any damaged ones or any open ones that do not close when tapped sharply with the back of a knife.

3 Put the fish trimmings and prawn trimmings in a saucepan with the onion and 1.2 litres/2 pints/5 cups water. Bring to the boil, then simmer gently for 30 minutes. Cool slightly and strain.

4 Soak the saffron in 15ml/1 tbsp boiling water. Heat 30ml/2 tbsp of the oil in a large sauté pan or saucepan. Add the gurnard or mullet and white fish and fry over a high heat for 1 minute. Drain.

5 Heat the remaining oil and fry the fennel, garlic, orange rind and thyme until beginning to colour. Make up the strained stock to about 1.2 litres/2 pints/5 cups with water.

COOK'S TIP
To save time, order the fish and ask the fishmonger to fillet the gurnard or mullet for you.

6 If using fresh tomatoes, plunge them into boiling water for 30 seconds, then refresh in cold water. Peel and chop. Add the stock to the pan with the saffron, tomatoes, tomato paste and bay leaves. Season, bring almost to the boil, then simmer gently, covered, for 20 minutes.

7 Stir in the gurnard or mullet, white fish and prawns and add the mussels. Cover the pan and cook for 3–4 minutes. Discard any mussels that do not open. Serve the soup hot with the rouille.

FISH AND OKRA SOUP

The inspiration for this soup originally came from North Africa. Chop the okra for a more authentic consistency, if you prefer.

2 │ Melt the butter in a large pan and sauté the onion for about 5 minutes until soft. Stir in the chopped tomatoes and okra, and fry gently for a further 10 minutes.

3 │ Add the fish, fish stock, chilli and seasoning. Bring to the boil, then reduce the heat and simmer for about 20 minutes or until the fish is cooked through and flakes easily.

4 │ Peel and slice the bananas. Stir into the soup and heat through. Serve sprinkled with parsley.

---

2 green bananas
50g/2oz/¼ cup butter
1 onion, finely chopped
2 tomatoes, peeled and finely chopped
115g/4oz okra, trimmed
225g/8oz smoked haddock or cod
fillet, cut into bite-size pieces
900ml/1½ pints/3¾ cups fish stock
1 chilli, seeded and chopped
salt and ground black pepper
chopped fresh parsley, to garnish

SERVES 4

1 │ Slit the skins of the green bananas and place in a large saucepan. Cover with water, bring to the boil and cook over a moderate heat for about 25 minutes or until the bananas are tender. Transfer to a plate and leave to cool.

FISH AND VEGETABLE SOUP

Liguria, in Italy, is famous for its fish soups. In this one, the fish are cooked in a broth with vegetables and then puréed. This mixture can also be used to dress pasta.

1kg/2¼lb mixed fish or fish pieces
(such as sole, whiting, red mullet,
salmon, haddock, etc)
90ml/6 tbsp olive oil, plus extra to serve
1 medium onion, finely chopped
1 celery stick, chopped
1 carrot, chopped
60ml/4 tbsp chopped fresh parsley
175ml/6fl oz/¾ cup dry white wine
3 medium tomatoes, peeled
and chopped
2 garlic cloves, finely chopped
1.5 litres/2½ pints/6 cups boiling water
salt and ground black pepper
rounds of French bread, to serve

SERVES 6

3 Pour in the wine, raise the heat, and cook until it reduces by about half. Stir in the tomatoes and garlic. Cook for 3–4 minutes, stirring occasionally. Add the boiling water, and bring back to the boil. Cook for a further 15 minutes.

4 Stir in the fish, and simmer for 10–15 minutes, or until it is tender. Season well.

5 Remove the fish from the soup. Discard any skin and bones. Purée the flesh in a food processor and return it to the soup. Season to taste. If the soup is too thick, add more water.

6 Heat the soup to simmering. Toast the bread, and sprinkle with olive oil. Place 2 or 3 rounds in each soup bowl before pouring over the soup.

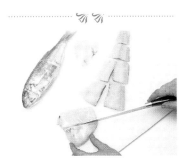

1 Scale and clean the fish, discarding all innards, but leaving the heads on. Cut into large pieces. Rinse well in cool water.

2 Heat the oil in a large saucepan and add the onion. Cook over a low heat until it softens. Stir in the celery and carrot, and cook for 5 minutes more. Add the parsley.

SPICED MUSSEL SOUP

Chunky and colourful, this Turkish fish soup is like a chowder in its consistency. It is flavoured with harissa sauce, more familiar in North African cookery.

1.5kg/3–3½lb fresh mussels
150ml/¼ pint/⅔ cup white wine
3 tomatoes
30ml/2 tbsp olive oil
1 onion, finely chopped
2 garlic cloves, crushed
2 celery sticks, thinly sliced
bunch of spring onions, thinly sliced
1 potato, diced
7.5ml/1½ tsp harissa sauce
45ml/3 tbsp chopped fresh parsley
ground black pepper
thick yogurt, to serve (optional)

SERVES 6

1 Scrub the mussels, discarding any that are damaged or any open ones that do not close when tapped with a knife.

2 Bring the wine to the boil in a large saucepan. Add the mussels and cover with a lid. Cook for 4–5 minutes until the mussels have opened wide. Discard any mussels that remain closed. Drain the mussels, reserving the cooking liquid. Reserve a few mussels in their shells for garnish and shell the rest.

3 Peel the tomatoes and dice them. Heat the oil in a pan and fry the onion, garlic, celery and spring onions for 5 minutes.

4 Add the shelled mussels, reserved liquid, potato, harissa sauce and tomatoes. Bring just to the boil, reduce the heat and cover. Simmer gently for 25 minutes, or until the potatoes are breaking up.

5 Stir in the parsley and pepper and add the reserved mussels. Heat through for 1 minute. Serve hot with a spoonful of yogurt, if you like.

GREEN LENTIL SOUP

Lentil soup is an Eastern Mediterranean classic, varying in its spiciness according to region. Red or puy lentils make an equally good substitute for the green lentils used here.

225g/8oz/1 cup green lentils
75ml/5 tbsp olive oil
3 onions, finely chopped
2 garlic cloves, thinly sliced
10ml/2 tsp cumin seeds, crushed
1.5ml/¼ tsp ground turmeric
600ml/1 pint/2½ cups chicken or vegetable stock
salt and ground black pepper
30ml/2 tbsp roughly chopped fresh coriander, to finish

SERVES 4–6

1 Put the lentils in a saucepan and cover with cold water. Bring to the boil and boil rapidly for 10 minutes. Drain.

2 Heat 30ml/2 tbsp of the oil in a pan and fry two of the onions with the garlic, cumin and turmeric for 3 minutes, stirring. Add the lentils, stock and 600ml/1 pint/2½ cups water. Bring to the boil, reduce the heat, cover and simmer gently for 30 minutes, until the lentils are soft.

3 Fry the third onion in the remaining oil until golden.

4 Use a potato masher to lightly mash the lentils and make the soup pulpy. Reheat gently and season with salt and pepper to taste. Pour the soup into bowls. Stir the fresh coriander into the fried onion and scatter over the soup. Serve with warm bread.

CHICK-PEA AND PARSLEY SOUP

Thick, tasty and comforting, this is perfect for wintry evenings.

225g/8oz/1⅓ cups chick-peas,
soaked overnight
1 small onion
1 bunch fresh parsley, about
40g/1½oz
30ml/2 tbsp olive oil and
sunflower oil, mixed
1.2 litres/2 pints/5 cups chicken stock
juice of ½ lemon
salt and ground black pepper
lemon wedges and finely pared strips
of rind, to garnish
crusty bread, to serve

SERVES 6

1 Drain the chick-peas and rinse them under cold water. Cook them in rapidly boiling water for 10 minutes, then simmer for 1–1½ hours until just tender. Drain.

2 Place the onion and parsley in a food processor or blender and process until finely chopped.

3 Heat the olive and sunflower oils in a saucepan or flameproof casserole dish and fry the onion mixture for 5 minutes over a low heat until the onion is slightly softened.

4 Add the chick-peas, cook gently for 1–2 minutes and add the stock. Season well with salt and pepper. Bring the soup to the boil, then cover and simmer for 20 minutes until the chick-peas are soft.

5 Allow the soup to cool a little. Part-purée the soup in a food processor or blender, or by mashing the chick-peas fairly roughly with a fork, so that the soup is thick but still has plenty of texture.

6 Return the soup to a clean pan, add the lemon juice and adjust the seasoning if necessary. Heat gently and then serve, garnished with lemon wedges and finely pared lemon rind, and accompanied by crusty bread.

COOK'S TIP
Chick-peas are easier to purée if the outer skin is rubbed away. If you don't have time to cook the chick-peas yourself use canned chick-peas.

MEDITERRANEAN BEAN SOUP

There are many versions of this wonderful soup. This one uses cannellini beans, leeks, cabbage and good olive oil — and tastes even better reheated.

45ml/3 tbsp extra virgin olive oil
1 onion, roughly chopped
2 leeks, roughly chopped
1 large potato, peeled and diced
2 garlic cloves, finely chopped
1.2 litres/2 pints/5 cups vegetable stock
400g/14oz canned cannellini beans, drained, liquid reserved
175g/6oz Savoy cabbage, shredded
45ml/3 tbsp chopped fresh flat leaf parsley
30ml/2 tbsp chopped fresh oregano
75g/3oz Parmesan cheese, shaved
salt and ground black pepper

For the garlic toasts
30–45ml/2–3 tbsp extra virgin olive oil
6 thick slices country bread
1 garlic clove, peeled and bruised

Serves 4

2 Stir in the cabbage and beans, with half of the herbs, season and cook for 10 minutes more. Spoon about one-third of the soup into a food processor or blender and process until fairly smooth. Return to the soup in the pan, taste for seasoning and then heat through for 5 minutes.

3 Meanwhile, make the garlic toasts. Drizzle a little oil over the slices of bread, then rub both sides of each slice with the garlic. Toast until browned on both sides. Ladle the soup into bowls. Sprinkle with the remaining herbs and the Parmesan shavings. Add a drizzle of olive oil and serve with the toasts.

1 Heat the oil and gently cook the onion, leeks, potato and garlic for 4–5 minutes. Pour on the stock and add the liquid from the beans. Cover and simmer for 15 minutes.

RIBOLLITA

Ribollita is rather like minestrone, but includes beans instead of pasta. In Italy it is traditionally served ladled over bread and a rich green vegetable, although you could omit this for a lighter version.

45ml/3 tbsp olive oil
2 onions, chopped
2 carrots, sliced
4 garlic cloves, crushed
2 celery sticks, thinly sliced
1 fennel bulb, trimmed and chopped
2 large courgettes, thinly sliced
400g/14oz can chopped tomatoes
30ml/2 tbsp home-made or
bought pesto
900ml/1½ pints/3¾ cups vegetable
stock
400g/14oz can haricot or borlotti
beans, drained
salt and ground black pepper

TO FINISH
450g/1lb young spinach
15ml/1 tbsp extra virgin olive oil, plus
extra for drizzling
6–8 slices white bread
Parmesan cheese shavings

SERVES 6–8

VARIATION
Use other dark greens, such as chard
or cabbage instead of the spinach;
shred and cook until tender.

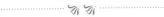

1 Heat the oil in a large saucepan.
Add the onions, carrots, garlic,
celery and fennel and fry gently for
10 minutes. Add the courgettes and
fry for a further 2 minutes.

2 Add the chopped tomatoes,
pesto, stock and beans and
bring to the boil. Reduce the heat,
cover and simmer gently for 25–30
minutes, until the vegetables are
completely tender. Season with salt
and pepper to taste.

3 To serve, fry the spinach in the
oil for 2 minutes or until wilted.
Spoon over the bread in soup bowls,
then ladle the soup over the spinach.
Serve with extra olive oil for drizzling
on to the soup and Parmesan cheese
to sprinkle on top.

MOROCCAN HARIRA

This is a hearty meat and vegetable soup, eaten during the month of Ramadan, when the Muslim population fast between sunrise and sunset.

450g/1lb well-flavoured tomatoes
225g/8oz lamb, cut into 1cm/½in pieces
2.5ml/½ tsp ground turmeric
2.5ml/½ tsp ground cinnamon
25g/1oz/2 tbsp butter
60ml/4 tbsp chopped fresh coriander
30ml/2 tbsp chopped fresh parsley
1 onion, chopped
50g/2oz/¼ cup split red lentils
75g/3oz/½ cup dried chick-peas, soaked overnight
4 baby onions or small shallots, peeled
25g/1oz/¼ cup soup noodles
salt and ground black pepper
chopped fresh coriander, lemon slices and ground cinnamon, to garnish

SERVES 4

1 Plunge the tomatoes into boiling water for 30 seconds, then refresh in cold water. Peel away the skins. Cut into quarters and remove the seeds. Chop roughly.

2 Put the lamb, turmeric, cinnamon, butter, coriander, parsley and onion into a large pan, and cook over a moderate heat, stirring, for 5 minutes. Add the chopped tomatoes and continue to cook for 10 minutes.

3 Rinse the lentils under running water and add to the pan with the drained chick-peas and 600ml/ 1 pint/2½ cups water. Season with salt and pepper. Bring to the boil, cover, and simmer gently for 1½ hours.

4 Add the baby onions and cook for a further 30 minutes. Add the noodles 5 minutes before the end of this cooking time. Garnish with the coriander, lemon slices and cinnamon.

CHICKEN SOUP WITH VERMICELLI

In Morocco, the cook – who is almost always the most senior female of the household – uses a whole chicken for this nourishing soup, to serve her large extended family. This is a slightly simplified version of the classic recipe, using chicken portions.

30ml/2 tbsp sunflower oil
15g/½oz/1 tbsp butter
1 onion, chopped
2 chicken legs or breast pieces, halved or quartered
seasoned flour, for dusting
2 carrots, cut into 4cm/1½in pieces
1 parsnip, cut into 4cm/1½in pieces
1.5 litres/2½ pints/6 cups chicken stock
1 cinnamon stick
a good pinch of paprika
a pinch of saffron strands
2 egg yolks
juice of ½ lemon
30ml/2 tbsp chopped fresh coriander
30ml/2 tbsp chopped fresh parsley
150g/5oz vermicelli
salt and ground black pepper
rustic bread, to serve

SERVES 4–6

1 Heat the oil and butter in a saucepan or flameproof casserole dish and fry the onion for 3–4 minutes until softened. Dust the chicken pieces in seasoned flour and fry gently until evenly browned.

2 Transfer the chicken to a plate and add the carrots and parsnip to the pan. Cook over a gentle heat for 3–4 minutes, stirring frequently, then return the chicken to the pan. Add the stock, cinnamon stick and paprika and season well with salt and black pepper.

3 Bring the soup to the boil, cover and simmer for 1 hour until the vegetables are very tender. While the soup is cooking, mix the saffron with 30ml/2 tbsp boiling water.

4 Beat the egg yolks with the lemon juice in a separate bowl and add the chopped coriander and parsley. As soon as the saffron water has cooled, stir it into the egg and lemon mixture.

VARIATION
Try using different root vegetables, such as swede and turnip, which will subtly vary the flavour of the soup.

5 When the vegetables are tender, transfer the chicken to a plate again. Spoon away any excess fat from the soup, then increase the heat a little and stir in the vermicelli. Cook for 5–6 minutes until the noodles are tender.

6 Meanwhile, remove the skin from the chicken and, if you like, bone and chop into bite-size pieces. If you prefer, simply skin the chicken and leave the pieces whole.

7 When the vermicelli is cooked, reduce the heat and stir in the chicken pieces and the egg, lemon and saffron mixture. Cook over a very low heat for 1–2 minutes, stirring all the time. Adjust the seasoning and serve with rustic bread.

MINESTRONE WITH PASTA AND BEANS

Although minestrone hails originally from northern Italy, it is now found all over that country.
This classic version includes pancetta for a pleasant touch of saltiness.

45ml/3 tbsp olive oil
115g/4oz pancetta, any rinds
removed, roughly chopped
2–3 celery sticks, finely chopped
3 medium carrots, finely chopped
1 medium onion, finely chopped
1–2 garlic cloves, crushed
400g/14oz canned chopped tomatoes
about 1 litre/1¾ pints/4 cups
chicken stock
400g/14oz canned cannellini beans,
drained and rinsed
50g/2oz/½ cup short-cut macaroni
30–60ml/2–4 tbsp chopped flat leaf
parsley, to taste
salt and ground black pepper
shaved Parmesan cheese, to serve

SERVES 4–6

[1] Heat the oil in a large saucepan,
but do not let the oil smoke as
this will spoil the subtle flavour of the
olive oil. Add the pancetta, fry for a
moment to release some of the fat,
then add the celery, carrots and
onion. Cook over a gentle heat for
5 minutes, stirring constantly with a
wooden spoon. Continue stirring
until the vegetables are tender but
not too soft.

[2] Add the garlic and tomatoes,
breaking them up well with a
wooden spoon. Pour in the stock.
Add salt and pepper to taste and
bring to the boil. Half-cover the pan,
reduce the heat and simmer gently
for about 20 minutes, until all the
vegetables are soft.

[3] Add the drained beans to the
pan with the macaroni. Bring to
the boil again. Cover, lower the heat
and continue to simmer for about 20
minutes more. Check the consistency
and add more stock if necessary. Stir
in the parsley and taste for seasoning.

[4] Serve hot, sprinkled with plenty
of Parmesan cheese. This hearty
soup makes a meal in itself if served
with chunks of crusty Italian bread.

VARIATION
Use long-grain rice instead of pasta,
and borlotti beans instead of
cannellini beans.

GALICIAN BROTH

This delicious main meal soup is very similar to the warming, chunky meat and potato broths of cooler climates. For extra colour, a few onion skins can be added when cooking the gammon, but remember to remove them before serving.

450g/1lb gammon, in one piece
2 bay leaves
2 onions, sliced
10ml/2 tsp paprika
675g/1½lb potatoes, cut into
large chunks
225g/8oz spring greens
425g/15oz can haricot or cannellini
beans, drained
salt and ground black pepper

SERVES 4

2 Bring to the boil then reduce the heat and simmer very gently for about 1½ hours until the meat is tender. Keep an eye on the pan to make sure it doesn't boil over.

4 Cut away the cores from the greens. Roll up the leaves and cut into thin shreds. Add to the pan with the beans and simmer for about 10 minutes. Season with salt and pepper to taste and serve hot.

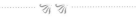

1 Soak the gammon overnight in cold water. Drain and put in a large saucepan with the bay leaves and onions. Pour over 1.5 litres/ 2½ pints/6¼ cups cold water.

3 Drain the meat, reserving the cooking liquid and leave to cool slightly. Discard the skin and any excess fat from the meat and cut into small chunks. Return to the pan with the paprika and potatoes. Cover and simmer gently for 20 minutes.

COOK'S TIP
Bacon knuckles can be used instead of the gammon. The bones will give the juices a delicious flavour.

ITALIAN LENTIL SOUP WITH TOMATOES

This is a classic rustic soup flavoured with rosemary. It is delicious served with garlic bread.

225g/8oz/1 cup dried green or
brown lentils
45ml/3 tbsp extra virgin olive oil
3 rindless streaky bacon rashers, cut
into small dice
1 onion, finely chopped
2 celery sticks, finely chopped
2 carrots, finely diced
2 rosemary sprigs, finely chopped
2 bay leaves
400g/14oz canned
plum tomatoes
1.75 litres/3 pints/7 cups
vegetable stock
salt and ground black pepper
fresh bay leaves and rosemary sprigs,
to garnish

SERVES 4

1 Place the lentils in a bowl and cover with cold water. Leave to soak for 2 hours. Rinse and drain.

2 Heat the oil in a large saucepan. Add the bacon and cook for about 3 minutes, then stir in the onion and cook for 5 minutes until softened. Stir in the celery, carrots, rosemary, bay leaves and lentils. Toss over the heat for 1 minute until thoroughly coated in the oil.

3 Tip in the tomatoes and stock and bring to the boil. Lower the heat, half-cover the pan, and simmer for about 1 hour, or until the lentils are perfectly tender. Stir the soup from time to time.

4 Remove the bay leaves, add salt and pepper to taste and serve in heated bowls, garnishing each portion with one or two fresh bay leaves and rosemary sprigs.

SPINACH AND RICE SOUP

Use very fresh, young spinach leaves to prepare this light and fresh-tasting soup.

675g/1½lb fresh spinach, washed
45ml/3 tbsp extra virgin olive oil
1 small onion, finely chopped
2 garlic cloves, finely chopped
1 small red chilli, seeded and
finely chopped
115g/4oz/generous ½ cup risotto rice
1.2 litres/2 pints/5 cups vegetable stock
60ml/4 tbsp grated Pecorino cheese
salt and ground black pepper

SERVES 4

1 Place the spinach in a pan with just the water that clings to its leaves. Add salt. Heat until wilted, then drain, reserving any liquid.

2 Chop the spinach finely using a large knife.

3 Heat the oil in a large saucepan and gently cook the onion, garlic and chilli for 4–5 minutes until softened. Stir in the rice until well coated, then pour in the stock and reserved spinach liquid. Bring to the boil, lower the heat and simmer for 10 minutes.

4 Add the spinach, with salt and pepper to taste. Cook for 5–7 minutes more, until the rice is tender. Check the seasoning and serve with the Pecorino cheese.

PISTOU

This is a delicious vegetable soup from Nice in the south of France, served with a sun-dried tomato pesto, and fresh Parmesan cheese.

---

1 courgette, diced
1 small potato, diced
1 shallot, chopped
1 carrot, diced
225g/8oz can chopped tomatoes
1.2 litres/2 pints/5 cups vegetable stock
50g/2oz French beans, cut into
1cm/½in lengths
50g/2oz/½ cup frozen petits pois
50g/2oz/½ cup small pasta shapes
60–90ml/4–6 tbsp home-made or
bought pesto
15ml/1 tbsp sun-dried tomato paste
salt and ground black pepper
freshly grated Parmesan cheese,
to serve

SERVES 4–6

1 Place the courgette, potato, shallot, carrot and tomatoes in a large pan. Add the vegetable stock and season with salt and pepper. Bring to the boil, then cover and simmer for 20 minutes.

2 Add the French beans, petits pois and pasta. Cook for a further 10 minutes, until the pasta is tender. Adjust the seasoning.

3 Ladle the soup into individual bowls. Mix together the pesto and sun-dried tomato paste, and stir a spoonful into each serving. Serve with grated Parmesan cheese to sprinkle into each bowl.

AVGOLEMONO

This is the most popular of Greek soups. The name means egg and lemon, two important ingredients which produce a light, nourishing soup. Orzo is Greek, rice-shaped pasta, but you can use any small shape.

1.75 litres/3 pints/7 cups
chicken stock
115g/4oz/1 cup orzo pasta
3 eggs
juice of 1 large lemon
salt and ground black pepper
lemon slices, to garnish

SERVES 4–6

1 Pour the stock into a large pan, and bring to the boil. Add the pasta and cook for 5 minutes.

2 Beat the eggs until frothy, then add the lemon juice and a tablespoon of cold water. Slowly stir in a ladleful of the hot chicken stock, then add one or two more. Return this mixture to the pan, take off the heat and stir well. Season with salt and pepper and serve at once, garnished with lemon slices. (Do not let the soup boil once the eggs have been added or it will curdle.)

109

MOROCCAN VEGETABLE SOUP

Creamy parsnip and pumpkin give this soup a wonderfully rich texture.

15ml/1 tbsp olive or sunflower oil
15g/¹⁄₂oz/1 tbsp butter
1 onion, chopped
225g/8oz carrots, chopped
225g/8oz parsnips, chopped
225g/8oz pumpkin
about 900ml/1¹⁄₂ pints/3³⁄₄ cups
vegetable or chicken stock
lemon juice, to taste
salt and ground black pepper

For the garnish
7.5ml/1¹⁄₂ tbsp olive oil
¹⁄₂ garlic clove, finely chopped
45ml/3 tbsp chopped fresh parsley and
coriander, mixed
a good pinch of paprika

Serves 4

2 Cut the pumpkin into chunks, discarding the skin and pith, and stir into the pan. Cover and cook for a further 5 minutes, then add the stock and seasoning, and slowly bring to the boil. Cover and simmer very gently for 35–40 minutes until all the vegetables are tender.

3 Allow the soup to cool slightly, then purée in a food processor or blender until smooth, adding a little extra water if necessary. Pour back into a clean pan and reheat.

4 To make the garnish, heat the oil in a small pan and add the garlic, parsley and coriander. Fry over a low heat for 1–2 minutes. Add the paprika and stir well.

5 Adjust the seasoning of the soup and stir in just enough lemon juice to taste.

6 Pour into warmed individual soup bowls. Spoon a little garnish on top and carefully swirl it into the soup.

1 Heat the oil and butter in a large pan and fry the onion for about 3 minutes until softened, stirring occasionally. Add the carrots and parsnips, stir well, cover and cook over a gentle heat for a further 5 minutes.

CREAMY COURGETTE SOUP

The beauty of this soup is its delicate colour, rich and creamy texture and subtle taste. If you prefer a more pronounced cheese flavour, use Gorgonzola instead of Dolcelatte.

30ml/2 tbsp olive oil
15g/½ oz/1 tbsp butter
1 medium onion, roughly chopped
900g/2lb courgettes, trimmed
and sliced
5ml/1 tsp dried oregano
about 600ml/1 pint/2½ cups vegetable
or chicken stock
115g/4oz Dolcelatte cheese, rind
removed, diced
300ml/½ pint/1¼ cups single cream
salt and ground black pepper
fresh oregano and extra Dolcelatte,
to garnish

SERVES 4–6

1 Heat the oil and butter in a large saucepan until foaming. add the onion and cook gently for about 5 minutes, stirring often, until softened but not browned.

2 Add the courgettes and oregano, with salt and pepper to taste. Cook over a medium heat for 10 minutes, stirring frequently.

3 Pour in the stock and bring to the boil, stirring. Lower the heat, half-cover the pan and simmer, stirring occasionally, for 30 minutes. Stir in the Dolcelatte until melted.

4 Process the soup in a food processor or blender until smooth, then press through a sieve into a clean pan.

5 Add two-thirds of the cream and stir over a low heat until hot, but not boiling. Check the consistency and add more stock if the soup is too thick. Taste for seasoning, then pour into heated bowls. Swirl in the remaining cream. Garnish with oregano and extra cheese, and serve.

COOK'S TIP
To save time, trim off and discard the ends of the courgettes, cut them into thirds, then chop them in a food processor fitted with the metal blade.

SPANISH GARLIC SOUP

This is a simple and satisfying soup, made with one of the most popular ingredients in the Mediterranean — garlic!

30ml/2 tbsp olive oil
4 large garlic cloves, peeled
4 slices French bread, 5mm/¼in thick
15ml/1 tbsp paprika
1 litre/1¾ pints/4 cups beef stock
1.5ml/¼ tsp ground cumin
pinch of saffron strands
4 eggs
salt and ground black pepper
chopped fresh parsley, to garnish

SERVES 4

1 Preheat the oven to 230°C/ 450°F/Gas 8. Heat the oil in a large pan. Add the whole garlic cloves and cook until golden. Remove and set aside. Fry the bread in the oil until golden, then set aside.

2 Add the paprika to the pan, and fry for a few seconds. Stir in the beef stock, cumin and saffron, then add the reserved garlic, crushing the cloves with the back of a wooden spoon. Season with salt and pepper then cook for about 5 minutes.

3 Ladle the soup into four ovenproof bowls and break an egg into each. Place the slices of fried bread on top of the egg (*left*) and place in the oven for about 3–4 minutes, until the eggs are set. Sprinkle with parsley and serve at once.

SPICY PUMPKIN SOUP

Pumpkin is popular all over the Mediterranean and it is an important ingredient in Middle Eastern cookery, which inspired this soup. Ginger and cumin give the soup its spicy flavour.

900g/2lb pumpkin, peeled and
seeds removed
30ml/2 tbsp olive oil
2 leeks, trimmed and sliced
1 garlic clove, crushed
5ml/1 tsp ground ginger
5ml/1 tsp ground cumin
900ml/1½ pints/3¾ cups chicken stock
salt and ground black pepper
coriander leaves, to garnish
60ml/4 tbsp natural yogurt, to serve

SERVES 4

[1] Cut the pumpkin into chunks. Heat the oil in a large pan and add the leeks and garlic. Cook gently until softened.

[2] Add the ginger and cumin and cook, stirring, for a further minute. Add the pumpkin and the chicken stock, and season with salt and pepper. Bring to the boil and simmer for 30 minutes, until the pumpkin is tender. Process the soup, in batches if necessary, in a blender or food processor.

[3] Reheat the soup and serve in warmed individual bowls, with a swirl of yogurt and a garnish of coriander leaves.

GREEN SOUP

This is a delicious and nutritious soup, ideal for warming cooler winter evenings.

1 onion, chopped
225g/8oz/2 cups leeks (trimmed
weight), sliced
225g/8oz unpeeled potatoes, diced
900ml/1½ pints/3¾ cups
vegetable stock
1 bay leaf
225g/8oz broccoli florets
175g/6oz/1½ cups frozen peas
30–45ml/2–3 tbsp chopped
fresh parsley
salt and ground black pepper
sprigs of parsley, to garnish

SERVES 4–6

1 Put the onion, leeks, potatoes, stock and bay leaf in a large saucepan and mix together. Cover, bring to the boil and simmer for 10 minutes, stirring.

2 Add the broccoli and peas, cover, return to the boil then lower the heat and simmer for a further 10 minutes, stirring occasionally.

3 Set aside to cool slightly, and remove and discard the bay leaf. Purée in a blender or food processor until smooth.

4 Add the parsley, season to taste and process briefly. Return to the saucepan and reheat gently until piping hot. Ladle into soup bowls and garnish with parsley sprigs.

114

ALMOND AND BROCCOLI SOUP

The creaminess of the toasted ground almonds combines perfectly with the slight bitterness of the broccoli in this delicious Spanish soup.

50g/2oz/½ cup ground almonds
675g/1½ lb broccoli
900ml/1½ pints/3¾ cups
vegetable stock
300ml/½ pint/1¼ cups milk
salt and ground black pepper

SERVES 4–6

3 Place the remaining toasted almonds, broccoli, stock and milk in a blender and process until smooth. Season to taste.

4 Pour the puréed mixture into a pan and heat to simmering. Serve, sprinkled with the reserved toasted almonds.

1 Preheat the oven to 180°C/ 350°F/Gas 4. Spread the ground almonds evenly on a baking sheet and toast them in the oven for about 10 minutes or until golden. Reserve one-quarter of the almonds and set aside for the garnish.

2 Cut the broccoli into small florets. Steam for 6–7 minutes or until tender.

115

FRESH TOMATO SOUP

Intensely flavoured sun-ripened tomatoes need little embellishment in this fresh-tasting soup. If you buy from the supermarket, choose the ripest looking ones and add the amount of sugar and vinegar necessary, depending on their natural sweetness. On a hot day this Italian soup is also delicious chilled.

1.5kg/3–3½lb ripe tomatoes
400ml/14fl oz/1⅔ cups chicken or
vegetable stock
45ml/3 tbsp sun-dried tomato paste
30–45ml/2–3 tbsp balsamic vinegar
10–15ml/2–3 tsp caster sugar
small handful basil leaves,
plus extra to garnish
salt and ground black pepper
toasted cheese croûtes and
crème fraîche, to serve

SERVES 6

1 Plunge the tomatoes into boiling water for 30 seconds, then refresh in cold water. Peel away the skins and quarter the tomatoes. Put them in a large saucepan and pour over the chicken or vegetable stock. Bring just to the boil, reduce the heat, cover and simmer gently for 10 minutes until the tomatoes are pulpy.

2 Stir in the tomato paste, vinegar, sugar and basil. Season with salt and pepper, then cook gently, stirring, for 2 minutes. Process the soup in a blender or food processor, then return to the pan and reheat gently. Serve in bowls topped with one or two toasted cheese croûtes and a spoonful of crème fraîche, garnished with basil leaves.

SPLIT PEA AND COURGETTE SOUP

Rich and satisfying — with just the slightest hint of spice — this hearty soup is good to come home to after a long walk.

175g/6oz/1 cup yellow split peas
1 medium onion, finely chopped
5ml/1 tsp sunflower oil
2 medium courgettes, finely diced
900ml/1½ pints/3¾ cups chicken stock
2.5ml/½ tsp ground turmeric
salt and ground black pepper
crusty bread, to serve

SERVES 4

1 Place the split peas in a bowl, cover with cold water and leave to soak for several hours or overnight. Drain, rinse in plenty of cold water and drain again.

2 Cook the onion in the oil in a covered pan, shaking occasionally, until soft. Reserve a handful of diced courgettes and add the rest to the pan. Cook, stirring, for 2–3 minutes.

3 Add the stock and turmeric to the pan and bring to the boil. Reduce the heat, then cover and simmer for 30–40 minutes, or until the split peas are tender. Season well.

4 When the soup is almost ready, bring a large saucepan of water to the boil, add the reserved diced courgettes and cook for 1 minute, then drain and add them to the soup. Serve hot, with warm crusty bread.

COOK'S TIP

For a quicker alternative, use split red lentils for this soup – they need no presoaking and cook very quickly. Adjust the amount of stock, if necessary.

JERUSALEM ARTICHOKE SOUP

For such an ugly vegetable, the Jerusalem artichoke has a surprisingly delicate flavour,
which makes a most delicious soup.

25–50g/1–2oz/2–4 tbsp butter
125g/4oz/1½ cups sliced mushrooms
450g/1lb Jerusalem artichokes
2 onions, chopped
300ml/½ pint/1¼ cups vegetable stock
300ml/½ pint/1¼ cups milk
salt and ground black pepper

SERVES 4

1 Melt the butter in a saucepan and sauté the mushrooms for 1 minute. Put them on a plate. Peel and slice the artichokes and then sauté them with the onions, adding a little more butter if needed. Do not let the vegetables brown.

2 Add the vegetable stock to the pan and simmer the artichokes until they are soft. Season to taste.

3 Purée in a food processor, adding the milk. Reheat the soup, stir in the mushrooms and serve.

118

SPINACH AND LEMON SOUP WITH MEATBALLS

Aarshe Saak is almost standard fare in many parts of the Middle East. In Greece it is normally made without the meatballs and is called Avgolemono.

2 large onions
45ml/3 tbsp oil
15ml/1 tbsp ground turmeric
100g/3½ oz/½ cup yellow split peas
1.2 litres/2 pints/5 cups water
225g/8oz minced lamb
450g/1lb spinach, chopped
50g/2oz/½ cup rice flour
juice of 2 lemons
1–2 garlic cloves, very finely chopped
30ml/2 tbsp chopped fresh mint
4 eggs, beaten
salt and ground black pepper

SERVES 6

1 Chop one of the onions. Heat 30ml/2 tbsp of the oil in a large shallow pan and fry the chopped onion until golden. Add the turmeric and split peas, then pour in the water and bring to the boil. Reduce the heat and simmer for 20 minutes, stirring occasionally.

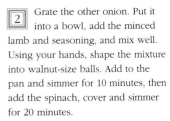

2 Grate the other onion. Put it into a bowl, add the minced lamb and seasoning, and mix well. Using your hands, shape the mixture into walnut-size balls. Add to the pan and simmer for 10 minutes, then add the spinach, cover and simmer for 20 minutes.

3 Mix the rice flour with about 250ml/8fl oz/1 cup cold water to make a smooth paste, then slowly add to the pan, stirring all the time to prevent lumps. Stir in the lemon juice, season with salt and pepper and cook over a gentle heat for 20 minutes.

4 Meanwhile, heat the remaining oil in a small pan and fry the garlic briefly until golden. Stir in the chopped mint.

5 Remove the soup from the heat and stir in the beaten eggs. Serve, sprinkled with the garlic and mint garnish.

COOK'S TIP
If preferred, use less lemon juice to begin with and then add more to taste once the soup is cooked.

CHILLED ALMOND SOUP

Unless you want to spend time pounding the ingredients for this dish by hand, a food processor is essential.
Then you'll find that this Spanish soup is very simple to make and refreshing to eat on a hot day.

115g/4oz fresh white bread
115g/4oz/1 cup blanched almonds
2 garlic cloves, sliced
75ml/5 tbsp olive oil
25ml/1½ tbsp sherry vinegar
salt and ground black pepper
toasted flaked almonds and
seedless green and black grapes,
halved and skinned, to garnish

SERVES 6

1   Break the bread into a bowl
and pour over 150ml/¼ pint/
⅔ cup cold water. Leave for 5 minutes.

2   Put the almonds and garlic in a
blender or food processor and
process until very finely ground.
Blend in the soaked white bread.

3   Gradually add the oil until the
mixture forms a smooth paste.
Add the sherry vinegar then 600ml/
1 pint/2½ cups cold water and
process until smooth.

4   Transfer to a bowl and season
with salt and pepper, adding a
little more water if the soup is very
thick. Chill for at least 2–3 hours.

5   Ladle the soup into bowls and
scatter with the toasted almonds
and skinned grapes.

GAZPACHO

There are many versions of this refreshingly chilled, pungent soup from southern Spain. All contain an intense blend of tomatoes, peppers, cucumber and garlic; perfect on a hot summer's evening.

900g/2lb ripe tomatoes
1 cucumber
2 red peppers, seeded and
roughly chopped
2 garlic cloves, crushed
175g/6oz/3 cups fresh white
breadcrumbs
30ml/2 tbsp white wine vinegar
30ml/2 tbsp sun-dried tomato paste
90ml/6 tbsp olive oil
salt and ground black pepper

To finish
1 slice white bread, crust removed
and cut into cubes
30ml/2 tbsp olive oil
6–12 ice cubes
small bowl of mixed chopped
garnishes, such as tomato, cucumber,
red onion, hard-boiled egg and flat
leaf parsley or tarragon leaves

Serves 6

Cook's Tip
The sun-dried tomato paste has been added to accentuate the flavour of the tomatoes. You might not need this if you use a really flavoursome variety.

1 | Plunge the tomatoes into boiling water for 30 seconds, then refresh in cold water. Peel away the skins and quarter. Peel and roughly chop the cucumber. Mix the tomatoes and cucumber in a bowl with the peppers, garlic, bread-crumbs, vinegar, tomato paste and olive oil and season lightly with salt and pepper.

2 | Process half the mixture in a blender or food processor until fairly smooth. Process the remaining mixture and mix with the first.

3 | Check the seasoning and add a little cold water if the soup is too thick. Chill for several hours.

4 | To finish, fry the bread in the oil until golden. Spoon the soup into bowls, adding one or two ice cubes to each. Serve accompanied by the croûtons and garnishes.

CHILLED TOMATO AND SWEET PEPPER SOUP

A recipe inspired by the Spanish gazpacho, the difference being that this soup is cooked first,
and then chilled.

2 red peppers, cored
and seeded
45ml/3 tbsp olive oil
1 onion, finely chopped
2 garlic cloves, crushed
675g/1½ lb ripe flavoursome tomatoes
150ml/¼ pint/⅔ cup red wine
600ml/1 pint/2½ cups chicken stock
salt and ground black pepper
snipped fresh chives, to garnish

FOR THE CROUTONS
2 slices white bread, crusts removed
60ml/4 tbsp olive oil

SERVES 4

1 Cut each pepper into quarters. Place skin side up on a grill rack and cook until the skins have charred. Transfer to a bowl and cover with a plate.

2 Heat the oil in a large pan. Add the onion and garlic and cook until soft. Meanwhile, remove the skin from the peppers and roughly chop them. Cut the tomatoes into chunks.

3 Add the peppers and tomatoes to the pan, then cover and cook gently for 10 minutes. Add the wine and cook for a further 5 minutes, then add the stock and salt and pepper and continue to simmer for 20 minutes.

4 To make the croûtons, cut the bread into cubes. Heat the oil in a small frying pan, add the bread and fry until golden. Drain on kitchen paper and store in an airtight box.

5 Process the soup in a blender or food processor until smooth. Pour into a clean glass or ceramic bowl and leave to cool thoroughly before chilling in the fridge for at least 3 hours. When the soup is cold, season to taste.

6 Serve the soup in bowls, topped with the croûtons and garnished with snipped chives.

MIDDLE EASTERN YOGURT AND CUCUMBER SOUP

Yogurt is used extensively in Middle Eastern cookery, and it is usually made at home. Sometimes it is added at the end of cooking a dish, to prevent it from curdling, but in this cold soup the yogurt is one of the basic ingredients.

🌿 🌿

1 large cucumber, peeled
300ml/½ pint/1¼ cups single cream
150ml/¼ pint/⅔ cup natural yogurt
2 garlic cloves, crushed
30ml/2 tbsp white wine vinegar
15ml/1 tbsp chopped fresh mint
salt and ground black pepper
sprigs of mint, to garnish

SERVES 4

🌿 🌿

1 Grate the cucumber coarsely. Place in a bowl with the cream, yogurt, garlic, vinegar and mint. Stir well and season to taste.

2 Chill for at least 2 hours before serving. Just before serving, stir the soup again. Pour into individual bowls and garnish with mint sprigs.

VEGETABLES

*Mediterranean vegetables are a veritable
treasure trove of taste and colour which beg to be
transformed into delectable dishes.*

A Mediterranean street market is a fascinating vision of colour, noise and photograph opportunities. The magnificent array of fruit and vegetable stalls in particular gives many "foodie" holiday-makers the urge to swap their hotel room for a kitchen in which to cook a feast of sweet, juicy local produce.

Mediterranean vegetables have an inviting irregularity about them. Uneven colourings, knobbly skins and unsymmetrical shapes are a sure indication that the flesh inside will be full of flavour, a far cry from the mass-produced, artificially grown and barely ripened produce of colder climes. The dishes cooked using them are a real joy to eat and even the simplest tossed salad of tomatoes and leaves, sprinkled with olive oil, herbs and seasoning, is worthy of serving solo – a meal in itself.

All around the Mediterranean, vegetables are the basis of everyday meals. This is due to the cost of meat and to the religious obligations of fasting. This austerity has led to imaginative cookery skills. Deep fried, roasted, baked, stuffed, marinated, grilled, steamed; mixed in pies, tarts, omelettes, stews and stuffings; vegetables are very versatile.

BELOW: At a finca – or farm – in Andalusia, vegetables grow alongside grape-drying beds.

RIGHT: Tomatoes, chillies, potatoes and strings of garlic are just some of the vegetables on sale at this market in southern Turkey.

BELOW: The golden harvest: pumpkins make marvellous soups, pies and vegetable bakes.

A stunning variety of mushrooms features highly in Italian and French cookery. In these countries markets are filled with wild varieties in the spring and autumn. The lovely shapes and flavours make interesting risottos and salads and may even be used to flavour pasta. Many mushroom varieties are dried for year-round availability. A small quantity goes a long way and can be used to enliven the flavour of everyday farmed mushrooms, though they need a little preparation beforehand.

Stuffed vegetables are greatly loved in many countries of the Mediterranean, particularly in Turkey, Greece and the Middle East. Tomatoes, aubergines, peppers, courgettes and onions are filled with couscous, rice, herbs, spices, dried fruits, nuts, cheese and sometimes meat. Large leaves like spinach, vine and cabbage are stuffed with interesting ingredients, packed in a pan and gently cooked so as to mingle all the flavours together.

Even the humble potato takes pride of place at the Mediterranean table. The Spanish make a delicious potato salad in which new potatoes are fried to give a crisp crust. Italian gnocchi is a distinctively shaped, puréed and poached potato dish flavoured with a variety of herbs, cheese or mild spices.

In France and Italy vegetable fritters of courgette or aubergine, deep fried in a light crisp batter, make a very enjoyable dish, often served with a ripe tomato sauce or garlicky herb dressing. Even the flowers of marrows are battered and fried. Ratatouille, a wonderful stew of lightly cooked vegetables, is traditionally French, although similar recipes stretch right across the Mediterranean.

No vegetable is considered too small to bother with, while salad "thinnings" are included in mixed leafy salads, the smallest artichokes, turnips, aubergines and broad beans are put to good use in many dishes.

MARINATED MUSHROOMS

This Spanish recipe makes a nice change from the French classic, mushrooms à la Grecque.
Make this dish the day before you eat it – the flavour will improve with keeping.

30ml/2 tbsp olive oil
1 small onion, very finely chopped
1 garlic clove, crushed
15ml/1 tbsp tomato purée
50ml/2fl oz/¼ cup dry white wine
2 cloves
pinch of saffron strands
225g/8oz button mushrooms,
trimmed
salt and ground black pepper
chopped fresh parsley, to garnish

SERVES 4

1. Heat the oil in a pan. Add the onion and garlic and cook until soft. Stir in the tomato purée, wine, 50ml/2fl oz/¼ cup water, cloves and saffron and season with salt and pepper. Bring to the boil, cover and simmer gently for 45 minutes, adding more water if it becomes too dry.

2. Add the mushrooms to the pan, then cover and simmer for a further 5 minutes. Remove from the heat and, still covered, allow to cool. Chill in the fridge overnight. Serve cold, sprinkled with chopped parsley.

POTATO AND ONION TORTILLA

One of the signature dishes of Spain, this delicious thick potato and onion omelette
is eaten at all times of the day, hot or cold.

300ml/½ pint/1¼ cups olive oil
6 large potatoes, peeled and sliced
2 Spanish onions, sliced
6 large eggs
salt and ground black pepper
cherry tomatoes, halved, to serve

SERVES 4

1. Heat the oil in a large non-stick frying pan. Stir in the potato, onion and a little salt. Cover and cook gently for 20 minutes until soft.

2. Beat the eggs in a large bowl. Remove the onion and potato from the pan with a slotted spoon and add to the eggs. Season with salt and pepper to taste. Pour off some of the oil, leaving about 60ml/4 tbsp in the pan. (Reserve the leftover oil for other cooking.) Heat the pan again.

3. When the oil is very hot, pour in the egg mixture. Cook for 2–3 minutes. Cover the pan with a plate and invert the omelette on to it. Slide it back into the pan and cook for a further 5 minutes, until golden brown and moist in the middle. Serve in wedges, with the tomatoes.

SWEET PEPPER AND COURGETTE FRITTATA

Eggs, cheese and vegetables form the basis of this excellent supper dish. Served cold, in wedges,
it also makes excellent picnic fare.

45ml/3 tbsp olive oil
1 red onion, thinly sliced
1 large red pepper, cored and
thinly sliced
1 large yellow pepper, cored and
thinly sliced
2 garlic cloves, crushed
1 medium courgette, thinly sliced
6 eggs
150g/5oz Italian cheese, such as
Fontina, Provolone or
Taleggio, grated
salt and ground black pepper
dressed mixed salad leaves, to garnish

SERVES 4

1 Heat 30ml/2 tbsp of the oil in a large heavy-based frying pan. Fry the onion and pepper slices over a low heat for about 10 minutes.

2 Add the remaining oil to the pan. When it is hot, tip in the garlic and courgette slices and fry for 5 minutes, stirring constantly.

3 Beat the eggs with salt and pepper in a bowl. Mix in the grated cheese.

4 Pour the egg and cheese mixture over the vegetables in the pan, stirring lightly to mix. Make sure that the base of the pan is evenly covered with egg. Cook over a low heat until the mixture is just set.

5 Allow the frittata to stand in the pan for about 5 minutes before cutting. This is delicious served hot or cold, with a salad garnish.

COOK'S TIP
Traditionally, a frittata is inverted on to a plate and returned to the pan upside down to cook the top, but it may be easier to brown the top lightly under a hot grill for a few minutes.

CHILLI CHEESE TORTILLA WITH FRESH TOMATO SALSA

Good either warm or cold, this is rather like a quiche without the pastry base.
Cheese and chillies are more than a match for each other.

45ml/3 tbsp sunflower
or olive oil
1 small onion, thinly sliced
2–3 fresh green jalapeño
chillies, sliced
200g/7oz cold cooked potato,
thinly sliced
120g/4¼ oz/generous 1 cup grated
Manchego, Mexican Queso Blanco
or Monterey Jack cheese
6 eggs, beaten
salt and ground black pepper
fresh herbs, to garnish

FOR THE SALSA
500g/1¼ lb fresh, flavoursome
tomatoes, peeled, seeded
and finely chopped
1 fresh mild green chilli, seeded
and finely chopped
2 garlic cloves, crushed
45ml/3 tbsp chopped fresh coriander
juice of 1 lime
2.5ml/½ tsp salt
pepper

SERVES 4

COOK'S TIP
You can brown the top of the tortilla
under a hot grill, using a frying pan
with a flameproof handle.
Alternatively, if you want to re-heat
the tortilla, place in an oven for a
few minutes.

1 Make the salsa. Put the chopped
tomatoes in a bowl and add the
chopped chilli, garlic, coriander, lime
juice, salt and pepper. Mix well and
set aside.

2 Heat half the oil in a large
omelette pan and gently fry the
onion and jalapeños for 5 minutes,
stirring once or twice, until softened.
Add the potato and cook for a further
5 minutes until lightly browned,
taking care to keep the slices whole.

3 Using a slotted spoon, transfer
the vegetables to a warm plate.
Wipe the pan with kitchen paper, add
the remaining oil. Heat well and
return the vegetable mixture to the
pan, season. Scatter the cheese over.

4 Pour in the beaten eggs, making
sure that they seep under the
vegetables. Cook the tortilla over a
gentle heat until set. Serve in wedges,
garnished with fresh herbs, with the
salsa on the side.

131

STUFFED TOMATOES AND PEPPERS

Colourful peppers and tomatoes make perfect containers for various meat and vegetable stuffings.
This rice and herb version uses typically Greek ingredients.

VARIATION

Small aubergines or large courgettes also make good vegetables for stuffing. Halve and scoop out the centres of the vegetables, then oil the vegetable cases and bake for about 15 minutes. Chop the centres, fry for 2–3 minutes to soften and add to the stuffing mixture. Fill the aubergine or courgette cases with the stuffing and bake as for the peppers and tomatoes.

2 large ripe tomatoes
1 green pepper
1 yellow or orange pepper
60ml/4 tbsp olive oil, plus extra
for sprinkling
2 onions, chopped
2 garlic cloves, crushed
50g/2oz/½ cup blanched
almonds, chopped
75g/3oz/scant ½ cup long grain rice,
boiled and drained
15g/½oz mint, roughly chopped
15g/½oz parsley, roughly chopped
25g/1oz/2 tbsp sultanas
45ml/3 tbsp ground almonds
salt and ground black pepper
chopped mixed herbs, to garnish

SERVES 4

 1   Preheat the oven to 190°C/ 375°F/Gas 5. Cut the tomatoes in half and scoop out the pulp and seeds using a teaspoon. Leave the tomatoes to drain on kitchen paper with cut sides down. Roughly chop the tomato pulp and seeds.

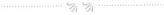 2   Halve the peppers, leaving the cores intact. Scoop out the seeds. Brush the peppers with 15ml/ 1 tbsp of the oil and bake on a baking tray for 15 minutes. Place the peppers and tomatoes in a shallow ovenproof dish and season with salt and pepper.

3   Fry the onions in the remaining oil for 5 minutes. Add the garlic and chopped almonds and fry for a further minute.

4 Remove the pan from the heat and stir in the rice, chopped tomatoes, mint, parsley and sultanas. Season well with salt and pepper and spoon the mixture into the tomatoes and peppers.

5 Pour 150ml/¼ pint/⅔ cup boiling water around the tomatoes and peppers and bake, uncovered, for 20 minutes. Scatter with the ground almonds and sprinkle with a little extra olive oil. Return to the oven and bake for a further 20 minutes, or until turning golden. Serve garnished with fresh herbs.

RATATOUILLE

A highly versatile vegetable stew from Provence. Ratatouille is delicious hot or cold, on its own or with eggs, pasta, fish or meat – particularly roast lamb.

900g/2lb ripe, flavoursome tomatoes
120ml/4fl oz/½ cup olive oil
2 onions, thinly sliced
2 red peppers, seeded and cut
into chunks
1 yellow or orange pepper, seeded and
cut into chunks
1 large aubergine, cut into chunks
2 courgettes, cut into thick slices
4 garlic cloves, crushed
2 bay leaves
15ml/1 tbsp chopped young thyme
salt and ground black pepper

SERVES 6

1. Plunge the tomatoes into boiling water for 30 seconds, then refresh in cold water. Peel away the skins and chop roughly.

2. Heat a little of the oil in a large, heavy-based pan and fry the onions for 5 minutes. Add the peppers and fry for a further 2 minutes. Drain. Add the aubergines and more oil and fry gently for 5 minutes. Add the remaining oil and courgettes and fry for 3 minutes. Drain.

3. Add the garlic and tomatoes to the pan with the bay leaves and thyme and a little salt and pepper. Cook gently until the tomatoes have softened and are turning pulpy.

4. Return all the vegetables to the pan and cook gently, stirring frequently, for about 15 minutes, until fairly pulpy but retaining a little texture. Season with more salt and pepper to taste.

COOK'S TIP
There are no specific quantities for the vegetables when making ratatouille so you can, to a large extent, vary the quantities and types of vegetables depending on what you have in the fridge. If the tomatoes are a little tasteless, add 30–45ml/2–3 tbsp tomato purée and a dash of sugar to the mixture along with the tomatoes.

COUSCOUS-STUFFED PEPPERS

Couscous is a form of semolina, and is used extensively in the Middle East. It makes a good basis for a stuffing, combined with other ingredients.

6 peppers
25g/1oz/2 tbsp butter
1 onion, finely chopped
5ml/1 tsp olive oil
2.5ml/½ tsp salt
175g/6oz/1 cup couscous
25g/1oz/2 tbsp raisins
30ml/2 tbsp chopped fresh mint
1 egg yolk
salt and ground black pepper
mint leaves, to garnish

SERVES 4

1 Preheat the oven to 200°C/
400°F/Gas 6. Carefully slit each pepper and remove the core and seeds. Melt the butter in a small pan and add the onion. Cook until soft.

2 To cook the couscous, bring 250ml/8fl oz/1 cup water to the boil. Add the oil and the salt, then remove the pan from the heat and add the couscous. Stir and leave to stand, covered, for 5 minutes. Stir in the cooked onion, raisins and mint, then season well with salt and pepper. Stir in the egg yolk.

3 Using a teaspoon, fill the peppers with the couscous mixture to only about three-quarters full, as the couscous will swell when cooked further. Place in a lightly oiled ovenproof dish and bake, uncovered, for about 20 minutes until tender. Serve hot or cold, garnished with the mint leaves.

AUBERGINES WITH TZATZIKI

Battered aubergine slices are irresistible with a minted cucumber dip.

2 medium-size aubergines
75g/3oz/¾ cup plain flour
1 egg
120–150ml/4–5fl oz/½–⅔ cup milk
oil for deep-frying
salt

FOR THE TZATZIKI
½ cucumber, peeled and diced
150ml/¼ pint/⅔ cup natural yogurt
1 garlic clove, crushed
15ml/1 tbsp chopped fresh mint

SERVES 4

1 To make the tzatziki, place the cucumber in a colander, sprinkle with salt and leave for 30 minutes. Rinse, drain well and pat dry on kitchen paper. Mix the yogurt, garlic, mint and cucumber in a bowl. Cover and chill.

2 Slice the aubergines lengthways. Sprinkle the slices with salt. Leave for 1 hour to draw out the bitter juices.

3 To make the batter, sift the flour and a pinch of salt into a large bowl, add the egg and milk and beat until smooth.

4 Rinse the aubergine slices and pat dry. Heat 1cm/½in of oil in a large frying pan. Dip the aubergine slices in the batter and fry them for 3–4 minutes until golden, turning once. Drain on kitchen paper and serve with the tzatziki.

AUBERGINE AND COURGETTE BAKE

Aubergines and courgettes are classic Mediterranean vegetables which absorb the most delicate of flavours. They are delicious cooked with olive oil, garlic, herbs and cheeses.

1 large aubergine
30ml/2 tbsp olive oil
1 large onion, chopped
1–2 garlic cloves, crushed
900g/2lb tomatoes, peeled
and chopped
a handful of basil leaves, shredded,
plus whole leaves, to garnish
15ml/1 tbsp chopped fresh parsley
2 courgettes, sliced lengthways
plain flour, for coating
75–90ml/5–6 tbsp sunflower oil
350g/12oz mozzarella cheese, sliced
25g/1oz Parmesan cheese, grated
salt and ground black pepper

SERVES 4–6

1 Grease a baking dish. Slice the aubergine, sprinkle with salt and set aside for 45–60 minutes. Heat the olive oil in a large frying pan. Fry the onion and garlic for 3–4 minutes until softened. Stir in the tomatoes, half the basil, the parsley and seasoning. Bring to the boil. Reduce the heat and cook, stirring, for 25–35 minutes until thickened to a pulp.

2 Rinse and dry the aubergines. Dust the aubergines and courgettes with flour. Preheat the oven to 180°C/350°F/Gas 4.

3 Heat the sunflower oil in another pan and fry the aubergine and courgette slices until golden. Spoon half the fried vegetables into the baking dish, pour over half the pulp and scatter with half the mozzarella and remaining basil. Repeat the layers. Sprinkle the Parmesan on top and bake for 30–35 minutes. Serve, garnished with basil.

GREEK SPINACH PIES

*These little horns of filo pastry are stuffed with a simple spinach and feta cheese filling
to make a quick and easy main course.*

225g/8oz fresh leaf spinach
2 spring onions, chopped
175g/6oz feta cheese, crumbled
1 egg, beaten
15ml/1 tbsp fresh dill, chopped
ground black pepper
*4 large sheets or 8 small sheets
of filo pastry*
olive oil, for brushing

SERVES 4

1 Preheat the oven to 190°C/ 375°F/Gas 5. Blanch the spinach in the tiniest amount of water until just wilted, then drain very well, pressing it through a sieve with the back of a wooden spoon.

2 Chop the spinach finely and mix with the onions, feta, egg, dill and ground black pepper. Lay out a sheet of filo pastry and brush with olive oil. If large, cut the pieces in two and sandwich them together. If small, fit another sheet on top and brush with olive oil.

3 Spread a quarter of the spinach filling on one corner of the filo, then roll it up firmly, but not too tightly. Shape into a crescent and place on a baking sheet.

4 Brush the pastry well with more oil and bake for about 20–25 minutes until golden and crisp. Cool slightly then remove to a wire rack to cool further.

CHUNKY VEGETABLE PAELLA

*This Spanish rice dish has become a firm family favourite the world over. There are many versions:
here is one which uses aubergine and chick-peas.*

good pinch saffron strands
1 aubergine, cut into thick chunks
90ml/6 tbsp olive oil
1 large onion, sliced
3 garlic cloves, crushed
1 yellow pepper, sliced
1 red pepper, sliced
10ml/2 tsp paprika
225g/8oz/1¼ cups risotto rice
600ml/1 pint/2½ cups stock
*450g/1lb fresh tomatoes, skinned
and chopped*
115g/4oz sliced mushrooms
115g/4oz cut green beans
1 × 400g/14oz can chick-peas
salt and ground black pepper

SERVES 6

1 Steep the saffron in 45ml/3 tbsp hot water. Sprinkle the aubergine with salt, leave to drain in a colander for 30 minutes, then rinse and drain.

2 In a large paella or frying pan, heat the oil and fry the onion, garlic, peppers and aubergine for about 5 minutes, stirring occasionally. Sprinkle in the paprika and stir again.

3 Mix in the rice, then pour in the stock, tomatoes, saffron and seasoning. Bring to a boil then simmer for 15 minutes, uncovered, shaking the pan frequently and stirring occasionally.

4 Stir in the mushrooms, green beans and chick-peas (with their liquor). Continue cooking for 10 minutes, then serve hot from the pan.

VEGETABLE MOUSSAKA

This is a flavoursome vegetarian alternative to the classic meat moussaka. Serve it with warm bread and a glass or two of rustic red wine.

450g/1lb aubergines, sliced
115g/4oz/½ cup whole green lentils
600ml/1 pint/2½ cups vegetable stock
1 bay leaf
45ml/3 tbsp olive oil
1 onion, sliced
1 garlic clove, crushed
225g/8oz mushrooms, sliced
400g/14oz can chick-peas, rinsed
and drained
400g/14oz can chopped tomatoes
30ml/2 tbsp tomato purée
10ml/2 tsp dried herbes de Provence
45ml/3 tbsp water
300ml/½ cup pint/1¼ cups
natural yogurt
3 eggs
50g/2oz/½ cup grated mature
Cheddar cheese
salt and ground black pepper
flat leaf parsley sprigs, to garnish

SERVES 6

1 Sprinkle the aubergine slices with salt and place in a colander. Cover and leave for about 30 minutes to allow the bitter juices to be extracted.

2 Meanwhile, place the lentils, stock and bay leaf in a saucepan. Cover, bring to the boil and simmer for about 20 minutes until the lentils are just tender. Drain well and keep warm.

3 Heat 15ml/1 tbsp of the oil in a large saucepan. Add the onion and garlic and cook for 5 minutes, stirring. Stir in the lentils, mushrooms, chick-peas, tomatoes, tomato purée, herbs and water. Bring to the boil, lower the heat, cover and simmer gently for 10 minutes.

COOK'S TIP
If the aubergines are young, there is no need to salt them.

4 Preheat the oven to 180°C/ 350°F/Gas 4. Rinse all the aubergine slices, drain and pat dry. Heat the remaining oil in a frying pan and fry the slices in batches for 3–4 minutes, turning once.

5 Season the lentil mixture with salt and pepper. Arrange a layer of aubergine slices in the bottom of a large, shallow, ovenproof dish or roasting tin, then spoon over a layer of the lentil mixture. Continue the layers until all the aubergine slices and lentil mixture have been used.

6 Beat together the yogurt and eggs, season with salt and pepper, and pour the mixture into the dish. Sprinkle the grated cheese on top and bake for about 45 minutes until the topping is golden brown and bubbling. Serve immediately, garnished with flat leaf parsley sprigs.

GRILLED AUBERGINE PARCELS

These are delicious little Italian bundles of tomatoes, mozzarella cheese and basil, wrapped in slices of aubergine.

2 large, long aubergines
225g/8oz mozzarella cheese
2 plum tomatoes
16 large basil leaves
30ml/2 tbsp olive oil
salt and ground black pepper

FOR THE DRESSING
60ml/4 tbsp olive oil
5ml/1 tsp balsamic vinegar
15ml/1 tbsp sun-dried tomato paste
15ml/1 tbsp lemon juice

FOR THE GARNISH
30ml/2 tbsp toasted pine nuts
torn basil leaves

SERVES 4

1 Remove the stalks from the aubergines and cut the aubergines lengthways into thin slices – the aim is to get 16 slices in total, disregarding the first and last slices (each about 5mm/¼in thick). If you have a mandolin, it will cut perfect, even slices for you. Otherwise, use a long-bladed, sharp knife.

2 Bring a large pan of salted water to the boil and cook the aubergine slices for about 2 minutes, until just softened. Drain the sliced aubergines, then dry on kitchen paper.

3 Cut the mozzarella cheese into eight slices. Cut each tomato into eight slices, not counting the first and last slices.

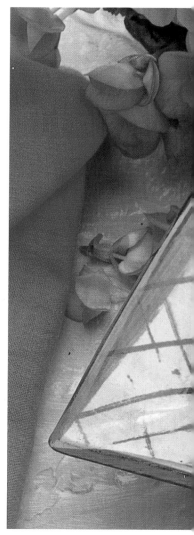

4 Take two aubergine slices and place on a flameproof tray or dish, in a cross (*left*). Place a slice of tomato in the centre, season with salt and pepper, then add a basil leaf, followed by a slice of mozzarella, another basil leaf, a slice of tomato and more seasoning.

5 Fold the ends of the aubergine slices around the mozzarella and tomato filling to make a neat parcel (*left*). Repeat with the rest of the assembled ingredients to make eight parcels. Chill the parcels for about 20 minutes.

6 To make the tomato dressing, whisk together the olive oil, vinegar, sun-dried tomato paste and lemon juice. Season to taste.

7 Preheat the grill. Brush the parcels with olive oil and cook for about 5 minutes on each side, until golden. Serve hot, with the dressing, sprinkled with pine nuts and basil.

POTATO AND PUMPKIN SOUFFLE

Serve this savoury soufflé with any rich meat dish, or simply with a mixed salad.

45ml/3 tbsp olive oil
1 garlic clove, sliced
675g/1½lb pumpkin flesh, cut into
2cm/¾in chunks
350g/12oz potatoes
25g/1oz/2 tbsp butter
90g/3½ oz/scant ½ cup ricotta cheese
50g/2oz/⅓ cup grated
Parmesan cheese
pinch of grated nutmeg
4 eggs, separated
salt and ground black pepper
chopped fresh parsley, to garnish

SERVES 4

1 Preheat the oven to 200°C/
400°F/Gas 6. Lightly grease a
1.75 litre/3 pint/7½ cup shallow,
oval baking dish.

2 Heat the oil in a large shallow
pan, add the garlic and
pumpkin and cook, stirring often to
prevent sticking, for 15–20 minutes or
until the pumpkin is tender.
Meanwhile, cook the potatoes in
boiling salted water for 20 minutes
until tender. Drain, leave until cool
enough to handle, then peel off the
skins. Place the potatoes and
pumpkin in a large bowl and mash
well with the butter.

3 Mash the ricotta with a fork
until smooth, then add to the
potato and pumpkin mixture, stirring
well with a wooden spoon.

4 Stir the Parmesan, nutmeg and
plenty of seasoning into the
potato and pumpkin mixture – it
should be smooth and creamy. Add
the egg yolks, one at a time, until
thoroughly mixed.

5 Whisk the egg whites with an
electric whisk until they form
stiff peaks, then fold gently into the
mixture. Spoon into the prepared
baking dish and bake for 30 minutes
until golden and firm. Serve hot,
garnished with parsley.

FRIED SPRING GREENS

*This dish can be served as a vegetable accompaniment, or it can be enjoyed simply on its own,
with some warm crusty bread.*

30ml/2 tbsp olive oil
25g/1oz/2 tbsp butter
75g/3oz rindless smoked streaky
bacon, chopped
1 large onion, thinly sliced
250ml/8fl oz/1 cup dry white wine
2 garlic cloves, finely chopped
900g/2lb spring greens, shredded
salt and ground black pepper

SERVES 4

1 Heat the oil and butter in a
large frying pan, and fry the
bacon for 2 minutes. Then add the
onions and fry for a further 3 minutes
until the onion is beginning to soften.

2 Add the wine and simmer
vigorously for 2 minutes to
reduce the liquid.

3 Reduce the heat. Add the garlic,
spring greens and seasoning.
Cover the pan and cook over a gentle
heat for about 15 minutes until the
greens are tender. Serve hot.

COOK'S TIP
Cooking the spring greens in a
covered pan helps them to retain
their brilliant colour.

HOT HALLOUMI WITH ROASTED PEPPERS

The best-known cheese from Cyprus is the salty, hard halloumi. Delicious served simply sliced or cubed, it takes on a wonderful texture when grilled or fried. A tumble of roasted sweet peppers makes a fine accompaniment.

2 red peppers
2 green peppers
2 yellow peppers
olive oil
30ml/2 tbsp balsamic or red
wine vinegar
small handful of raisins (optional)
300g/11oz halloumi cheese,
thickly sliced
salt and ground black pepper
flat leaf parsley, to garnish
sesame seed bread, to serve (optional)

SERVES 4

2 Pour about 30ml/2 tbsp olive oil over the peppers. Add the vinegar and raisins, if using, with salt and pepper to taste. Toss lightly and leave the mixture to cool.

3 When you are ready to serve, divide the pepper salad among four plates. Heat olive oil to a depth of about 5mm/¼in in a large heavy-based frying pan. Fry the halloumi slices over a medium-high heat for 2–3 minutes, until golden, turning them halfway through cooking.

4 Drain the halloumi thoroughly on kitchen paper and serve with the roasted peppers and a parsley garnish. Offer chunks of sesame seed bread, if you like.

1 Preheat the oven to 220°C/ 425°F/Gas 7. Cut all the peppers in quarters, discard the cores and seeds, then place cut side down on a non-stick baking sheet. Roast for 15–20 minutes until the skins start to blacken and blister. Remove and cover with several layers of kitchen paper. Set aside for 30 minutes, then peel off the skins. Slice the flesh into a bowl. Save any roasting juices and mix these with the peppers.

MALFATTI WITH GRILLED PEPPER SAUCE

The Italians use ricotta, which is a rich but light cream cheese, in sweet and savoury dishes.
For this recipe, it is beaten into deliciously light spinach dumplings, called malfatti,
which are served with a smoky pepper and tomato sauce.

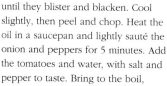

500g/1¼lb young leaf spinach
1 onion, finely chopped
1 garlic clove, crushed
15ml/1 tbsp extra virgin olive oil
350g/12oz/1½ cups ricotta cheese
3 eggs, beaten
50g/2oz/½ cup natural-coloured
dried breadcrumbs
50g/2oz/½ cup plain flour
50g/2oz/⅔ cup freshly grated
Parmesan cheese
freshly grated nutmeg
25g/1oz/2 tbsp butter, melted
salt and ground black pepper

FOR THE SAUCE
2 red peppers, quartered and cored
30ml/2 tbsp extra virgin olive oil
1 onion, chopped
400g/14oz can chopped tomatoes
150ml/¼ pint/⅔ cup water

SERVES 4

1 Make the sauce. Grill the pepper quarters, skin side up, until they blister and blacken. Cool slightly, then peel and chop. Heat the oil in a saucepan and lightly sauté the onion and peppers for 5 minutes. Add the tomatoes and water, with salt and pepper to taste. Bring to the boil, then simmer gently for 15 minutes. Purée in a food processor, return to the clean pan and set aside.

2 Trim any thick stalks from the spinach, wash well if necessary, then blanch in a pan of boiling water for about 1 minute. Drain, refresh under cold water and drain again. Squeeze dry, then chop finely.

3 Put the finely chopped onion, garlic, olive oil, ricotta, eggs and breadcrumbs in a bowl. Add the spinach and mix well. Stir in the flour and 5ml/1 tsp salt with half of the Parmesan, then season to taste with pepper and nutmeg.

4 Roll the mixture into 12 small logs and chill lightly.

5 Bring a large saucepan of water to the boil. Carefully drop in the malfatti in batches and cook for 5 minutes. Remove with a fish slice and toss with the melted butter.

6 To serve, reheat the sauce and divide it among four plates. Arrange four malfatti on each and sprinkle over the remaining Parmesan. Serve at once.

POLPETTES

Delicious little fried morsels of potato and Greek feta cheese, flavoured with dill and lemon juice.

500g/1¼lb potatoes
115g/4oz feta cheese
4 spring onions, chopped
45ml/3 tbsp chopped fresh dill
1 egg, beaten
15ml/1 tbsp lemon juice
flour for dredging
45ml/3 tbsp olive oil
salt and ground black pepper

SERVES 4

[1] Boil the potatoes in their skins in lightly salted water until soft. Drain, then peel while still warm. Place in a bowl and mash. Crumble the feta cheese into the potatoes and add the spring onions, dill, egg and lemon juice and season with salt and pepper. (The cheese is salty, so taste before you add salt.) Stir well.

[2] Cover the mixture and chill until firm. Divide the mixture into walnut-size balls, then flatten them slightly. Dredge with flour. Heat the oil in a frying pan and fry the polpettes until golden brown on each side. Drain on kitchen paper and serve at once.

MARROW WITH GNOCCHI

A simple way with marrow, this dish makes an excellent accompaniment to grilled meat, but it is also good with a vegetarian dish, or simply served with grilled tomatoes.

1 small marrow, cut into
bite-size chunks
50g/2oz butter
400g/14oz packet gnocchi
½ garlic clove, crushed
salt and ground black pepper
chopped fresh basil, to garnish

SERVES 4

1 Preheat the oven to 180°C/ 350°F/Gas 4. Butter an ovenproof dish and place the marrow in a single layer. Dot with the butter.

2 Place a double layer of buttered greaseproof paper over the top. Cover with an ovenproof plate or lid, so that it presses the marrow down, and then place a heavy, ovenproof weight on top of that.

3 Put in the oven to bake for about 15 minutes, by which time the marrow should just be tender. Cook the gnocchi in a large saucepan of boiling salted water for 2–3 minutes, or according to the instructions on the packet. Drain well.

4 Stir the garlic and gnocchi into the marrow. Season and then replace the greaseproof paper over the marrow and bake for another 5 minutes (the weights are not necessary).

5 Just before serving, sprinkle the mixture with a little chopped fresh basil.

COURGETTE FRITTERS WITH PISTOU

These delicious fritters are a speciality of Southern France. The pistou sauce provides a lovely contrast in flavour, but you could substitute other sauces, like a garlicky tomato one or a herb dressing.

FOR THE PISTOU
15g/½oz basil leaves
4 garlic cloves, crushed
75g/3oz/1 cup grated
Parmesan cheese
finely grated rind of 1 lemon
150ml/¼ pint/⅔ cup olive oil

FOR THE FRITTERS
450g/1lb courgettes, grated
75g/3oz/¾ cup plain flour
1 egg, separated
15ml/1 tbsp olive oil
oil for shallow frying
salt and ground black pepper

SERVES 4

1 To make the pistou, crush the basil leaves and garlic with a pestle and mortar to make a fairly fine paste. Transfer the paste to a bowl and stir in the grated cheese and lemon rind. Gradually blend in the oil, a little at a time, until combined, then transfer to a small serving dish.

2 To make the fritters, put the grated courgettes in a sieve over a bowl and sprinkle with plenty of salt. Leave for 1 hour then rinse thoroughly. Dry well on kitchen paper.

3 Sift the flour into a bowl and make a well in the centre, then add the egg yolk and oil. Measure 75ml/5 tbsp water and add a little to the bowl.

4 Whisk the egg yolk and oil, gradually incorporating the flour and water to make a smooth batter. Season and leave for 30 minutes.

5 Stir the courgettes into the batter. Whisk the egg white until stiff, then fold into the batter.

6 Heat 1cm/½in of oil in a frying pan. Add dessertspoons of batter to the oil and fry for 2 minutes until golden. Drain the fritters on kitchen paper and keep warm while frying the rest. Serve with the sauce.

AUBERGINE PARMIGIANA

A classic Italian dish, this features blissfully tender sliced aubergines layered with melting creamy mozzarella, fresh Parmesan and a good home-made tomato sauce.

3 medium aubergines, thinly sliced
olive oil, for brushing
300g/11oz mozzarella cheese, sliced
115g/4oz/1⅓ cups freshly grated
Parmesan cheese
30–45ml/2–3 tbsp natural-coloured
dried breadcrumbs
basil sprigs, to garnish
salt and ground black pepper

FOR THE SAUCE
30ml/2 tbsp olive oil
1 onion, finely chopped
2 garlic cloves, crushed
400g/14oz can chopped tomatoes
5ml/1 tsp granulated sugar
about 6 basil leaves

SERVES 4–6

[2] Preheat the oven to 200°C/
400°F/Gas 6. Spread out the aubergine slices on non-stick baking sheets, brush the tops with olive oil and bake for 10–15 minutes until softened.

[3] Make the sauce. Heat the oil in a saucepan and sauté the onion and garlic for 5 minutes. Add the canned tomatoes and sugar, with salt and pepper to taste. Bring to the boil, then lower the heat and simmer for about 10 minutes until reduced and thickened. Tear the basil leaves into small pieces and add them to the tomato sauce.

[4] Layer the aubergines in a greased baking dish with the mozzarella, the tomato sauce and the Parmesan, ending with Parmesan mixed with breadcrumbs. Bake for 20–25 minutes until golden brown and bubbling. Stand for 5 minutes before serving, garnished with basil.

[1] Layer the aubergine slices in a colander, sprinkling each layer with a little salt. Let the juices drain over a sink for about 20 minutes, then rinse the slices thoroughly under cold running water and pat dry with kitchen paper.

SPINACH WITH RAISINS AND PINE NUTS

Raisins and pine nuts are frequent partners in Spanish recipes. Here, tossed with wilted spinach and croûtons, they make a delicious snack or main meal accompaniment.

50g/2oz/⅓ cup raisins
1 thick slice crusty white bread
45ml/3 tbsp olive oil
25g/1oz/⅓ cup pine nuts
500g/1¼lb young spinach,
stalks removed
2 garlic cloves, crushed
salt and ground black pepper

SERVES 4

 Put the raisins in a small bowl with boiling water and leave to soak for 10 minutes. Drain.

 Cut the bread into cubes and discard the crusts. Heat 30ml/ 2 tbsp of the oil and fry the bread until golden. Drain.

 Heat the remaining oil in the pan. Fry the pine nuts until beginning to colour. Add the spinach and garlic and cook quickly, turning the spinach until it has just wilted.

 Toss in the raisins and season lightly with salt and pepper. Transfer to a warmed serving dish. Scatter with croûtons and serve hot.

VARIATION
Use Swiss chard or spinach beet instead of the spinach, cooking them a little longer.

SPICED TURNIPS WITH SPINACH AND TOMATOES

*Sweet baby turnips, tender spinach and ripe tomatoes make tempting partners
in this simple Eastern Mediterranean vegetable stew.*

450g/1lb plum or other
well-flavoured tomatoes
60ml/4 tbsp olive oil
2 onions, sliced
450g/1lb baby turnips, peeled
5ml/1 tsp paprika
2.5ml/½ tsp caster sugar
60ml/4 tbsp chopped fresh coriander
450g/1lb fresh young spinach,
stalks removed
salt and ground black pepper

SERVES 6

1 Plunge the tomatoes into a bowl of boiling water for 30 seconds, then refresh in a bowl of cold water. Peel away the tomato skins and chop roughly. Heat the olive oil in a large frying pan or sauté pan and fry the onion slices for about 5 minutes until golden.

2 Add the baby turnips, tomatoes and paprika to the pan with 60ml/4 tbsp water and cook until the tomatoes are pulpy. Cover with a lid and continue cooking until the baby turnips have softened.

3 Stir in the sugar and coriander, then add the spinach and a little salt and pepper and cook for a further 2–3 minutes until the spinach has wilted. Serve warm or cold.

TUNISIAN BROAD BEANS

*Peeling the broad beans is a bit time-consuming, but well worth the effort, and this dish is so delicious
that you will never want to eat broad beans any other way.*

350g/12oz frozen broad beans
15g/½ oz/1 tbsp butter
4–5 spring onions, sliced
15ml/1 tbsp chopped fresh coriander
5ml/1 tsp chopped fresh mint
2.5–5ml/½–1 tsp ground cumin
10ml/2 tsp olive oil
salt

SERVES 4

1 Simmer the broad beans in water for 3–4 minutes until tender. Drain and, when cool enough to handle, peel away the outer skin, so you are left with the bright green centres. Put these in a bowl.

2 Melt the butter in a small pan and gently fry the spring onions for 2–3 minutes. Add the broad beans and then stir in the coriander, mint, cumin and a pinch of salt. Stir in the olive oil and serve immediately.

COURGETTES WITH MOROCCAN SPICES

*The combination of onion and garlic with chilli, paprika and cumin gives the courgettes
a deliciously spicy flavour.*

500g/1¼ lb courgettes
lemon juice, chopped fresh coriander
and parsley, to serve

FOR THE SPICY *CHARMOULA*
1 onion
1–2 garlic cloves, crushed
¼ red or green chilli, seeded and
finely sliced
2.5ml/½ tsp paprika
2.5ml/½ tsp ground cumin
45ml/3 tbsp olive oil
salt and ground black pepper

SERVES 4

1 Preheat the oven to 180°C/ 350°F/Gas 4. Cut all the courgettes into quarters lengthways, and place in a shallow dish.

COOK'S TIP
Buy young courgettes with tender skin – older courgettes may need to be peeled.

2 Finely chop the onion and blend with the other *charmoula* ingredients and 60ml/4 tbsp water. Pour over the courgettes. Cover and bake for 15 minutes.

3 Baste the courgettes with the *charmoula,* and return to the oven, uncovered, for 5–10 minutes until they are tender. Sprinkle with lemon juice and herbs, and serve.

ROASTED PLUM TOMATOES AND GARLIC

These are so simple to prepare yet taste absolutely wonderful. Use a large, shallow earthenware dish that will allow the tomatoes to sear and char in a hot oven.

8 plum tomatoes, halved
12 garlic cloves
60ml/4 tbsp extra virgin olive oil
3 bay leaves
salt and ground black pepper
45ml/3 tbsp fresh oregano leaves,
to garnish

SERVES 4

1 Preheat the oven to 230°C/ 450°F/Gas 8. Select a shallow flameproof dish which will hold all the tomatoes snugly in a single layer. Place the tomatoes in the dish and push the whole, unpeeled garlic cloves between them.

2 Brush the tomatoes with the oil, add the bay leaves and sprinkle black pepper over the top. Bake for about 45 minutes until the tomatoes have softened and are sizzling in the pan. They should be charred around the edges. Season, garnish and serve.

TAGINE OF ONIONS

This is a typically sweet dish, much appreciated in Morocco, where cooks might even add three or four times the amount of cinnamon and twice the amount of sugar listed here. This recipe is especially good with kebabs.

675g/1½lb red or Spanish onions,
finely sliced
90ml/6 tbsp olive or sunflower oil,
or a mixture of both
pinch of saffron
2.5ml/½ tsp ground ginger
5ml/1 tsp ground black pepper
5ml/1 tsp ground cinnamon
15ml/1 tbsp granulated sugar

SERVES 4

3 Preheat the oven to 160°C/ 325°F/Gas 3 and pour the onions and the marinade into an ovenproof dish or casserole.

4 Fold a piece of foil into three and place over the top of the dish or casserole, securing with a lid.

5 Cook in the hot oven for 45 minutes or until the onions are very soft. Increase the oven temperature to 200°C/400°F/Gas 6, remove the lid and foil and cook for 5–10 minutes more until the onions are lightly glazed. Serve with grilled meats or a vegetarian alternative.

1 Place the onions in a shallow dish. Spread them out evenly.

2 Mix the oil, saffron, ginger, pepper, cinnamon and sugar and pour over the onions. Stir gently to mix and then set aside for 2 hours.

OKRA WITH CORIANDER AND TOMATOES

Okra is frequently combined with tomatoes and mild spices in various parts of the Mediterranean.
Buy okra only if it is soft and velvety, not dry and shrivelled.

🌿 🌿

450g/1lb tomatoes or 400g/14oz can
chopped tomatoes
450g/1lb fresh okra
45ml/3 tbsp olive oil
2 onions, thinly sliced
10ml/2 tsp coriander seeds, crushed
3 garlic cloves, crushed
2.5ml/½ tsp caster sugar
finely grated rind and juice
of 1 lemon
salt and ground black pepper

SERVES 4

🌿 🌿

1 If using fresh tomatoes, plunge them into boiling water for 30 seconds, then refresh in cold water. Peel away the skins and chop.

2 Trim off any stalks from the okra and leave whole. Heat the oil in a sauté pan and fry the onions and coriander for 3–4 minutes until beginning to colour.

3 Add the okra and garlic and fry for 1 minute. Gently stir in the tomatoes and sugar and simmer gently for about 20 minutes, until the okra is tender, stirring once or twice. Stir in the lemon rind and juice and add salt and pepper to taste, adding a little more sugar if necessary. Serve warm or cold.

RADICCHIO AND CHICORY GRATIN

Salad vegetables such as radicchio and chicory take on a different flavour when cooked in this way.
The creamy sauce combines wonderfully with the bitter leaves.

2 heads radicchio, quartered
lengthways
2 heads chicory, quartered lengthways
25g/1oz/¼ cup drained sun-dried
tomatoes in oil, roughly chopped,
plus 30ml/2 tbsp oil from the jar
25g/1oz/2 tbsp butter
15g/½ oz/1 tbsp plain flour
250ml/8fl oz/1 cup milk
pinch of grated nutmeg
50g/2oz/½ cup grated
Emmental cheese
salt and ground black pepper
chopped fresh parsley, to garnish

SERVES 4

1 Preheat the oven to 180°C/ 350°F/Gas 4. Grease a baking dish. Arrange the radicchio and chicory quarters in the dish. Scatter over the tomatoes and brush the leaves with oil. Season and cover with foil. Bake for 15 minutes, then remove the foil and bake for a further 10 minutes.

2 Make the sauce. Place the butter in a small saucepan and melt over a moderate heat. When the butter is foaming, add the flour and cook for 1 minute, stirring. Remove from the heat and gradually add the milk, whisking. Return to the heat and bring to the boil, still whisking. Simmer for 2–3 minutes to thicken. Season to taste and add the nutmeg.

3 Pour the sauce over the vegetables and sprinkle with the grated Emmental. Bake for about 20 minutes until golden. Serve immediately, garnished with parsley.

BAKED COURGETTES

*When very small and very fresh courgettes are used for this recipe, it is both simple and delicious.
The creamy, tangy goat's cheese contrasts well with the delicate flavour of the young courgettes.*

8 small courgettes, about 450g/1lb
total weight
15ml/1 tbsp olive oil, plus extra
for greasing
75–115g/3–4oz goat's cheese, cut into
thin strips
small bunch of fresh mint,
finely chopped
freshly ground black pepper

SERVES 4

|3| Insert pieces of goat's cheese into the slits. Add a little mint and sprinkle with the remaining olive oil and the ground black pepper.

|4| Wrap each courgette in a foil rectangle, place on a baking sheet and bake for about 25 minutes until tender.

|1| Preheat the oven to 180°C/350°F/Gas 4. Cut out eight rectangles of foil, each large enough to encase a courgette. Brush each rectangle with a little olive oil, on one side only.

|2| Trim the courgettes by cutting off the top and tail. Cut a thin slit along the length of each.

COOK'S TIP
The courgettes can be unwrapped and finished under the grill.

SPANISH POTATOES

*This is an adaptation of a peppery potato dish, of which there are several versions. All of them are fried
and mildly spiced with the added tang of wine vinegar. Serve with cold meats or as a tapas.*

675g/1½ lb small new potatoes
75ml/5 tbsp olive oil
2 garlic cloves, sliced
2.5ml/½ tsp crushed chillies
2.5ml/½ tsp ground cumin
10ml/2 tsp paprika
30ml/2 tbsp red or white
wine vinegar
1 red or green pepper, seeded
and sliced
coarse sea salt, to serve (optional)

SERVES 4

1 Cook the potatoes in boiling salted water until almost tender.
Drain and, if preferred, peel them.
Cut into chunks.

2 Heat the oil in a large frying or sauté pan and fry the potatoes,
turning them frequently until golden.

3 Meanwhile, crush together the garlic, chillies and cumin using
a pestle and mortar. Mix with the paprika and wine vinegar.

4 Add the garlic mixture to the potatoes with the sliced pepper
and cook, stirring, for 2 minutes.
Serve warm, or leave until cold.
Scatter with coarse sea salt, if you like, to serve.

ROASTED POTATOES WITH RED ONIONS

These mouth-watering potatoes are a fine accompaniment to just about anything. The key is to use small, firm potatoes. The smaller they are cut, the quicker they will cook.

675g/1½ lb small firm potatoes
25g/1oz/2 tbsp butter
30ml/2 tbsp olive oil
2 red onions, cut into chunks
8 garlic cloves, unpeeled
30ml/2 tbsp chopped fresh rosemary
salt and ground black pepper

SERVES 4

COOK'S TIP
Salt the potatoes a few minutes before the end of cooking, this will help them maintain their shape.

1 Preheat the oven to 230°C/ 450°F/Gas 8. Use a potato peeler to remove the potato skins. Try and do this as thinly as possible to retain the vitamins and minerals which lie just below the surface. Use a knife to cut the potatoes into quarters. Rinse them with water. To ensure that the potatoes remain crisp, they should be completely dry before cooking. Place the butter and oil in a roasting tin and place in the oven to heat.

2 When the butter has melted and is foaming, add the potatoes, red onions, garlic and rosemary. Toss well and then spread out in one layer.

3 Place the tin in the oven and roast for about 25 minutes until the potatoes are golden and tender when tested with a fork. Shake the tin from time to time to redistribute the potatoes. When they are cooked, season with salt and pepper.

GREEN BEANS WITH TOMATOES

This is a real summer favourite, using the best ripe plum tomatoes and French beans.

30ml/2 tbsp olive oil
1 large onion, finely sliced
2 garlic cloves, finely chopped
6 large ripe plum tomatoes, peeled,
  seeded and coarsely chopped
150ml/¼ pint/⅔ cup dry white wine
450g/1lb French green beans, sliced
  in half lengthways
16 stoned black olives
10ml/2 tsp lemon juice
salt and ground black pepper

SERVES 4

1 Heat the oil in a deep frying pan. Add the onion and garlic and cook for about 5 minutes until the onion is soft but not brown.

2 Add the chopped tomatoes, white wine, beans, olives and lemon juice. Cook over a gentle heat for a further 20 minutes, stirring from time to time, until the liquid is thickened and the beans are tender. Season with salt and pepper to taste and serve at once.

SALADS

·················· ❧ ❧ ··················

*Summer and salads are synonymous, and
nowhere is there a wider variety of these
flavoursome dishes than in the Mediterranean.*

LEFT: Some of these plump Moroccan olives will find their way into salads, but the majority will be pressed for oil.

salt and pepper. There are many variations, using different ingredients such as lemon juice, mustard, herbs, garlic and cream, and the types of oils and vinegars can be varied too. Extra virgin olive oil gives the finest flavour of all the olive oils, but a mixture of peanut oil and olive oil will produce a lighter dressing. Nut oils, such as walnut, complement salads containing nuts. The Italians favour a good red wine vinegar, but there is also the sour/sweet flavour of balsamic vinegar to consider – delicious with grilled vegetables. Spanish sherry vinegar is another good flavour to try. Herb-infused vinegars are also useful, particularly if the fresh herbs are unavailable.

There is an abundant variety of salad leaves in the Mediterranean, ranging in colour, taste and texture. The French favour a mixture of leaves called "mesclun", which can be bought in the markets by the handful. Dandelion leaves are popular too, as well as frisée, chicory, oak leaf lettuce and many more. In Italy, radicchio and rocket are preferred, and Spaniards favour romaine lettuce. In the Middle East, however, leaf salads are less popular. Salads

The climate of the Mediterranean countries has ensured that salads and cold dishes have always been popular. There is an abundance of wonderful ingredients, particularly vegetables, which are combined to produce delicious results. In its simplest form, a salad in France, Spain or Italy would consist of lettuce, or perhaps a mixture of a few different salad leaves, dressed with vinaigrette. A salad may be eaten after the main course, often before the cheese is served. Vinaigrette is the basic salad dressing. Originally a French classic, it is now used world-wide. As its name suggests, vinegar is a main ingredient, combined with three times its quantity of olive oil, and seasoned with

RIGHT: Visiting a Turkish market is more than a mere shopping trip; it's a chance to catch up on local news.

ABOVE: A quiet landscape near Carmona, in the beautiful region of Andalusia.

of cooked or raw vegetables, dressed with a lemony vinaigrette, are more typical of these countries. Fresh herbs also play an important part, sometimes served alone, between courses, to cleanse the palate. These basic leaf salads are spontaneous, depending on what is available in the market, and need no recipes.

The markets of the Mediterranean offer some of the best vegetables and fruit in the world. From huge vine-ripened tomatoes to tiny artichokes, all are lovingly displayed, waiting to be picked up and dropped into a basket to be taken home. The inspiration for salads is endless. Fruit too, is included; grapes and oranges make refreshing additions to some of our recipes.

Apart from the simple salads, there are the composed salads – specific ingredients, with a special dressing, which are dishes on their own, to be eaten as a lunch dish, or perhaps a starter. These salads include all sorts of foodstuffs: olives, sausage, nuts, cheese, anchovies; morsels chosen for a contrast in taste, texture and colour.

This chapter includes some of the classic salads of the region, including Salad Niçoise, Panzanella and Greek Salad, which are sure to transport any-one who has eaten them in their native countries straight to a little village on the coast of the Mediterranean. Some salads are substantial enough to be served as a main meal, such as Roasted Peppers with Tomatoes and Anchovies or Broad Bean, Mushroom and Chorizo Salad. Bread and a glass of wine should complete the picture!

PROVENCAL SALAD

*There are probably as many versions of this salad as there are cooks in Provence. With good French
bread, this regional classic makes a wonderful summer lunch or light supper.*

225g/8oz French beans
450g/1lb new potatoes, peeled and cut
into 2.5cm/1in pieces
white wine vinegar and olive oil,
for sprinkling
1 small cos or round lettuce, washed
4 ripe plum tomatoes, quartered
1 small cucumber, peeled, seeded
and diced
1 green or red pepper, thinly sliced
4 hard-boiled eggs, peeled
and quartered
24 Niçoise or black olives
225g/8oz can tuna in brine, drained
50g/2oz can anchovy fillets in olive
oil, drained
basil leaves, to garnish
garlic croûtons, to serve

FOR THE ANCHOVY VINAIGRETTE
20ml/4 tbsp Dijon mustard
50g/2oz can anchovy fillets in olive
oil, drained
1 garlic clove, crushed
60ml/4 tbsp lemon juice or
white wine vinegar
120ml/4fl oz/½ cup sunflower oil
120ml/4fl oz/½ cup extra virgin
olive oil
ground black pepper

SERVES 4–6

1 First make the anchovy
vinaigrette. Place the mustard,
anchovies and garlic in a bowl and
blend together by pressing the garlic
and anchovies against the sides of the
bowl. Season generously with pepper.

2 Using a small whisk, blend in
the lemon juice or wine vinegar.
Slowly whisk in the sunflower oil in a
thin stream, followed by the olive oil,
whisking until the dressing is smooth
and creamy.

3 Drop the French beans into a
large saucepan of boiling water
and boil for 3 minutes until tender,
yet crisp. Transfer the beans to a
colander with a slotted spoon, then
rinse under cold running water. Drain
again and set aside.

COOK'S TIP
To make garlic croûtons, thinly slice a
French stick into 2.5cm/1in cubes.
Place the bread in a single layer on
a baking sheet and bake in a
180°C/350°F/Gas 4 oven for
7–10 minutes or until golden, turning
once. Rub the toast with a garlic clove
and serve hot or cool.

4 Cook the potatoes in the same
boiling water, for 15 minutes
until just tender, then drain.
Sprinkle with a little vinegar, olive oil
and vinaigrette.

5 Arrange the lettuce on a platter,
with the tomatoes, cucumber,
pepper, beans and potatoes.

6 Arrange the eggs, olives, tuna
and anchovies on top and
garnish with the basil leaves. Drizzle
with the remaining vinaigrette and
serve with garlic croûtons.

TOMATO AND FETA CHEESE SALAD

Sweet sun-ripened tomatoes are rarely more delicious than when served with feta cheese and olive oil.
This salad, popular in Greece and Turkey, is enjoyed as a light meal with pieces of crispy bread.

2 Slice the tomatoes thickly and arrange in a shallow dish.

3 Crumble the cheese over the tomatoes, sprinkle with olive oil, then strew with olives and fresh basil sprigs. Season with freshly ground black pepper and serve at room temperature.

900g/2lb tomatoes
200g/7oz feta cheese
120ml/4fl oz/½ cup olive oil,
preferably Greek
12 black olives
4 fresh basil sprigs
freshly ground black pepper

SERVES 4

1 Remove the tough cores from the tomatoes with a small knife.

COOK'S TIP
Feta cheese has a strong flavour and can be quite salty. The least salty variety is imported from Greece and Turkey, and is available from specialist delicatessens.

ROCKET AND GRILLED CHEVRE SALAD

For this recipe, look out for a cylinder-shaped goat's cheese, or for small individual cheeses with a weight of about 50g/2oz, which can be cut into halves.

about 15ml/1 tbsp olive oil
about 15ml/1 tbsp vegetable oil
4 slices of French bread
45ml/3 tbsp walnut oil
15ml/1 tbsp lemon juice
225g/8oz goat's cheese
generous handful of rocket leaves
about 115g/4oz curly endive
salt and ground black pepper

FOR THE SAUCE
45ml/3 tbsp apricot jam
60ml/4 tbsp white wine
5ml/1 tsp Dijon mustard

SERVES 4

[1] Heat both the oils in a frying pan and fry the slices of French bread on one side only, until lightly golden. Drain on kitchen paper.

[2] To make the sauce, heat the jam in a small saucepan until warm but not boiling. Push through a sieve, into a clean pan, then stir in the wine and mustard. Heat gently and keep warm until ready to serve.

[3] Mix the walnut oil and lemon juice and season with a little salt and pepper.

[4] Preheat the grill a few minutes before serving the salad. Cut the goat's cheese into 50g/2oz rounds and place each piece on a French bread croûton, untoasted side up.

[5] Toss the rocket and curly endive in the walnut oil dressing and arrange on four individual serving plates. Place the croûtons under the grill for 3–4 minutes until the cheese melts. When the cheese croûtons are ready, arrange on each salad and pour over a little of the apricot sauce.

GOAT'S CHEESE SALAD WITH BUCKWHEAT, FRESH FIGS AND WALNUTS

*The robust flavours of goat's cheese and buckwheat combine especially well with ripe figs and walnuts.
The olive and nut oil dressing contains no vinegar and depends instead on the acidity of the cheese.
Enjoy with a gutsy red wine from the south of France.*

175g/6oz/1 cup couscous
30ml/2 tbsp toasted buckwheat
1 hard-boiled egg
30ml/2 tbsp chopped fresh parsley
60ml/4 tbsp extra virgin olive oil
45ml/3 tbsp walnut oil
115g/4oz rocket
½ frisée lettuce
175g/6oz crumbly white goat's cheese
*50g/2oz/½ cup broken
walnuts, toasted*
*4 ripe figs, trimmed and almost cut
into four (leave the pieces joined
at the base)*

SERVES 4

COOK'S TIP

Goat's cheeses vary in strength from
the youngest, which are soft and mild,
to strongly-flavoured cheeses which
have a firm and crumbly texture. The
crumbly type is best suited to salads
and sweet fruit such as figs.

1 Place the couscous and
buckwheat in a bowl, cover
with boiling water and leave to soak
for 15 minutes until softened. Place in
a sieve if necessary to drain off any
remaining water, then spread the
couscous and buckwheat on a metal
tray and allow to cool.

2 Roll the hard-boiled egg on a
hard surface to break the shell,
then peel the egg. Rinse it under the
tap to ensure that no pieces of shell
are left on the surface. Carefully
grate the egg on the finest side of a
cheese grater, ensuring that it does
not break up into lumps.

3 Toss the egg, parsley, couscous
and buckwheat in a bowl using
a spoon or a fork. Combine the two
oils and use half the oil to moisten
the couscous mixture.

4 Wash the rocket and lettuce
leaves in water and spin to dry
them. Dress with the remaining
walnut and olive oils and distribute
the salad between four large plates.

5 Pile the couscous in the centre
of the leaves, crumble on the
goat's cheese, scatter with toasted
walnuts and add the figs. Arrange so
that the salad looks attractive.

MOROCCAN FISH SALAD

This salad is similar to the classic Salade Niçoise and uses slightly-spiced fresh tuna or swordfish steaks, along with broad beans and French beans. Olives and hard-boiled eggs make this a very pretty salad.

about 900g/2lb fresh tuna or
swordfish, sliced into 2cm/¾ in steaks
olive oil, for brushing

FOR THE SALAD
450g/1lb French beans
450g/1lb broad beans
1 cos lettuce
450g/1lb cherry tomatoes, halved,
unless very small
30ml/2 tbsp coarsely chopped
fresh coriander
3 shelled hard-boiled eggs
45ml/3 tbsp olive oil
10–15ml/2–3 tsp lime or lemon juice
1 garlic clove, crushed
175–225g/6–8oz/1½–2 cups pitted
black olives
salt

FOR THE *CHARMOULA*
1 onion
2 garlic cloves
1 bunch fresh parsley
1 bunch fresh coriander
10ml/2 tsp paprika
45ml/3 tbsp olive oil
30ml/2 tbsp white wine vinegar
15ml/1 tbsp lime or lemon juice

SERVES 6

1. First make the *charmoula*. Place all the ingredients in a food processor, add 45ml/3 tbsp water and process for 30–40 seconds until it is all finely chopped.

2. Prick the tuna or swordfish steaks all over with a fork, place in a shallow dish and pour over the *charmoula*, turning the fish so that each piece is well coated. Cover with clear film and leave in a cool place for 2–4 hours.

3. To prepare the salad, cook the French beans and broad beans in boiling salted water until tender. Drain and refresh under cold water. Discard the outer shells from the broad beans and place them in a large serving bowl with the French beans.

4. Tear the lettuce leaves into pieces. Add to the salad with the tomatoes and coriander. Cut the eggs into eighths. Mix the olive oil with the citrus juice and garlic.

5. Brush the steaks with the marinade together with a little olive oil and grill for 5–6 minutes on each side until the fish is tender. Brush with marinade and more olive oil when turning the fish. Allow the fish to cool and then break the steaks into large pieces. Toss into the salad with the olives and dressing. Decorate with the eggs and serve.

ROASTED PEPPERS WITH TOMATOES AND ANCHOVIES

This is a Sicilian-style salad, using some typical ingredients from the Italian island. The flavour
improves if the salad is made and dressed an hour or two before serving.

1 red pepper
1 yellow pepper
4 sun-dried tomatoes in oil, drained
4 ripe plum tomatoes, sliced
2 canned anchovies, drained
and chopped
15ml/1 tbsp capers, drained
15ml/1 tbsp pine nuts
1 garlic clove, very thinly sliced

FOR THE DRESSING
75ml/5 tbsp extra virgin olive oil
15ml/1 tbsp balsamic vinegar
5ml/1 tsp lemon juice
chopped fresh mixed herbs
salt and freshly ground
black pepper

SERVES 4

1 Cut the peppers in half, and
remove the seeds and stalks.
Cut into quarters and cook, skin side
up, under a hot grill until the skin
chars. Transfer to a bowl, and cover
with a plate. Leave to cool. Peel the
peppers and cut into strips.

2 Thinly slice the sun-dried
tomatoes. Arrange the peppers
and fresh tomatoes on a serving dish.
Scatter over the anchovies, sun-dried
tomatoes, capers, pine nuts and garlic.

3 To make the dressing, mix
together the olive oil, vinegar,
lemon juice and chopped herbs and
season with salt and pepper. Pour
over the salad just before serving.

175

SEACOOD SALAD

SEAFOOD SALAD

Squid, mussels and prawns with a simple dressing make a fresh-tasting salad.

115g/4oz prepared squid rings
1 large carrot
6 crisp lettuce leaves, torn
into pieces
10cm/4in piece cucumber,
finely diced
12 fresh mussels, in their
shells, steamed
115g/4oz cooked, peeled prawns
15ml/1 tbsp drained capers

FOR THE DRESSING
30ml/2 tbsp freshly squeezed
lemon juice
45ml/3 tbsp olive oil
15ml/1 tbsp chopped fresh parsley
sea salt and freshly ground
black pepper

SERVES 6

3 Arrange the mussels, prawns and squid rings over the salad and scatter the capers over the top.

4 Whisk the dressing ingredients in a small bowl and drizzle over the salad. Chill before serving.

1 Place the squid in a vegetable steamer or sieve and steam for 3 minutes until the squid just turns white. Remove the steamer from the pan and cool under cold running water. Drain on kitchen paper.

2 Using a swivel-style vegetable peeler, cut the carrot into wafer-thin ribbons. Place the lettuce on a serving plate. Scatter over the carrot ribbons, followed by the finely diced cucumber.

COOK'S TIP
For a change, use any type of cooked seafood or fish in this salad – try steamed clams or cockles, prawns in their shells or cubes of firm fish.

AVOCADO, CRAB AND CORIANDER SALAD

The sweet richness of crab combines especially well with ripe avocado, fresh coriander and tomato.

675g/1½ lb small new potatoes
1 fresh mint sprig
900g/2lb boiled crabs, or 275g/10oz
frozen crab meat, thawed
1 Batavian endive or
butterhead lettuce
175g/6oz lamb's lettuce or young
spinach leaves
1 large ripe avocado, peeled
and sliced
175g/6oz cherry tomatoes
a pinch of ground nutmeg
salt and ground black pepper

FOR THE DRESSING
75ml/5 tbsp olive oil,
preferably Tuscan
15ml/1 tbsp lime juice
45ml/3 tbsp chopped fresh coriander
2.5ml/ ½ tsp caster sugar

SERVES 4

3 Turn the crab on its back and push away the rear leg section with the thumb and forefinger of each hand. Remove the flesh from inside the shell.

4 Discard the soft gills ("dead men's fingers"); the crab uses these gills to filter impurities in its diet. Apart from these and the shell, everything else is edible, both the white and dark meat.

5 Split the central body section open with a knife and remove the white and dark flesh with a toothpick or skewer.

6 Combine all the dressing ingredients in a screw-top jar and shake. Distribute the salad leaves among four plates. Top with avocado, crab, tomatoes and the warm new potatoes. Season with salt, pepper and freshly grated nutmeg, and serve.

1 Scrape or peel the potatoes. Put in a pan with water to cover, add salt and a sprig of mint. Bring to the boil, then simmer for 20 minutes. Drain, cover and keep warm until needed.

2 Remove the legs and claws from each crab, if using. Crack these open with the back of a chopping knife and then remove the white meat and set it aside.

SALAD NICOISE

Made with good quality ingredients, this Provençal salad makes a simple yet unbeatable summer lunch or supper dish. Serve with country-style bread and chilled white wine.

FOR THE DRESSING
90ml/6 tbsp extra virgin olive oil
2 garlic cloves, crushed
15ml/1 tbsp white wine vinegar
salt and ground black pepper

FOR THE SALAD
115g/4oz French beans, trimmed
115g/4oz mixed salad leaves
½ small cucumber, thinly sliced
4 ripe tomatoes, quartered
200g/7oz can tuna in oil, drained
50g/2oz can anchovies, drained
4 eggs, hard-boiled
½ bunch radishes, trimmed
50g/2oz/½ cup small black olives
flat leaf parsley, to garnish

SERVES 4

1 To make the dressing, whisk together the oil, garlic and vinegar and season to taste with salt and pepper.

2 Halve the French beans and cook in a saucepan of boiling water for 2 minutes until only just tender, then drain.

3 Mix the salad leaves, cucumber, tomatoes and beans in a large, shallow salad bowl. Flake the tuna. Halve the anchovies lengthways. Shell and quarter the eggs.

4 Scatter the radishes, tuna, anchovies, eggs and olives over the salad. Pour over the dressing and toss together lightly. Serve garnished with parsley.

COUSCOUS SALAD

Couscous salad is popular throughout the Mediterranean region. This salad has a delicate flavour and is excellent with grilled chicken or kebabs.

275g/10oz/1⅔ cups couscous
525ml/18fl oz/2¼ cups boiling
vegetable stock
16–20 black olives
2 small courgettes
25g/1oz/¼ cup flaked
almonds, toasted
60ml/4 tbsp olive oil
15ml/1 tbsp lemon juice
15ml/1 tbsp chopped fresh coriander
15ml/1 tbsp chopped fresh parsley
a good pinch of ground cumin
a good pinch of cayenne pepper
salt

SERVES 4

3 Carefully mix the courgettes, olives and toasted almonds into the couscous.

4 Whisk together the olive oil, lemon juice, herbs, spices and a pinch of salt. Stir into the salad.

1 Place the couscous in a bowl and pour over the boiling stock. Stir with a fork and then set aside for 10 minutes for the stock to be absorbed. Fluff up with a fork.

2 Halve the olives, discarding the stones by using the tip of a knife. Top and tail both the courgettes, cut them into slices along the length, then cut each slice into small strips.

CURLY ENDIVE SALAD WITH BACON

This country-style salad is popular in France. When they are in season, dandelion leaves often replace the endive and the salad is sometimes sprinkled with chopped hard-boiled egg.

225g/8oz curly endive or
escarole leaves
75–90ml/5–6 tbsp extra virgin
olive oil
175g/6oz piece of smoked bacon, diced,
or 6 thick-cut pancetta rashers, cut
crossways into thin strips
50g/2oz white bread, cubed
1 small garlic clove, finely chopped
15ml/1 tbsp red wine vinegar
10ml/2 tsp Dijon mustard
salt and ground black pepper

SERVES 4

3 Add another 30ml/2 tbsp oil to the pan and fry the cubes of bread over a medium-high heat, turning frequently, until evenly browned. Remove the croûtons with a slotted spoon and drain on kitchen paper. Wipe the pan clean.

4 Stir the garlic, vinegar and mustard into the pan with the remaining oil and heat until just warm, whisking to combine. Season to taste, then pour the dressing over the salad and sprinkle with the fried bacon and croûtons.

1 Tear the lettuce into bite-size pieces and put in a salad bowl.

2 Heat 15ml/1 tbsp of the oil in a medium non-stick frying pan over a low–medium heat and add the bacon. Fry gently until well browned, stirring occasionally. Remove the bacon with a slotted spoon and drain on kitchen paper.

FATTOUSH

This simple peasant salad has become a popular dish all over Syria and the Lebanon.

1 yellow or red pepper
1 large cucumber
4–5 tomatoes
1 bunch spring onions
30ml/2 tbsp finely chopped
fresh parsley
30ml/2 tbsp finely chopped fresh mint
30ml/2 tbsp finely chopped
fresh coriander
2 garlic cloves, crushed
75ml/5 tbsp olive oil
juice of 2 lemons
salt and ground black pepper
2 pitta breads

SERVES 4

VARIATION
If you prefer, make this salad in the traditional way. After toasting the pitta bread until crisp, crush it in your hand and then sprinkle it over the salad before serving.

COOK'S TIP
Although the recipe calls for only 30ml/2 tbsp of each herb, parsley, mint and coriander, if you have plenty to hand, then you can add as much as you like to this delicious aromatic salad.

1 Slice the pepper, discarding the seeds and core, then roughly chop the cucumber and tomatoes. Place them in a large salad bowl and mix together.

2 Trim and slice the spring onions. Add to the cucumber, tomatoes and pepper with the finely chopped parsley, mint and coriander.

3 To make the dressing, mix the garlic with the olive oil and lemon juice in a jug, then season to taste with salt and black pepper. Pour the dressing over the salad and toss lightly to mix.

4 Toast the pitta bread in a toaster or under a hot grill until crisp and then serve it alongside the salad.

TABBOULEH

This classic Lebanese salad makes an ideal substitute for a rice dish on a buffet table.
It is excellent served with cold sliced lamb.

175g/6oz/1 cup fine bulgur wheat
juice of 1 lemon
45ml/3 tbsp olive oil
40g/1½oz fresh parsley,
finely chopped
45ml/3 tbsp fresh mint, chopped
4–5 spring onions, chopped
1 green pepper, seeded and sliced
salt and ground black pepper
2 large tomatoes, diced, and black
olives, to garnish

SERVES 4

1 Put the bulgur wheat in a bowl. Add enough cold water to cover the wheat and let it stand for at least 30 minutes and up to 2 hours.

2 Drain in a cloth and squeeze to remove excess water. Spread on kitchen paper to dry the bulgur wheat completely.

3 Place the bulgur wheat in a large bowl, add the lemon juice, the oil and a little seasoning. Allow to stand for 1–2 hours if possible.

4 Add the chopped parsley, mint, spring onions and green pepper, and mix well. Garnish with diced tomatoes and olives, and serve.

SWEET AND SOUR ONION SALAD

This recipe is primarily from Provence in the south of France but there are influences from other Mediterranean countries, too.

450g/1lb baby onions, peeled
50ml/2fl oz/¼ cup wine vinegar
45ml/3 tbsp olive oil
40g/1½oz/3 tbsp caster sugar
45ml/3 tbsp tomato purée
1 bay leaf
2 parsley sprigs
65g/2½oz/½ cup raisins
salt and ground black pepper

SERVES 6

1 Put all the ingredients in a pan with 300ml/½ pint/1¼ cups water. Bring to the boil and simmer gently, uncovered, for 45 minutes, or until the onions are tender and most of the liquid has evaporated.

2 Remove the bay leaf and parsley, check the seasoning, and transfer to a serving dish. Serve at room temperature.

PANZANELLA

In this lively Italian speciality, a sweet tangy blend of tomato juice, rich olive oil and red wine vinegar is soaked up in a colourful salad of roasted peppers, anchovies and toasted ciabatta.

225g/8oz ciabatta (about ⅔ loaf)
150ml/¼ pint/⅔ cup olive oil
3 red peppers
3 yellow peppers
50g/2oz can anchovy fillets
675g/1½lb ripe plum tomatoes
4 garlic cloves, crushed
60ml/4 tbsp red wine vinegar
50g/2oz capers
115g/4oz/1 cup pitted black olives
salt and ground black pepper
basil leaves, to garnish

SERVES 4–6

1 Preheat the oven to 200°C/ 400°F/Gas 6. Cut the ciabatta into 2cm/¾in chunks and drizzle with 50ml/2fl oz/¼ cup of the oil. Grill lightly until just golden.

2 Put the peppers on a foil-lined baking sheet and bake for about 45 minutes until the skin begins to char. Remove from the oven, cover with a cloth and leave to cool slightly.

3 Pull the skin off the peppers and cut them into quarters, discarding the stalk ends and seeds. Drain and then roughly chop the anchovies. Set aside.

4 To make the tomato dressing, peel and halve the tomatoes. Scoop the seeds into a sieve set over a bowl. Using the back of a spoon, press the tomato pulp in the sieve to extract as much juice as possible. Discard the pulp and add the remaining oil, the garlic and vinegar to the juices.

5 Layer the toasted bread, peppers, tomatoes, anchovies, capers and olives in a large salad bowl. Season the tomato dressing with salt and pepper and pour it over the salad. Leave to stand for about 30 minutes. Serve garnished with plenty of basil leaves.

RADICCHIO, ARTICHOKE AND WALNUT SALAD

The distinctive, earthy taste of Jerusalem artichokes makes a lovely contrast to the sharp freshness of radicchio and lemon. Serve warm or cold as an accompaniment to grilled steak or barbecued meats.

1 large radicchio or 150g/5oz
radicchio leaves
40g/1½oz/6 tbsp walnut pieces
45ml/3 tbsp walnut oil
500g/1¼lb Jerusalem artichokes
pared rind and juice of 1 lemon
coarse sea salt and ground
black pepper
flat leaf parsley, to garnish (optional)

SERVES 4

1 If using a whole radicchio, cut it into 8–10 wedges. Put the wedges or leaves in a flameproof dish. Scatter over the walnuts, then spoon over the oil and season. Grill for 2–3 minutes.

2 Peel the artichokes and cut up any large ones so the pieces are all roughly the same size. Add the artichokes to a pan of boiling salted water with half the lemon juice and cook for 5–7 minutes until tender. Drain. Preheat the grill to high.

3 Toss the artichokes into the salad with the remaining lemon juice and the pared rind. Season with coarse salt and pepper. Grill until beginning to brown. Serve at once garnished with torn pieces of parsley, if you like.

GREEK SALAD

*Anyone who has spent a holiday in Greece will have eaten a version of this salad – the Greeks'
equivalent to a mixed salad. Its success relies on using the freshest of ingredients, and a good olive oil.*

1 small cos lettuce, sliced
450g/1lb flavoursome tomatoes,
cut into eighths
1 cucumber, seeded and chopped
200g/7oz feta cheese, crumbled
4 spring onions, sliced
50g/2oz/½ cup black olives, stoned
and halved

FOR THE DRESSING
90ml/6 tbsp good olive oil
25ml/1½ tbsp lemon juice
salt and ground black pepper

SERVES 6

1 Put all the main salad
ingredients into a large bowl.
Whisk together the olive oil and
lemon juice, then season with salt
and pepper, and pour the dressing
over the salad. Mix well and
serve immediately.

SPICED AUBERGINE SALAD

*Serve this Middle-Eastern-influenced salad with warm pitta bread as a starter or to accompany
a main course rice pilaff.*

2 small aubergines, sliced
75ml/5 tbsp olive oil
50ml/2fl oz/¼ cup red wine vinegar
2 garlic cloves, crushed
15ml/1 tbsp lemon juice
2.5ml/½ tsp ground cumin
2.5ml/½ tsp ground coriander
½ cucumber, thinly sliced
2 flavoursome tomatoes,
thinly sliced
30ml/2 tbsp natural yogurt
salt and ground black pepper
chopped flat leaf parsley, to garnish

SERVES 4

1 Preheat the grill. Brush the
aubergine slices lightly with
some of the oil and cook under a
high heat, turning once, until golden
and tender. Cut into quarters.

2 Mix together the remaining oil,
vinegar, garlic, lemon juice,
cumin and coriander. Season with salt
and pepper and mix thoroughly. Add
the warm aubergines, stir well and
chill for at least 2 hours. Add the
cucumber and tomatoes. Transfer to a
serving dish and spoon the yogurt on
top. Sprinkle with parsley.

WARM BROAD BEAN AND FETA SALAD

This recipe is loosely based on a typical medley of fresh-tasting Greek salad ingredients – broad beans, tomatoes and feta cheese. It's lovely warm or cold as a starter or main course accompaniment.

900g/2lb broad beans, shelled, or
350g/12oz shelled frozen beans
60ml/4 tbsp olive oil
175g/6oz plum tomatoes, halved, or
quartered if large
4 garlic cloves, crushed
115g/4oz firm feta cheese, cut
into chunks
45ml/3 tbsp chopped fresh dill
12 black olives
salt and ground black pepper
chopped fresh dill, to garnish

SERVES 4–6

1 Cook the fresh or frozen broad beans in boiling, salted water until just tender. Drain and set aside.

2 Meanwhile, heat the oil in a heavy-based frying pan and add the tomatoes and garlic. Cook until the tomatoes are beginning to colour.

3 Add the feta to the pan and toss the ingredients together for 1 minute. Mix with the drained beans, dill, olives and salt and pepper. Serve garnished with chopped dill.

HALLOUMI AND GRAPE SALAD

In Eastern Europe, firm salty halloumi cheese is often served fried for breakfast or supper. In this recipe it is tossed with sweet, juicy grapes which really complement its distinctive flavour.

FOR THE DRESSING
60ml/4 tbsp olive oil
15ml/1 tbsp lemon juice
2.5ml/½ tsp caster sugar
salt and ground black pepper
15ml/1 tbsp chopped fresh thyme or dill

FOR THE SALAD
150g/5oz mixed green salad leaves
75g/3oz seedless green grapes
75g/3oz seedless black grapes
250g/9oz halloumi cheese
45ml/3 tbsp olive oil
fresh young thyme leaves or dill,
to garnish

SERVES 4

1 To make the dressing, mix together the olive oil, lemon juice and sugar. Season. Stir in the thyme or dill and set aside.

2 Toss together the salad leaves and the green and black grapes, then transfer to a large serving plate.

3 Thinly slice the cheese. Heat the oil in a large frying pan. Add the cheese and fry briefly until turning golden on the underside. Turn the cheese with a fish slice and cook the other side.

4 Arrange the cheese over the salad. Pour over the dressing and garnish with thyme or dill.

TURKISH SALAD

This classic salad is a wonderful combination of textures and flavours. The saltiness of the cheese is perfectly balanced by the refreshing salad vegetables.

1 cos lettuce heart
1 green and 1 red pepper
½ cucumber
4 tomatoes
1 red onion
225g/8oz feta cheese, crumbled
black olives, to garnish

FOR THE DRESSING
45ml/3 tbsp olive oil
45ml/3 tbsp lemon juice
1 garlic clove, crushed
15ml/1 tbsp chopped fresh parsley
15ml/1 tbsp chopped fresh mint
salt and ground black pepper

SERVES 4

1 Chop the lettuce into bite-size pieces. Seed the peppers, remove the cores and cut the flesh into thin strips. Chop the cucumber and slice or chop the tomatoes. Cut the onion in half, then slice finely. Place the chopped lettuce, peppers, cucumber, tomatoes and onion in a large bowl. Scatter the feta over the top and toss lightly.

2 To make the dressing, whisk together the olive oil, lemon juice and garlic in a small bowl. Stir in the parsley and mint. Season with salt and pepper to taste.

3 Pour the dressing over the salad, toss lightly and serve at once, garnished with a handful of black olives.

PERSIAN SALAD

This simple salad works very well with baked Italian dishes – don't add the dressing until just before you are ready to serve.

4 tomatoes
½ cucumber
1 onion
1 cos lettuce heart

FOR THE DRESSING
30ml/2 tbsp olive oil
juice of 1 lemon
1 garlic clove, crushed
salt and ground black pepper

SERVES 4

1 Cut the tomatoes and cucumber into small cubes. Finely chop the onion and tear the lettuce into pieces. Place the cubed tomatoes, cucumber, onion and lettuce in a large salad bowl and mix them lightly together.

2 To make the dressing, pour the olive oil into a small bowl. Add the lemon juice, garlic and seasoning and whisk together well. Pour over the salad and toss lightly to mix. Sprinkle with black pepper and serve with meat or rice dishes.

BROAD BEAN, MUSHROOM AND CHORIZO SALAD

Broad beans are used in both their fresh and dried forms in various Mediterranean countries.
This Spanish salad could be served as either a first course or lunch dish.

225g/8oz shelled broad beans
175g/6oz chorizo sausage
60ml/4 tbsp extra virgin olive oil
225g/8oz brown cap
mushrooms, sliced
handful of fresh chives
salt and ground black pepper

SERVES 4

1 Cook the broad beans in boiling, salted water for about 7–8 minutes. Drain and refresh under cold water.

2 Remove the skin from the sausage and cut it into small chunks. Heat the oil in a frying pan, add the chorizo and cook for 2–3 minutes. Tip the chorizo and oil into the mushrooms and mix well. Leave to cool. Chop half the chives. If the beans are large, peel away the tough outer skins. Stir the beans and snipped chives into the mushroom mixture, and season to taste. Serve at room temperature, garnished with the remaining chives.

AVOCADO, ORANGE AND ALMOND SALAD

The Mediterranean is not particularly known for its avocados, but the climate is perfect and they are
grown in many parts of the region. This salad has a Spanish influence.

2 oranges
2 flavoursome tomatoes
2 small avocados
60ml/4 tbsp extra virgin olive oil
30ml/2 tbsp lemon juice
15ml/1 tbsp chopped fresh parsley
1 small onion, sliced into rings
salt and ground black pepper
25g/1oz/¼ cup flaked almonds
and 10–12 black olives,
to garnish

SERVES 4

1 Peel the oranges and slice into thick rounds. Plunge the tomatoes into boiling water for 30 seconds, then refresh in cold water. Peel away the skins, cut into quarters, remove the seeds and chop roughly.

2 Cut the avocados in half, remove the stones and carefully peel away the skin. Cut into chunks.

3 Mix together the olive oil, lemon juice and parsley. Season with salt and pepper. Toss the avocados and tomatoes in half of the dressing.

4 Arrange the sliced oranges on a plate and scatter over the onion rings. Drizzle with the rest of the dressing. Spoon the avocados, tomatoes, almonds and olives on top.

TRICOLORE SALAD

A popular salad, this dish depends for its success on the quality of its ingredients. Mozzarella di bufala is the best cheese to serve uncooked. Whole ripe plum tomatoes give up their juices to blend with extra virgin olive oil for a natural dressing.

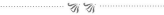

150g/5oz mozzarella di bufala cheese, thinly sliced
4 large plum tomatoes, sliced
sea salt flakes, to season
1 large avocado
about 12 basil leaves or a small handful of flat leaf parsley leaves
45–60ml/3–4 tbsp extra virgin olive oil
freshly ground black pepper

SERVES 2

1 Arrange the sliced cheese and tomatoes randomly on two salad plates. Crush over a few good pinches of sea salt flakes. This will help to draw out some of the juices from the tomatoes. Set aside in a cool place to marinate for 30 minutes.

2 Just before serving, cut the avocado in half using a large sharp knife and twist to separate. Lift out the stone and remove the peel.

3 Slice the avocado flesh crossways into half-moons, or cut it into large chunks or cubes if that is easier.

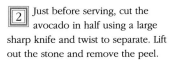

4 Place the avocado on the salad, then sprinkle with the basil or parsley. Drizzle over the olive oil, add a little more salt if liked and some black pepper. Serve the salad at room temperature, with chunks of crusty Italian ciabatta.

VARIATION
A light sprinkling of balsamic vinegar added just before serving would give this salad a refreshing tang, while a few thinly sliced red onion rings would add extra colour and flavour.

SPANISH ASPARAGUS AND ORANGE SALAD

Complicated salad dressings are rarely found in Spain – they simply rely on the wonderful flavour of a good quality olive oil.

225g/8oz asparagus, trimmed and cut
into 5cm/2in pieces
2 large oranges
2 flavoursome tomatoes, cut
into eighths
50g/2oz romaine lettuce leaves,
shredded
30ml/2 tbsp extra virgin olive oil
2.5ml/½ tsp sherry vinegar
salt and ground black pepper

SERVES 4

COOK'S TIP
Cos or Little Gem lettuce can be used
in place of romaine.

1. Cook the asparagus in boiling, salted water for 3–4 minutes, until just tender. Drain and refresh under cold water.

2. Grate the rind from half an orange and reserve. Peel all the oranges and cut into segments. Squeeze out the juice from the membrane and reserve the juice.

3. Put the asparagus, orange segments, tomatoes and lettuce into a salad bowl. Mix together the oil and vinegar and add 15ml/1 tbsp of the reserved orange juice and 5ml/1 tsp of the rind *(left)*. Season with salt and pepper. Just before serving, pour the dressing over the salad and mix gently to coat.

GLOBE ARTICHOKES WITH GREEN BEANS AND AIOLI

Just like the French aïoli, there are many recipes for the Spanish equivalent. This one is exceptionally garlicky, a perfect partner to freshly cooked vegetables.

FOR THE AIOLI
6 large garlic cloves, sliced
10ml/2 tsp white wine vinegar
250ml/8fl oz/1 cup olive oil
salt and ground black pepper

FOR THE SALAD
225g/8oz green beans
3 small globe artichokes
15ml/1 tbsp olive oil
pared rind of 1 lemon
coarse salt for sprinkling
lemon wedges, to garnish

SERVES 4–6

1. To make the aïoli, put the garlic and vinegar in a blender or mini food processor. With the machine switched on, gradually pour in the olive oil until the mixture is thickened and smooth. (Alternatively, crush the garlic to a paste with the vinegar and gradually beat in the oil using a hand whisk.) Season with salt and pepper to taste.

2. To make the salad, cook the beans in boiling water for 1–2 minutes until slightly softened. Drain.

3. Trim the artichoke stalks close to the base. Cook the artichokes in a large pan of salted water for about 30 minutes, or until you can easily pull away a leaf from the base. Drain well.

4. Using a sharp knife, halve the artichokes lengthways and ease out the choke using a teaspoon.

5. Arrange the artichokes and beans on serving plates and drizzle with the oil. Scatter with the lemon rind and season with coarse salt and a little pepper. Spoon the aïoli into the artichoke hearts and serve warm, garnished with lemon wedges. To eat artichokes, pull the leaves from the base one at a time and use to scoop a little of the sauce. It is only the fleshy end of each leaf and the base (or "heart") of the artichoke that is eaten.

COOK'S TIP
Mediterranean baby artichokes are sometimes available and are perfect for this kind of salad as, unlike the larger ones, they can be eaten whole. Cook them until just tender, then cut in half to serve.
Canned artichoke hearts, thoroughly drained and sliced, can be substituted when fresh ones are not available.

MOROCCAN COOKED SALAD

A version of a North African favourite, this cooked salad is served as a side dish with a main course.
Make this one the day before serving to improve the flavour.

2 flavoursome tomatoes, quartered
2 onions, chopped
½ cucumber, halved lengthways,
seeded and sliced
1 green pepper, halved, seeded
and chopped
30ml/2 tbsp lemon juice
45ml/3 tbsp olive oil
2 garlic cloves, crushed
30ml/2 tbsp chopped fresh coriander
salt and ground black pepper
sprigs of coriander, to garnish

SERVES 4

[1] Put the tomatoes, onions, cucumber and green pepper into a pan, add 60ml/4 tbsp water and simmer for 5 minutes. Leave to cool.

[2] Mix together the lemon juice, olive oil and garlic. Strain the vegetables, then transfer to a bowl. Pour over the dressing, season with salt and pepper and stir in the chopped coriander. Serve at once, garnished with coriander, if you like.

SCHLADA

Though Schlada is a salad, it is actually the Moroccan cousin of the Spanish soup Gazpacho. In addition to the usual ingredients, Schlada contains ground cumin and spicy paprika.

3 green peppers, quartered
4 large tomatoes
2 garlic cloves, finely chopped
30ml/2 tbsp olive oil
30ml/2 tbsp lemon juice
good pinch of paprika
pinch of ground cumin
¼ preserved lemon
salt and ground black pepper
fresh coriander and flat leaf parsley,
to garnish

SERVES 4

1 Grill the peppers, skin side up, until the skins are blackened, place in a plastic bag and tie the ends. Leave for about 10 minutes until the peppers are cool enough to handle, then peel away the skins.

2 Cut the peppers into small pieces, discarding the seeds and core, and place in a serving dish.

3 Peel the tomatoes by placing in boiling water for 1 minute, then plunging into cold water. Peel off the skins, then quarter the tomatoes, discarding the core and seeds. Chop roughly and add to the peppers. Scatter the garlic on top and chill for 1 hour.

4 Blend together the olive oil, lemon juice, paprika and cumin and pour over the salad. Season with salt and pepper.

5 Rinse the preserved lemon in cold water and remove the flesh and pith. Cut the peel into slivers and sprinkle over the salad. Garnish with coriander and flat leaf parsley.

CACIK

This refreshing yogurt dish is served all over the Eastern Mediterranean, whether as part of a mezze with marinated olives and pitta bread, or as an accompaniment to meat dishes. Greek tzatziki is very similar.

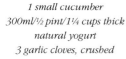

1 small cucumber
300ml/½ pint/1¼ cups thick
natural yogurt
3 garlic cloves, crushed
30ml/2 tbsp chopped fresh mint
30ml/2 tbsp chopped fresh dill
or parsley
salt and ground black pepper
mint or parsley and dill, to garnish
olive oil, olives and pitta bread,
to serve

SERVES 6

1 Finely chop the cucumber and layer in a colander with plenty of salt. Leave for 30 minutes. Wash the cucumber in several changes of cold water and drain thoroughly. Pat dry on kitchen paper.

2 Mix together the yogurt, garlic and herbs and season with salt and pepper. Stir in the cucumber. Garnish with herbs, drizzle over a little olive oil and serve with olives and pitta bread.

GARDEN SALAD

This wonderful salad, which looks just as good as it tastes, is just the thing to eat on a hot sunny day.

1 cos lettuce
175g/6oz rocket
1 small frisée lettuce
fresh chervil and tarragon sprigs
15ml/1 tbsp snipped fresh chives
handful of mixed edible flower heads,
such as nasturtiums or marigolds

FOR THE DRESSING
45ml/3 tbsp olive oil
15ml/1 tbsp white wine vinegar
2.5ml/½ tsp French mustard
1 garlic clove, crushed
a pinch of sugar

SERVES 4

1 Mix together the cos, rocket and frisée leaves and herbs.

2 Make the dressing by whisking all the ingredients together in a large bowl. Toss the salad leaves in the bowl with the dressing, sprinkle the flower heads decoratively and serve at once. If you prefer, use only half the dressing initially, and serve the rest separately, in a small jug.

COOK'S TIP
You can use any fresh, edible flowers from your garden in this beautiful, light salad.

SPINACH AND ROAST GARLIC SALAD

Don't worry about the amount of garlic in this salad. During roasting, the garlic becomes sweet and subtle and loses its pungent taste.

12 garlic cloves, unpeeled
60ml/4 tbsp extra virgin olive oil
450g/1lb baby spinach leaves
50g/2oz/½ cup pine nuts,
lightly toasted
juice of ½ lemon
salt and ground black pepper

SERVES 4

1. Preheat the oven to 190°C/ 375°F/Gas 5. Place the garlic in a small roasting dish, toss in about 30ml/2 tbsp of the olive oil and bake for about 15 minutes until the garlic cloves are slightly charred around the edges and have softened.

2. While still warm, tip the garlic into a salad bowl. Add the spinach, pine nuts, lemon juice, remaining olive oil and seasoning. Toss well. Serve immediately, inviting guests to squeeze the garlic purée out of the skins to eat.

MOROCCAN DATE, ORANGE AND CARROT SALAD

A colourful and unusual salad with exotic ingredients — fresh dates and orange flower water — combined with crisp leaves, carrots, oranges and toasted almonds.

1 Little Gem lettuce
2 carrots, finely grated
2 oranges
*115g/4oz fresh dates, stoned and cut
into eighths, lengthways*
*25g/1oz/¼ cup toasted whole
almonds, chopped*
30ml/2 tbsp lemon juice
5ml/1 tsp caster sugar
1.5ml/¼ tsp salt
15ml/1 tbsp orange flower water

SERVES 4

1 Separate the lettuce leaves and arrange them in the bottom of a salad bowl or on individual serving plates. Place the grated carrot in a mound on top.

2 Peel and segment the oranges and arrange them around the carrot. Pile the dates on top, then sprinkle with the almonds. Mix together the lemon juice, sugar, salt and orange flower water and sprinkle over the salad. Serve chilled.

203

BLACK AND ORANGE SALAD

This dramatic salad is typically North African and contrasts both colours and flavours – the dark black olives with the brightly-fleshed oranges, and the juxtaposition of tastes, sweet and savoury. A striking and refreshing salad suitable for any dinner party.

3 oranges
115g/4oz/1 cup pitted black olives
15ml/1 tbsp chopped fresh coriander
15ml/1 tbsp chopped fresh parsley
30ml/2 tbsp olive oil
15ml/1 tbsp lemon juice
2.5ml/½ tsp paprika
2.5ml/½ tsp ground cumin

SERVES 4

1 Using a knife, cut away the peel and white pith from the oranges, then cut the flesh into thick wedges.

2 Place the oranges in a salad bowl and add the black olives, coriander and parsley.

3 Whisk together the olive oil, lemon juice, paprika and cumin until it is of one consistency. Pour the dressing over the salad and toss gently. Rearrange the ingredients attractively. Chill for about 30 minutes and serve.

ROCKET AND CORIANDER SALAD

Rocket leaves have a wonderful, peppery flavour and, mixed with coriander, make a favourite salad. However, unless you grow your own rocket, or have a plentiful supply, you may well have to use extra spinach or another green leaf in order to pad this salad out.

115g/4oz or more rocket leaves
115g/4oz young spinach leaves
1 large bunch (about 25g/1oz)
    fresh coriander
2–3 fresh parsley sprigs
1 garlic clove, crushed
45ml/3 tbsp olive oil
10ml/2 tsp white wine vinegar,
    or herb vinegar
pinch of paprika
salt
cayenne pepper

SERVES 4

1 Wash the rocket and spinach leaves, ensuring that all grit is washed off, and place in a large salad bowl. Chop the coriander and parsley and add to the rest of the salad, mixing the different leaves together thoroughly.

2 In a small jug, blend together the garlic, olive oil, vinegar, paprika, salt and cayenne pepper.

3 Pour the dressing over the salad, coating all the leaves, and serve immediately.

FISH AND
SEAFOOD

❧ ❦ ❧

Mediterranean fishermen reap a rich harvest of
fish and seafood, which are often simply grilled or
fried, or used as the basis of a soup or stew.

The Mediterranean sea is tiny in relation to the world's larger seas and oceans. It is also relatively shallow, warm, low in natural food supplies and more polluted. Despite all these factors, the Mediterranean Sea has hundreds of different species of fish and crustacea, marketed in the Mediterranean and beyond. Visit a large fish market in any part of the region and you will be amazed at the fantastic variety of fish, many of which are wholly unknown, except to the locals and, of course, the fishermen themselves.

Above: Fishermen in Crete bring home the day's catch, packed in salt.

Left: Safely back in harbour, a Cretan fishing boat bobs gently on the calm sea.

A visit to a Mediterranean restaurant, bar or taverna, illustrates how this freshly caught fish, cooked simply, can be quite unbeatable in terms of flavour and texture. Few of us ever forget the arrival of a hot, steaming bowl of garlicky mussels or crisp prawns, dripping in garlic and olive oil. Perfectly fresh fish, grilled or barbecued with a basting of olive oil, garlic and herbs, needs little more embellishment, except perhaps a crisp salad, bread and light wine.

On a more elaborate scale, fish stew and soups are typically Mediterranean. A varied mixture of fish such as conger eel, gurnard, John Dory, monkfish, bass, bream and red mullet is combined with aromatic flavourings like saffron, herbs, garlic and orange peel and cooked in an intensely flavoured fish stock made from all fish trimmings. The *bourride* of France and the *brodetto* of Italy are classic examples but similar variations can be found all over the Mediterranean.

ABOVE: A Moroccan cook patiently prepares the family meal of fish kebabs.

batter and deep fried. When served piping hot, this is delicious as a light snack or starter with a scattering of *gremolata* (a blend of garlic, parsley and lemon zest) or simply squeezed with lemon. The Spanish also love fried fish and use much the same technique, sometimes simply dredging the fish with seasoned flour before frying in light olive oil.

Taking into consideration the availability of so much fresh produce it is surprising that salt cod is so well loved in various parts of the Mediterranean; the kite-shaped, leathery pieces are a common sight in many market-places. The Spanish and Portuguese fished for cod in the Atlantic, salted it and sun-dried it at sea as a means of preservation. These familiar, stiff yellow-tinged boards of fish, which once were associated with the frugal eating of Lent, are now a highly esteemed luxury. Perhaps the most famous dish is the *brandade* of France, a smooth purée of salt cod, flavoured with garlic and olive oil.

On the eastern side of the Mediterranean the types of fish available are much the same, although the cooking methods vary. Baking fish whole is the most widespread practice, often on a bed of tomatoes, lemons, onions, herbs, and sometimes with slightly sweet and spicy flavourings such as raisins and cinnamon. *Plaki* is a well-loved example, perfect for fish such as grey mullet, sea bream and bass, which absorb all the wonderful flavours. Middle Eastern and North African fish dishes emphasize the accompanying sauce – the choice of fish being the pick of the catch. A simple blend of tahini with olive oil and lemon juice is very classical.

Squid and octopus both play an important role in Mediterranean cookery. Squid, from the tiniest, which are lovely seared in olive oil with garlic and herbs, to huge specimens, rich with stuffings, typify Mediterranean cooking techniques. Octopus too, is highly esteemed particularly in the eastern Mediterranean where it is frequently stewed with red wine or used in salads.

Small oily fish thrive in the Mediterranean and the freshly grilled or barbecued sardines prepared in cafes and tavernas around the region cannot be rivalled anywhere else in the world. Sardines and large anchovies are sometimes stuffed with a slightly tangy mixture of ingredients, such as capers, olives, pine nuts, lemons and dried fruit, that provides a perfect contrast to the rich oiliness of the fish itself. Other interesting recipes are the short term preserving of fried sardines in olive oil and vinegar or the delicious combination of sardines with fresh herbs and spaghetti or macaroni.

The technique of frying fish in a light batter is typical of the Mediterranean. *Fritto Misto* is an Italian version in which a medley of seafood, such as mussels, squid, red mullet, prawns and whitebait, is coated in a light crisp

BAKED FISH WITH TAHINI SAUCE

This North African recipe evokes all the colour and rich flavours of Mediterranean cuisine.
Choose any whole white fish, such as sea bass, hake, bream or snapper.

1 whole fish, about 1.1kg/2½lb,
scaled and cleaned
10ml/2 tsp coriander seeds
4 garlic cloves, sliced
10ml/2 tsp harissa sauce
90ml/6 tbsp olive oil
6 plum tomatoes, sliced
1 mild onion, sliced
3 preserved lemons or 1 fresh lemon
plenty of fresh herbs, such as bay
leaves, thyme and rosemary
salt and ground black pepper

FOR THE SAUCE
75ml/3fl oz/⅓ cup light tahini
juice of 1 lemon
1 garlic clove, crushed
45ml/3 tbsp finely chopped fresh
parsley or coriander
extra herbs, to garnish

SERVES 4

1 Preheat the oven to 200°C/
400°F/Gas 6. Grease the base
and sides of a large shallow
ovenproof dish or roasting tin.

2 Slash the fish diagonally on
both sides with a sharp knife.
Finely crush the coriander seeds and
garlic with a pestle and mortar. Mix
with the harissa sauce and about
60ml/4 tbsp of the olive oil.

3 Spread a little of the harissa,
coriander and garlic paste inside
the cavity of the fish. Spread the
remainder over each side of the fish
and set aside.

4 Scatter the tomatoes, onion and
preserved or fresh lemon into
the dish. (Thinly slice the lemon if
using fresh.) Sprinkle with the
remaining oil and season with salt
and pepper. Lay the fish on top and
tuck plenty of herbs around it.

5 Bake, uncovered, for about
25 minutes, or until the fish has
turned opaque – test by piercing the
thickest part with a knife.

6 Meanwhile, make the sauce. Put
the tahini, lemon juice, garlic
and parsley or coriander in a small
saucepan with 120ml/4fl oz/½ cup
water and add a little salt and pepper.
Cook gently until smooth and heated
through. Serve in a separate dish.

COOK'S TIP
If you can't get a suitable large fish,
use small whole fish such as red
mullet or even cod or haddock steaks.
Remember to reduce the cooking
time slightly.

SEA BASS WITH AN ALMOND CRUST

This is a surprising — and quite delicious — way to cook fish. The almond crust is almost a biscuit, and its sweetness complements the flavour of the sea bass, as well as keeping the fish deliciously moist and succulent. Lime wedges are the perfect garnish.

4 Preheat the oven to 190°C/ 375°F/Gas 5. Grease a shallow ovenproof dish, large enough to take the whole fish, using about 15g/ 1/2 oz/1 tbsp of the butter. Scatter the sliced onion in the dish. Dissolve the saffron threads in 15ml/1 tbsp boiling water and add to the dish with some salt and pepper.

5 Stuff the fish with half of the almond mixture and place it on top of the onion. Using a spatula, spread the remaining almond paste evenly over the top of the fish.

6 Melt the remaining butter, pour over the fish and then bake in the oven, uncovered, for about 45–50 minutes (35–40 minutes if you are cooking 2 smaller fish) until the fish flakes easily and the almond topping is crusty.

7 Transfer the fish to a warmed serving plate and arrange the onion slices around the edge. Garnish with lime wedges and flat leaf parsley, and serve at once.

1 large or 2 small sea bass, about 1.5kg/ 3–3 1/2 lb total weight, cleaned and scaled, with head and tail left on
15ml/1 tbsp sunflower oil
175g/6oz/1 1/2 cups blanched almonds
about 65g/2 1/2 oz/1/3 cup butter, softened
2.5–5ml/1/2–1 tsp ground cinnamon
25g/1oz/1/4 cup icing sugar
1 onion, finely sliced
a good pinch of saffron strands
salt and ground black pepper
lime wedges and sprigs of fresh flat leaf parsley, to garnish

SERVES 4

1 Rinse the fish in cold running water and pat dry.

2 Heat the oil in a small frying pan and fry the almonds for 2–3 minutes over a brisk heat until golden, stirring frequently. Drain on kitchen paper until cool and then grind in a spice or coffee mill.

3 Pour the ground almonds into the bowl of a food processor and blend with 25g/1oz/2 tbsp of the butter, the ground cinnamon, icing sugar and 60ml/4 tbsp water to make a smooth paste.

GRILLED SEA BASS WITH FENNEL

—

This dish is served in almost every fish restaurant on the French Mediterranean coast.
Traditionally fennel twigs are used but, as they are hard to find, this recipe uses fennel seeds.

1 sea bass, weighing 1.75kg/4–4½lb,
cleaned
60–90ml/4–6 tbsp olive oil
10–15ml/2–3 tsp fennel seeds
2 large fennel bulbs, trimmed and
thinly sliced (reserve any fronds)
60ml/4 tbsp Pernod
salt and ground black pepper

SERVES 6–8

1 | With a sharp knife, make three or four deep cuts in both sides of the fish. Brush the fish with olive oil and season with salt and pepper. Sprinkle the fennel seeds in the stomach cavity and in the cuts. Set aside while you cook the fennel.

2 | Preheat the grill. Put the slices of fennel in a flameproof dish or on the grill rack and brush with oil. Grill for 4 minutes on each side until tender. Transfer to a large platter.

3 | Place the fish on the oiled grill rack and position about 10–13cm/4–5in away from the heat. Grill for 10–12 minutes on each side, brushing with oil occasionally.

4 | Transfer the fish to the platter on top of the fennel. Garnish with fennel fronds. Heat the Pernod in a small pan, light it and pour it, flaming, over the fish. Serve at once.

PAN-FRIED RED MULLET WITH BASIL AND CITRUS

Red mullet is popular all over the Mediterranean. This Italian recipe combines it with oranges and lemons, which grow in abundance.

4 red mullet, weighing about 225g/
8oz each, filleted
90ml/6 tbsp olive oil
10 peppercorns, crushed
2 oranges, one peeled and sliced,
and one squeezed
1 lemon
30ml/2 tbsp plain flour
15g/½oz/1 tbsp butter
2 drained canned anchovies, chopped
60ml/4 tbsp shredded fresh basil
salt and ground black pepper

SERVES 4

1 Place the fish fillets in a shallow dish in a single layer. Pour over the olive oil and sprinkle with the crushed peppercorns. Lay the orange slices on top of the fish. Cover the dish, and leave to marinate in the fridge for at least 4 hours.

2 Halve the lemon. Remove the skin and pith from one half using a small sharp knife, and slice thinly. Squeeze the juice from the other half.

3 Lift the fish out of the marinade, and pat dry on kitchen paper. Reserve the marinade and orange slices. Season the fish with salt and pepper and dust lightly with flour.

4 Heat 45ml/3 tbsp of the marinade in a frying pan. Add the fish and fry for 2 minutes on each side. Remove from the pan and keep warm. Discard the marinade that is left in the pan.

5 Melt the butter in the pan with any of the remaining original marinade. Add the anchovies and cook until completely softened.

6 Stir in the orange and lemon juice, then check the seasoning and simmer until slightly reduced. Stir in the basil. Pour the sauce over the fish and garnish with the reserved orange slices and the lemon slices.

COOK'S TIP
If you prefer, use other fish fillets for this dish, such as lemon sole, haddock or hake.

BAKED FISH WITH NUTS

This speciality comes from Egypt and is as delicious as it is unusual.
Make sure you use good-quality hazelnuts and pine nuts.

45ml/3 tbsp oil
4 small red mullet
1 large onion, finely chopped
75g/3oz/¾ cup hazelnuts, chopped
75g/3oz/¾ cup pine nuts
3–4 tomatoes, sliced
45–60ml/3–4 tbsp finely chopped
fresh parsley
250ml/8fl oz/1 cup fish stock
salt and ground black pepper
sprigs of parsley, to garnish
new potatoes or rice, and vegetables or
salad, to serve

SERVES 4

2 Heat the remaining oil in a large pan or flameproof casserole and fry the finely chopped onion for 3–4 minutes until golden. Add the chopped hazelnuts and pine nuts, and stir-fry for a few minutes.

3 Stir in the tomatoes, cook for a few minutes and then add the parsley, stock and seasoning. Simmer for 10–15 minutes, stirring occasionally.

4 Place the fish in an ovenproof dish and spoon the sauce over. Bake in the oven for 20 minutes or until the fish is cooked through and flakes easily when pierced with a fork.

5 Serve the fish at once, garnished with parsley and accompanied by new potatoes or rice, and vegetables or salad.

1 Preheat the oven to 190°C/375°F/Gas 5. Heat about 30ml/2 tbsp of the oil in a frying pan and fry the fish, two at a time, until crisp on both sides.

VARIATION
Other small whole fish, such as snapper or trout, can be used for this recipe if mullet is unavailable.

MONKFISH PARCELS

Delicate dumplings, with a fish forcemeat filling, make an elaborate light lunch dish.

175g/6oz/1½ cups strong plain flour,
plus extra for rolling
2 eggs
115g/4oz skinless monkfish
fillet, diced
grated rind of 1 lemon
1 garlic clove, chopped
1 small red chilli, seeded and sliced
45ml/3 tbsp chopped fresh parsley
30ml/2 tbsp single cream

For the tomato oil
2 tomatoes, peeled, seeded and
finely diced
45ml/3 tbsp extra virgin olive oil
30ml/1 tbsp fresh lemon juice
salt and ground black pepper

Serves 4

1. Place the flour, eggs and 2.5ml/ ½ tsp salt in a food processor; pulse until the mixture forms a soft dough. Knead briefly, then wrap in clear film and chill.

2. Process the fish, lemon rind, garlic, chilli and parsley until very fine. Add the cream, season and whizz to a thick purée.

3. Make the tomato oil by stirring the diced tomatoes with the olive oil and lemon juice in a bowl. Add salt to taste. Cover and chill.

4. Roll out the dough on a lightly floured surface and cut out 32 rounds with a 4cm/1½ in plain cutter. Divide the monkfish filling among half the rounds, then cover with the remaining rounds. Pinch the edges tightly to seal, trying to exclude as much as air as possible.

5. Bring a large saucepan of water to simmering point and poach the parcels, in batches, for about 3 minutes or until they rise to the surface. Drain and serve hot, drizzled with the tomato oil.

STUFFED SWORDFISH ROLLS

This is a very tasty dish, with strong flavours from the tomato, olive and caper sauce — and from the salty Pecorino cheese. If you like, substitute Parmesan cheese, which is milder.

30ml/2 tbsp olive oil
1 small onion, finely chopped
1 celery stick, finely chopped
450g/1lb ripe Italian plum
  tomatoes, chopped
115g/4oz/1 cup stoned green olives,
  half chopped, half left whole
45ml/3 tbsp drained bottled capers
4 swordfish steaks, each 1cm/1/2in
  thick and 115g/4oz in weight
1 egg
50g/2oz/2/3 cup grated
  Pecorino cheese
25g/1oz/1/2 cup fresh white
  breadcrumbs
salt and ground black pepper
sprigs of fresh parsley, to garnish

SERVES 4

1 Heat the oil in a large heavy-based frying pan. Add the onion and celery and cook gently for about 3 minutes, stirring frequently. Stir in the tomatoes, olives and capers, with salt and pepper to taste. Bring to the boil, then lower the heat, cover and simmer for 15 minutes. Stir the sauce occasionally.

2 Remove the fish skin and place each steak between two sheets of clear film. Pound lightly with a rolling pin until each steak is reduced to about 5mm/1/4in thick.

3 Beat the egg in a bowl and add the cheese, breadcrumbs and a few spoonfuls of the sauce. Stir well to mix to a moist stuffing. Spread one-quarter of the stuffing over each swordfish steak, then roll up.

4 Secure the rolls with cocktail sticks, add them to the sauce and bring to the boil. Lower the heat, cover and simmer for about 30 minutes, turning once. Add a little water as the sauce reduces.

5 Remove the rolls from the sauce and discard the cocktail sticks. Place on warmed dinner plates and spoon the sauce over and around. Garnish with the parsley and serve.

FISH BOULETTES IN HOT TOMATO SAUCE

This is an unusual dish that needs scarcely any preparation and produces very little washing up, as it is all cooked in one pan. It serves four people as a main course, but also makes a great starter for eight.

675g/1½lb cod, haddock or
white fish fillets
pinch of saffron strands
½ bunch flat leaf parsley
1 egg
25g/1oz/½ cup white breadcrumbs
25ml/1½ tbsp olive oil
15ml/1 tbsp lemon juice
salt and ground black pepper
fresh flat leaf parsley and lemon
wedges, to garnish

FOR THE SAUCE
1 onion, very finely chopped
2 garlic cloves, crushed
6 tomatoes, peeled, seeded
and chopped
1 green or red chilli, seeded and
finely sliced
90ml/6 tbsp olive oil
150ml/¼ pint/⅔ cup water
15ml/1 tbsp lemon juice

SERVES 4

1 Skin the fish and, if necessary, remove any bones. Cut the fish into large chunks and place in a blender or a food processor.

2 Soak the saffron in 30ml/2 tbsp boiling water for a few minutes and pour into the blender or food processor with the parsley, egg, breadcrumbs, olive oil and lemon juice. Season well and process for 10–20 seconds until the fish is finely chopped and the ingredients are mixed.

3 Mould the mixture into small balls about the size of walnuts. Put them in a single layer on a plate.

4 To make the sauce, place the onion, garlic, tomatoes, chilli, olive oil and water in a saucepan. Bring to the boil and then simmer, partially covered, for 10–15 minutes until the sauce is slightly reduced.

5 Add the lemon juice and then place the fish balls in the simmering sauce. Cover and simmer very gently for 12–15 minutes until the fish boulettes are cooked through, turning them over occasionally.

6 Serve the boulettes and sauce immediately, garnished with flat leaf parsley and lemon wedges.

MARINATED SALMON TROUT STEAKS

Marinating the fish in a mixture of saffron, egg yolks and garlic is simplicity itself, and the results are sensational, especially when served with herb-flavoured rice.

2–3 saffron strands
2 egg yolks
1 garlic clove, crushed
4 salmon trout steaks
oil, for deep-frying
salt and ground black pepper
lemon wedges, rice and green salad,
to serve

SERVES 4

1 Soak the saffron in 15ml/1 tbsp boiling water and then beat the mixture into the egg yolks. Season with garlic, salt and pepper.

2 Place the fish steaks in a shallow dish and coat with the egg mixture. Cover with clear film and marinate for up to 1 hour.

3 Heat the oil in a deep-fryer until very hot and then fry the fish, one steak at a time, for 10 minutes until they are golden brown. Drain each one on kitchen paper. Serve with lemon wedges, accompanied by rice and a green salad.

VARIATION
Any type of fish can be used in this recipe. Try a combination of plain and smoked for a delicious change, such as smoked and unsmoked cod or haddock.

PAN-FRIED SARDINES

This delicious fish recipe is a favourite in many countries.

10g/¼ oz fresh parsley
3–4 garlic cloves, crushed
8–12 sardines, prepared
30ml/2 tbsp lemon juice
50g/2oz/½ cup plain flour
2.5ml/½ tsp ground cumin
60ml/4 tbsp vegetable oil
salt and ground black pepper
naan bread and salad, to serve

SERVES 4

1 Finely chop the parsley and mix in a small bowl with the garlic.

2 Pat the parsley and garlic mixture all over the outsides and insides of the sardines. Sprinkle them with the lemon juice and set aside, covered, in a cool place for about 2 hours to absorb the flavours.

3 Place the flour on a large plate and season with cumin, salt and pepper. Roll the sardines in the flour, coating each fish thoroughly.

4 Heat the oil in a large frying pan and fry the fish in batches for 5 minutes on each side until crisp. Keep warm in the oven while cooking the remaining fish. Serve with naan bread and salad.

COOK'S TIP
If you don't have a garlic crusher, you can crush the garlic using the flat side of a large knife blade instead.

FISH PLAKI

Greece has so much coastline, it is no wonder that fish is popular all over the country. Generally, it is treated very simply, but this recipe is a little more involved, baking the fish with onions and tomatoes.

300ml/½ pint/1¼ cups olive oil
2 onions, thinly sliced
3 large flavoursome tomatoes,
roughly chopped
3 garlic cloves, thinly sliced
5ml/1 tsp sugar
5ml/1 tsp chopped fresh dill
5ml/1 tsp chopped fresh mint
5ml/1 tsp chopped fresh celery leaves
15ml/1 tbsp chopped fresh parsley
6 white fish steaks
juice of 1 lemon
salt and ground black pepper
extra dill, mint or parsley, to garnish

SERVES 6

1. Heat the oil in a large sauté pan or flameproof dish. Add the onions and cook until pale golden. Add the tomatoes, garlic, sugar, dill, mint, celery leaves and parsley with 300ml/½ pint/1¼ cups water. Season with salt and pepper, then simmer, uncovered, for 25 minutes, until the liquid has reduced by one-third.

2. Add the fish steaks and cook gently for 10–12 minutes, until the fish is just cooked. Remove from the heat and add the lemon juice (*left*). Cover and leave to stand for about 20 minutes before serving. Arrange the cod in a dish and spoon the sauce over. Garnish with herbs and serve warm or cold.

SICILIAN SPAGHETTI WITH SARDINES

*A traditional dish from Sicily, with ingredients that are common
to many parts of the Mediterranean.*

12 fresh sardines, cleaned and boned
250ml/8fl oz/1 cup olive oil
1 onion, chopped
25g/1oz/¼ cup dill sprigs
50g/2oz/½ cup pine nuts
25g/1oz/3 tbsp raisins, soaked
in water
50g/2oz/1 cup fresh breadcrumbs
450g/1lb spaghetti
plain flour for dusting
salt

SERVES 4

1 | Wash the sardines and pat dry on kitchen paper. Open them out flat, then cut in half lengthways.

2 | Heat 30ml/2 tbsp of the oil in a pan, add the onion and fry until golden. Add the dill and cook gently for a minute or two. Add the pine nuts and raisins and season with salt. Dry-fry the breadcrumbs in a frying pan until golden. Set aside.

3 | Cook the spaghetti in boiling, salted water according to the instructions on the packet, until *al dente*. Heat the remaining oil in a pan. Dust the sardines with flour and fry in the hot oil for 2–3 minutes. Drain on kitchen paper.

4 | Drain the spaghetti and return to the pan. Add the onion mixture and toss well. Transfer the spaghetti mixture to a serving platter and arrange the fried sardines on top. Sprinkle with the toasted breadcrumbs and serve immediately.

MONKFISH COUSCOUS

Since fish needs very little cooking, it is quickest and easiest to cook the couscous using this simple method. However, if you prefer to steam couscous, steam it over the onions and peppers.

675g/1½lb monkfish
30ml/2 tbsp olive oil
1 onion, thinly sliced into rings
25g/1oz/3 tbsp raisins
40g/1½oz/¼ cup cashew nuts
1 small red pepper, cored, seeded
and sliced
1 small yellow pepper, cored, seeded
and sliced
4 tomatoes, peeled, seeded and sliced
350ml/12fl oz/1½ cups fish stock
15ml/1 tbsp chopped fresh parsley
salt and ground black pepper

FOR THE COUSCOUS
275g/10oz/1⅔ cups couscous
525ml/18fl oz/2¼ cups boiling
vegetable stock or water

SERVES 4

[4] Heat the remaining oil in the pan and add the remaining onion rings. Cook for 4–5 minutes until golden, and then add the pepper slices. Cook over a fairly high heat for 6–8 minutes until the peppers are soft, stirring occasionally. Add the tomatoes and fish stock, reduce the heat and simmer for 10 minutes, stirring several times.

[5] Meanwhile, prepare the couscous. Place in a bowl, pour over the boiling stock or water and stir once or twice. Set aside for 10 minutes so that the couscous can absorb the liquid, then fluff up with a fork. Cover and keep warm.

[6] Add the fish to the peppers and onion, partially cover and simmer for 6–8 minutes until the fish is tender, stirring gently. Season well.

[7] Pile the couscous on to a large serving plate. Pour over the monkfish mixture, with all of the sauce. Sprinkle with the parsley and the reserved onion rings, raisins and cashew nuts and serve.

[1] Bone and skin the monkfish, if necessary, and cut into bite-size chunks using a sharp knife.

[2] Heat half the oil in a saucepan and fry a quarter of the onion rings for 5–6 minutes until dark golden brown. Drain on kitchen paper.

[3] Add the raisins to the pan and stir-fry for 30–60 seconds until they begin to plump up. Add to the plate with the onion rings. Add the cashew nuts to the pan and stir-fry for 30–60 seconds until golden. Place on the plate with the onion and raisins, and set aside.

MONKFISH WITH TOMATOES AND OLIVES

This makes a really delicious lunch or light supper dish. Alternatively, serve this medley of monkfish, tomatoes and black olives as a starter for six to eight people.

8 tomatoes
675g/1½lb monkfish
30ml/2 tbsp plain flour
5ml/1 tsp ground coriander
2.5ml/½ tsp ground turmeric
25g/1oz/2 tbsp butter
2 garlic cloves, finely chopped
15–30ml/1–2 tbsp olive oil
40g/1½oz/4 tbsp pine nuts, toasted
small pieces of preserved lemon
12 black olives, pitted
salt and ground black pepper
whole slices of preserved lemon and
chopped fresh parsley, to garnish

SERVES 4

1 Peel the tomatoes by plunging them briefly in boiling water, then cold water. Quarter them, remove the cores and seeds and chop the flesh roughly.

2 Cut the fish into bite-size chunks. Mix the flour, coriander, turmeric and seasoning in a bowl. Dust the fish with the seasoned flour and set aside.

3 Melt the butter in a medium non-stick frying pan. Fry the tomatoes and garlic over a gentle heat for 6–8 minutes until most of the liquid has evaporated.

4 Push the tomatoes to the edge of the frying pan, moisten the pan with a little olive oil and fry the monkfish pieces in a single layer over a moderate heat for 3–5 minutes, turning frequently. You may have to do this in batches, so as the first batch of fish pieces cooks, place them on top of the tomatoes and fry the rest, adding more oil, if needed.

5 When all the fish is cooked, add the pine nuts and stir, scraping the bottom of the pan to incorporate the tomatoes. The sauce should be thick and slightly charred in places.

6 Rinse the preserved lemon in cold water, discard the pulp and cut the peel into strips. Stir into the sauce with the olives. Adjust the seasoning and serve, garnished with whole slices of preserved lemon and a scattering of chopped parsley.

FRESH TUNA AND TOMATO STEW

A deliciously simple dish that relies on good basic ingredients.
For real Italian flavour serve with polenta or pasta.

12 baby onions, peeled
900g/2lb ripe tomatoes
675g/1½lb fresh tuna
45ml/3 tbsp olive oil
2 garlic cloves, crushed
45ml/3 tbsp chopped fresh herbs
2 bay leaves
2.5ml/½ tsp caster sugar
30ml/2 tbsp sun-dried tomato paste
150ml/¼ pint/⅔ cup dry white wine
salt and ground black pepper
baby courgettes and fresh herbs,
to garnish

SERVES 4

VARIATION
Two large mackerel make a more
readily available alternative to the
tuna. Fillet them and cut into chunks
or simply lay the whole fish over the
sauce and cook, covered with a lid
until the mackerel is cooked through.
Sage, rosemary or oregano all go
extremely well with this dish. Choose
whichever you prefer, or use a
mixture of one or two.

1 Leave the onions whole and
cook in a pan of boiling water
for 4–5 minutes until softened. Drain.

2 Plunge the tomatoes into
boiling water for 30 seconds,
then refresh in cold water. Peel away
the skins and chop roughly.

3 Cut the tuna into 2.5cm/1in
chunks. Heat the oil in a large
frying or sauté pan and quickly fry
the tuna until browned. Drain.

4 Add the onions, garlic,
tomatoes, chopped herbs, bay
leaves, sugar, tomato paste and wine
and bring to the boil, breaking up the
tomatoes with a wooden spoon.

5 Reduce the heat and simmer
gently for 5 minutes. Return the
fish to the pan and cook for a further
5 minutes. Season, and serve hot,
garnished with baby courgettes and
fresh herbs.

BRANDADE DE MORUE

*Salt cod is popular in Spain and France, and it can be found cooked in a number of ways. This recipe is
a purée, flavoured with garlic and olive oil, which is made all over southern France.*

675g/1½lb salt cod
300ml/½ pint/1¼ cups olive oil
250ml/8fl oz/1 cup milk
1 garlic clove, crushed
grated nutmeg
lemon juice, to taste
white pepper

FOR THE CROUTES
50ml/2fl oz/¼ cup olive oil
6 slices white bread, crusts removed
1 garlic clove, halved
parsley sprigs, to garnish

SERVES 6

1 Soak the salt cod in cold water for at least 24 hours, changing the water several times. Drain.

2 To make the croûtes, heat the oil in a frying pan. Cut the bread slices in half diagonally and fry in the oil until golden. Drain on kitchen paper, then rub on both sides with garlic.

3 Put the cod in a large pan, with enough cold water to cover. Cover and bring to the boil. Simmer gently for 8–10 minutes, until just tender. Drain and cool. Flake the fish and discard any skin and bone.

4 Heat the oil in a pan until very hot. In a separate pan, scald the milk. Transfer the fish to a blender or food processor and, with the motor running, slowly pour in the hot oil, followed by the milk, until the mixture is smooth and stiff. Transfer to a bowl and beat in the crushed garlic. Season with nutmeg, lemon juice and white pepper. Leave the *brandade* to cool and then chill until almost ready to serve.

5 Spoon the *brandade* into a shallow serving bowl and surround with the croûtes. Garnish with parsley and serve cold.

SEA BASS AND FENNEL TAGINE

This is a delicious tagine in which the fish is flavoured with charmoula, a specially selected blend of herbs and spices used especially in fish dishes.

675g/1½lb sea bass, monkfish or
cod fillets
225g/8oz raw Mediterranean prawns
30ml/2 tbsp olive oil
1 onion, chopped
1 fennel bulb, sliced
225g/8oz small new potatoes, halved
475ml/16fl oz/2 cups fish stock
lemon wedges, to serve

FOR THE *CHARMOULA*
2 garlic cloves, crushed
20ml/4 tsp ground cumin
20ml/4 tsp paprika
pinch of chilli powder or
cayenne pepper
30ml/2 tbsp chopped fresh parsley
30ml/2 tbsp chopped fresh coriander
45ml/3 tbsp white vinegar
15ml/1 tbsp lemon juice

SERVES 4

1 First make the *charmoula* by mixing the crushed garlic, spices, herbs, vinegar and lemon juice together in a bowl.

2 Skin the fish if necessary and remove any bones, then cut into large bite-size chunks. Top and tail the prawns and pull away the shells. Using a sharp knife, cut along the back of each prawn and pull away and discard the dark thread.

3 Place the fish and prawns in two separate shallow dishes, add half the *charmoula* marinade to each dish and stir well to coat evenly. Cover with clear film and set aside in a cool place for 30 minutes–2 hours.

4 Heat the olive oil in a large flameproof casserole and fry the onion for 2 minutes. Add the sliced fennel and continue cooking over a gentle heat for 5–6 minutes until the onion and fennel are flecked with brown. Add the potatoes and fish stock and cook for a further 10–15 minutes until the potatoes are tender.

5 Add the marinated fish, stir gently and cook for 4 minutes, then add the prawns and any remaining marinade and cook for a further 5–6 minutes until the fish is tender and the prawns are pink. Serve with lemon wedges.

229

BRODETTO

The different regions of Italy have their own variations of this dish, but all require a good fish stock. Make sure you buy some of the fish whole so that you can simply simmer them, remove the cooked flesh and strain the deliciously flavoured juices to make the stock.

900g/2lb mixture of fish fillets or
steaks, such as monkfish, cod,
haddock, halibut or hake
900g/2lb mixture of conger eel, red or
grey mullet, snapper or small
white fish
1 onion, halved
1 celery stick, roughly chopped
225g/8oz squid
225g/8oz fresh mussels
675g/1½lb ripe tomatoes
60ml/4 tbsp olive oil
1 large onion, thinly sliced
3 garlic cloves, crushed
5ml/1 tsp saffron strands
150ml/¼ pint/⅔ cup dry white wine
90ml/6 tbsp chopped fresh parsley
salt and ground black pepper
croûtons, to serve

SERVES 4–5

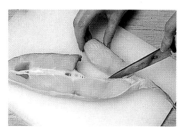

1 Remove any skin and bones from the fish fillets or steaks, cut the fish into large pieces and reserve. Place the bones in a pan with all the remaining fish.

2 Add the halved onion and the celery and just cover with water. Bring almost to the boil, then reduce the heat and simmer gently for about 30 minutes. Lift out the fish and remove the flesh from the bones. Reserve the stock.

3 To prepare the squid, twist the head and tentacles away from the body. Cut the head from the tentacles. Discard the body contents and peel away the mottled skin. Wash the tentacles and bodies and dry on kitchen paper.

COOK'S TIP
To make the croûtons, cut thin slices from a long thin stick of bread and shallow fry in a little butter until golden.

4 Scrub the mussels, discarding any that are damaged or open ones that do not close when tapped.

5 Plunge the tomatoes into boiling water for 30 seconds, then refresh in cold water. Peel away the skins and chop roughly.

6 Heat the oil in a large saucepan or sauté pan. Add the sliced onion and the garlic and fry gently for 3 minutes. Add the squid and the uncooked white fish, which you reserved earlier, and fry quickly on all sides. Drain.

7 Add 475ml/16fl oz/2 cups strained reserved fish stock, the saffron and tomatoes to the pan. Pour in the wine. Bring to the boil, then reduce the heat and simmer for about 5 minutes. Add the mussels, cover, and cook for 3–4 minutes until the mussels have opened. Discard any that remain closed.

8 Season the sauce with salt and pepper and put all the fish in the pan. Cook gently for 5 minutes. Scatter with the parsley and serve with the croûtons.

SARDINE GRATIN

*In Sicily and other countries in the Western Mediterranean, sardines are filled with a robust stuffing,
flavoursome enough to compete with the rich oiliness of the fish itself.*

15ml/1 tbsp light olive oil
½ small onion, finely chopped
2 garlic cloves, crushed
40g/1½oz/⅓ cup blanched
almonds, chopped
25g/1oz/3 tbsp sultanas,
roughly chopped
10 pitted black olives
30ml/2 tbsp capers, roughly chopped
30ml/2 tbsp roughly chopped
fresh parsley
50g/2oz/1 cup breadcrumbs
16 large sardines, scaled and gutted
25g/1oz/⅓ cup grated
Parmesan cheese
salt and ground black pepper
flat leaf parsley, to garnish

SERVES 4

ABOVE: *Brodetto (top) and Sardine Gratin (bottom).*

1 Preheat the oven to 200°C/
400°F/Gas 6. Lightly oil a large
shallow ovenproof dish.

2 Heat the oil in a frying pan and
fry the onion and garlic gently
for 3 minutes. Stir in the almonds,
sultanas, olives, capers, parsley and
25g/1oz/¼ cup of the breadcrumbs.
Season lightly with salt and pepper.

3 Make 2–3 diagonal cuts on each
side of the sardines. Pack the
stuffing into the cavities and lay the
sardines in the prepared dish.

4 Mix the remaining breadcrumbs
with the cheese and scatter over
the fish. Bake for about 20 minutes
until the fish is cooked through. Test
by piercing one sardine through the
thickest part with a knife. Garnish
with parsley and serve immediately
with a leafy salad.

MOROCCAN PAELLA

This is a Moroccan version of the traditional Spanish dish. It is especially popular on the coast.

2 large boneless chicken breasts
about 150g/5oz prepared squid
275g/10oz cod or haddock fillets
8–10 raw king prawns, shelled
8 scallops, trimmed and halved
350g/12oz raw mussels, in shells
250g/9oz/1⅓ cups long grain rice
30ml/2 tbsp sunflower oil
1 bunch spring onions, cut into strips
2 small courgettes, cut into strips
1 red pepper, cored, seeded and
cut into strips
400ml/14fl oz/1⅔ cups chicken stock
250ml/8fl oz/1 cup puréed
canned tomatoes
salt and ground black pepper
sprigs of fresh coriander and lemon
wedges, to garnish

FOR THE MARINADE
2 red chillies, seeded
good handful of fresh coriander
10–15ml/2–?3 tsp ground cumin
15ml/1 tbsp paprika
2 garlic cloves
45ml/3 tbsp olive oil
60ml/4 tbsp sunflower oil
juice of 1 lemon

SERVES 6

1 First make the marinade. Place
all the ingredients in a food
processor with 5ml/1 tsp salt and
process until thoroughly blended.

2 Skin the chicken and cut into
bite-size pieces. Place these in
a glass or ceramic bowl.

3 Slice the squid into rings. Skin
the fish, if necessary, and cut
into bite-size chunks. Place the fish
and shellfish (apart from the mussels)
in a separate glass or ceramic bowl.
Divide the marinade between the fish
and chicken and stir well. Cover with
clear film and leave to marinate for
about 2 hours.

4 Scrub the mussels, discarding
any that do not close when
tapped sharply, and reserve in a
bowl in the fridge until ready to use.
Place the rice in a bowl, cover with
boiling water and set aside for about
30 minutes.

5 Drain the chicken and fish, and
reserve the marinade from each
separately. Heat the oil in a wok,
balti pan or paella pan and fry the
chicken pieces for a few minutes
until lightly browned.

6 Add the spring onions to the
pan, fry for 1 minute and then
add the courgettes and red pepper
strips and fry for a further 3–4 minutes
until slightly softened. Remove the
chicken and then the vegetables to
separate plates.

7 Use a spatula to scrape all the
marinade into the pan and cook
for 1 minute. Drain the rice, add to
the pan and stir-fry for 1 minute. Add
the chicken stock, puréed tomatoes
and reserved chicken, season with salt
and pepper and stir well. Bring the
mixture to the boil, then cover the
pan with a large lid or foil and
simmer very gently for 15–20 minutes
until the rice is almost tender.

8 Add the reserved vegetables to
the pan and place all the fish
and mussels on top. Cover again with
a lid or foil and cook over a moderate
heat for 10–12 minutes until the fish is
cooked and the mussels have opened.

9 Discard any mussels that have
not opened during the cooking.
Serve, garnished with sprigs of fresh
coriander and lemon wedges.

SEAFOOD RISOTTO

Risotto is one of Italy's most popular rice dishes and it is made with everything from pumpkin to squid ink. On the Mediterranean shores, seafood is the most obvious addition.

60ml/4 tbsp sunflower oil
1 onion, chopped
2 garlic cloves, crushed
225g/8oz/generous 1 cup arborio rice
105ml/7 tbsp white wine
1.5 litres/2½ pints/6 cups hot
fish stock
350g/12oz mixed seafood, such as
raw prawns, mussels, squid rings
or clams
grated rind of ½ lemon
30ml/2 tbsp tomato purée
15ml/1 tbsp chopped fresh parsley
salt and ground black pepper

SERVES 4

1 Heat the oil in a heavy-based pan, add the onion and garlic and cook until soft. Add the rice and stir to coat the grains with oil. Add the wine and cook over a moderate heat, stirring for a few minutes until the liquid is absorbed.

2 Add 150ml/¼ pint/⅔ cup of the hot stock and cook, stirring constantly, until the liquid is absorbed by the rice. Continue stirring and adding stock in 150ml/¼ pint/⅔ cup quantities, until half is left.

3 Stir in the seafood and cook for 2–3 minutes. Remove any mussels that are closed after cooking. Add the remaining stock until the rice is cooked. It should be creamy and the grains *al dente*.

4 Stir in the lemon rind, tomato purée and parsley. Season with salt and pepper and serve warm.

ITALIAN PRAWN SKEWERS

Simple and delicious mouthfuls from the Amalfi Coast.

900g/2lb raw tiger prawns, peeled
60ml/4 tbsp olive oil
45ml/3 tbsp vegetable oil
75g/3oz/¾ cup very fine dry
breadcrumbs
1 garlic clove, crushed
15ml/1 tbsp chopped fresh parsley
salt and ground black pepper
lemon wedges, to serve

SERVES 4

1 Slit the prawns down their backs and remove the dark vein. Rinse in cold water and pat dry.

2 Put the olive oil and vegetable oil in a large bowl and add the prawns, mixing them to coat evenly. Add the breadcrumbs, garlic and parsley and season with salt and pepper. Toss the prawns thoroughly, to give them an even coating of breadcrumbs. Cover and leave to marinate for 1 hour.

3 Thread the prawns on to four metal or wooden skewers, curling them up as you do so, so that the tail is skewered in the middle.

4 Preheat the grill. Place the skewers in the grill pan and cook for about 2 minutes on each side, until the breadcrumbs are golden. Serve with lemon wedges.

SHELLFISH AND MUSHROOM RISOTTO

The creamy nature of short grain rice, cooked with onions and a simple stock, provides the basis for this delicious combination of shellfish and mushrooms.

45ml/3 tbsp olive oil
1 medium onion, chopped
225g/8oz assorted wild and cultivated
mushrooms, trimmed and sliced
450g/1lb/2¼ cups arborio or
carnaroli rice
1.2 litres/2 pints/5 cups chicken or
vegetable stock, boiling
150ml/¼ pint/⅔ cup white wine
115g/4oz raw prawns, peeled
225g/8oz live mussels
225g/8oz clams
1 medium squid, cleaned, trimmed
and sliced
3 drops truffle oil (optional)
75ml/5 tbsp chopped fresh parsley
and chervil
celery salt and cayenne pepper
bread, to serve

SERVES 4

 3 Pour in the stock and wine. Add the prawns, mussels, clams and squid. Stir and simmer for 15 minutes. Discard any mussels that remain shut.

4 Add the truffle oil if using, stir in the herbs, cover and stand for 10 minutes. Season to taste with celery salt and a pinch of cayenne pepper, and serve with bread.

1 Heat the oil in a large pan and fry the onion for 6–8 minutes until soft but not brown.

2 Add the mushrooms and soften until their juices begin to run. Stir in the rice and heat through.

TRUFFLE AND LOBSTER RISOTTO

To capture the precious qualities of the fresh truffle, partner it with lobster and serve in a silky smooth risotto. Both truffle shavings and oil are added towards the end of cooking to preserve their flavour.

50g/2oz/¼ cup unsalted butter
1 medium onion, chopped
400g/14oz/2 cups arborio rice
1 thyme sprig
1.2 litres/2 pints/5 cups chicken stock
150ml/¼ pint/⅔ cup dry white wine
1 freshly cooked lobster
45ml/3 tbsp chopped fresh parsley and
chervil, plus sprigs to garnish
3–4 drops truffle oil
2 hard-boiled eggs, sliced
1 fresh black or white truffle

SERVES 4

3 Remove the rice mixture from the heat, stir in the chopped lobster meat, herbs and truffle oil. Cover the pan with a tight-fitting lid and leave to stand for 5 minutes.

4 Divide among warmed dishes and arrange the sliced lobster and hard-boiled egg, with shavings of fresh truffle on top. Garnish with herb sprigs and serve immediately.

1 Melt the butter in a large shallow pan, add the onion and fry gently until soft, without allowing it to colour. Add the rice and thyme and stir well to coat evenly with fat. Pour in the stock and wine, stir once and cook uncovered for 15 minutes.

2 Twist off the lobster tail, cut the underside with scissors and remove the white tail meat. Slice half of the meat then roughly chop the remainder. Break open the claws and remove the flesh in one piece.

STUFFED SQUID

This Greek delicacy is best made with large squid as they are less fiddly to stuff.
If you have to make do with small squid, buy about 450g/1lb.

For the stuffing
30ml/2 tbsp olive oil
1 large onion, finely chopped
2 garlic cloves, crushed
50g/2oz/1 cup fresh breadcrumbs
60ml/4 tbsp chopped fresh parsley
115g/4oz halloumi cheese, grated
salt and ground black pepper

To finish
4 squid tubes, each about
18cm/7in long
900g/2lb ripe tomatoes
45ml/3 tbsp olive oil
1 large onion, chopped
5ml/1 tsp caster sugar
120ml/4fl oz/½ cup dry white wine
several rosemary sprigs
toasted pine nuts and flat leaf parsley,
to garnish

Serves 4

1 To make the stuffing, heat the oil in a frying pan and fry the onion for 3 minutes. Remove the pan from the heat and add the garlic, breadcrumbs, parsley, cheese and a little salt and pepper. Stir until thoroughly blended.

2 Dry the squid tubes on kitchen paper and fill with the prepared stuffing using a teaspoon. Secure the ends of the squid tubes with wooden cocktail sticks.

VARIATION
If you would prefer a less rich filling, halve the quantity of cheese and breadcrumbs in the stuffing and add 225g/8oz cooked spinach.

3 Plunge the tomatoes into boiling water for 30 seconds, then refresh in cold water. Peel away the skins and chop roughly.

4 Heat the oil in a frying pan or sauté pan. Add the squid and fry on all sides. Remove from the pan.

5 Add the onion to the pan and fry gently for 3 minutes. Stir in the tomatoes, sugar and wine and cook rapidly until the mixture becomes thick and pulpy.

6 Return the squid to the pan with the rosemary. Cover and cook gently for 30 minutes. Slice the squid and serve on individual plates with the sauce. Scatter over the pine nuts and garnish with parsley.

OCTOPUS AND RED WINE STEW

Unless you're happy to clean and prepare octopus for this Greek dish, buy one that's ready for cooking.

900g/2lb prepared octopus
450g/1lb onions, sliced
2 bay leaves
450g/1lb ripe tomatoes
60ml/4 tbsp olive oil
4 garlic cloves, crushed
5ml/1 tsp caster sugar
15ml/1 tbsp chopped fresh oregano
or rosemary
30ml/2 tbsp chopped fresh parsley
150ml/¼ pint/⅔ cup red wine
30ml/2 tbsp red wine vinegar
chopped fresh herbs, to garnish
warm bread and pine nuts, to serve

SERVES 4

1 Put the octopus in a saucepan of gently simmering water with a quarter of the onions and the bay leaves. Cook gently for 1 hour.

2 While the octopus is cooking, plunge the tomatoes into boiling water for 30 seconds, then refresh in cold water. Peel away the skins and chop roughly.

3 Drain the octopus and, using a sharp knife, cut it into bite-size pieces. Discard the head.

4 Heat the oil in a saucepan and fry the octopus, the remaining onions and the garlic for 3 minutes. Add the tomatoes, sugar, oregano or rosemary, parsley, wine and vinegar and cook, stirring, for 5 minutes until pulpy.

5 Cover the pan and cook over the lowest possible heat for about 1½ hours until the sauce is thickened and the octopus is tender. Garnish with fresh herbs and serve with plenty of warm bread, and pine nuts to scatter on top.

GRILLED KING PRAWNS WITH ROMESCO SAUCE

*This sauce, from the Catalan region of Spain, is served with fish and seafood.
Its main ingredients are sweet pepper, tomatoes, garlic and almonds.*

24 raw king prawns
30–45ml/2–3 tbsp olive oil
flat leaf parsley, to garnish
lemon wedges, to serve

FOR THE SAUCE
2 flavoursome tomatoes
60ml/4 tbsp olive oil
1 onion, chopped
4 garlic cloves, chopped
1 canned pimiento, chopped
2.5ml/½ tsp dried chilli flakes
or powder
75ml/5 tbsp fish stock
30ml/2 tbsp white wine
10 blanched almonds
15ml/1 tbsp red wine vinegar
salt

SERVES 4

1 To make the sauce, immerse the tomatoes in boiling water for about 30 seconds, then refresh them under cold water. Peel away the skins and roughly chop the flesh.

2 Heat 30ml/2 tbsp of the oil in a pan, add the onion and 3 of the garlic cloves and cook until soft. Add the pimiento, tomatoes, chilli, fish stock and wine, then cover and simmer for 30 minutes.

3 Toast the almonds under the grill until golden. Transfer to a blender or food processor and grind coarsely. Add the remaining 30ml/ 2 tbsp of oil, the vinegar and the last garlic clove and process until evenly combined. Add the tomato and pimiento sauce and process until smooth. Season with salt.

4 Remove the heads from the prawns leaving them otherwise unshelled and, with a sharp knife, slit each one down the back and remove the dark vein. Rinse and pat dry on kitchen paper. Preheat the grill. Toss the prawns in olive oil, then spread out in the grill pan. Grill for about 2–3 minutes on each side, until pink. Arrange on a serving platter with the lemon wedges, and the sauce in a small bowl. Serve at once, garnished with parsley.

ZARZUELA

———

Zarzuela means "light opera" or "musical comedy" in Spanish and the classic fish stew of the same name should be as lively and colourful as the zarzuela itself. This feast of fish includes lobster and other shellfish, but you can modify the ingredients to suit the occasion and availability.

1 cooked lobster
24 fresh mussels or clams
1 large monkfish tail
225g/8oz squid rings
15ml/1 tbsp plain flour
90ml/6 tbsp olive oil
12 large raw prawns
450g/1lb ripe tomatoes
2 large mild onions, chopped
4 garlic cloves, crushed
30ml/2 tbsp brandy
2 bay leaves
5ml/1 tsp paprika
1 red chilli, seeded and chopped
300ml/½ pint/1¼ cups fish stock
15g/½oz/2 tbsp ground almonds
30ml/2 tbsp chopped fresh parsley
salt and ground black pepper

SERVES 6

1 Using a large knife, cut the lobster in half lengthways. Remove the dark intestine that runs down the length of the tail. Crack the claws using a hammer.

2 Scrub the mussels, discarding any that are damaged or open ones that do not close when tapped with a knife. Cut the monkfish fillets away from the central cartilage and cut each fillet into three.

3 Toss the monkfish and squid in seasoned flour. Heat the oil in a large frying pan. Add the monkfish and squid and fry quickly; remove from the pan. Fry the prawns on both sides, then remove from the pan.

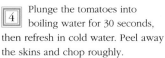

4 Plunge the tomatoes into boiling water for 30 seconds, then refresh in cold water. Peel away the skins and chop roughly.

5 Add the onions and two-thirds of the garlic to the frying pan and fry for 3 minutes. Add the brandy and ignite with a taper. When the flames die down, add the tomatoes, bay leaves, paprika, chilli and stock.

6 Bring to the boil, reduce the heat and simmer gently for 5 minutes. Add the mussels or clams, cover and cook for 3–4 minutes, until the shells have opened.

7 Remove the mussels or clams from the sauce and discard any that remain closed.

8 Arrange all the fish, including the lobster, in a large flameproof serving dish. Blend the ground almonds to a paste with the remaining garlic and parsley and stir into the sauce. Season with salt and pepper.

9 Pour the sauce over the fish and lobster and cook gently for about 5 minutes until hot. Serve immediately with a green salad and plenty of warmed bread.

HAKE AND CLAMS WITH SALSA VERDE

Hake is one of the most popular fish in Spain and here it is cooked in a sauce flavoured with parsley, lemon juice and garlic.

4 hake steaks, about 2cm/¾in thick
50g/2oz/½ cup plain flour for dusting,
plus 30ml/2 tbsp
60ml/4 tbsp olive oil
15ml/1 tbsp lemon juice
1 small onion, finely chopped
4 garlic cloves, crushed
150ml/¼ pint/⅔ cup fish stock
150ml/¼ pint/⅔ cup white wine
90ml/6 tbsp chopped fresh parsley
75g/3oz/¾ cup frozen petits pois
16 fresh clams
salt and ground black pepper

SERVES 4

1　Preheat the oven to 180°C/
350°F/Gas 4. Season the fish with salt and pepper, then dust both sides with flour. Heat 30ml/2 tbsp of the oil in a large sauté pan, add the fish and fry for about 1 minute on each side. Transfer to an ovenproof dish and sprinkle with lemon juice.

2　Clean the pan, then heat the remaining oil. Add the onion and garlic and cook until soft. Stir in 30ml/2 tbsp flour and cook for about 1 minute. Gradually add the stock and wine, stirring until thickened and smooth. Add 75ml/5 tbsp of the parsley and the petits pois and season with salt and pepper.

3　Pour the sauce over the fish, and bake in the oven for 15–20 minutes, adding the clams to the dish 3–4 minutes before the end of the cooking time. Discard any clams that do not open, then sprinkle with the remaining parsley before serving.

BLACK PASTA WITH SQUID SAUCE

Tagliatelle flavoured with squid ink looks amazing and tastes deliciously of the sea.
You can find it in good Italian delicatessens.

105ml/7 tbsp olive oil
2 shallots, chopped
3 garlic cloves, crushed
45ml/3 tbsp chopped fresh parsley
675g/1½lb cleaned squid, cut
into rings and rinsed
150ml/¼ pint/⅔ cup dry white wine
400g/14oz can chopped tomatoes
2.5ml/½ tsp dried chilli flakes
or powder
450g/1lb squid ink tagliatelle
salt and ground black pepper

SERVES 4

1 Heat the oil in a pan and add the shallots. Cook until pale golden, then add the garlic. When the garlic colours a little, add 30ml/2 tbsp of the parsley, stir, then add the squid and stir again. Cook for 3–4 minutes, then add the wine.

2 Simmer for a few seconds, then add the tomatoes and chilli flakes (*right*) and season with salt and pepper. Cover and simmer gently for about 1 hour, until the squid is tender. Add more water if necessary.

3 Cook the pasta in plenty of boiling, salted water, according to the instructions on the packet, or until *al dente*. Drain and return the tagliatelle to the pan. Add the squid sauce and mix well. Sprinkle each serving with the remaining chopped parsley and serve at once.

MOUCLADE OF MUSSELS

This recipe is quite similar to Moules Marinière, but has the additional flavouring of fennel and mild curry. Traditionally the mussels are shelled and piled into scallop shells, but nothing beats a bowlful of steaming hot, garlicky mussels, served in their own glistening shells.

1.75kg/4½lb fresh mussels
250ml/8fl oz/1 cup dry white wine
good pinch of grated nutmeg
3 thyme sprigs
2 bay leaves
1 small onion, finely chopped
50g/2oz/¼ cup butter
1 fennel bulb, thinly sliced
4 garlic cloves, crushed
2.5ml/½ tsp curry paste or powder
30ml/2 tbsp plain flour
150ml/¼ pint/⅔ cup double cream
ground black pepper
chopped fresh dill, to garnish

SERVES 6

1. Scrub the mussels, discarding any that are damaged or open ones that do not close when tapped with a knife.

2. Put the wine, nutmeg, thyme, bay leaves and onion in a large saucepan and bring just to the boil. Tip in the mussels and cover with a lid. Cook for 4–5 minutes until the mussels have opened.

3. Drain the mussels, reserving all the juices. Discard any mussels that remain closed.

4. Melt the butter in a large clean pan and gently fry the fennel slices and garlic for about 5 minutes until softened.

5. Stir in the curry paste or powder and flour and cook for 1 minute. Remove from the heat and gradually blend in the cooking juices from the mussels. Return to the heat and cook, stirring, for 2 minutes.

6. Stir in the cream and a little pepper. Add the mussels to the pan and heat through for 2 minutes. Serve hot, garnished with dill.

VARIATION

Saffron is a popular addition to a mouclade. Soak 2.5ml/½ tsp saffron strands in a little boiling water and add to the sauce with the stock.

MEAT

❦

While aromatic Mediterranean herbs
complement tender grilled meats, robust local
wines enrich succulent, long-simmered stews.

Although Mediterranean meat dishes are overshadowed by the popular vegetables and seafood of the area, they are in fact a celebration of simple, yet creative, traditional seasonal cooking. The countryside around the Mediterranean can be quite harsh and animals often survive on meagre grazing to be slaughtered young. Lamb and goat are favourite meats, particularly flavoured with wild herbs and spit-roasted whole to celebrate spring feast days. In the rugged, less-sophisticated regions such as Corsica, parts of Greece and the Middle East, where there are no lush green fields, cattle are a rare sight. In times past, beef was considered a luxury and the meat of young kid is still particularly popular.

Many rural families kept a pig, fattened on kitchen scraps to be slaughtered in autumn when the meat was preserved for food during the chilly winter months. Every last edible bit of the carcass was utilized in wonderful dry sausages, like salami, and cured hams, which are still popular today, and are appreciated all over the world.

ABOVE: Sunlight dapples the walls of this farmhouse overlooking Lake Trasimeno, in Umbria.

Jews and Muslims are forbidden by their religion to eat pork, so there are no pork recipes from their communities. In the Middle East, lamb and mutton are the only traditional meats, but beef is now becoming more popular. Although they do not exclude specific meats, the Roman Catholic and Greek Orthodox Churches used to observe strict fast days, when meat would not be consumed. Therefore many festive dishes were created using meat to celebrate the end of these annual fasts.

Sparse grazing and poverty often produced miserable beasts that yielded poor-quality meat, giving tough and stringy cuts. Marinating in wine or yogurt and cooking slowly at a low temperature tenderized and improved the flavour of the meat. Indeed, these methods created some of the most delicious casseroles and stews, still popular today, even though the meat is probably of better

RIGHT: This French shepherd has a magnificent view of the Provençal countryside.

BELOW: Sacks of spices and grains invite inspection at a Tunisian market.

quality. *Daubes* from France, *tagines* from Morocco and *estofados* from Spain have all been been handed down through generations. As meat was a luxury, those frugal housekeepers added pulses, rice and potatoes to ensure the meal was enough for the entire family.

Grilling is another popular cooking method, originating from the need to cook over the hot embers of an open fire. The meat is threaded on to skewers, or sometimes a trimmed branch of rosemary or bay, with chunks of onion and other vegetables added for flavour. This basic form of cooking results in succulent, smoky-flavoured meat, particularly in Greece and the Middle East, where the technique has been mastered to perfection.

Mincing is another old-fashioned way of dealing with tough or inferior meat and transforming it into succulent patties, meatballs or sauces for pasta. Along with savoury bakes and fillings for pastries these dishes are widely eaten throughout the Mediterranean. Rice, bulgur wheat and potatoes were originally added to make a little meat go a long way, with onions and tomatoes for additional flavour and volume. Spices, nuts and dried fruits also feature with minced meat, for example in delicious fillings for little parcels of filo pastry or hearty pilaffs. Layered bakes extend modest portions of meat into hearty and filling dishes. In Greece, a sauce of minced lamb layered with aubergines or potatoes and Béchamel sauce makes superb Moussaka. Turkish cooking is renowned for the variety and quality of its stuffed vegetables. Served hot or cold, aubergines, peppers or cabbage leaves rely on only a little meat for flavour, with rice or other grains for extra bulk.

Goat is not readily available outside the Mediterranean, so this chapter includes authentic recipes for dishes such as Corsican Beef Stew with Macaroni, Turkish Lamb Pilaff and Greek Lamb Sausages with Tomato Sauce. As with most dishes in this book, once cooked and ready to eat, some simple side dishes and some good company is all that is needed to make an enjoyable meal.

MOUSSAKA

Like many popular classics, a real moussaka bears little resemblance to the imitations experienced in many Greek tourist resorts. This one is mildly spiced, moist but not dripping in grease, and encased in a golden baked crust.

900g/2lb aubergines
120ml/4fl oz/½ cup olive oil
2 large tomatoes
2 large onions, sliced
450g/1lb minced lamb
1.5ml/¼ tsp ground cinnamon
1.5ml/¼ tsp ground allspice
30ml/2 tbsp tomato purée
45ml/3 tbsp chopped fresh parsley
120ml/4fl oz/½ cup dry white wine
salt and ground black pepper

FOR THE SAUCE
50g/2oz/4 tbsp butter
50g/2oz/½ cup plain flour
600ml/1 pint/2½ cups milk
1.5ml/¼ tsp grated nutmeg
25g/1oz/⅓ cup grated
Parmesan cheese
45ml/3 tbsp toasted breadcrumbs

SERVES 6

1 Cut the aubergines into 5mm/¼in thick slices. Layer the slices in a colander, sprinkling each layer with plenty of salt. Leave to stand for 30 minutes.

2 Rinse the aubergines in several changes of cold water. Squeeze gently with your fingers to remove the excess water, then pat them dry on kitchen paper.

3 Heat some of the oil in a large frying pan. Fry the aubergine slices in batches until golden on both sides, adding more oil when necessary. Leave the fried aubergine slices to drain on kitchen paper.

4 Plunge the tomatoes into boiling water for 30 seconds, then refresh in cold water. Peel away the skins and chop roughly.

5 Preheat the oven to 180°C/350°F/Gas 4. Heat 30ml/2 tbsp oil in a saucepan. Add the onions and lamb and fry gently for 5 minutes, stirring and breaking up the lamb with a wooden spoon.

VARIATION
Sliced and sautéed courgettes or potatoes can be used instead of the aubergines in this dish.

6 Add the tomatoes, cinnamon, allspice, tomato purée, parsley, wine and pepper and bring to the boil. Reduce the heat, cover with a lid and simmer gently for 15 minutes.

7 Spoon alternate layers of the aubergines and meat mixture into a shallow ovenproof dish, finishing with a layer of aubergines.

8 To make the sauce, melt the butter in a small pan and stir in the flour. Cook, stirring, for 1 minute. Remove from the heat and gradually blend in the milk. Return to the heat and cook, stirring, for 2 minutes, until thickened. Add the nutmeg, cheese and salt and pepper. Pour the sauce over the aubergines and sprinkle with the breadcrumbs. Bake for 45 minutes until golden. Serve hot, sprinkled with extra black pepper, if you like.

KLEFTIKO

For this Greek recipe, marinated lamb steaks or chops are slow-cooked to develop an unbeatable, meltingly tender flavour. The dish is sealed, like a pie, with a flour dough lid to trap succulence and flavour, although a tight-fitting foil cover, if less attractive, will serve equally well.

juice of 1 lemon
15ml/1 tbsp chopped fresh oregano
4 lamb leg steaks or chump chops
with bones
30ml/2 tbsp olive oil
2 large onions, thinly sliced
2 bay leaves
150ml/¼ pint/⅔ cup dry white wine
225g/8oz/2 cups plain flour
salt and ground black pepper

SERVES 4

COOK'S TIP
They are not absolutely essential for this dish, but lamb steaks or chops with bones will provide lots of additional flavour. Boiled potatoes make a delicious accompaniment.

1 Mix together the lemon juice, oregano and salt and pepper, and brush over both sides of the lamb steaks or chops. Leave to marinate for at least 4 hours or overnight.

2 Preheat the oven to 160°C/ 325°F/Gas 3. Drain the lamb, reserving the marinade, and dry the lamb with kitchen paper. Heat the olive oil in a large frying pan or sauté pan and fry the lamb over a high heat until browned on both sides.

3 Transfer the lamb to a shallow pie dish. Scatter the sliced onions and bay leaves around the lamb, then pour over the white wine and the reserved marinade.

4 Mix the flour with sufficient water to make a firm dough. Moisten the rim of the pie dish. Roll out the dough on a floured surface and use to cover the dish so that it is tightly sealed.

5 Bake for 2 hours, then break away the dough crust and serve the lamb hot with boiled potatoes.

SPICED ROAST LAMB

This is a particularly toothsome Turkish version of roast lamb.

2.75kg/6lb leg of lamb
3–4 large garlic cloves, halved
60ml/4 tbsp olive oil
10ml/2 tsp paprika
10ml/2 tsp Dijon mustard
juice of 1 lemon
2.5ml/½ tsp dried thyme
2.5ml/½ tsp dried rosemary
2.5ml/½ tsp sugar
120ml/4fl oz/½ cup white wine
salt and ground black pepper
fresh thyme, to garnish
rice and salad, to serve

SERVES 6–8

1. Trim the fat from the lamb and make several incisions in the meat with a sharp knife. Press the garlic halves into the slits. Mix together the olive oil, paprika, mustard, lemon juice, herbs, sugar and seasoning and rub this paste all over the meat. Place the joint in a shallow dish and allow to stand in a cool place for 1–2 hours.

2. Preheat the oven to 200°C/400°F/Gas 6. Place the joint in a roasting tin, add the white wine and cook for 20 minutes. Reduce the heat to 160°C/325°F/Gas 3 and cook for a further 2 hours, basting from time to time. Serve garnished with thyme, and accompanied by rice and a salad of young leaves and herbs.

COOK'S TIP
If you can spare the time, it is better to leave the meat to rest for 15 minutes before carving. This makes the flesh firmer, which in turn makes it easier to carve.

ROAST LEG OF LAMB WITH SAFFRON

Even such a tiny quantity of saffron imparts a delicate flavour to the meat.

2.75kg/6lb leg of lamb
4 garlic cloves, halved
60ml/4 tbsp olive oil
juice of 1 lemon
2–3 saffron strands, soaked in
15ml/1 tbsp boiling water
5ml/1 tsp dried mixed herbs
450g/1lb potatoes
2 large onions
salt and ground black pepper
fresh flat leaf parsley, to garnish

SERVES 6–8

1. Make several incisions in the meat and press the garlic halves into the slits. Mix the oil, lemon juice, saffron and herbs in a small bowl. Rub this mixture over the meat, then leave to marinate at room temperature for 2 hours.

2. Preheat the oven to 180°C/350°F/Gas 4. Peel all the potatoes and cut them crossways into thick slices. Cut the onions into thick slices.

3. Layer the potatoes and onions in a large roasting tin. Lift the lamb out of the marinade and place the meat on the top of the potatoes and onions, fat side up.

4. Pour any remaining marinade over the lamb and roast for 2 hours, basting occasionally. Remove the lamb from the oven, cover loosely with foil and leave in a warm place to rest for about 10–15 minutes before carving. Serve, surrounded by the potatoes and onions, and garnished with parsley.

LAMB WITH RED PEPPERS AND RIOJA

Plenty of garlic, peppers, herbs and red wine give this lamb stew a lovely rich flavour.
Slice through the pepper stalks, rather than remove them,
as this makes the dish look extra special.

900g/2lb lean lamb fillet
15ml/1 tbsp plain flour
60ml/4 tbsp olive oil
2 red onions, sliced
4 garlic cloves, sliced
10ml/2 tsp paprika
1.5ml/¼ tsp ground cloves
400ml/14fl oz/1⅔ cups red Rioja
150ml/¼ pint/⅔ cup lamb stock
2 bay leaves
2 thyme sprigs
3 red peppers, halved and seeded
salt and ground black pepper
bay leaves and thyme sprigs,
to garnish
green beans and saffron rice or boiled
potatoes, to serve

SERVES 4

1 Preheat the oven to 160°C/
325°F/Gas 3. Cut the lamb into chunks. Season the flour, add the lamb and toss lightly to coat.

2 Heat the oil in a frying pan and fry the lamb, stirring, until browned. Transfer to an ovenproof dish. Lightly fry the onions in the pan with the garlic, paprika and cloves.

VARIATION
Use any lean cubed pork instead of the lamb and a white Rioja instead of the red. A mixture of red, yellow and orange peppers looks very effective.

3 Add the Rioja, stock, bay leaves and thyme and bring to the boil, stirring. Pour the contents of the pan over the meat. Cover with a lid and bake for 30 minutes.

4 Remove the dish from the oven. Stir the red peppers into the stew and season lightly with salt and pepper. Bake for a further 30 minutes until the meat is tender. Garnish the stew with bay leaves and sprigs of thyme and serve with green beans and saffron rice or boiled potatoes.

ROAST LAMB WITH ROSEMARY

In Italy, lamb is traditionally served at Easter. This simple roast with potatoes owes its wonderful flavour to the addition of fresh rosemary and garlic. It makes the perfect Sunday lunch at any time of year, served with one or two lightly-cooked fresh vegetables, such as broccoli, spinach or baby carrots.

½ leg of lamb, about 1.4kg/3lb
2 garlic cloves, cut lengthways into
thin slivers
105ml/7 tbsp olive oil
leaves from 4 sprigs of fresh rosemary,
finely chopped
about 250ml/8fl oz/1 cup lamb or
vegetable stock
675g/1½ lb potatoes, cut into
2.5cm/1in cubes
a few fresh sage leaves, chopped
salt and ground black pepper

SERVES 4

1 Preheat the oven to 230°C/
450°F/Gas 8. Using the point
of a sharp knife, make several deep
incisions in the lamb, especially near
the bone, and insert a sliver of garlic
into each.

COOK'S TIP

If you like, the cooking juices can be
strained and used to make a thin
gravy with stock and red wine.

2 Place the lamb in a roasting tin
and rub it all over with 45ml/
3 tbsp of the oil. Sprinkle over about
half of the chopped rosemary, patting
it on firmly, and season with plenty of
salt and pepper. Roast for 30 minutes,
turning once.

3 Lower the oven temperature to
190°C/375°F/Gas 5. Turn the
lamb over again. Carefully pour in
125ml/4fl oz/½ cup of the stock.

4 Roast for a further 1¼–1½ hours
until the lamb is tender, turning
the joint two or three times more and
adding the rest of the stock in two or
three batches. Baste the lamb each
time it is turned.

5 Meanwhile, put the potatoes in
a separate roasting tin and toss
with the remaining oil and rosemary
and the sage. Roast the potatoes on
the same shelf as the lamb, if possible,
for 45 minutes, turning the potatoes
several times until golden and tender.

6 Transfer the lamb to a carving
board, cover with foil and leave
for 10 minutes before carving. Serve
with the roast potatoes and accompanied
by a green vegetable, baby carrots or
roasted Mediterranean vegetables.

VARIATION

Tuck one or two rosemary leaves into
each slit in the lamb, as well as the
garlic, for a more intense flavour.

LAMB CASSEROLE WITH GARLIC AND BROAD BEANS

This recipe has a Spanish influence and makes a substantial meal, served with potatoes. It is based on stewing lamb with a large amount of garlic and sherry — the addition of broad beans gives colour.

 2 Heat the remaining oil in the pan, add the onion and cook for about 5 minutes until soft. Return the meat to the casserole.

3 Add the garlic cloves, bay leaf, paprika and sherry. Season with salt and pepper. Bring to the boil, then cover and simmer very gently for 1½–2 hours, until the meat is tender.

45ml/3 tbsp olive oil
1.5kg/3–3½lb lamb fillet, cut into 5cm/2in cubes
1 large onion, chopped
6 large garlic cloves, unpeeled
1 bay leaf
5ml/1 tsp paprika
120ml/4fl oz/½ cup dry sherry
115g/4oz shelled fresh or frozen broad beans
30ml/2 tbsp chopped fresh parsley
salt and ground black pepper

SERVES 6

1 Heat 30ml/2 tbsp of the oil in a large flameproof casserole. Add half the meat and brown well on all sides. Transfer to a plate. Brown the rest of the meat in the same way and remove from the casserole.

4 Add the broad beans about 10 minutes before the end of the cooking time. Stir in the parsley just before serving.

BRAISED LAMB WITH APRICOTS AND HERB DUMPLINGS

This is a rich and fruity lamb casserole, topped with light, herby dumplings, which is delicious served with baked jacket potatoes and a green vegetable.

30ml/2 tbsp sunflower oil
675g/1½ lb lean lamb fillet, cut into
2.5cm/1in cubes
350g/12oz button onions
1 garlic clove, crushed
225g/8oz/3 cups button mushrooms
175g/6oz/¾ cup small ready-to-eat
dried apricots
250ml/8fl oz/1 cup well-flavoured
lamb or beef stock
250ml/8fl oz/1 cup red wine
15ml/1 tbsp tomato purée
salt and ground black pepper
sprigs of fresh herbs, to garnish

FOR THE DUMPLINGS
115g/4oz/1 cup self-raising flour
50g/2oz/scant ½ cup shredded
vegetable suet
15–30ml/1–2 tbsp chopped fresh
mixed herbs

SERVES 6

VARIATIONS
Use lean beef or pork in place of the lamb, and substitute shallots or double quantities of caramelized red and white onions for the button onions, if you prefer. Prunes, dates or even figs can be used instead of apricots.

1. Preheat the oven to 160°C/ 325°F/Gas 3. Heat the oil in a large, flameproof casserole, add the lamb and cook gently until browned all over, stirring occasionally. Remove the meat from the casserole using a slotted spoon, set aside and keep warm.

2. Add the button onions, garlic and mushrooms to the oil remaining in the casserole. Cook gently for about 5 minutes, stirring occasionally to incorporate any sediment on the bottom.

3. Return all the meat to the casserole, add the dried apricots, lamb or beef stock, red wine and tomato purée. Season to taste with salt and pepper and stir with a wooden spoon to mix.

4. Bring to the boil, stirring, then remove the casserole from the heat and cover. Transfer the casserole to the oven and cook for 1½–2 hours until the lamb is cooked and tender, stirring once or twice and adding a little extra stock, if necessary.

5. Meanwhile, make the dumplings. Place the flour, suet, herbs and seasoning in a bowl and stir to mix. Add enough cold water to make a soft, elastic dough. Divide the dough into small, marble-size pieces and, using lightly floured hands, roll each piece into a small ball.

6. Remove the lid from the casserole and place the dumplings on the top of the braised lamb and vegetables. Do not place the dumplings too close together; they must have room to rise.

7. Increase the oven temperature to 190°C/375°F/Gas 5. Return the casserole to the oven and cook for a further 20–25 minutes until the herb dumplings are cooked. Serve straight from the casserole, garnished with fresh herb sprigs.

MOROCCAN LAMB STEW

Known locally as Tagine, after the conical-shaped pottery dish in which it is cooked, this colourful, spicy stew combines French colonial and African influences.

.... 🌿 🌿 ....

225g/8oz/1⅓ cups dried chick-peas
soaked in cold water overnight
60ml/4 tbsp olive oil
10ml/2 tsp sugar
10ml/2 tsp ground cumin
5ml/1 tsp ground cinnamon
5ml/1 tsp ground ginger
2.5ml/½ tsp ground turmeric
2.5ml/½ tsp powdered saffron
or paprika
1.4kg/3lb lamb shoulder, trimmed of
all fat and cut into 5cm/2in cubes
2 onions, coarsely chopped
3 garlic cloves, finely chopped
2 tomatoes, peeled, seeded
and chopped
75g/3oz/⅔ cup raisins, soaked in
warm water
10–24 pitted black olives,
such as Kalamata
2 preserved lemons, thinly sliced, or
grated rind of 1 unwaxed lemon
60–90ml/4–6 tbsp chopped
fresh coriander
salt and ground black pepper
450g/1lb/2⅔ cups couscous, to serve

SERVES 6–8

.... 🌿 🌿 ....

COOK'S TIP
Preserved lemons are frequently used
in Moroccan cooking. They are
available in delicatessens and
specialist food halls but, if you can't
find them, a little grated lemon rind
makes an adequate substitute.
Be sure to use unwaxed lemons,
which are widely available.

1 Drain the chick-peas, rinse under cold running water and place in a large saucepan, then cover with water and boil vigorously for 10 minutes. Drain the chick-peas and return to a clean saucepan. Cover with fresh cold water and bring to the boil over a high heat, then reduce the heat and simmer, covered, for about 1–1½ hours until tender. Remove the pan from the heat and add a little salt.

2 In a large bowl, combine half of the olive oil with the sugar, cumin, cinnamon, ginger, turmeric, saffron or paprika, 5ml/1 tsp salt and pepper. Add the lamb, toss to coat well and set aside for 20 minutes.

3 In a large heavy frying pan, heat the remaining oil and fry the lamb in batches until well browned. Transfer to a large flameproof casserole.

4 Add the onions to the pan and stir them constantly until well browned. Stir in the garlic and tomatoes with 250ml/8fl oz/1 cup water, stirring and scraping the base of the pan. Pour into the casserole and add enough water to just cover, then bring to the boil over a high heat, skimming off any foam that rises to the surface. Reduce the heat to low and simmer for about 1 hour, or until the meat is tender when pierced with a sharp knife.

5 Drain the chick-peas, reserving the liquid. Pour on to the lamb in the casserole with about 250ml/8fl oz/1 cup of the liquid. Stir in all the raisins with their soaking liquid and simmer for 30 minutes more. Stir in the olives and sliced preserved lemons or lemon rind, and simmer for 20–30 minutes more, then mix in half of the chopped coriander.

6 About 30 minutes before serving, prepare the couscous according to the instructions on the packet. Spoon the couscous on to a warmed serving dish, spoon the lamb stew on top, mounding it up in the centre, and sprinkle with the remaining fresh coriander.

GREEK LAMB SAUSAGES WITH TOMATO SAUCE

*The Greek name for these sausages is soudzoukakia. They are more like elongated meatballs than the
type of sausage we are accustomed to. Passata is sieved tomato, which can be bought in cartons or jars.*

50g/2oz/1 cup fresh breadcrumbs
150ml/¼ pint/⅔ cup milk
675g/1½lb minced lamb
30ml/2 tbsp grated onion
3 garlic cloves, crushed
10ml/2 tsp ground cumin
30ml/2 tbsp chopped fresh parsley
flour for dusting
olive oil for frying
600ml/1 pint/2½ cups passata
5ml/1 tsp sugar
2 bay leaves
1 small onion, peeled
salt and ground black pepper
flat leaf parsley, to garnish

SERVES 4

1 Mix together the breadcrumbs and milk. Add the lamb, onion, garlic, cumin and parsley and season with salt and pepper.

2 Shape the mixture with your hands into little fat sausages, about 5cm/2in long and roll them in flour. Heat about 60ml/4 tbsp olive oil in a frying pan.

3 Fry the sausages for about 8 minutes, turning them until evenly browned. Remove and place on kitchen paper to drain.

4 Put the passata, sugar, bay leaves and whole onion in a pan and simmer for 20 minutes. Add the sausages and cook for 10 minutes more. Serve garnished with parsley.

TURKISH LAMB PILAU

Here we have a delicious combination of rice, lamb, spices, nuts and fruit – a typical Middle Eastern dish.

40g/1½oz/3 tbsp butter
1 large onion, finely chopped
450g/1lb lamb fillet, cut into
small cubes
2.5ml/½ tsp ground cinnamon
30ml/2 tbsp tomato purée
45ml/3 tbsp chopped fresh parsley
115g/4oz/½ cup ready-to-eat dried
apricots, halved
75g/3oz/¾ cup pistachio nuts
450g/1lb long grain rice, rinsed
salt and ground black pepper
flat leaf parsley, to garnish

SERVES 4

1 Heat the butter in a large heavy-based pan. Add the onion and cook until soft and golden. Add the cubed lamb and brown on all sides. Add the cinnamon and season with salt and pepper. Cover and cook gently for 10 minutes.

2 Add the tomato purée and enough water to cover the meat. Stir in the parsley, bring to the boil, cover and simmer very gently for 1½ hours, until the meat is tender. Chop the pistachio nuts.

3 Add enough water to the pan to make up to about 600ml/1 pint/ 2½ cups liquid. Add the apricots, pistachio nuts and rice, bring to the boil, cover tightly and simmer for about 20 minutes, until the rice is cooked. (You may need to add a little more water, if necessary.) Transfer to a warmed serving dish and garnish with parsley before serving.

LEBANESE KIBBEH

Kibbeh is popular in many parts of the southern and eastern Mediterranean. This version comes from the Lebanon, where it is the national dish.

· · · · · · · · · · · · · · · · · · · 🌿 🌿 · · · · · · · · · · · · · · · · · · ·

115g/4oz/⅔ cup bulgur wheat
450g/1lb finely minced lean lamb
1 large onion, grated
15g/½oz/1 tbsp butter, melted
salt and ground black pepper
sprigs of mint, to garnish
rice, to serve

FOR THE FILLING
30ml/2 tbsp oil
1 onion, finely chopped
225g/8oz minced lamb or veal
50g/2oz/⅔ cup pine nuts
2.5ml/½ tsp ground allspice

FOR THE YOGURT DIP
600ml/1 pint/2½ cups Greek yogurt
2–3 garlic cloves, crushed
15–30ml/1–2 tbsp chopped fresh mint

SERVES 6

· · · · · · · · · · · · · · · · · · · 🌿 🌿 · · · · · · · · · · · · · · · · · · ·

1 Preheat the oven to 190°C/
375°F/Gas 5. Rinse the bulgur wheat in a sieve and squeeze out any excess moisture. Mix the lamb, onion and seasoning, kneading the mixture to make a thick paste. Add the bulgur wheat.

2 To make the filling, heat the oil in a frying pan and fry the onion until golden. Add the lamb or veal and cook, stirring, until evenly browned, then add the pine nuts, allspice and salt and pepper.

3 Oil a large baking dish and spread half of the meat and bulgur wheat mixture over the bottom. Spoon the filling over it and top with a second layer of meat and bulgur wheat, pressing down firmly with the back of a spoon.

4 Pour the melted butter over the top of the *kibbeh* and then bake in the oven for 40–45 minutes until browned on top.

5 Meanwhile, make the yogurt dip. Mix together the yogurt and garlic, spoon into a serving bowl and sprinkle with the chopped mint.

6 Cut the cooked *kibbeh* into squares or rectangles and serve, garnished with mint and accompanied by the yogurt dip. Serve with rice.

LAMB WITH SPLIT PEAS

Khoreshe Ghaimeh is a traditional Persian dish and is always served at parties and religious ceremonies. It is a great favourite with children, too.

25g/1oz/2 tbsp butter or margarine
1 large onion, chopped
450g/1lb lean lamb, cubed
5ml/1 tsp ground turmeric
5ml/1 tsp ground cinnamon
5ml/1 tsp curry powder
300ml/½ pint/1¼ cups water
2–3 saffron strands
100g/3½ oz/½ cup yellow split peas
3 limu amani (dried limes)
3–4 tomatoes, chopped
30ml/2 tbsp oil
2 large potatoes, chopped
salt and freshly ground black pepper
rice, to serve

SERVES 4

COOK'S TIP
Dried limes are available in all Iranian or Middle Eastern shops. However, if you have difficulty obtaining them, use the juice of either 2 fresh limes, 2 fresh oranges or 1 fresh lemon instead, and reduce the water by the same amount. If you prefer, you can use lean stewing beef in place of the lamb in this traditional dish.

1 Melt the butter or margarine in a large saucepan or flameproof casserole and fry the onion for about 4 minutes until golden, stirring occasionally. Add the meat and cook over a high heat for a further 3–4 minutes until brown.

2 Add the turmeric, cinnamon and curry powder and cook for about 2 minutes, stirring frequently.

3 Stir in the water, season well and bring to the boil, then cover and simmer over a low heat for about 30–35 minutes, until the meat is half-cooked. Stir the saffron into about 15ml/1 tbsp boiling water, then add it to the meat.

4 Stir in the split peas, limes and tomatoes. Simmer, covered, for 35 minutes more until the meat is tender.

5 Heat the oil in a frying pan and fry the potatoes for 10–15 minutes, until cooked and golden. Lift out the dried limes and discard. Spoon the meat on to a large serving dish and scatter the potatoes on top. Serve with rice.

STUFFED KIBBEH

Kibbeh is a tasty North African speciality of minced meat and bulgur wheat.
The patties are sometimes stuffed with additional meat and deep fried.
Moderately spiced, they're good with yogurt or Cacik sauce.

450g/1lb lean lamb (or lean minced
lamb or beef)
oil for deep frying
avocado slices and coriander sprigs,
to serve

FOR THE KIBBEH
225g/8oz/1⅓ cups bulgur wheat
1 red chilli, seeded and
roughly chopped
1 onion, roughly chopped
salt and ground black pepper

FOR THE STUFFING
1 onion, finely chopped
50g/2oz/⅔ cup pine nuts
30ml/2 tbsp olive oil
7.5ml/1½ tsp ground allspice
60ml/4 tbsp chopped fresh coriander

SERVES 4–6

1 If necessary, roughly cut up the lamb and process the pieces in a blender or food processor until minced. Divide the minced meat into two equal portions.

2 To make the kibbeh, soak the bulgur wheat for 15 minutes in cold water. Drain well, then process in the blender or food processor with the chilli, onion, half the meat and plenty of salt and pepper.

3 To make the stuffing, fry the onion and pine nuts in the oil for 5 minutes. Add the allspice and remaining minced meat and fry gently, breaking up the meat with a wooden spoon, until browned. Stir in the coriander and a little seasoning.

4 Turn the kibbeh mixture out on to a work surface and shape into a cake. Cut into 12 wedges.

5 Flatten one piece in the palm of your hand and spoon a little stuffing into the centre. Bring the edges of the kibbeh up over the stuffing to enclose it. Make into a firm egg-shaped mould between the palms of the hands, ensuring that the filling is completely encased. Repeat with the other kibbeh.

6 Heat oil to a depth of 5cm/2in a large pan until a few kibbeh crumbs sizzle on the surface.

7 Lower half the kibbeh into the oil and fry for about 5 minutes until golden. Drain on kitchen paper and keep them hot while cooking the remainder. Serve with avocado slices and coriander sprigs.

LAMB AND CELERY KHORESH

This unusual stew, known in the Middle East as Khoreshe Karafs, has a lovely fresh taste.

1 large onion, chopped
40g/1½ oz/3 tbsp butter
450g/1lb lean lamb, cubed
5ml/1 tsp ground turmeric
2.5ml/½ tsp ground cinnamon
600ml/1 pint/2½ cups water
1 head of celery, chopped
25g/1oz fresh parsley, chopped
1 small bunch fresh mint, chopped
juice of 1 lemon
salt and ground black pepper
mint leaves, to garnish

SERVES 4

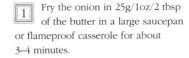

1 Fry the onion in 25g/1oz/2 tbsp of the butter in a large saucepan or flameproof casserole for about 3–4 minutes.

2 Add the meat and cook for 2–3 minutes until brown, stirring frequently. Then stir in the turmeric, cinnamon and salt and pepper.

3 Add the water and bring to the boil, then reduce the heat, cover and simmer for 30 minutes until the meat is half-cooked.

4 Melt the remaining butter in a frying pan and fry the celery for 8–10 minutes, until tender, stirring frequently. Add the parsley and mint, and fry for a further 3–4 minutes.

5 Stir the celery and herbs into the meat. Add the lemon juice and simmer, covered, for a further 25–30 minutes until the meat is completely tender.

6 Serve in a heated bowl, garnished with mint leaves and accompanied by rice. A salad of dressed cherry tomatoes and pared cucumber would be the perfect side-dish.

LAMB WITH SPINACH AND PRUNES

*If you like fresh spinach you will love this lightly spiced sweet-and-sour dish.
It is traditionally served with rice.*

45ml/3 tbsp oil
1 large onion, chopped
450g/1lb lean lamb, cubed
2.5ml/½ tsp grated nutmeg
5ml/1 tsp ground cinnamon
600ml/1 pint/2½ cups water
150g/5oz chives or spring onions, green parts included, finely chopped
450g/1lb fresh spinach, chopped
250g/9oz/1¼ cups prunes, soaked
juice of 1 lemon
salt and ground black pepper

SERVES 4

1 Heat 30ml/2 tbsp of the oil in a large pan and fry the onion for 3–4 minutes until golden. Add the lamb and fry until brown on all sides. Sprinkle with the nutmeg and cinnamon, and stir the mixture well.

2 Add the water, bring to the boil and spoon off any foam that rises to the surface. Season with salt and pepper, cover and simmer over a low heat for 40–45 minutes until the meat is nearly cooked.

3 Heat the remaining oil in another large pan, add the chives or spring onions, stir-fry for a few minutes and then add the spinach. Cover and cook over a medium heat for 2–3 minutes until the spinach has wilted, then add this mixture to the meat, with the prunes and lemon juice.

4 Cook, covered, for a further 20–25 minutes, until the meat is completely tender. Serve with rice.

MEAT DUMPLINGS WITH YOGURT SAUCE

These Lebanese meat dumplings are braised in yogurt sauce, a speciality known as Shish Barak.
Mint and garlic give the lamb a lovely flavour.

30ml/2 tbsp oil
1 large onion, chopped
60ml/4 tbsp pine nuts or
chopped walnuts
450g/1lb minced lamb
25g/1oz/2 tbsp butter
3 garlic cloves, crushed
15ml/1 tbsp chopped fresh mint
salt and ground black pepper
mint leaves, to garnish

FOR THE DOUGH
225g/8oz/2 cups plain flour
5ml/1 tsp salt

FOR THE YOGURT SAUCE
2 litres/3½ pints/8 cups yogurt
1 egg, beaten
15ml/1 tbsp cornflour, blended with
15ml/1 tbsp cold water
salt and white pepper

SERVES 4

1 First make the dough. Mix together the flour and salt and then stir in enough water to bind the dough. Knead lightly, then leave to rest for 1 hour.

2 Heat the oil in a large frying pan and fry the onion for 3–4 minutes until soft. Add the pine nuts or walnuts and fry until golden. Stir in the meat and cook until brown. Season, then remove the pan from the heat and set it aside.

3 Roll out the dough thinly on a floured board. Cut into small rounds 5–6cm/2–2½in in diameter. Place 5ml/1 tsp of the meat filling on each one, fold the pastry over and firmly press the edges together. It is important not to over-fill the pastries or they may burst. Bring the ends together to form a handle.

4 Make the yogurt sauce. Pour the yogurt into a saucepan and beat in the egg and the cornflour mixture. Season with salt and white pepper and slowly bring to the boil, stirring constantly. Cook over a gentle heat until the sauce thickens and then carefully drop in the dumpling. Simmer for 20 minutes.

5 Spoon the dumplings and sauce on to warmed serving plates. Melt the butter in a small frying pan and fry the garlic until golden. Stir in the mint, cook briefly and then pour over the dumplings. Garnish with mint leaves. Serve with rice and a salad.

KOFTAS IN TOMATO SAUCE

—

There are many varieties of kofta in the Mediterranean and Middle East. This is a popular version from Turkey.

350g/12oz minced lamb or beef
25g/1oz/½ cup fresh breadcrumbs
1 onion, grated
45ml/3 tbsp chopped fresh parsley
15ml/1 tbsp chopped fresh mint
5ml/1 tsp ground cumin
5ml/1 tsp ground turmeric
45ml/3 tbsp oil for frying
salt and ground black pepper
noodles, to serve
mint leaves, to garnish

FOR THE TOMATO SAUCE
15ml/1 tbsp olive oil
1 onion, chopped
400g/14oz can plum tomatoes
15ml/1 tbsp tomato purée
juice of ½ lemon
salt and ground black pepper

SERVES 4

2 Meanwhile, place the minced lamb or beef in a large bowl and mix in the breadcrumbs, grated onion, herbs and spices and a little salt and pepper.

3 Knead the mixture by hand until thoroughly blended and then shape it into walnut-size balls and place on a plate.

4 Heat the oil in a frying pan and fry the meatballs, in batches if necessary, until evenly browned. Transfer them to the pan of tomato sauce. Cover the pan and simmer gently for about 30 minutes. Serve with noodles and garnish with mint leaves.

COOK'S TIP
Instead of using either minced lamb or beef, use a mixture of the two, or add a little chopped bacon.

1 First make the tomato sauce. Heat the oil in a large saucepan or flameproof casserole and fry the onion until golden. Stir in the canned tomatoes, tomato purée, lemon juice and seasoning, bring to the boil and then reduce the heat and simmer for about 10 minutes.

SKEWERED LAMB WITH CORIANDER YOGURT

Although lamb is the most commonly used meat for Turkish kebabs, lean beef or pork work equally well.
For colour you can alternate pieces of pepper, lemon or onions, although this is not traditional.

900g/2lb lean boneless lamb
1 large onion, grated
3 bay leaves
5 thyme or rosemary sprigs
grated rind and juice of
1 lemon
2.5ml/½ tsp caster sugar
75ml/3fl oz/⅓ cup olive oil
salt and ground black pepper
sprigs of rosemary, to garnish
grilled lemon wedges, to serve

FOR THE CORIANDER YOGURT
150ml/¼ pint/⅔ cup thick
natural yogurt
15ml/1 tbsp chopped fresh mint
15ml/1 tbsp chopped fresh coriander
10ml/2 tsp grated onion

SERVES 4

1. To make the coriander yogurt, mix together the yogurt, mint, coriander and grated onion and transfer to a small serving dish.

2. To make the kebabs, cut the lamb into small chunks and put in a bowl. Mix together the grated onion, herbs, lemon rind and juice, sugar and oil, then add salt and pepper and pour over the lamb.

3. Mix the ingredients together and leave to marinate in the fridge for several hours or overnight.

4. Drain the meat and thread on to skewers. Arrange on a grill rack and cook under a preheated grill for about 10 minutes until browned, turning occasionally. Transfer to a plate and garnish with rosemary. Serve with the grilled lemon wedges and the coriander yogurt.

COOK'S TIP
Cover the tips of wooden skewers with foil so they don't char.

MINCED MEAT KEBABS

These kebabs are often served with rice, into which is stirred raw egg yolk and melted butter.
Traditionally, the kebabs are barbecued over open fires, but they can also be cooked
under a very hot grill.

450g/1lb lean lamb
450g/1lb lean beef
1 large onion, grated
2 garlic cloves, crushed
15ml/1 tbsp sumac (optional)
2–3 saffron strands, soaked in 15ml/
1 tbsp boiling water
10ml/2 tsp bicarbonate of soda
6–8 tomatoes, halved
15ml/1 tbsp melted butter
salt and ground black pepper

SERVES 4

1 Mince the lamb and beef two or three times until very finely minced, place in a large bowl and add the grated onion, garlic, *sumac*, if using, soaked saffron, bicarbonate of soda, and salt and pepper. Knead by hand until the mixture becomes glutinous.

COOK'S TIP
It helps to have a bowl of water nearby in which to dip your fingers to stop the meat sticking to them while you knead it.

2 Take a small handful of meat and roll it into a ball. If the ball seems crumbly, knead the mixture in the bowl for a few minutes.

3 Shape the ball around a flat skewer, moulding it around the skewer. Repeat until you have three or four balls on each skewer, pressing them tightly to prevent the meat from falling off.

4 Thread the tomatoes on to separate skewers. Cook the meat and the tomato kebabs over a barbecue or under a hot grill for about 10 minutes, basting them with melted butter and turning them occasionally.

CORIANDER LAMB KEBABS WITH AN ALMOND CHANTERELLE SAUCE

The delicate sweetness of lamb combines well with chanterelles, which are used here to make this especially delicious almond sauce.

8 lamb cutlets, trimmed
225g/8oz chanterelle
mushrooms, trimmed
25g/1oz/2 tbsp unsalted butter
25g/1oz/¼ cup whole
almonds, toasted
50g/2oz white bread, crusts removed
250ml/8fl oz/1 cup milk
45ml/3 tbsp olive oil
2.5ml/½ tsp caster sugar
10ml/2 tsp lemon juice
salt and cayenne pepper, to taste

FOR THE MARINADE
45ml/3 tbsp olive oil
15ml/1 tbsp lemon juice
10ml/2 tsp ground coriander
½ garlic clove, crushed
10ml/2 tsp clear honey

SERVES 4

1 Put the lamb in a shallow dish. Make the marinade. Mix the oil, lemon juice, ground coriander, garlic and honey in a bowl. Spoon over the lamb, coating each cutlet, then cover and leave for at least 30 minutes.

2 Fry the chanterelles gently in butter for 3–4 minutes without colouring. Set aside.

3 Place the almonds in a food processor and grind finely. Add half of the chanterelles, the bread, milk, oil, sugar and lemon juice, then process together well.

4 Thread the lamb cutlets on to four metal skewers, and cook under a moderately hot grill for 6–8 minutes on each side. Season the almond mixture with salt and cayenne, then spoon this over the kebabs. Top with the remaining chanterelles and serve with new potatoes and dressed green leaves.

SKEWERED LAMB WITH RED ONION SALSA

This summery tapas dish is ideal for outdoor eating, but if the weather fails, the skewers can be cooked under a conventional grill. The simple salsa makes a refreshing accompaniment – make sure that you use a mild-flavoured red onion, which is fresh and crisp, and a tomato which is ripe and full of flavour.

225g/8oz lean lamb
2.5ml/½ tsp ground cumin
5ml/1 tsp ground paprika
15ml/1 tbsp olive oil
salt and ground black pepper

FOR THE SALSA
1 red onion, finely sliced
1 large tomato, seeded and chopped
15ml/1 tbsp red wine vinegar
3–4 fresh basil or mint leaves,
roughly torn
small mint leaves, to garnish

SERVES 4

COOK'S TIP
To make an alternative sauce to the red onion salsa, stir chopped fresh mint or basil and a little lemon juice into a small pot of Greek-style yogurt. Drizzle the mixture over the cooked kebabs before serving.

VARIATION
For a more fiery flavour, prepare the salsa the day before and spike it with a chopped red chilli.

1 Cut the lamb into cubes, removing some of the fat, but leaving a little on the meat to prevent it from drying out too much when grilled or barbecued. Place the lamb cubes in a bowl with the cumin, paprika, olive oil and plenty of salt and pepper. Toss well until the lamb is coated with spices.

2 Cover the bowl with clear film and leave in a cool place for several hours, or in the fridge overnight, so that the lamb absorbs the spicy flavours. Stir the meat cubes from time to time, if convenient.

3 Spear the lamb cubes on to four small skewers – if using wooden skewers, soak them first in cold water for at least 30 minutes to prevent them from burning. Do not pack the cubes too closely.

4 To make the salsa, put the sliced onion, tomato, vinegar and basil or mint leaves in a small bowl, and stir together until thoroughly blended. Season to taste with salt, garnish with mint, then set the salsa aside while you cook the skewered lamb.

5 Cook the skewered lamb over hot coals or under a preheated grill for about 5–10 minutes, turning the skewers frequently, until the lamb is well browned but still slightly pink in the centre. Serve hot, with the red onion salsa.

LAMB KOUTLETS

Koutlets are very tasty and are equally popular served either hot at a buffet or cold on a picnic.

3 eggs
1 onion, grated
30ml/2 tbsp chopped fresh parsley
450g/1lb new potatoes, peeled
450g/1lb finely minced lean lamb
115g/4oz/1 cup dried breadcrumbs
oil, for frying
salt and ground black pepper
mint leaves, to garnish

MAKES 12–15

1 Beat the eggs in a large bowl, add the onion and parsley, season with salt and pepper, and beat together well.

2 Cook the potatoes in a large saucepan of boiling salted water for 20 minutes until tender, then drain and leave to cool. When the potatoes are cold, grate them coarsely and stir into the egg mixture together with minced lamb. Knead by hand for 3 minutes until thoroughly mixed.

3 Take a handful of meat and roll it into a ball. Next, roll each ball in the breadcrumbs and then mould into triangles, about 13cm/5in long. Cover with the breadcrumb patting them on firmly.

4 Heat the oil in a frying pan and fry the *koutlets* over a medium heat for 8–12 minutes until golden brown, turning occasionally. Garnish with mint and serve hot, with pitta bread and a salad.

DILL AND BROAD BEAN MEATBALLS

This is another recipe for kofta, this time using lean minced beef instead of the more common lamb.

115g/4oz/generous ½ cup long grain rice
450g/1lb minced lean beef
115g/4oz/1 cup plain flour
3 eggs, beaten
115g/4oz/1 cup broad beans, skinned
30ml/2 tbsp chopped fresh dill
25g/1oz/2 tbsp butter or margarine
1 large onion, chopped
2.5ml/½ tsp ground turmeric
1.2 litres/2 pints/5 cups water
salt and ground black pepper
chopped fresh parsley, to garnish
naan bread, to serve

SERVES 4

1 Put the rice in a saucepan, cover with water and boil for about 4 minutes until half-cooked. Drain and place in a bowl with the meat, flour, eggs and seasoning. Knead thoroughly by hand until well blended.

2 Add the skinned broad beans and dill, and knead again thoroughly until the mixture resembles a firm paste. Shape the mixture into large balls and set aside on a plate. This is easier to do if you wet your hands first.

3 Melt the butter or margarine in a large saucepan or flameproof casserole and fry the onion for about 4 minutes until golden. Stir in the turmeric, cook for 30 seconds then add the water and bring to boil over a high heat.

4 Add the meatballs to the pan, reduce the heat and simmer for 45–60 minutes until the meatballs are cooked through and the sauce is reduced to about 250ml/8fl oz/1 cup. Garnish with parsley and serve with warm naan bread.

LAMB TAGINE WITH ARTICHOKES AND PRESERVED LEMON

You can also use stewing or braising beef for this tagine, if you prefer.

675g/1½ lb leg of lamb, trimmed and
cut into cubes
2 onions, very finely chopped
2 garlic cloves, crushed
60ml/4 tbsp chopped fresh parsley
60ml/4 tbsp chopped fresh coriander
a good pinch of ground ginger
5ml/1 tsp ground cumin
90ml/6 tbsp olive oil
350–400ml/12–14fl oz/1½–1⅔ cups
water or stock
1 preserved lemon
400g/14oz can artichoke hearts,
drained and halved
15ml/1 tbsp chopped fresh mint
1 egg, beaten (optional)
salt and ground black pepper
couscous and mint, to serve

SERVES 4–6

2 Heat a large heavy-based saucepan and stir in the meat with all the marinade. Cook for 5–6 minutes until the meat is evenly brown, then stir in enough water or stock to just cover the meat. Bring to the boil, cover and simmer for 45–60 minutes until the meat is just tender.

3 Rinse the preserved lemon under cold water, discard the flesh and cut the peel into pieces. Stir into the meat and simmer for a further 15 minutes, then add the artichoke hearts and mint.

4 Simmer for a few minutes more to warm through. If you wish to thicken the sauce, remove the pan from the heat and stir in some or all of the beaten egg. Garnish with mint and serve with couscous.

1 Place the meat in a shallow dish. Stir together the onions, garlic, parsley, coriander, ginger, cumin, seasoning and olive oil. Stir into the meat, cover with clear film and set aside to marinate for at least 3 hours or preferably overnight.

BEEF ROLLS WITH GARLIC AND TOMATO SAUCE

Italy has many regional variations on the technique of wrapping thin slices of beef around a richly flavoured stuffing. This recipe incorporates some of the classic ingredients.

4 thin slices of rump steak, (about
115g/4oz each)
4 slices smoked ham
150g/5oz Pecorino cheese, grated
2 garlic cloves, crushed
75ml/5 tbsp chopped fresh parsley
2 eggs, soft-boiled and shelled
45ml/3 tbsp olive oil
1 large onion, finely chopped
150ml/¼ pint/⅔ cup passata
75ml/3fl oz/⅓ cup red wine
2 bay leaves
150ml/¼ pint/⅔ cup beef stock
salt and ground black pepper
flat leaf parsley, to garnish

SERVES 4

1 Preheat the oven to 160°C/
325°F/Gas 3. Lay the beef slices
on a sheet of greaseproof paper.
Cover the beef with another sheet of
greaseproof paper or clear film and
beat with a mallet or rolling pin until
very thin.

2 Lay a ham slice over each. Mix
the cheese in a bowl with the
garlic, parsley, eggs and a little salt
and pepper. Stir well until all the
ingredients are evenly mixed.

3 Spoon the stuffing on to the
ham and beef slices. Fold two
opposite sides of the meat over the
stuffing, then roll up the meat to form
neat parcels. Secure with string.

4 Heat the oil in a frying pan.
Add the parcels and fry quickly
on all sides to brown. Transfer to an
ovenproof dish.

5 Add the onion to the frying pan
and fry for 3 minutes. Stir in the
passata, wine, bay leaves and stock
and season with salt and pepper.
Bring to the boil, then pour the sauce
over the meat in the dish.

6 Cover the dish and bake in the
oven for 1 hour. Drain the meat
and remove the string. Spoon on to
warmed serving plates. Taste the sauce,
adding extra salt and pepper if
necessary, and spoon it over the meat.
Serve garnished with flat leaf parsley.

CORSICAN BEEF STEW WITH MACARONI

Pasta is eaten in many parts of the Mediterranean. In Corsica, it is often served with gravy as a sauce and, in this case, in a rich beef stew.

25g/1oz dried mushrooms
(ceps or porcini)
6 garlic cloves
900g/2lb stewing beef, cut into
5cm/2in cubes
115g/4oz lardons, or thick streaky
bacon cut into strips
45ml/3 tbsp olive oil
2 onions, sliced
300ml/½ pint/1¼ cups dry white wine
30ml/2 tbsp passata
pinch of ground cinnamon
sprig of rosemary
1 bay leaf
225g/8oz/2 cups large macaroni
50g/2oz/⅔ cup freshly grated
Parmesan cheese
salt and ground black pepper

SERVES 4

1 Soak the dried mushrooms in warm water for 30 minutes. Drain, set the mushrooms aside and reserve the liquid. Cut three of the garlic cloves into thin strips and insert into the pieces of beef by making little slits with a sharp knife. Push the lardons or pieces of bacon into the beef with the garlic. Season the meat with salt and pepper.

3 Stir in the white wine, passata, mushrooms, cinnamon, rosemary and bay leaf and season with salt and pepper. Cook gently for 30 minutes, stirring often. Strain the mushroom liquid and add to the stew with enough water to cover. Bring to the boil, cover and simmer very gently for 3 hours, until the meat is very tender.

2 Heat the oil in a heavy-based pan, add half the beef and brown well on all sides. Repeat with the remaining beef. Transfer to a plate. Add the sliced onions to the pan and cook until lightly browned. Crush the remaining garlic and add to the onions with the meat.

4 Cook the macaroni in a large pan of boiling, salted water for 10 minutes, or until *al dente*. Lift the pieces of meat out of the gravy and transfer to a warmed serving platter. Drain the pasta and layer in a serving bowl with the gravy and cheese. Serve with the meat.

PROVENCAL BEEF AND OLIVE DAUBE

A daube is a French method of braising meat with wine and herbs. This version from the Nice area in the south of France also includes black olives and tomatoes.

1.5kg/3–3½lb topside beef
225g/8oz lardons, or thick streaky
bacon cut into strips
225g/8oz carrots, sliced
1 bay leaf
1 thyme sprig
2 parsley stalks
3 garlic cloves
225g/8oz/2 cups pitted
black olives
400g/14oz can chopped tomatoes
crusty bread, flageolet beans or pasta,
to serve

FOR THE MARINADE
120ml/4fl oz/½ cup extra virgin
olive oil
1 onion, sliced
4 shallots, sliced
1 celery stick, sliced
1 carrot, sliced
150ml/¼ pint/⅔ cup red wine
6 peppercorns
2 garlic cloves, sliced
1 bay leaf
1 thyme sprig
2 parsley stalks
salt

SERVES 6

1 To make the marinade, heat the oil in a large shallow pan, add the onion, shallots, celery and carrot. Cook for 2 minutes, then lower the heat and add the red wine, peppercorns, garlic, bay leaf, thyme and parsley stalks. Season with salt, then cover and leave to simmer gently for 15–20 minutes. Set aside.

2 Place the beef in a large glass or earthenware dish and pour over the cooled marinade. Cover the dish and leave to marinate in a cool place or in the fridge for 12 hours, turning the meat once or twice.

3 Preheat the oven to 160°C/325°F/Gas 3. Lift the meat out of the marinade and fit snugly into an ovenproof casserole. Add the lardons or bacon and carrots, along with the herbs and garlic. Strain in all the marinade. Cover the casserole with greaseproof paper, then the lid and cook in the oven for 2½ hours.

4 Remove the casserole from the oven and stir in the olives and tomatoes. Re-cover the casserole, return to the oven and cook for a further 30 minutes. Serve the meat cut into thick slices, accompanied by crusty bread, beans or pasta.

BEEF STEW WITH TOMATOES, WINE AND PEAS

*There are as many versions of this Italian recipe as there are cooks. This one is very traditional,
perfect for a winter lunch or dinner. Serve it with boiled or mashed potatoes
to soak up the deliciously rich sauce.*

30ml/2 tbsp plain flour
10ml/2 tsp chopped fresh thyme or
5ml/1 tsp dried thyme
1kg/2¼ lb braising or stewing steak,
cut into large cubes
45ml/3 tbsp olive oil
1 medium onion, roughly chopped
450g/1lb jar passata
250ml/8fl oz/1 cup beef stock
250ml/8fl oz/1 cup red wine
2 garlic cloves, crushed
30ml/2 tbsp tomato purée
275g/10oz/2 cups shelled fresh peas
5ml/1 tsp sugar
salt and ground black pepper
sprigs of fresh thyme, to garnish

SERVES 4

3   Add the onion to the pan,
scraping the base of the pan to
mix in any sediment. Cook gently for
about 3 minutes, until softened, then
add in the passata, stock, wine, garlic
and tomato purée. Bring to the boil,
stirring. Return the beef to the pan
and coat with the sauce. Cover and
cook in the oven for 1½ hours.

1   Preheat the oven to 160°C/
325°F/Gas 3. Put the plain flour
in a shallow dish and season with the
thyme and salt and pepper. Add the
beef cubes and turn them in the
mixture to coat evenly.

2   Heat the olive oil in a large
flameproof casserole, add the
beef and brown on all sides over a
medium to high heat. Remove with a
slotted spoon and drain on kitchen
paper. It may be necessary to cook
the beef in batches.

4   Stir in the peas and sugar.
Return the casserole to the oven
and cook for 30 minutes more, or
until the beef is tender. Check the
seasoning and garnish with fresh
thyme before serving.

CALF'S LIVER WITH BALSAMIC VINEGAR

This sweet and sour liver dish is a speciality of Venice. Serve it very simply, with a side vegetable such as lightly cooked green beans.

15ml/1 tbsp plain flour
2.5ml/½ tsp finely chopped fresh sage
4 thin slices of calf's liver, cut into serving pieces
45ml/3 tbsp olive oil
25g/1oz/2 tbsp butter
2 small red onions, sliced and separated into rings
150ml/¼ pint/²⁄₃ cup dry white wine
45ml/3 tbsp balsamic vinegar
a pinch of granulated sugar
salt and ground black pepper
fresh sage sprigs, to garnish

SERVES 2

1 Spread out the flour in a shallow bowl. Season it with the sage and plenty of salt and pepper. Turn the liver in the flour until well coated.

2 Heat 30ml/2 tbsp of the oil with half of the butter in a wide heavy-based saucepan or frying pan until foaming.

3 Add the onion rings and cook gently, stirring frequently, for about 5 minutes until softened but not coloured. Remove the onion rings with a fish slice and set them aside on a plate.

4 Heat the remaining oil and butter in the pan until foaming, add the liver and cook over a medium heat for 2–3 minutes on each side. Never overcook calf's liver because it can soon become tough; it is most tender when served slightly pink. Transfer to warmed dinner plates and keep hot.

5 Add the wine and vinegar to the pan, then stir to mix with the pan juices and any sediment. Return the onions and add the sugar, and heat through, stirring. Spoon the sauce over the liver, garnish with sage and serve at once.

CALF'S LIVER WITH HONEY

Liver is prepared in many ways all over the Mediterranean — this is a quick and easy, slightly contemporary treatment from France. Cook the liver until it is browned on the outside but still rosy pink in the centre.

4 slices calf's liver, each about 175g/
6oz and 1.5cm/½in thick
plain flour, for dusting
25g/1oz/2 tbsp butter
30ml/2 tbsp vegetable oil
30ml/2 tbsp sherry vinegar or red
wine vinegar
30–45ml/2–3 tbsp chicken stock
15ml/1 tbsp clear honey
salt and ground black pepper
watercress sprigs, to garnish

SERVES 4

1 Wipe the liver slices with damp kitchen paper, then season both sides with a little salt and pepper, and dust the slices lightly with flour, shaking off any excess. Place the floured slices on a board.

2 In a large heavy frying pan, melt half of the butter with the oil over a high heat and swirl the pan to mix them together.

3 Add the liver slices to the pan and cook for 1–2 minutes until browned on one side, then turn and cook for a further 1 minute. Transfer to heated plates and keep warm.

4 Stir the vinegar, stock and honey into the pan and boil for about 1 minute, stirring constantly, then add the remaining butter, stirring until melted and smooth. Spoon the liquid over the liver slices, garnish with watercress and serve.

COOK'S TIP
Use a mild-flavoured honey, such as acacia, for the sauce.

POLPETTINI WITH FONTINA

*In this Italian dish, meatballs are filled with Fontina cubes, then rolled in crumbs and fried.
They are delicious served with noodles and a rich tomato sauce.*

500g/1¼lb lean minced beef
500g/1¼lb lean minced pork
3 garlic cloves, crushed
grated rind and juice of 1 lemon
2 slices of day-old bread, crumbed
40g/1½ oz/½ cup freshly grated
Parmesan cheese
2.5ml/½ tsp ground cinnamon
5ml/1 tsp dried oregano
2 eggs, beaten
5ml/1 tsp salt
150g/5oz Fontina cheese, cut into
16 cubes
115–150g/4–5oz/1–1¼ cups
dried breadcrumbs
olive oil, for shallow frying
ground black pepper
fresh herbs and freshly grated
Parmesan cheese, to garnish

SERVES 6–8

1 Preheat the oven to 180°C/ 350°F/Gas 4. Put the lean minced beef and pork into a bowl. Add the garlic, lemon rind and juice, breadcrumbs, Parmesan, cinnamon and oregano and stir. Beat in the eggs, salt and plenty of pepper.

2 Using clean hands occasionally dipped into cold water, knead the mixture to ensure that all the ingredients are well distributed, then shape it into 16 balls. Cup each ball in turn in your hand and press a piece of Fontina into the centre. Reshape each ball, making sure the cheese is well covered.

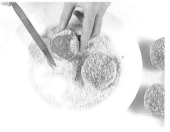

3 Roll the meatballs in the dried breadcrumbs. Heat the olive oil in a large frying pan. Add the meatballs in batches and cook them quickly all over, until lightly browned and sealed. Transfer them to a roasting tin and bake for 20 minutes or until cooked through. Garnish with fresh herbs and Parmesan, and serve.

POLPETTES WITH MOZZARELLA AND TOMATO

These Italian meatballs are made with beef and topped with mozzarella cheese and tomato.

½ slice white bread, crusts removed
45ml/3 tbsp milk
675g/1½lb minced beef
1 egg, beaten
50g/2oz/⅔ cup dry breadcrumbs
vegetable oil for frying
2 beefsteak or other large
tomatoes, sliced
15ml/1 tbsp chopped fresh oregano
1 mozzarella cheese, cut into 6 slices
6 drained canned anchovies, cut in
half lengthways
salt and ground black pepper

SERVES 6

 Preheat the oven to 200°C/
400°F/Gas 6. Put the bread and milk into a small saucepan and heat very gently, until the bread absorbs all the milk. Mash it to a pulp and leave to cool.

2 Put the beef into a bowl with the bread mixture and the egg and season with salt and pepper. Mix well, then shape the mixture into six patties. Sprinkle the breadcrumbs on to a plate and dredge the patties, coating them thoroughly.

3 Heat about 5mm/¼in oil in a large frying pan. Add the patties and fry for 2 minutes on each side, until brown. Transfer to a greased ovenproof dish, in a single layer.

 Lay a slice of tomato on top of each patty, sprinkle with oregano and season with salt and pepper. Place the mozzarella slices on top. Arrange two strips of anchovy, placed in a cross on top of each slice of mozzarella.

5 Bake for 10–15 minutes, until the mozzarella has melted. Serve hot, straight from the dish.

PEPPERS STUFFED WITH MINCED BEEF

This lunch or buffet dish makes a pleasant change from vegetables stuffed with rice or wheat.

2 Sauté the minced beef in a non-stick frying pan until it is no longer red. Transfer to a plate. Pour half of the oil into the frying pan and sauté the onion and celery over a high heat until the onion starts to brown. Trim the mushrooms and add to the pan. Then stir in the partly-cooked beef. Season with the cinnamon, salt and pepper. Cook over a low heat for about 30 minutes.

1 onion
2 celery sticks
4 red peppers
450g/1lb minced lean beef
60ml/4 tbsp olive oil
50g/2oz button mushrooms
pinch of ground cinnamon
salt and ground black pepper
chervil or flat leaf parsley, to garnish
green salad, to serve

SERVES 4

1 Dice the onion and celery. Cut the tops off the peppers and remove the seeds and membranes.

3 Preheat the oven to 190°C/375°F/Gas 5. Cut a sliver off the base of each pepper to make sure that they stand level, spoon in the beef and vegetable mixture and then replace the lids. Arrange in an oiled baking dish, drizzle the remaining oil on top, and bake for 30 minutes. Garnish with a herb, then serve with a green salad.

TANGY BEEF AND HERB KHORESH

Lamb, beef or poultry stews with herbs, spices and vegetables or fruit are all called khoresh and are among the best-loved Persian dishes. Like this beef stew, Khoreshe Gormeh Sabzi, they are mildly spiced and are ideal to serve as a simple but delicious dish for a dinner party.

45ml/3 tbsp oil
1 large onion, chopped
450g/1lb lean stewing beef, cubed
15ml/1 tbsp fenugreek leaf
10ml/2 tsp ground turmeric
2.5ml/½ tsp ground cinnamon
600ml/1 pint/2½ cups water
25g/1oz fresh parsley, chopped
25g/1oz fresh chives, snipped
425g/15oz can red kidney beans
juice of 1 lemon
salt and ground black pepper

SERVES 4

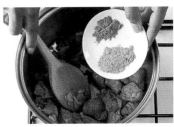

[1] Heat 30ml/2 tbsp of the oil in a large saucepan or flameproof casserole and fry the onion for about 3–4 minutes until light golden. Add the beef and fry for 5–10 minutes more, until brown, stirring so that the meat is coloured on all sides.

[2] Add the fenugreek, turmeric and cinnamon and cook for about 1 minute, stirring, then add the water and bring to the boil. Cover and simmer over a low heat for 45 minutes, stirring occasionally with a wooden spoon.

[3] Heat the remaining oil in a small frying pan and fry the parsley and chives over a moderate heat for 2–3 minutes, stirring the mixture frequently.

[4] Drain the kidney beans and stir them into the beef with the fried herbs and lemon juice. Season with salt and pepper.

[5] Simmer the stew for a further 30–35 minutes, until the meat is tender. Serve with rice.

BEEF TAGINE WITH SWEET POTATOES

This warming dish is eaten during the winter in Morocco, where, especially in the mountains, the weather can be surprisingly cold. Tagines, by definition, are cooked on the hob (or, more often in Morocco, over coals). However, this also works well cooked in the oven.

675–900g/1½–2lb braising or
stewing beef
30ml/2 tbsp sunflower oil
a good pinch of ground turmeric
1 large onion, chopped
1 red or green chilli, seeded
and chopped
7.5ml/1½ tsp paprika
a good pinch of cayenne pepper
2.5ml/½ tsp ground cumin
450g/1lb sweet potatoes
15ml/1 tbsp chopped fresh parsley
15ml/1 tbsp chopped fresh coriander
15g/½ oz/1 tbsp butter
salt and ground black pepper

SERVES 4

3 Add the onion, chilli, paprika, cayenne pepper and cumin to the casserole, with just enough water to cover the meat. Cover tightly and cook in the oven for 1–1½ hours until the meat is very tender, checking occasionally and adding a little extra water to keep the stew moist.

4 Meanwhile, peel the sweet potatoes and slice them straight into a bowl of salted water. Transfer to a pan, bring to the boil and simmer for 3 minutes until just tender. Drain.

5 Stir the herbs into the meat. Arrange the potato slices over the meat and dot with the butter. Cover. Bake for 10 minutes more.

6 Increase the oven temperature to 200°C/400°F/Gas 6 or heat the grill. Remove the lid of the casserole and cook in the oven or under the grill for a further 5–10 minutes until the potatoes are golden.

1 Cube the beef. Heat the oil in a flameproof casserole and fry the meat, with the turmeric and seasoning for 3–4 minutes until evenly brown, stirring frequently.

2 Cover the pan tightly and cook for 15 minutes over a fairly gentle heat, without lifting the lid. Preheat the oven to 180°C/350°F/Gas 4.

PORK WITH MARSALA AND JUNIPER

Although most frequently used in desserts, Sicilian marsala gives savoury dishes a rich, fruity and alcoholic tang. Use good quality butcher's pork which won't be drowned by the flavour of the sauce.

25g/1oz dried cep or
porcini mushrooms
4 pork escalopes
10ml/2 tsp balsamic vinegar
8 garlic cloves
15g/½oz/1 tbsp butter
45ml/3 tbsp marsala
several rosemary sprigs
10 juniper berries, crushed
salt and ground black pepper
noodles and green vegetables,
to serve

SERVES 4

1. Put the dried mushrooms in a bowl and just cover with hot water. Leave to stand.

2. Brush the pork with 5ml/1 tsp of the vinegar and season with salt and pepper. Put the garlic cloves in a small pan of boiling water and cook for 10 minutes until soft. Drain and set aside.

3. Melt the butter in a large frying pan. Add the pork and fry quickly until browned on the underside. Turn the meat over and cook for another minute.

4. Add the marsala, rosemary, mushrooms, 60ml/4 tbsp of the mushroom juices, the garlic cloves, juniper and remaining vinegar.

5. Simmer gently for about 3 minutes until the pork is cooked through. Season lightly with salt and ground black pepper and serve hot with noodles and green vegetables.

CASSOULET

Cassoulet is a classic French dish in which a feast of various meats is baked slowly with beans under a golden crumb crust. It is hearty and rich, perfect for a winter gathering.

675g/1½lb/3½ cups dried
haricot beans
900g/2lb salt belly pork
4 large duck breasts
60ml/4 tbsp olive oil
2 onions, chopped
6 garlic cloves, crushed
2 bay leaves
1.5ml/¼ tsp ground cloves
60ml/4 tbsp tomato purée
8 good-quality sausages
4 tomatoes
75g/3oz/1½ cups stale breadcrumbs
salt and ground black pepper

SERVES 6–8

1. Put the beans in a large bowl and cover with plenty of cold water. Leave to soak overnight. If using salted belly pork, soak it overnight in water.

2. Drain the beans thoroughly and put them in a large saucepan with fresh water to cover. Bring to the boil and boil rapidly for 10 minutes. Drain and set the beans aside.

3. Cut the pork into large pieces, discarding the rind. Halve the duck breasts.

4. Heat 30ml/2 tbsp of the oil in a frying pan and fry the pork in batches, until browned.

5. Put the beans in a large, heavy-based saucepan with the onions, garlic, bay leaves, ground cloves and tomato purée. Stir in the browned pork and just cover with water. Bring to the boil, then reduce the heat to the lowest setting and simmer, covered, for about 1½ hours until the beans are tender.

6. Preheat the oven to 180°C/ 350°F/Gas 4. Heat the rest of the oil in a frying pan and fry the duck breasts and sausages until browned. Cut the sausages into smaller pieces.

7. Plunge the tomatoes into boiling water for 30 seconds, then refresh in cold water. Peel away the skins and cut them into quarters.

8. Transfer the bean mixture to a large earthenware pot or ovenproof dish and stir in the fried sausages and duck breasts and chopped tomatoes with salt and pepper to taste.

9. Sprinkle with an even layer of breadcrumbs and bake in the oven for 45 minutes to 1 hour until the crust is golden. Serve hot.

VARIATION
You can easily alter the proportions and types of meat and vegetables in a cassoulet. Turnips, carrots and celeriac make suitable vegetable substitutes while cubed lamb and goose can replace the pork and duck.

SPANISH PORK AND SAUSAGE CASSEROLE

Another pork dish from the Catalan region of Spain, which uses the spicy butifarra sausage. You can find these sausages in some Spanish delicatessens but, if not, sweet Italian sausages will do.

30ml/2 tbsp olive oil
4 boneless pork chops, about 175g/6oz
4 butifarra or sweet Italian sausages
1 onion, chopped
2 garlic cloves, chopped
120ml/4fl oz/½ cup dry white wine
4 plum tomatoes, chopped
1 bay leaf
30ml/2 tbsp chopped fresh parsley
salt and ground black pepper
green salad and baked potatoes,
to serve

SERVES 4

1 Heat the oil in a large deep frying pan. Cook the pork chops over a high heat until browned on both sides, then transfer to a plate.

2 Add the sausages, onion and garlic to the pan and cook over a moderate heat until the sausages are browned and the onion softened, turning the sausages two or three times during cooking. Return the chops to the pan.

3 Stir in the wine, tomatoes and bay leaf, and season with salt and pepper. Add the parsley. Cover the pan and cook for 30 minutes.

4 Remove the sausages from the pan and cut into thick slices. Return them to the pan and heat through. Serve hot, accompanied by a green salad and baked potatoes.

COOK'S TIP
Vine tomatoes, which are making a welcome appearance in our supermarkets, can be used instead of plum tomatoes.

BLACK BEAN STEW

This simple Spanish stew uses a few robust ingredients to create a deliciously intense flavour, rather like a French cassoulet.

🌾 🌾

275g/10oz/1⅓ cups black beans
675g/1½lb boneless belly pork rashers
60ml/4 tbsp olive oil
350g/12oz baby onions
2 celery sticks, thickly sliced
10ml/2 tsp paprika
150g/5oz chorizo sausage, cut
into chunks
600ml/1 pint/2½ cups light chicken or
vegetable stock
2 green peppers, seeded and cut into
large pieces
salt and ground black pepper

SERVES 5–6

🌾 🌾

1. Put the beans in a bowl and cover with plenty of cold water. Leave to soak overnight. Drain the beans into a saucepan and cover with fresh water. Bring to the boil and boil rapidly for 10 minutes. Drain.

2. Preheat the oven to 160°C/325°F/Gas 3. Cut away any rind from the pork and cut the meat into large chunks.

3. Heat the oil in a large frying pan and fry the onions and celery for 3 minutes. Add the pork and fry for 5–10 minutes until the pork is browned.

4. Add the paprika and chorizo and fry for a further 2 minutes. Transfer to an ovenproof dish with the beans and mix together.

5. Add the stock to the pan and bring to the boil. Season lightly, then pour over the meat and beans. Cover and bake for 1 hour.

6. Stir the green peppers into the stew and return to the oven for a further 15 minutes. Serve hot.

🌾 🌾

COOK'S TIP
This is the sort of stew to which you can add a variety of winter vegetables such as chunks of leek, turnip, celeriac and even little potatoes.

🌾 🌾

AFELIA

This lightly-spiced pork stew makes a really delicious supper dish served simply, as it would be in Cyprus, with warmed bread, a leafy salad and a few olives.

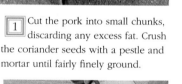

675g/1½lb pork fillet, boneless leg or
chump steaks
20ml/4 tsp coriander seeds
2.5ml/½ tsp caster sugar
45ml/3 tbsp olive oil
2 large onions, sliced
300ml/½ pint/1¼ cups red wine
salt and ground black pepper
fresh coriander, to garnish

SERVES 4

COOK'S TIP
A coffee grinder can also be used
to grind the coriander seeds.
Alternatively, use 15ml/1 tbsp
ground coriander.

1 Cut the pork into small chunks,
discarding any excess fat. Crush
the coriander seeds with a pestle and
mortar until fairly finely ground.

2 Mix the coriander seeds with
the sugar and salt and pepper
and rub all over the meat. Leave to
marinate for up to 4 hours.

 Preheat the oven to 160°C/
325°F/Gas 3. Heat 30ml/2 tbsp
of the oil in a frying pan over a high
heat. Brown the meat quickly, then
transfer to an ovenproof dish.

4 Add the remaining oil to the
pan and fry the onions until
beginning to colour. Stir in the wine
and a little salt and pepper and bring
just to the boil.

5 Pour the onion and wine
mixture over the meat and
cover with a lid. Bake for 1 hour, or
until the meat is very tender. Serve
scattered with fresh coriander.

ROAST LOIN OF PORK STUFFED WITH FIGS, OLIVES AND ALMONDS

Pork is a popular meat in Spain, and this recipe using fruit and nuts in the stuffing is of Catalan influence, where the combination of meat and fruit is quite common.

2. Remove any string from the pork and unroll the belly flap, cutting away any excess fat or meat, to enable you to do so. Spread half the stuffing over the flat piece and roll up, starting from the thick side. Tie at intervals with string.

3. Pour the remaining oil into a small roasting tin and put in the pork. Roast for 1 hour 15 minutes. Form the remaining stuffing mixture into balls and add to the roasting tin around the meat, 15–20 minutes before the end of cooking time.

60ml/4 tbsp olive oil
1 onion, finely chopped
2 garlic cloves, chopped
75g/3oz/1½ cups fresh breadcrumbs
4 ready-to-eat dried figs, chopped
8 pitted green olives, chopped
25g/1oz/¼ cup flaked almonds
15ml/1 tbsp lemon juice
15ml/1 tbsp chopped fresh parsley
1 egg yolk
900g/2lb boned loin of pork
salt and ground black pepper

SERVES 4

1. Preheat the oven to 200°C/400°F/Gas 6. Heat 45ml/3 tbsp of the oil in a pan, add the onion and garlic, and cook gently until softened. Remove the pan from the heat and stir in the breadcrumbs, figs, olives, almonds, lemon juice, parsley and egg yolk. Season to taste.

COOK'S TIP
Keep a tub of breadcrumbs in the freezer. They can be used frozen.

4. Remove the pork from the oven and let it rest for 10 minutes. Carve into thick slices and serve with the stuffing balls and any juices from the tin. This is also good served cold.

POULTRY
AND GAME

Poultry and game play key roles in the cuisines of
all Mediterranean countries and the addition of
fruit creates sensational flavour combinations.

Poultry and game have always played important roles in Mediterranean cooking. This is largely due to the dry, rugged and, in some places, mountainous land which does not provide good pasture for cattle. Chickens and ducks are more accessible as they can be kept on a small, garden-sized plot.

Chicken is without doubt the most popular poultry, used creatively in a wide range of dishes. In spite of their scraggy appearance, the hand-reared, traditionally corn-fed birds, are full of flavour, with meat that also has a firm texture. The cooking methods are varied and interesting, but they have many similarities. In both the east

and west Mediterranean, cooks have long acknowledged the fact that savoury dishes are complemented by the tang of fresh, dried or preserved fruits, the rich earthiness of nuts and the lively warmth of spices.

In the Middle East, where chickens were kept mainly for their eggs, only older birds graduated to the cooking pot. They required long, slow stewing with richly seasoned stuffings and sauces enhance the dishes. These recipes are ideal for improving the mild young

BELOW: Verdant farmland rimmed by craggy mountains in southern Spain.

RIGHT: *Lord of all he surveys, this Greek cockerel patrols his perimeter wall.*

BELOW: *Lemons are a favourite flavouring for chicken dishes, notably in Chicken with Lemons and Olives.*

supermarket chickens, even if the cooking time is shorter. Preserved lemons are superb with chicken: tucked in or around a whole bird, during long, slow cooking they impart a fresh aromatic flavour but without the acidity of fresh citrus. Sweet fresh pomegranates are an entirely different but equally popular flavouring for chicken. The jewel-like segments are crushed to release their juice or made into an unusual preserve with lemon, sugar and a few seasonings.

Spain has numerous excellent chicken and rabbit recipes, and duck and goose also feature prominently, particularly cooked with pears, apples or figs to counteract the richness of these fatty poultry. Even a plain roast is served with a delicious raisin, pine nut and sherry sauce or spicy chorizo sausage is used to pep up many simple casseroles,

Mediterranean cooking is also known for small game birds: pigeon, partridge and quail migrate across the sea and huntsmen take full advantage of their seasonal availability and regular routes. Italian cooks prepare many types of small birds, including delicious pigeon dishes, often with rich sauces and accompanied by crisply grilled or creamy polenta.

OLIVE OIL ROASTED CHICKEN WITH MEDITERRANEAN VEGETABLES

This is a delicious French alternative to a traditional roast chicken. Use a corn-fed or free-range bird, if available. This recipe also works well with guinea fowl.

1.75kg/4–4½lb roasting chicken
150ml/¼ pint/⅔ cup extra virgin
olive oil
½ lemon
few sprigs of fresh thyme
450g/1lb small new potatoes
1 aubergine, cut into 2.5cm/1in cubes
1 red pepper, seeded and quartered
1 fennel bulb, trimmed and quartered
8 large garlic cloves, unpeeled
coarse salt and ground black pepper

SERVES 4

2 Remove the chicken from the oven and season with salt. Turn the chicken right side up, and baste with the juices from the pan. Surround the bird with the potatoes, roll them in the pan juices, and return the roasting pan to the oven, to continue roasting.

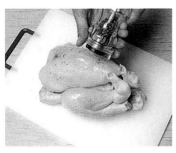

1 Preheat the oven to 200°C/ 400°F/Gas 6. Rub the chicken all over with olive oil and season with pepper. Place the lemon half inside the bird, with a sprig or two of thyme. Put the chicken breast side down in a large roasting pan. Roast for about 30 minutes.

3 After 30 minutes, add the aubergine, red pepper, fennel and garlic cloves to the pan. Drizzle with the remaining oil, and season with salt and pepper. Add any remaining thyme to the vegetables. Return to the oven, and cook for 30–50 minutes more, basting and turning the vegetables occasionally.

4 To find out if the chicken is cooked, push the tip of a sharp knife between the thigh and breast. If the juices run clear, it is done. The vegetables should be tender and just beginning to brown. Serve the chicken and vegetables from the pan, or transfer the vegetables to a serving dish, joint the chicken and place it on top. Serve the skimmed juices in a gravy boat.

ROAST CHICKEN WITH ALMONDS

Despite the wide availability of alternatives, roast chicken remains a top family favourite around the Mediterranean. It is delectable with a fruity almond stuffing.

1.5kg/3–3½ lb chicken
pinch of ground ginger
pinch of ground cinnamon
pinch of saffron, dissolved in 30ml/
2 tbsp boiling water
2 onions, chopped
300ml/½ pint/1¼ cups chicken stock
45ml/3 tbsp flaked almonds
15ml/1 tbsp plain flour
salt and ground black pepper
lemon wedges and coriander,
to garnish

FOR THE STUFFING
50g/2oz/⅓ cup couscous
120ml/4fl oz/½ cup chicken stock
20g/¾ oz/1½ tbsp butter
1 shallot, finely chopped
½ small cooking apple
25ml/1½ tbsp flaked almonds
30ml/2 tbsp ground almonds
30ml/2 tbsp chopped fresh coriander
a good pinch of paprika
pinch of cayenne pepper

SERVES 4

1 Preheat the oven to 180°C/
350°F/Gas 4. First prepare the almond stuffing. Place the couscous in a bowl, bring the chicken stock to the boil and pour it over the couscous. Stir with a fork and then set aside for 10 minutes for the couscous to swell. Meanwhile, melt the butter in a small frying pan and fry the shallot for 2–3 minutes until soft.

2 Fluff up the couscous and stir in the shallot and all the butter from the pan. Peel, core and chop the apple and add to the couscous with the remaining stuffing ingredients. Season and stir well.

3 Loosely push the couscous mixture into the neck end of the chicken. Truss the chicken.

4 Mix the ginger and cinnamon with the saffron water. Rub the chicken with salt and pepper, and then pour over the spiced water.

5 Place the chicken in a small roasting tin or dish so that it fits snugly. Spoon the chopped onions and stock around the chicken. Cover the dish with a foil tent.

6 Cook for 1¼ hours and then increase the oven temperature to 200°C/400°F/Gas 6. Transfer the chicken to a plate and strain the cooking liquid into a jug, reserving the onions. Return the chicken to the roasting tin with the onions, baste with a little of the cooking liquid and scatter the flaked almonds over the top. Return to the oven and cook for about 30 minutes, until the chicken is golden brown and cooked through.

7 Remove and discard the fat from the reserved cooking liquid, and pour into a small saucepan. Mix the flour with 30ml/2 tbsp cold water, stir into the pan of cooking liquid and heat gently, stirring, to make a smooth sauce. Garnish the chicken and serve with the sauce.

CHICKEN WITH LEMONS AND OLIVES

Preserved lemons and limes are frequently used in Mediterranean cookery, particularly in North Africa where their gentle flavour enhances all kinds of meat and fish dishes.

2.5ml/½ tsp ground cinnamon
2.5ml/½ tsp ground turmeric
1.5kg/3–3½lb chicken
30ml/2 tbsp olive oil
1 large onion, thinly sliced
5cm/2in piece fresh root
ginger, grated
600ml/1 pint/2½ cups chicken stock
2 preserved lemons or limes, or fresh
ones, cut into wedges
75g/3oz/½ cup pitted brown olives
15ml/1 tbsp clear honey
60ml/4 tbsp chopped fresh coriander
salt and ground black pepper

coriander sprigs, to garnish

SERVES 4

1. Preheat the oven to 190°C/ 375°F/Gas 5. Mix the ground cinnamon and turmeric in a bowl with a little salt and pepper and rub all over the chicken skin to give an even coating.

2. Heat the oil in a large sauté or shallow frying pan and fry the chicken on all sides until it turns golden. Transfer the chicken to an ovenproof dish.

3. Add the sliced onion to the pan and fry for 3 minutes. Stir in the grated ginger and the chicken stock and bring just to the boil. Pour over the chicken, cover with a lid and bake in the oven for 30 minutes.

4. Remove the chicken from the oven and add the lemons or limes, brown olives and honey. Bake, uncovered, for a further 45 minutes until the chicken is tender.

5. Stir in the coriander and season to taste. Garnish with coriander sprigs and serve at once.

CHICKEN IN A SALT CRUST

*Cooking food in a casing of salt gives a deliciously moist, tender flavour that, surprisingly, is not too
salty. The technique is used in both Italy and France for chicken and whole fish,
although chicken is easier to deal with.*

1.75kg/4–4½lb chicken
about 2.25kg/5lb coarse sea salt

FOR THE GARLIC PUREE
450g/1lb onions, quartered
2 large heads of garlic
120ml/4fl oz/½ cup olive oil
salt and ground black pepper

FOR THE ROASTED TOMATOES
AND PEPPERS
450g/1lb plum tomatoes
3 red peppers, seeded and quartered
1 red chilli, seeded and finely chopped
90ml/6 tbsp olive oil
flat leaf parsley, to garnish

SERVES 6

[1] Preheat the oven to 220°C/
425°F/Gas 7. Choose a deep
ovenproof dish into which the whole
chicken will fit snugly. Line the dish
with a double thickness of heavy foil,
allowing plenty of excess foil to
overhang the top edge of the
ovenproof dish.

[2] Truss the chicken tightly so that
the salt cannot fall into the
cavity. Sprinkle a thin layer of salt in
the foil-lined dish then place the
chicken on top.

[3] Pour the remaining salt all
around and over the top of the
chicken until it is completely encased.
Sprinkle the top with a little water.

[4] Cover tightly with the foil and
bake the chicken on the lower
oven shelf for 1¾ hours. Meanwhile,
put the onions in a small heavy-based
saucepan. Break up the heads of
garlic, but leave the skins on. Add to
the pan with the olive oil and a little
salt and pepper.

[5] Cover and cook over the lowest
possible heat for about 1 hour
or until the garlic is completely soft.

This recipe makes a really stunning
main course when you want to serve
something a little different. Take the
salt-crusted chicken to the table
garnished with plenty of fresh mixed
herbs. Once you've scraped away the
salt, transfer the chicken to a clean
plate to carve it.

[6] Plunge the tomatoes into
boiling water for 30 seconds,
then refresh in cold water. Peel away
the skins and quarter. Put the red
peppers, tomatoes and chilli in a
shallow ovenproof dish and sprinkle
with the oil. Bake on the shelf above
the chicken for 45 minutes or until
the peppers are slightly charred.

[7] Squeeze the garlic out of the
skins. Process the onions, garlic
and pan juices in a blender or food
processor until smooth. Return the
purée to the clean saucepan.

[8] To serve the chicken, open out
the foil and ease it out of the
dish. Place on a large serving platter.
Transfer the roasted pepper mixture
to a serving dish and garnish with
parsley. Reheat the garlic purée.
Crack open the salt crust on the
chicken and brush away the salt
before carving and serving with the
garlic purée and pepper mixture.

CHICKEN WITH RED WINE

The robust red wine and red pesto give this sauce a rich colour and an almost spicy flavour, while the grapes add a delicious suggestion of sweetness. Serve the stew with grilled polenta or warm crusty bread, and accompany with a piquant salad, such as rocket or watercress, tossed in a well-flavoured dressing.

45ml/3 tbsp olive oil
4 part-boned chicken breasts, skinned
1 medium red onion
30ml/2 tbsp red pesto
300ml/½ pint/1¼ cups red wine
300ml/½ pint/1¼ cups water
115g/4oz red grapes, halved
lengthways and seeded, if necessary
salt and ground black pepper
fresh basil leaves, to garnish

SERVES 4

VARIATIONS

Use green pesto instead of red, and substitute a dry white wine for the red, then finish with seedless green grapes. A few spoonfuls of mascarpone cheese can be added at the end, if liked, to enrich the sauce.

1 Heat 30ml/2 tbsp of the oil in a large frying pan, add the chicken breasts and sauté over a medium heat for about 5 minutes until they have changed colour on all sides. Remove with a slotted spoon and drain on kitchen paper.

2 Cut the onions in half, through the root. Trim off the root, then slice the onion halves lengthways to create thin wedges.

3 Heat the remaining oil in the pan, add the onion wedges and red pesto, and cook gently, stirring constantly, for about 3 minutes until the onion is softened, but not browned.

4 Add the red wine and water to the pan and bring to the boil, stirring all the time. Then return the sautéed chicken breasts to the pan and add salt and freshly ground black pepper to taste.

5 Reduce the heat, then cover the pan and simmer gently for about 20 minutes or until the chicken is tender, stirring occasionally to stop it sticking to the bottom of the pan.

6 Add the grapes to the pan and cook over a low to medium heat until heated through. Check the seasoning, then add more salt and pepper if necessary. Serve the chicken hot, garnished with fresh basil leaves.

CHICKEN WITH MORELS

Morels are among the best-flavoured dried mushrooms and, although they are expensive, a little goes a long way. You can, of course, use fresh mushrooms if you prefer.

40g/1½ oz dried morels
250ml/8fl oz/1 cup chicken stock
50g/2oz/4 tbsp butter
5 or 6 shallots, finely sliced
100g/3½oz button mushrooms,
finely sliced
2.5ml/½ tsp dried thyme
30–45ml/2–3 tbsp brandy
175ml/6fl oz/¾ cup double or
whipping cream
4 skinless boneless chicken breasts,
about 200g/7oz each
15ml/1 tbsp vegetable oil
175ml/6fl oz/¾ cup dry
sparkling wine
salt and ground black pepper

SERVES 4

1 Put the morels in a strainer and rinse well under cold running water, shaking to remove as much sand as possible. Place in a saucepan with the stock and bring to the boil over a medium-high heat. Remove the pan from the heat and leave to stand for 1 hour.

2 Remove the morels from the cooking liquid and strain the liquid through a fine sieve or muslin-lined strainer and reserve for the sauce. Reserve a few whole morels and slice the rest.

3 Melt half of the butter in a frying pan over a medium heat. Add the shallots and cook for 2 minutes until softened. Add the sliced morels and button mushrooms and cook, stirring frequently, for 2–3 minutes more. Season and add the thyme, brandy and 100ml/3½fl oz/7 tbsp of the cream. Reduce the heat and simmer gently for 10–12 minutes until any liquid has evaporated, stirring occasionally. Remove the morel mixture from the pan and set aside.

4 Pull off the fillets from the chicken breasts (the finger-shaped pieces on the underside) and reserve for another use. Make a pocket in each chicken breast by cutting a slit along the thicker edge with a sharp knife, taking care not to cut all the way through. Using a small spoon, fill each pocket with one-quarter of the mushroom mixture and then, if necessary, close with a cocktail stick.

5 Melt the remaining butter with the oil in a heavy frying pan over a medium-high heat and cook the chicken breasts on one side for 6–8 minutes until golden. Transfer the chicken breasts to a plate. Add the sparkling wine to the pan and boil to reduce by half. Add the strained morel cooking liquid and boil to reduce by half again.

6 Add the remaining cream and cook over a medium heat for 2–3 minutes until the sauce thickens just enough to coat the back of a spoon. Adjust the seasoning. Return the chicken to the pan with any accumulated juices and the reserved whole morels, and simmer for about 5 minutes over a medium heat until the chicken breasts are hot and the juices run clear when the meat is pierced with a knife. Serve at once.

CHICKEN WITH TOMATOES AND PRAWNS

This Piedmontese dish was created for Napoleon after the battle of Marengo.
Versions of it appear in both Italian and French recipe books.

················· 🌾 🌾 ·················

120ml/4fl oz/½ cup olive oil
8 chicken thighs on the bone, skinned
1 onion, finely chopped
1 celery stick, finely chopped
1 garlic clove, crushed
350g/12oz ripe Italian plum tomatoes,
 peeled and roughly chopped
250ml/8fl oz/1 cup dry white wine
2.5ml/½ tsp finely chopped
 fresh rosemary
175g/6oz large raw prawns
15g/½oz/1 tbsp butter
8 small triangles of thinly sliced white
 bread, without crusts
salt and ground black pepper
finely chopped flat leaf parsley,
 to garnish

SERVES 4

················· 🌾 🌾 ·················

1 Heat about 30ml/2 tbsp of the oil in a frying pan, add the chicken thighs and sauté over a medium heat for about 5 minutes until they have changed colour on all sides. Transfer the chicken to a flameproof casserole.

2 Add the onion and celery to the frying pan and cook gently, stirring frequently, for about 3 minutes until softened. Add the garlic, tomatoes, wine and rosemary to the pan. Season well with salt and pepper. Shell half the prawns, then add all the prawns to the tomato sauce and heat until they are cooked.

3 Pour the tomato sauce over the chicken. Cover and cook gently for 40 minutes or until the chicken is tender when pierced.

4 About 10 minutes before serving, add the remaining oil and the butter to the frying pan and heat until the mixture is hot but not smoking. Add the triangles of white bread and shallow-fry for about 2 minutes on each side, or until they are crisp and golden. Drain on kitchen paper. Season.

5 Dip one of the tips of each fried bread triangle in parsley to garnish. Serve the dish piping hot, decorated with the bread triangles.

MOROCCAN ROAST CHICKEN

In Morocco, a whole chicken is commonly cooked on a spit over hot charcoal. However, it is still excellent roasted in a hot oven and can be cooked whole, halved or in quarters.

1.75kg/4–4½lb chicken
2 small shallots
1 garlic clove
1 fresh parsley sprig
1 fresh coriander sprig
5ml/1 tsp salt
7.5ml/1½ tsp paprika
pinch of cayenne pepper
5–7.5ml/1–1½ tsp ground cumin
about 40g/1½oz/3 tbsp butter
½–1 lemon (optional)
sprigs of fresh parsley or coriander,
to garnish

SERVES 4–6

1 Unless cooking whole, cut the chicken in half or into quarters using poultry shears or a sharp knife.

2 Place the shallots, garlic, herbs, salt and spices in a food processor or blender and process until the shallots are finely chopped. Add the butter and process to make a smooth paste.

3 Thoroughly rub the paste over the skin of the chicken and then allow it to stand for 1–2 hours.

4 Preheat the oven to 200°C/400°F/Gas 6 and place the chicken in a roasting tin. Quarter the lemon, if using, place one or two quarters around the chicken pieces (or in the body cavity if the chicken is whole) and squeeze a little juice over the skin. Roast for 1–1¼ hours (2–2½ hours for a whole bird) until the chicken is cooked through and the meat juices run clear. Baste occasionally with the juices in the roasting tin. If the skin browns too quickly, cover the chicken loosely with foil.

5 Allow the chicken to stand for 5–10 minutes, covered in foil, before carving, and then serve garnished with sprigs of fresh parsley or coriander.

PAN-FRIED CHICKEN

The essence of this dish is to cook it quickly over a fierce heat. It therefore works best with small quantities, as larger amounts would have less contact with the pan and would braise rather than fry.

2 skinless, boneless chicken breasts
1 small red or green chilli, seeded and
finely sliced
2 garlic cloves, finely sliced
3 spring onions, sliced
4–5 wafer-thin slices fresh root ginger
2.5ml/$^{1}/_{2}$ tsp ground coriander
2.5ml/$^{1}/_{2}$ tsp ground cumin
30ml/2 tbsp olive oil
25ml/1$^{1}/_{2}$ tbsp lemon juice
30ml/2 tbsp pine nuts
15ml/1 tbsp raisins (optional)
oil, for frying
15ml/1 tbsp chopped fresh coriander
15ml/1 tbsp chopped fresh mint
salt and ground black pepper
sprigs of fresh mint and lemon
wedges, to garnish

SERVES 2 AS A MAIN COURSE,
4 AS A STARTER

1 Cut the chicken breasts horizontally into three or four thin pieces: this will speed up the cooking. Place in a shallow bowl until they are needed.

2 Mix together the chilli, garlic, spring onions, spices, olive oil, lemon juice, pine nuts and raisins, if using. Season with salt and pepper, and then pour over the chicken pieces, stirring gently so that each piece is coated. Cover and leave in a cool place for 1–2 hours.

3 Brush a wok, balti pan or cast-iron frying pan with oil and heat. Add the chicken slices and stir-fry them over a fairly high heat for 3–4 minutes until the chicken is browned on both sides.

4 Add the remaining marinade and continue to cook over a high heat for 6–8 minutes until the chicken is cooked through. (The timing will depend on the thickness of the chicken, but make sure that it is completely cooked.)

5 Reduce the heat and stir in the coriander and mint. Cook for 1 minute and serve immediately, garnished with mint sprigs and lemon wedges. Serve with bread as a starter or, if preferred, with rice or couscous as a main course.

HUNTER'S CHICKEN

This traditional dish sometimes has strips of green pepper in the sauce for extra colour and flavour instead of the fresh mushrooms.

15g/¹/₂oz/1 cup dried porcini
mushrooms
30ml/2 tbsp olive oil
15g/¹/₂ oz/1 tbsp butter
4 chicken pieces, on the bone, skinned
1 large onion, finely sliced
400g/14oz can chopped tomatoes
150ml/¹/₄ pint/²/₃ cup red wine
1 garlic clove, crushed
leaves of 1 sprig of fresh rosemary,
finely chopped
115g/4oz/1³/₄ cups fresh field
mushrooms, finely sliced
salt and ground black pepper
fresh rosemary sprigs, to garnish

SERVES 4

3 Add the onion and chopped porcini to the pan. Cook gently, stirring frequently, for about 3 minutes until the onion has softened but not browned. Stir in the chopped tomatoes, wine and reserved mushroom soaking liquid, then add the crushed garlic and chopped rosemary, with salt and ground black pepper to taste. Bring to the boil over a medium heat, stirring all the time with a wooden spoon.

4 Return the chicken to the pan and spoon the sauce over the top. Cover the pan and simmer gently for 30 minutes.

5 Add the fresh mushrooms and stir well to mix into the sauce. Continue simmering gently for about 10 minutes, until the chicken is tender. Taste for seasoning. Serve hot, with creamed potato or polenta, if you like. Garnish with rosemary.

1 Put the porcini mushrooms in a bowl, add 250ml/8fl oz/1 cup warm water and soak for 20–30 minutes. Squeeze the porcini over the bowl. Strain the liquid and reserve. Finely chop the porcini.

2 Heat the oil and butter in a flameproof casserole. Sauté the chicken over a medium heat for 5 minutes. Drain on kitchen paper.

CHICKEN KDRA WITH CHICK-PEAS AND ALMONDS

A kdra is a type of tagine that is traditionally cooked with smen, a strong Moroccan butter, and a lot of onions. The almonds in this recipe are precooked until soft, adding an interesting texture and flavour.

75g/3oz/3/4 cup blanched almonds
75g/3oz/1/2 cup chick-peas,
soaked overnight
4 part-boned chicken breasts, skinned
50g/2oz/1/4 cup butter
2.5ml/1/2 tsp saffron strands
2 Spanish onions, finely sliced
900ml/11/2 pints/33/4 cups
chicken stock
1 small cinnamon stick
60ml/4 tbsp chopped fresh flat leaf
parsley, plus extra to garnish
lemon juice, to taste
salt and ground black pepper

SERVES 4

1 Simmer the almonds in a pan of water for 2 hours until soft. Drain. Cook the chick-peas for 1½ hours until soft. Drain. Place the chick-peas in a bowl of cold water and rub off the skins. Put the chicken pieces, butter, half the saffron and seasoning in a pan. Heat until the butter melts.

2 Add the onions and stock, bring to the boil and then add the chick-peas and cinnamon stick. Cover the pan and cook very gently for 45–60 minutes until the chicken is completely tender.

3 Transfer the chicken to a serving plate and keep warm. Bring the sauce to the boil, then simmer until well reduced, stirring frequently. Add the almonds, parsley and remaining saffron, and cook for a further 2–3 minutes. Sharpen the sauce with a little lemon juice, then pour over the chicken and serve, garnished with the extra parsley.

CHICKEN WITH TOMATOES AND HONEY

Honey is surprisingly good in savoury dishes such as this one, making it rich rather than sweet.

30ml/2 tbsp sunflower oil
25g/1oz/2 tbsp butter
4 chicken quarters or 1 whole
chicken, quartered
1 onion, grated or finely chopped
1 garlic clove, crushed
a good pinch of ground ginger
5ml/1 tsp ground cinnamon
1.5kg/3–3½lb tomatoes, peeled, cored
and roughly chopped
30ml/2 tbsp clear honey
50g/2oz/1/2 cup blanched almonds
15ml/1 tbsp sesame seeds
salt and ground black pepper

SERVES 4

1 Heat the oil and butter in a large casserole. Add the chicken pieces and cook over a medium heat for about 3 minutes until the chicken is lightly browned.

2 Add the onion, garlic, ginger, cinnamon, tomatoes and seasoning, and heat gently until the tomatoes begin to bubble.

3 Lower the heat, cover and simmer gently for 1 hour, stirring and turning the chicken occasionally, until it is completely cooked through.

4 Transfer the chicken pieces to a plate. Increase the heat and cook the tomato mixture, stirring frequently, until the sauce is reduced to a thick purée. Stir in the honey, cook for 1 minute and then return the chicken to the pan and cook for 2–3 minutes to heat through. Dry-fry the almonds and sesame seeds until golden, or toast them under the grill.

5 Transfer the chicken and sauce to a warmed serving dish and sprinkle with the almonds and sesame seeds. Serve at once, with crusty bread.

CHICKEN WITH CHORIZO

*The addition of chorizo sausage and sherry gives a warm, interesting flavour to this simple
Spanish casserole. Serve with rice or boiled potatoes.*

1 medium chicken, jointed, or
4 chicken legs, halved
10ml/2 tsp ground paprika
60ml/4 tbsp olive oil
2 small onions, sliced
6 garlic cloves, thinly sliced
150g/5oz chorizo sausage
400g/14oz can chopped tomatoes
12–16 bay leaves
75ml/5 tbsp medium sherry
salt and ground black pepper
rice or potatoes, to serve

SERVES 4

1 Preheat the oven to 190°C/
375°F/Gas 5. Coat the chicken
pieces in the paprika, making sure
they are evenly covered, then season
with salt. Heat the olive oil in a frying
pan and fry the chicken until brown.

2 Transfer to an ovenproof dish.
Add the onions to the pan and
fry quickly. Add the garlic and sliced
chorizo and fry for 2 minutes.

3 Add the tomatoes, two of the
bay leaves and sherry and bring
to the boil. Pour over the chicken and
cover with a lid. Bake for 45 minutes.
Remove the lid and season to taste.
Cook for a further 20 minutes until
the chicken is tender and golden.
Serve with rice or boiled potatoes,
garnished with bay leaves.

CIRCASSIAN CHICKEN

This is a Turkish dish, which is popular all over the Middle East. The chicken is poached and served cold with a flavoursome walnut sauce.

🍗 🍗

1.5kg/3–3½ lb chicken
2 onions, quartered
1 carrot, sliced
1 celery stick, trimmed and sliced
6 peppercorns
3 slices bread, crusts removed
2 garlic cloves, roughly chopped
400g/14oz/3½ cups chopped walnuts
15ml/1 tbsp walnut oil
salt and ground black pepper
chopped walnuts and paprika,
to garnish

SERVES 6

🍗 🍗

1 Place the chicken in a large pan, with the onions, carrot, celery and peppercorns. Add enough water to cover, and bring to the boil. Simmer for about 1 hour, uncovered, until the chicken is tender. Leave to cool in the stock. Drain the chicken, reserving the stock.

2 Tear up the bread and soak in 90ml/6 tbsp of the chicken stock. Transfer to a blender or food processor, with the garlic and walnuts, and add 250ml/8fl oz/1 cup of the remaining stock. Process until smooth, then transfer to a pan.

3 Over a low heat, gradually add more chicken stock to the sauce, stirring constantly, until it is of a thick pouring consistency. Season with salt and pepper, remove from the heat and leave to cool in the pan. Skin and bone the chicken, and cut into bite-size chunks.

4 Place in a bowl and add a little of the sauce. Stir to coat the chicken, then arrange on a serving dish. Spoon the remaining sauce over the chicken, and drizzle with the walnut oil. Sprinkle with walnuts and paprika and serve at once.

PAN-FRIED CHICKEN WITH PESTO

Pan-fried chicken, served with warm pesto, makes a deliciously quick main course. Serve with boiled pasta or rice noodles and braised vegetables, such as baby carrots and celery.

15ml/1 tbsp olive oil
4 skinless, boneless chicken breasts
fresh basil leaves, to garnish

FOR THE PESTO
90ml/6 tbsp olive oil
50g/2oz/½ cup pine nuts
50g/2oz/⅔ cup freshly grated
Parmesan cheese
50g/2oz/1 cup fresh basil leaves
15g/½ oz/¼ cup fresh parsley
2 garlic cloves, crushed
salt and ground black pepper

SERVES 4

[1] Heat the 15ml/1 tbsp oil in a frying pan. Add the chicken breasts and cook gently for about 15 minutes, turning several times, until the chicken is tender, lightly browned and thoroughly cooked.

[2] Meanwhile, make the pesto. Place the olive oil, pine nuts, Parmesan cheese, basil leaves, parsley, garlic, salt and pepper in a blender or food processor, and process until smooth and well mixed.

[3] Remove the chicken from the pan, cover and keep hot. Reduce the heat slightly, then add the pesto to the pan and cook gently for a few minutes, stirring constantly, until the pesto has warmed through.

[4] Pour the warm pesto over the chicken, then garnish with basil leaves. Serve with braised baby carrots and celery, if you like.

CHICKEN CASSEROLE WITH SPICED FIGS

The Spanish Catalans have various recipes for fruit with meat. This is quite an unusual one, but it uses one of the fruits most strongly associated with the Mediterranean — the fig.

FOR THE FIGS
150g/5oz/⅔ cup granulated sugar
120ml/4fl oz/½ cup white
wine vinegar
1 lemon slice
1 cinnamon stick
450g/1lb fresh figs

FOR THE CHICKEN
120ml/4fl oz/½ cup medium sweet
white wine
pared rind of ½ lemon
1.5kg/3–3½lb chicken, jointed into
eight pieces
50g/2oz lardons, or thick streaky
bacon cut into strips
15ml/1 tbsp olive oil
50ml/2fl oz/¼ cup chicken stock
salt and ground black pepper

SERVES 4

1 Put the sugar, vinegar, lemon slice and cinnamon stick in a pan with 120ml/4fl oz/½ cup water. Bring to the boil, then simmer for 5 minutes. Add the figs, cover, and simmer for 10 minutes. Remove from heat, cover, and leave for 3 hours.

2 Preheat the oven to 180°C/ 350°F/Gas 4. Drain the figs, and place in a bowl. Add the wine and lemon rind. Season the chicken. In a large frying pan cook the lardons or streaky bacon strips until the fat melts and they turn golden. Transfer to a shallow ovenproof dish, leaving any fat in the pan. Add the oil to the pan and brown the chicken pieces all over.

3 Drain the figs, adding the wine to the pan with the chicken. Boil until the sauce has reduced and is syrupy. Transfer the contents of the frying pan to the ovenproof dish and cook in the oven, uncovered, for about 20 minutes. Add the figs and chicken stock, cover and return to the oven for a further 10 minutes. Serve with a green salad.

PERSIAN CHICKEN WITH WALNUT SAUCE

This distinctive dish is traditionally served on festive occasions in Iran.

30ml/2 tbsp olive oil
4 chicken pieces (leg or breast)
1 large onion, grated
250ml/8fl oz/1 cup water
115g/4oz/1 cup finely
chopped walnuts
75ml/5 tbsp pomegranate purée
15ml/1 tbsp tomato purée
30ml/2 tbsp lemon juice
15ml/1 tbsp sugar
3–4 saffron strands, dissolved in
15ml/1 tbsp boiling water
salt and freshly ground black pepper

SERVES 4

1 Heat 15ml/1 tbsp of the oil in a large frying pan and sauté the chicken pieces until golden brown. Add half of the grated onion and fry until slightly softened, then add the water and seasoning, and bring to the boil. Cover the pan, reduce the heat and simmer for 15 minutes.

COOK'S TIP
Pomegranate purée is available from Middle Eastern delicatessens.

2 Heat the remaining oil in a frying pan and fry the rest of the onion for 2–3 minutes until soft. Add the chopped walnuts and fry for a further 2–3 minutes over a low heat, stirring frequently so that the walnuts do not burn.

3 Stir in the pomegranate and tomato purées, lemon juice, sugar and the dissolved saffron. Season to taste and simmer over a low heat for 5 minutes.

4 Pour the walnut sauce over the chicken, ensuring that all the pieces are well coated. Cover and simmer for 30–35 minutes until the meat is cooked and the oil from the walnuts has risen to the surface.

5 Serve at once with Persian rice and salad leaves such as baby cos or Little Gem.

CHICKEN WITH OLIVES

Olives and lemon make a wonderful combination, one which is used traditionally in the Middle East and north Africa.

30ml/2 tbsp olive oil
1.5kg/3–3¹/2lb chicken
1 large onion, sliced
15ml/1 tbsp fresh root ginger, grated
3 garlic cloves, crushed
5ml/1 tsp paprika
250ml/8fl oz/1 cup chicken stock
2–3 saffron strands, soaked in 15ml/
1 tbsp boiling water
4–5 spring onions, chopped
15–20 pitted black and green olives
juice of ¹/2 lemon
salt and ground black pepper

SERVES 4

1 Heat the oil in a large saucepan and sauté the chicken on all sides until golden.

2 Add the onion, ginger, garlic, paprika and seasoning, and continue frying over a moderate heat, coating the chicken with the mixture.

3 Add the chicken stock and saffron, and bring to the boil. Cover and simmer for 45 minutes until the chicken is almost done.

4 Add the spring onions and cook for a further 15 minutes until the chicken is well cooked and the surrounding sauce is reduced to about half. Add the olives.

5 Stir in the lemon juice. Cook over a medium heat for a further 5 minutes. Place the chicken on a large, deep plate and pour over the sauce. Serve with rice or flat bread and a salad of mixed leaves and cherry tomatoes, if you like.

CHICKEN THIGHS WITH LEMON AND GARLIC

This recipe uses classic flavourings for chicken. Versions of it can be found in Spain and Italy.
This particular recipe, however, is of French origin.

600ml/1 pint/2½ cups chicken stock
20 large garlic cloves
25g/1oz/2 tbsp butter
15ml/1 tbsp olive oil
8 chicken thighs
1 lemon, peeled, pith removed and
sliced thinly
30ml/2 tbsp plain flour
150ml/¼ pint/⅔ cup dry white wine
salt and ground black pepper
chopped fresh parsley or basil,
to garnish
new potatoes or rice, to serve

SERVES 4

1   Put the stock into a pan and bring to the boil. Add the garlic cloves, cover and simmer gently for 40 minutes. Heat the butter and oil in a sauté or frying pan, add the chicken thighs and cook gently on all sides until golden. Transfer them to an ovenproof dish. Preheat the oven to 190°C/375°F/Gas 5.

2   Strain the stock and reserve it. Distribute the garlic and lemon slices among the chicken pieces. Add the flour to the fat in the pan in which the chicken was browned, and cook, stirring, for 1 minute. Add the wine, stirring constantly and scraping the bottom of the pan, then add the stock. Cook, stirring, until the sauce has thickened and is smooth. Season with salt and pepper.

3   Pour the sauce over the chicken, cover, and cook in the oven for 40–45 minutes. If a thicker sauce is required, lift out the chicken pieces, and reduce the sauce by boiling rapidly, until it reaches the desired consistency. Scatter over the chopped parsley or basil and serve with boiled new potatoes or rice.

CHICKEN AND APRICOT FILO PIE

The filling for this pie has a Middle Eastern flavour – minced chicken combined with apricots,
bulgur wheat, nuts and spices.

75g/3oz/½ cup bulgur wheat
75g/3oz/6 tbsp butter
1 onion, chopped
450g/1lb minced chicken
50g/2oz/¼ cup ready-to-eat dried
apricots, finely chopped
25g/1oz/¼ cup blanched almonds,
chopped
5ml/1 tsp ground cinnamon
2.5ml/½ tsp ground allspice
50ml/2fl oz/¼ cup Greek yogurt
15ml/1 tbsp snipped fresh chives
30ml/2 tbsp chopped fresh parsley
6 large sheets filo pastry
salt and ground black pepper
chives, to garnish

SERVES 6

1 Preheat the oven to 200°C/400°F/Gas 6. Put the bulgur wheat in a bowl with 120ml/4fl oz/½ cup boiling water. Soak for 5–10 minutes, until the water is absorbed.

2 Heat 25g/1oz/2 tbsp of the butter in a pan, and gently fry the onion and chicken until pale golden.

3 Stir in the apricots, almonds and bulgur wheat and cook for a further 2 minutes. Remove from the heat and stir in the cinnamon, allspice, yogurt, chives and parsley. Season to taste with salt and pepper.

4 Melt the remaining butter. Unroll the filo pastry and cut into 25cm/10in rounds. Keep the pastry rounds covered with a clean, damp dish towel to prevent drying.

5 Line a 23cm/9in loose-based flan tin with three of the pastry rounds, brushing each one with butter as you layer them. Spoon in the chicken mixture, cover with three more pastry rounds, brushed with melted butter as before.

6 Crumple the remaining rounds and place them on top of the pie, then brush over any remaining melted butter. Bake the pie for about 30 minutes, until the pastry is golden brown and crisp. Serve Chicken and Apricot Filo Pie hot or cold, cut in wedges and garnished with chives.

BISTEEYA

Bisteeya is one of the most elaborate and intriguing dishes in Moroccan cuisine. It is often the centrepiece at feasts and banquets, and is normally made using pigeon, which is then layered with a wafer-thin pastry known as ouarka and cooked in a tin over hot coals. This simplified version uses chicken and filo.

30ml/2 tbsp sunflower oil, plus extra
for brushing
25g/1oz/2 tbsp butter
3 chicken quarters, preferably breasts
1½ Spanish onions, grated or
finely chopped
a good pinch of ground ginger
a good pinch of saffron strands
10ml/2 tsp ground cinnamon, plus
extra for dusting
40g/1½oz/4 tbsp flaked almonds
1 large bunch fresh coriander,
finely chopped
1 large bunch fresh parsley,
finely chopped
3 eggs, beaten
about 175g/6oz filo pastry
5–10ml/1–2 tsp icing sugar (optional),
plus extra for dusting
salt and ground black pepper

SERVES 4

1 Heat the oil and butter in a large saucepan or flameproof casserole and brown the chicken pieces for about 4 minutes. Add the onions, ginger, saffron, 2.5ml/½ tsp of the cinnamon and enough water so that the chicken braises, rather than boils (about 300ml/½ pint/1¼ cups). Season well.

2 Bring to the boil, cover and simmer for 45–55 minutes over a gentle heat, until the chicken is tender and completely cooked. Meanwhile, dry-fry the almonds until golden and set aside.

3 Transfer the chicken to a plate and, when cool enough to handle, remove the skin and bones and cut the flesh into pieces.

4 Stir the coriander and parsley into the pan and simmer the sauce until well-reduced and thick. Add the beaten eggs and cook over a very gentle heat until the eggs are lightly scrambled.

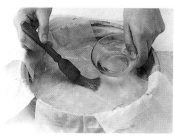

5 Preheat the oven to 180°C/ 350°F/Gas 4. Oil a round shallow flameproof dish, about 25cm/10in in diameter. Place one or two sheets of filo pastry in a single layer over the bottom of the dish, so that it is completely covered and the edges of the pastry sheets hang over the sides. Brush lightly with oil and add two more layers of filo, brushing each layer lightly with oil.

6 Place the chicken on the pastry and then spoon the egg and herb mixture over the top.

7 Place a single layer of filo pastry on top of the filling (you may need to use more than one sheet of filo pastry) and scatter with the almonds. Sift the remaining cinnamon and the icing sugar, if using, on top.

8 Fold the edges of the filo over the almonds and then make four further layers of filo (using one or two sheets per layer, depending on size), brushing each layer with a little oil. Tuck the filo edges under the pie (as if you were making a bed!) and brush the top layer with oil.

9 Bake the pie in the oven for 40–45 minutes until golden. Dust the top with icing sugar, if using, and use the extra cinnamon to make criss-cross or diagonal lines. Serve immediately.

CHICKEN AND AUBERGINE KHORESH

*This aubergine and pepper stew is often served on festive occasions in Iran
and is believed to have been a favourite with royalty.*

2 Add the crushed garlic, chopped tomatoes and their liquid, water and seasoning. Bring to the boil, then reduce the heat and simmer slowly, covered, for 10 minutes.

3 Meanwhile, heat the remaining oil and fry the aubergines in batches until light golden. Transfer to a plate with a spatula. Add the peppers to the pan and fry for a few minutes until slightly softened.

4 Place the aubergines over the chicken or chicken pieces and then add the peppers. Sprinkle the lemon juice and cinnamon over the top, then cover and continue cooking over a low heat for about 45 minutes, or until the chicken is cooked through.

5 Transfer the chicken to a serving plate and spoon the aubergines and peppers around the edge. Reheat the sauce if necessary, adjust the seasoning and pour over the chicken. Serve with rice.

60ml/4 tbsp oil
*1 whole chicken or 4 large
chicken pieces*
1 large onion, chopped
2 garlic cloves, crushed
400g/14oz can chopped tomatoes
250ml/8fl oz/1 cup water
3 aubergines, sliced
*3 peppers (preferably red, green and
yellow), seeded and sliced*
30ml/2 tbsp lemon juice
15ml/1 tbsp ground cinnamon
salt and ground black pepper

SERVES 4

1 Heat 15ml/1 tbsp of the oil in a large saucepan or flameproof casserole, and fry the chicken or chicken pieces on all sides for about 10 minutes or until golden all over. Add the onion and fry for 4–5 minutes more, until the onion is golden brown.

VARIATION
Substitute courgettes for some or all
of the aubergines, if you like.

YOGURT CHICKEN AND RICE

This rice dish is very unusual, but tastes absolutely superb.

40g/1¹/₂oz/3 tbsp butter
1.5kg/3–3¹/₂lb chicken
1 large onion, chopped
250ml/8fl oz/1 cup chicken stock
2 eggs
475ml/16fl oz/2 cups natural yogurt
2–3 saffron strands, dissolved in
15ml/1 tbsp boiling water
5ml/1 tsp ground cinnamon
450g/1lb/2¹/₃ cups basmati rice, soaked
in water for 20 minutes
75g/3oz zereshk (small dried berries)
salt and ground black pepper

SERVES 6

1   Melt 25g/1oz/2 tbsp of the butter and fry the chicken and onion for 4–5 minutes until the onion is softened and the chicken browned.

2   Add the chicken stock, salt and pepper, and bring to the boil. Then reduce the heat and simmer for about 45 minutes, or until the chicken is cooked and the stock reduced by half. Skin and bone the chicken. Cut the flesh into large pieces and place in a bowl. Reserve the stock.

3   Beat the eggs and mix with the yogurt. Add the saffron water and cinnamon and season with more salt and black pepper. Pour over the chicken and leave to marinate for up to 2 hours.

4   Drain the rice, then boil in salted water for 5 minutes. Reduce the heat and simmer very gently for 10 minutes until half-cooked. Drain and rinse in lukewarm water, then drain again.

5   Transfer the chicken from the yogurt mixture to a dish and mix half the rice into the yogurt.

6   Preheat the oven to 160°C/325°F/Gas 3 and grease a large 10cm/4in deep flameproof dish.

7   Place the rice and yogurt mixture in the bottom of the dish, arrange the chicken pieces in a layer on top and then add the plain rice. Sprinkle with the *zereshk*.

8   Mix the remaining butter with the chicken stock and pour over the rice. Cover tightly with foil and a lid. Cook in the oven for 35–45 minutes.

9   Leave the dish to cool for a few minutes. Place on a cold, damp cloth (which will help lift the rice from the bottom of the dish), then run a knife around the edges of the dish. Place a large flat plate over the dish and turn out. You should have a rice "cake" which can be cut into wedges. Serve hot with a salad.

MUSHROOM PICKER'S CHICKEN PAELLA

A good paella is based on a few well-chosen ingredients. Here, wild mushrooms are combined with chicken and vegetables.

45ml/3 tbsp olive oil
1 medium onion, chopped
1 small bulb fennel, sliced
225g/8oz/3 cups assorted wild and
cultivated mushrooms, such as ceps,
bay boletus, chanterelles and oyster
mushrooms, trimmed and sliced
1 garlic clove, crushed
3 large chicken legs, chopped through
the bone
350g/12oz/1¾ cups short grain
Spanish or Italian rice
900ml/1½ pints/3¾ cups chicken
stock, boiling
pinch of saffron strands or 1 sachet
of saffron powder
1 thyme sprig
400g/14oz can butter beans, drained
75g/3oz/¾ cup frozen peas

SERVES 4

 1 Heat the olive oil gently in a 35cm/14in paella pan or a large frying pan. Add the onion and fennel and fry, stirring, over a gentle heat for 3–4 minutes.

2 Add the mushrooms and garlic, and cook until the juices begin to run, then increase the heat to evaporate the juices. Push the onion and mushrooms to one side. Add the chicken pieces and fry briefly.

3 Stir in the rice, pour in the stock, then stir in the saffron, thyme, butter beans and peas. Bring to a simmer and then cook gently for 15 minutes without stirring.

4 Remove from the heat and cover the surface of the paella with a circle of oiled greaseproof paper. Cover the paper with a clean dish towel and leave for about 5 minutes before serving the paella.

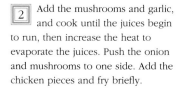

COOK'S TIP
For a vegetarian mushroom paella, omit the chicken, replace the chicken stock with vegetable stock and, if you can, include chicken of the woods in your choice of mushrooms.

CHICKEN WITH PIMIENTOS

"Pimiento" is the Spanish word for the sweet bell-shaped pepper, which is a favourite ingredient in many Mediterranean recipes.

2 Heat half the oil in a large frying pan and sauté the onion, garlic and peppers for 3 minutes. Transfer to an ovenproof dish. Add the chicken pieces to the pan. Fry them until browned on all sides, then add them to the dish.

3 Add the remaining oil to the pan and, when it is hot, fry the tomatoes for a few minutes. Stir in seasoning, sugar and 15ml/1 tbsp water, then spoon the mixture over the chicken. Cook, uncovered, in the oven for 30 minutes.

4 Remove the chicken from the oven and carefully pour the free juices from the dish into a small pan. Return the chicken to the oven and bake for 30 minutes more, covering the dish with foil if the chicken starts to get too brown.

5 When the chicken is almost cooked, skim the fat from the juices in the saucepan and reheat. Stir the olives into the vegetables surrounding the chicken mixture, garnish with flat leaf parsley and serve with rice. Pour the pan juices into a jug and pass round as extra gravy.

2kg/4¹/₂lb roasting chicken
3 ripe tomatoes
2 large red peppers
60–90ml/4–6 tbsp olive oil
1 large onion, sliced
2 garlic cloves, crushed
15ml/1 tbsp sugar
salt and ground black pepper
75g/3oz/¹/₂ cup pitted black olives
flat leaf parsley, to garnish

SERVES 6

1 Preheat the oven to 190°C/ 375°F/Gas 5. Joint the chicken, then cut it into eight pieces and set aside. Peel and chop the tomatoes and seed and slice the red peppers.

POUSSINS WITH BULGUR WHEAT AND DRY VERMOUTH

Vermouth is a valuable asset in the kitchen. It appears twice in this recipe, first to flavour the bulgur wheat stuffing and then in the glaze for the poussins.

2 Heat half of the oil and fry the onion and carrots for 10 minutes, then remove the pan from the heat and stir in the nuts, celery seeds and well-drained bulgur wheat.

3 Stuff the poussins with the bulgur wheat mixture. Place them in a roasting tin, brush with oil and sprinkle with salt and pepper. Roast for 45–55 minutes until cooked.

4 Meanwhile, spread out the red onions, aubergines, squashes and baby carrots on a baking sheet.

50g/2oz/⅓ cup bulgur wheat
150ml/¼ pint/⅔ cup dry white vermouth
60ml/4 tbsp olive oil
1 large onion, finely chopped
2 carrots, finely chopped
75g/3oz/1 cup pine nuts, chopped
5ml/1 tsp celery seeds
4 poussins
3 red onions, quartered
4 baby aubergines, halved
4 patty pan squashes
12 baby carrots
45ml/3 tbsp corn or golden syrup
salt and ground black pepper

SERVES 4

1 Preheat the oven to 200°C/ 400°F/Gas 6. Put the bulgur wheat in a heatproof bowl, pour over half of the vermouth and cover with boiling water. Set aside until needed.

5 Mix the corn syrup with the remaining vermouth and oil in a small bowl. Season with salt and pepper. Brush the syrup mixture over the vegetables and roast them for 35–45 minutes until golden. Cut each poussin in half and serve with the roasted vegetables.

GRILLED POUSSINS WITH CITRUS GLAZE

This recipe is suitable for many kinds of small birds, including pigeons, snipe and partridges.
It would also work with quail, but in such a case decrease the cooking time and spread the citrus mixture
over, rather than under, the fragile skin.

2 poussins (about 675g/1½lb each)
50g/2oz/¼ cup butter, softened
30ml/2 tbsp olive oil
2 garlic cloves, crushed
2.5ml/½ tsp dried thyme
1.5ml/¼ tsp cayenne pepper,
or to taste
grated rind and juice of
1 unwaxed lemon
grated rind and juice of
1 unwaxed lime
30ml/2 tbsp clear honey
salt and ground black pepper
fresh dill, to garnish

SERVES 4

[1] Using kitchen scissors, cut along both sides of the backbone of each bird; remove and discard the spine. Cut the birds in half along the breast bone, and then press down firmly with a rolling pin to flatten.

[2] Place the butter in a small bowl, then beat in 15ml/1 tbsp of the olive oil, the garlic, thyme, cayenne, salt and black pepper, half the lemon and lime rind, and 15ml/1 tbsp each of the lemon and lime juice.

[3] Carefully loosen the skin of each poussin breast with your fingertips. Using a round-bladed knife or small palette knife, spread the butter mixture evenly between the skin and the breast meat.

[4] Preheat the grill and line a grill pan with foil. In a small bowl, mix together the remaining olive oil, lemon and lime juices, and the honey. Place the bird halves, skin side up, on the grill pan and brush with the citrus juice mixture.

[5] Grill on one side for 10–12 minutes, basting once or twice with the juices. Turn over and grill for 7–10 minutes, basting once, or until the meat juices run clear when the thigh is pierced with a knife. Garnish with the dill. Serve with grilled tomatoes and a salad.

351

POUSSINS WITH COURGETTES AND APRICOT STUFFING

If possible, buy very small or baby poussins for this recipe. If these are not available,
buy slightly larger poussins and serve half a poussin per person.

4 small poussins
about 40g/1½oz/3 tbsp butter
5–10ml/1–2 tsp ground coriander
1 large red pepper
1 red chilli
15–30ml/1–2 tbsp olive oil
120ml/4fl oz/½ cup chicken stock
30ml/2 tbsp cornflour
salt and ground black pepper
fresh flat leaf parsley, to garnish

FOR THE STUFFING
525ml/18fl oz/2¼ cups chicken or
vegetable stock
275g/10oz/1⅔ cups couscous
2 small courgettes
8 ready-to-eat dried apricots
15ml/1 tbsp chopped fresh
flat leaf parsley
15ml/1 tbsp chopped fresh coriander
juice of ½ lemon

SERVES 4

☐1 First make the stuffing. Bring the stock to the boil and pour it over the couscous in a large bowl. Stir once, then set aside for 10 minutes so that the couscous absorbs the liquid.

☐2 Meanwhile, top and tail the courgettes and then grate them coarsely. Roughly chop the apricots and add to the courgettes. Preheat the oven to 200°C/400°F/Gas 6.

☐3 When the couscous has swollen, fluff up with a fork and then spoon 90ml/6 tbsp into a separate bowl and add the courgettes and chopped apricots. Add the herbs, seasoning and lemon juice, and stir to make a fairly loose stuffing. Set aside the remaining couscous for serving.

☐4 Spoon the stuffing loosely into the body cavities of the poussins and secure with string or cocktail sticks. Place the birds in a medium to large roasting tin, so that they fit comfortably but not too closely. Rub the butter into the skins and sprinkle with ground coriander and a little salt and pepper.

☐5 Cut the red pepper into medium-size strips and finely slice the chilli, discarding the seeds and core from both. Place in the roasting tin, around the poussins, and spoon over the olive oil.

☐6 Roast for 20 minutes, then reduce the oven temperature to 180°C/350°F/Gas 4. Pour the chicken stock around the poussins and baste each bird with the stock and red pepper/chilli mixture. Return the tin to the oven and cook for a further 30–35 minutes, basting occasionally with the stock, until the poussins are cooked through and the meat juices run clear.

☐7 When the poussins are cooked, transfer them to a warmed serving plate. Mix the cornflour with 45ml/3 tbsp cold water, stir into the stock and peppers in the roasting tin.

☐8 Heat gently, stirring all the time, until the sauce is slightly thickened. Check the seasoning and transfer to a jug, or pour directly over the poussins. Garnish the birds with fresh flat leaf parsley and serve at once with the reserved couscous.

DUCK BREASTS WITH A WALNUT AND POMEGRANATE SAUCE

This is an extremely exotic sweet-and-sour dish which originally came from Persia.

60ml/4 tbsp olive oil
2 onions, very thinly sliced
2.5ml/½ tsp ground turmeric
400g/14oz/3½ cups walnuts,
roughly chopped
1 litre/1¾ pints/4 cups duck or
chicken stock
6 pomegranates
30ml/2 tbsp caster sugar
60ml/4 tbsp lemon juice
4 duck breasts, about 225g/8oz each
salt and ground black pepper

SERVES 6

COOK'S TIP
Choose pomegranates with shiny,
brightly coloured skins. The juice
stains, so take care when cutting
them. Only the seeds are used in
cooking; the pith is discarded.

1 Heat half the oil in a frying pan. Add the onions and turmeric, and cook gently until soft. Transfer to a pan, add the walnuts and stock, then season with salt and pepper. Stir, then bring to the boil and simmer the mixture, uncovered, for 20 minutes.

2 Cut the pomegranates in half and scoop out the seeds into a bowl. Reserve the seeds of one pomegranate. Transfer the remaining seeds to a blender or food processor, and process to break them up. Strain through a sieve, to extract the juice, and stir in the sugar and lemon juice.

3 Score the skin of the duck breasts in a lattice fashion with a sharp knife. Heat the remaining oil in a frying pan or char grill and place the duck breasts in it, skin side down.

4 Cook gently for 10 minutes, pouring off the fat from time to time, until the skin is dark golden and crisp. Turn them over and cook for a further 3–4 minutes. Transfer to a plate and leave to rest.

5 Deglaze the frying pan or char grill with the pomegranate juice mixture, stirring with a wooden spoon, then add the walnut and stock mixture and simmer for 15 minutes until the sauce has thickened slightly. Serve the duck breasts sliced, drizzled with a little sauce, and garnished with the reserved pomegranate seeds. Serve the remaining sauce separately.

APPLE-STUFFED DUCK

Stuffing the duck breasts with whole apples keeps the slices moist and gives an attractive appearance when they are served cold.

.... 🌿 🌿 ....

40g/1¹/₂oz/¹/₄ cup raisins or sultanas
30ml/2 tbsp brandy
3 large onions
30ml/2 tbsp oil
175g/6oz/3 cups fresh breadcrumbs
2 small dessert apples,
preferably Cox's
2 large duck breasts, including
the skin
salt and ground black pepper
mixed leaf salad, to serve

SERVES 4 AS A HOT DISH; MORE WHEN
SERVED COLD AS PART OF A BUFFET

1 Soak the dried fruit in the brandy. Preheat the oven to 220°C/425°F/Gas 7.

2 Chop 1 of the onions finely and sauté in the oil until golden. Season with salt and pepper, and add 50ml/2fl oz/¹/₄ cup water. Bring to the boil, add the breadcrumbs and enough extra water to make a moist but not sloppy stuffing.

3 Core and peel the apples. Drain the raisins and press them into the centre of the apples. Flatten the duck breasts and spread out, skin down.

4 Divide the stuffing between them and spread it over the meat. Place an apple at one end of each duck breast and carefully roll up to enclose the apple and stuffing. Secure with a length of cotton or fine string. Quarter the remaining onions. Prick the duck skin in several places to release the fat.

5 Arrange on a rack in a roasting tin with the onions underneath. Roast for about 35 minutes. Pour off the fat, reduce the oven temperature to 160°C/325°F/Gas 3 and roast for a further 30–45 minutes.

6 Serve hot with mixed, roast vegetables or, to serve cold, chill and then cut each breast into 5 or 6 thin slices. Arrange on a platter and bring to room temperature before serving. Serve with a mixed leaf salad.

DUCK STEW WITH OLIVES

This method of preparing duck has its roots in Provence. The sweetness of the onions balances the saltiness of the olives.

2 Heat 15ml/1 tbsp of the duck fat in a large flameproof casserole and cook the onions, covered, over a low-medium heat until evenly browned, stirring frequently. Sprinkle with flour and continue cooking, uncovered, for 2 minutes, stirring frequently.

3 Stir in the wine and bring to the boil, then add the duck pieces, stock and bouquet garni. Bring to the boil, then simmer, covered, for about 40 minutes, stirring occasionally.

4 Rinse the olives in several changes of cold water. If they are very salty, put in a saucepan, cover with water and bring to the boil, then drain and rinse. Add the olives to the casserole and continue cooking for a further 20 minutes until the duck is very tender.

5 Transfer the duck pieces, onions and olives to a plate. Strain the cooking liquid, skim off all the fat and return the liquid to the pan. Boil to reduce by about one-third, then adjust the seasoning and return the duck and vegetables to the casserole. Simmer gently for a few minutes to heat through. Serve.

🌿 🌿

2 ducks, each about 1.5kg/3–3¹/₂lb,
quartered, or 8 duck leg quarters
225g/8oz baby onions
30ml/2 tbsp plain flour
350ml/12fl oz/1¹/₂ cups dry red wine
500ml/17fl oz/generous 2¹/₄ cups
duck or chicken stock
bouquet garni
115g/4oz/²/₃ cup pitted green or black
olives, or a combination
salt and freshly ground
black pepper

SERVES 6–8

1 Put the duck pieces, skin side down, in a large frying pan over a medium heat and cook for about 12 minutes until well browned, turning to colour evenly. Cook in batches if necessary. Pour off and reserve the fat from the pan.

SPICED DUCK WITH PEARS

———

This delicious casserole is based on a Catalan dish that uses goose or duck. The sautéed pears are added towards the end of cooking, along with picarda sauce, a pounded pine nut and garlic paste which both flavours and thickens.

6 duck portions, either breast or
leg pieces
15ml/1 tbsp olive oil
1 large onion, thinly sliced
1 cinnamon stick, halved
2 thyme sprigs
475ml/16fl oz/2 cups chicken stock

TO FINISH
3 firm ripe pears
30ml/2 tbsp olive oil
2 garlic cloves, sliced
25g/1oz/⅓ cup pine nuts
2.5ml/½ tsp saffron strands
25g/1oz/2 tbsp raisins
salt and ground black pepper
young thyme sprigs or parsley,
to garnish

SERVES 6

[1] Preheat the oven to 180°C/
350°F/Gas 4. Fry the duck
portions in the olive oil for about
5 minutes until the skin is golden.
Transfer the duck to an ovenproof
dish and drain off all but 15ml/1 tbsp
of the fat left in the pan.

[2] Add the onion to the pan and
fry for 5 minutes. Add the
cinnamon stick, thyme and stock and
bring to the boil. Pour over the duck
and bake in the oven for 1¼ hours.

[3] Meanwhile, peel, core and
halve the pears and fry quickly
in the oil until beginning to turn
golden on the cut sides. Pound the
garlic, pine nuts and saffron in a
mortar, with a pestle, to make a thick,
smooth paste.

[4] Add the paste to the casserole
along with the raisins and
pears. Bake for a further 15 minutes
until the pears are tender.

[5] Season to taste with salt and
pepper and garnish with parsley
or thyme. Serve with mashed potatoes
and a green vegetable, if liked.

COOK'S TIP
A good stock is essential for this dish.
Buy a large duck (plus two extra duck
breasts if you want portions to be
generous) and joint it yourself, using
the giblets and carcass for stock.
Alternatively buy duck portions and a
carton of chicken stock.

QUAIL WITH FRESH FIGS

The fig trees in the south of France are laden with ripe purple fruit in early autumn,
coinciding with the quail-shooting season.

8 oven-ready quail
6 firm ripe figs, quartered
15g/½ oz/1 tbsp butter
90ml/6 tbsp dry sherry
300ml/½ pint/1¼ cups chicken stock
1 garlic clove, finely chopped
2–3 thyme sprigs
1 bay leaf
7.5ml/1½ tsp cornflour, mixed to a
paste with 15ml/1 tbsp water
salt and ground black pepper
green salad, to serve

SERVES 4

2 Melt the butter in a deep frying pan or heavy flameproof casserole over a medium-high heat. Cook the quail for 5–6 minutes, turning to brown all sides evenly; cook in batches if necessary.

3 Add the sherry and boil for 1 minute, then add the stock, garlic, thyme and bay leaf. Bring to the boil, reduce the heat and simmer gently, covered, for 20 minutes.

4 Add the remaining fig quarters and continue cooking for a further 5 minutes until the meat juices run clear when the thigh of a quail is pierced with a knife. Transfer the quail and figs to a warmed serving dish, cut off the trussing string and cover to keep warm.

5 Bring the cooking liquid to the boil, then stir in the cornflour paste. Cook gently for 3 minutes, stirring frequently, until the liquid is thickened, then strain into a sauce boat. Serve the quail and figs with the sauce and a green salad.

1 Season the quail inside and out. Put a fig quarter in the cavity of each quail and tie the legs with string.

COOK'S TIP
Farmed quail are available all year
and are an excellent buy.

360

DUCK BREASTS WITH CHICORY

A plum and sherry purée is the perfect accompaniment for glazed duck breasts with chicory.

15ml/1 tbsp lemon juice
4 heads of chicory
4 duck breasts, about 115–175g/
4–6oz each
15ml/1 tbsp clear honey
15ml/1 tbsp sunflower oil
salt and ground black pepper

FOR THE PURÉE
1 cooking apple, peeled, cored
and sliced
175g/6oz plums, halved and stoned
15ml/1 tbsp soft light brown sugar
150ml/¼ pint/⅔ cup vegetable stock
45ml/3 tbsp sherry
10ml/2 tsp balsamic vinegar

SERVES 4

2 Stir the lemon juice into a saucepan of lightly salted water and bring to the boil. Cut the heads of chicory lengthways into quarters and add to the pan. Cook for 3 minutes, then drain and set aside.

4 Brush the chicory pieces with oil and place them alongside the duck. Bake for 6 minutes more.

5 Stir the sherry and balsamic vinegar into the purée and season to taste with salt and pepper. Arrange the chicory pieces on a platter. Slice the duck breasts and fan them out on top of the chicory. Spoon the purée over the top and serve.

3 Score the duck breasts, brush with honey and sprinkle with a little salt. Transfer to a baking sheet and bake for 6–9 minutes, depending on weight.

1 Preheat the oven to 220°C/ 425°F/Gas 7. Make the plum purée. Put the apple, plums, sugar and stock into a saucepan. Bring to the boil, lower the heat and simmer for 10 minutes until the fruit is soft. Press the fruit through a strainer into a bowl and set it aside.

PIGEON BREASTS WITH PANCETTA

Mild succulent pigeon breasts are easy to cook and make an impressive main course for a special dinner.
Serve this Italian-style dish with polenta and some simple green vegetables.

4 whole pigeons
2 large onions
2 carrots, roughly chopped
1 celery stick, trimmed and
   roughly chopped
25g/1oz dried porcini mushrooms
50g/2oz pancetta
25g/1oz/2 tbsp butter
30ml/2 tbsp olive oil
2 garlic cloves, crushed
150ml/¼ pint/⅔ cup red wine
salt and ground black pepper
flat leaf parsley, to garnish
cooked oyster mushrooms, to serve

SERVES 4

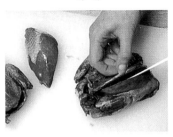

1 To prepare a pigeon, cut down the length of the bird, just to one side of the breastbone. Gradually scrape away the meat from the breastbone until the breast comes away completely. Do the same on the other side then repeat with the remaining pigeons.

2 Put the pigeon carcasses in a large saucepan. Halve one of the onions, leaving the skin on. Add to the pan with the carrots and celery and just cover with water. Bring to the boil, reduce the heat and simmer very gently, uncovered, for about 1½ hours to make a dark, rich stock. Leave to cool slightly, then strain through a large sieve into a bowl.

3 Cover the dried mushrooms with 150ml/¼ pint/⅔ cup hot water and soak for 30 minutes. Cut the pancetta into small dice.

4 Peel and finely chop the remaining onion. Melt half the butter with the oil in a large frying pan. Add the onion and pancetta and fry very gently for 3 minutes. Add the pigeon breasts, skin sides down and fry for 2 minutes until browned. Turn over and fry for a further 2 minutes.

5 Add the mushrooms, with the soaking liquid, garlic, wine and 250ml/8fl oz/1 cup of the stock. Bring just to the boil, then reduce the heat and simmer gently for 5 minutes until the pigeon breasts are tender, but still a little pink in the centre.

6 Lift out the pigeon breasts and keep them hot. Return the sauce to the boil and boil rapidly to reduce slightly. Gradually whisk in all the remaining butter and season with salt and pepper to taste.

7 Transfer the pigeon breasts to warmed serving plates and pour over the sauce. Serve at once, garnished with sprigs of parsley and accompanied by oyster mushrooms.

COOK'S TIP
If buying pigeons from a butcher, order them in advance and ask him to remove the breasts for you. You can also joint the legs and fry these with the breasts, although there is little meat on them and you might prefer to let them flavour the stock.

MOROCCAN PIGEON PIE

This recipe is based upon a classic Moroccan dish called Pastilla, which is a filo pastry pie, filled with an unusual but delicious mixture of pigeon, eggs, spices and nuts. If pigeon is unavailable, chicken makes a good substitute.

3 pigeons
50g/2oz/4 tbsp butter
1 onion, chopped
1 cinnamon stick
2.5ml/½ tsp ground ginger
30ml/2 tbsp chopped fresh coriander
45ml/3 tbsp chopped fresh parsley
pinch of ground turmeric
15ml/1 tbsp caster sugar
1.5ml/¼ tsp ground cinnamon
115g/4oz/1 cup toasted almonds,
finely chopped
6 eggs, beaten
salt and ground black pepper
cinnamon and icing sugar, to garnish

FOR THE PASTRY
175g/6oz/¾ cup butter, melted
16 sheets filo pastry
1 egg yolk

SERVES 6

 Wash the pigeons and place in a pan with the butter, onion, cinnamon stick, ginger, coriander, parsley and turmeric. Season with salt and pepper. Add just enough water to cover and bring to the boil. Cover and simmer gently for about 1 hour, until the pigeon flesh is very tender.

2 Strain off the stock and reserve. Skin and bone the pigeons, and shred the flesh into bite-size pieces. Preheat the oven to 180°C/350°F/Gas 4. Mix together the sugar, cinnamon and almonds, and set aside.

3 Measure 150ml/¼ pint/⅔ cup of the reserved stock into a small pan. Add the eggs and mix well. Stir over a low heat until creamy and very thick and almost set. Season with salt and pepper.

4 Brush a 30cm/12in diameter ovenproof dish with some of the melted butter and lay the first sheet of pastry in the dish. Brush this with butter and continue with five more sheets of pastry. Cover with the almond mixture, then half the egg mixture. Moisten with a little stock.

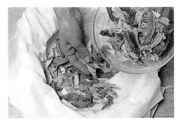

5 Layer four more sheets of filo pastry, brushing with butter as before. Lay the pigeon meat on top, then add the remaining egg mixture and more stock. Cover with all the remaining pastry, brushing each sheet with butter, and tuck in any overlap.

6 Brush the pie with egg yolk and bake for 40 minutes. Raise the oven temperature to 200°C/400°F/Gas 6, and bake for 15 minutes more, until the pastry is crisp and golden. Garnish with a lattice design of cinnamon and icing sugar. Serve hot.

WOOD PIGEON AND CHESTNUT CASSEROLE WITH PORT

Relish the flavours of autumn in this delicious, warming casserole.

30ml/2 tbsp oil
4 pigeons, halved
1 onion, chopped
6 streaky bacon rashers, chopped
25g/1oz/2 tbsp plain flour
400ml/14fl oz/1⅔ cups game or
chicken stock
150ml/¼ pint/⅔ cup orange juice
30ml/2 tbsp port
225g/8oz/2 cups shelled chestnuts
25g/1oz/2 tbsp butter
2 oranges, sliced
salt and ground black pepper
watercress sprigs, to garnish

SERVES 4

COOK'S TIP
To shell fresh chestnuts, make a cross
with a sharp knife on each nut. Cook
in a hot oven for 15 minutes until the
shells crack, then peel.

 Preheat the oven to 180°C/
350°F/Gas 4. Heat the oil in a
shallow flameproof casserole and
sauté the pigeons until browned.
Transfer them to a bowl.

2 Add the chopped onion and
bacon to the pan and sauté
until golden. Stir in the flour and cook
for 1 minute until it begins to brown.
Pour in the stock, orange juice and
port, with salt and pepper to taste.
Bring to the boil, stirring constantly,
then return the pigeons to the
casserole. Cover, place in the oven
and cook for 30 minutes.

3 Stir the chestnuts into the
casserole, return to the oven
and cook for 30 minutes more.

4 Just before serving, melt the
butter in a frying pan. Fry the
orange slices until golden on both
sides. Garnish the pigeon casserole
with the orange slices and watercress
sprigs. Serve at once.

366

RABBIT WITH PUY LENTILS AND PORT

Port gives this rustic dish from France a wonderfully warm and rich flavour.

15ml/1 tbsp plain flour
450g/1lb diced boneless rabbit
15ml/1 tbsp olive oil
2 onions, sliced
1 garlic clove, crushed
225g/8oz/3 cups mushrooms, sliced
45ml/3 tbsp port
400ml/14fl oz/1²/₃ cups chicken or
vegetable stock
5ml/1 tsp red wine vinegar
30ml/2 tbsp chopped fresh parsley,
plus extra to garnish
15ml/1 tbsp tomato purée
175g/6oz/³/₄ cup Puy lentils
12 slices French bread
30ml/2 tbsp olive purée
15g/¹/₂ oz/1 tbsp butter
salt and ground black pepper

SERVES 4

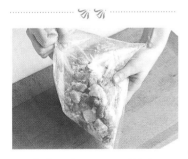

1   Preheat the oven to 180°C/ 350°F/Gas 4. Put the plain flour into a plastic bag, season with salt and pepper, and add the rabbit. Shake until evenly coated in flour.

2   Heat the oil in a flameproof casserole and fry the rabbit until all the pieces are browned.

3   Stir in the sliced onions, garlic and mushrooms. Add the port, stock, vinegar, parsley and tomato purée. Stir well, then bring the mixture to the boil.

4   Cover the casserole with a lid, transfer it to the oven and cook for 40 minutes. Meanwhile, bring a saucepan of lightly salted water to the boil. Add the lentils and cook for 35 minutes until tender.

5   Spread the French bread with the olive purée. Drain the lentils, stir them into the casserole and put the bread on top, with the topping uppermost. Dot with butter.

6   Return the casserole to the oven and cook, uncovered, for a further 10 minutes. Serve garnished with lots of chopped parsley.

RABBIT SALMOREJO

Small pieces of jointed rabbit, conveniently sold in packs at the supermarket, make an interesting alternative to chicken in this light, spicy sauté from Spain. Serve with a simple dressed salad.

675g/1½lb rabbit portions
300ml/½ pint/1¼ cups dry white wine
15ml/1 tbsp sherry vinegar
several oregano sprigs
2 bay leaves
90ml/6 tbsp olive oil
175g/6oz baby onions, peeled and
left whole
1 red chilli, seeded and finely chopped
4 garlic cloves, sliced
10ml/2 tsp paprika
150ml/¼ pint/⅔ cup chicken stock
salt and ground black pepper
flat leaf parsley sprigs, to garnish

SERVES 4

1 Put the rabbit in a bowl. Add the wine, vinegar, oregano and bay leaves and toss together lightly. Cover and leave to marinate for several hours or overnight.

2 Drain the rabbit, reserving the marinade, and pat dry on kitchen paper. Heat the oil in a large sauté or frying pan. Add the rabbit and fry on all sides until golden, then remove with a slotted spoon. Fry the onions until beginning to colour.

3 Remove the onions from the pan and add the chilli, garlic and paprika. Cook, stirring for about a minute. Add the reserved marinade, with the stock. Season lightly.

4 Return the rabbit to the pan with the onions. Bring to the boil, then reduce the heat and cover with a lid. Simmer very gently for about 45 minutes until the rabbit is tender. Serve garnished with a few sprigs of flat leaf parsley, if you like.

COOK'S TIP
If more convenient, rather than cooking on the hob, transfer the stew to an ovenproof dish and bake in the oven at 180°C/350°F/Gas 4 for about 50 minutes.

GRAINS AND PULSES

*Mediterranean cooks are responsible for creating fabulous
risottos, paella, pizzas and pasta dishes as well as for
using pulses in aromatic salads and succulent stews.*

The countries surrounding the Mediterranean produce a seemingly inexhaustible quantity and variety of grains and pulses. Wheat, the most ancient cereal grown in the region, predominates and it is processed in many forms for use in dishes common to the entire area as well as in unusual local specialities. Centuries of trading and travel have resulted in the exchanging and marrying of methods, ingredients and seasonings so that dishes originally associated with one country, are found in various forms in different areas of the Mediterranean.

Pasta, for example, consumed with gusto in Italy, is known as *rishta* in the eastern Mediterranean, as *fideos* in Spain and as *macaroni* or *koshari* in Egypt.

Bread is a staple food all over the Mediterranean. It is remarkable that a product of the same basic ingredients can be so varied in flavour and texture. There are plain Italian breads made with olive oil – focaccia and ciabatta – as well as a feast of richly flavoured breads with added ingredients, such as sun-dried tomatoes and herbs. Crisp grissini breadsticks or little toasts, crostini, are also bread

BELOW: Spain produces a wide range of grains of all types, seen here at a typical market.

products. Visit any part of France and see how important freshly baked breads are to the French. All over France, bakeries stay open all through the day, turning out batch after batch of hot bread, from rich brioches to crisp baguettes. Freshly baked breads are vital to the French and bakers do not depend on preservatives as the bread has to be prepared fresh every day.

Festive breads are still widely enjoyed. Among the most elaborate, there is the braided Greek Easter Bread, flavoured with nuts and fruit and adorned with hard-boiled eggs that are dyed red. According to legend, these will keep those who eat them safe from harm.

Unleavened or slightly leavened flat breads of the eastern Mediterranean and North Africa are eaten with every meal. There is well-known pitta which, in fact, varies widely in shape and size. The Turks bake a huge, flat loaf that inflates like a balloon during baking – it is carried ceremoniously to the table to be shared by diners who appreciate its soft, chewy texture for mopping up spicy sauces. Pitta bread is often used instead of cutlery, as a scoop or, when slit, it forms a pocket that is a perfect container for salads, beans, falafel or grilled meat.

Wheat flour is also used to make the fine pastries of North Africa, Lebanon, Greece and Turkey. Popular filo pastry is skilfully stretched into an almost transparent sheet which is then brushed with olive oil or melted butter and folded into layers that are light and crisp when cooked. Filo is used in many sweet or savoury classics from tiny finger-sized pastries to the rich Moroccan pastilla, a spicy pigeon pie seasoned with cloves and cinnamon.

Couscous is another wheat product. It is a kind of coarsely ground wheat that gives its name to the traditional stew of spiced meat or vegetables that is ladled over the steamed couscous. At its most splendid, the mound of couscous with its delectable topping is served as a finale at a special feast or banquet when guests have already enjoyed several delicate courses.

ABOVE: The fertile Guadalquivir valley in Spain.

Rice has been central to Mediterranean cookery for twelve thousand years. The Moors brought rice to Europe in the eighth century through the eastern Mediterranean trade routes from Persia and Asia. With its strong Moorish tradition, southern Spain, particularly Valencia, is the country's main producer of rice. The national dish of paella originates from the coastal cities and fishing ports of Andalucia, but rice is more widely used than for this one dish. Many rich, saffron-flavoured rice recipes are popular, and they are good with *zarzuela*, an extravagant feast of fish and crustacea.

Italians also consume a lot of rice, predominantly arborio, a short grain, starchy rice that makes soft creamy risottos, this is preferred to the dry, long grain varieties used further south. Risotto alla Milanese, a subtle dish enriched with saffron, wine and Parmesan, is just one example, many others use fresh or dried mushrooms. By

way of contrast, the fiery, dry pilaffs of Turkey and the Middle East are heavily spiced and flavoured with herbs, dried fruits, nuts and vegetables.

Chick-peas are among the most popular of the Mediterranean pulses and form the basis of creamy pastes, like hummus. Along with other beans and pulses they are the base for many piping-hot soups and they are also widely used in cold, garlic dressed salads.

Traditionally a peasant food, beans are cooked slowly during which time their flavour is enhanced by adding inexpensive highly seasoned meats or garlic-cured sausages. Served with locally produced vegetables, beans are the heart of many delicious stews, such as the traditional *cassoulet* of France.

Before cooking dried beans, soak them in water overnight. Boil them rapidly for ten minutes to destroy any natural toxins, then simmer until the beans are tender. Add salt only towards the end of the cooking time – if added sooner, salt will toughen the beans.

PERSIAN RICE

Plain rice in Iran is called Chelo. The rice is soaked in salted water before cooking, and it is important not to skimp on this process. The longer it is soaked, the better the flavour of the finished rice.

350g/12oz/1¾ cups long grain rice
about 20ml/4 tsp salt
40g/1½oz/3 tbsp butter, melted
2–3 saffron strands, soaked in 15ml/
1 tbsp boiling water (optional)

SERVES 4

|1| Soak the rice in lukewarm water, salted with 15ml/3 tsp salt, for at least 2 hours.

|2| When the rice has soaked and you are ready to cook, fill a non-stick pan with fresh water, add 5ml/1 tsp salt and bring to the boil.

|3| Drain the rice well and stir it into the boiling water. Boil for 5 minutes, then reduce the heat and simmer for about 10 minutes until half-cooked. Drain and rinse in lukewarm water. Wash and dry the pan.

|4| Heat 30ml/2 tbsp of the melted butter in the saucepan. Keep the heat low so that it does not brown. Add about 15ml/1 tbsp water and stir in the rice. Cook the rice over a very low heat for 10 minutes, then pour over the remaining butter.

|5| Cover the pan with a clean dish towel and secure with a tight-fitting lid, lifting back the corners of the cloth over the lid.

|6| Steam for 30–40 minutes. The dish towel will absorb the excess steam and will turn the bottom of the rice into a crisp, golden crust known as *tahdiq*. Many regard this as the best part of the rice. If liked, mix 30–45ml/2–3 tbsp of the rice with the saffron water and sprinkle over the top. Serve.

PLAIN RICE

This is a simplified and slightly quicker version of Persian rice (Chelo).

750ml/1¼ pints/3 cups water
5ml/1 tsp salt
350g/12oz/1¾ cups basmati rice
40g/1½ oz/3 tbsp butter

SERVES 4

|1| Place the water and salt in a non-stick saucepan and pour in the rice. Set aside to soak for at least 30 minutes and for up to 2 hours.

|2| Bring the water and rice to the boil, then reduce the heat and simmer for 10–15 minutes until all the water has been absorbed.

|3| Add the butter to the rice, cover the pan with a tight-fitting lid and steam over a very low heat for about 30 minutes.

SPICED RICE

In the countries that border the eastern Mediterranean, rice is served for everyday meals and feasts.
Spices, nuts and dried fruit can be used to turn boiled rice into a special dish.

225g/8oz/generous 1 cup basmati rice
30ml/2 tbsp oil
2.5cm/1in cinnamon stick
1.5ml/¼ tsp ground turmeric
1.5ml/¼ tsp tomato purée
15ml/1 tbsp raisins
25g/1oz/¼ tsp toasted almonds,
to serve
salt and freshly ground black pepper

SERVES 4-6

1 First make simple boiled rice: using a sieve, rinse the rice in cold running water until the water runs clear.

2 Add the rice to a saucepan of fast boiling water, add 5ml/1 tsp salt and boil for about 5–7 minutes or until the grains are tender. Drain and rinse with a little boiling water.

3 To make fried rice, heat the oil in a large frying pan. Add the cinnamon stick and the turmeric and then the boiled rice. Stir well and heat thoroughly. Mix in the tomato purée and the raisins, and taste to check the seasoning.

4 Remove the cinnamon stick, spoon the rice into a dish and serve, sprinkled with the almonds.

COOK'S TIP
Pouring water through the boiled rice removes the excess starch.

BULGUR PILAFF

Bulgur – or cracked wheat – is much easier to cook than rice. For every 1 cup of grain, you simply need
2 cups of liquid. Then you can add herbs, nuts or dried fruits to make the pilaff more interesting.

about 60ml/4 tbsp oil
2 onions, finely chopped
350g/12oz/2 cups bulgur wheat
1 litre/1¾ pints/4 cups hot chicken or
vegetable stock
2–3 fresh mint or flat leaf
parsley sprigs
3–4 ready-to-eat dried apricots, sliced
45ml/3 tbsp pine nuts, toasted
salt and ground black pepper
1 fresh mint sprig, to garnish

SERVES 8

1 Heat the oil in a large frying pan. When it is hot, toss in the onions. Stir over a medium to high heat until the onions have browned slightly.

2 Wash the bulgur wheat and drain it thoroughly, squeezing out any excess moisture. Add the bulgur wheat to the sautéed onion and stir for a few minutes to coat the grains with the oil, adding a little more if necessary.

3 Add the stock. Bring to the boil, switch off the heat and cover.

4 Allow to stand for 10 minutes. Meanwhile, chop the herbs. Check the pilaff seasoning and add the apricots. To serve, spoon the hot bulgur wheat into a large dish and sprinkle over the herbs and toasted pine nuts. Garnish with mint.

SWEET RICE

In Iran, sweet rice (Shirin Polo) is always served at wedding banquets and on other traditional special occasions.

3 oranges
90ml/6 tbsp sugar
5–6 carrots, cut into julienne strips
40g/1¹/₂oz/3 tbsp butter, melted
50g/2oz/¹/₂ cup mixed chopped
pistachios, almonds and pine nuts
675g/1¹/₂lb/3¹/₂ cups basmati rice,
soaked in salted water for 2 hours
2–3 saffron strands, soaked in 15ml/
1 tbsp boiling water
salt, to taste

SERVES 8-10

2 Simmer the peel in water for 10 minutes, drain and repeat until the bitterness of the peel has gone.

3 Add 45ml/3 tbsp of sugar and 60ml/4 tbsp water to the peel. Boil until the water is reduced by half. Set aside. Fry the carrots in 15ml/ 1 tbsp of butter for 3 minutes. Add the remaining sugar and 60ml/4 tbsp water, and simmer for 10 minutes until the water has evaporated.

4 Stir the carrots and half of the nuts into the orange peel mixture and set aside. Drain the rice, boil in salted water for 5 minutes, then reduce the heat and simmer for 10 minutes. Drain and rinse.

1 Cut the peel from the oranges. Scrape off any pith. Cut the peel into thin shreds and place in a pan.

5 Heat 15ml/1 tbsp of the butter in the pan and add 45ml/3 tbsp water. Fork in a little rice and spoon on some carrot mixture. Make layers until the mixture has been used up.

6 Cook gently for 10 minutes. Pour over the remaining butter and cover with a clean dish towel. Secure the lid and steam for 30–45 minutes. Serve garnished with the remaining nuts and the saffron water.

RICE WITH FRESH HERBS

Chives and spring onions give this easy rice dish a lovely fresh flavour.

350g/12oz/1¾ cups basmati rice, soaked
in salted water for 2 hours
30ml/2 tbsp chopped fresh parsley
30ml/2 tbsp chopped fresh coriander
30ml/2 tbsp finely snipped fresh chives
15ml/1 tbsp finely chopped fresh dill
3–4 spring onions, finely chopped
2–3 saffron strands (optional)
50g/2oz/¹/₄ cup butter
5ml/1 tsp ground cinnamon
salt

SERVES 4

1 Drain the rice, then boil in a pan of salted water for 5 minutes. Reduce the heat and simmer for 10 minutes.

2 Stir in the herbs and spring onions, and mix well with a fork. Simmer for a few minutes more, then drain but do not rinse. Wash and dry the pan. If using the saffron, soak the strands in 15ml/1 tbsp boiling water and set aside.

3 Heat half of the butter in the pan, add 15ml/1 tbsp water, then stir in the rice. Cook over a very low heat for 10 minutes, by which time it will be half-cooked. Add the remaining butter, the cinnamon and saffron water, if using, and cover with a clean dish towel. Secure with a tight-fitting lid, and steam over a low heat for 30–40 minutes. Serve at once.

SWEET AND SOUR RICE

Persian Zereshk Polo is flavoured with fruit and spices and is usually served with chicken dishes.

50g/2oz zereshk
40g/1¹/₂oz/3 tbsp butter, melted
50g/2oz/¹/₃ cup raisins
30ml/2 tbsp sugar
5ml/1 tsp ground cinnamon
5ml/1 tsp ground cumin
350g/12oz/1¾ cups basmati rice, soaked
in salted water for 2 hours
2–3 saffron strands, soaked in 15ml/
1 tbsp boiling water
pinch of salt

SERVES 4

1 Thoroughly wash the *zereshk* in cold water at least 4–5 times to rinse off any bits of grit.

2 Heat 15ml/1 tbsp of the butter in a small frying pan and stir-fry the raisins for 1–2 minutes.

3 Add the *zereshk*, fry for a few seconds, then add the sugar, and half of the ground spices. Cook briefly and then set aside.

4 Drain the rice. Boil in salted water for 5 minutes. Reduce the heat and simmer for 10 minutes.

5 Drain the rice again; rinse well, then wash and dry the pan. Heat half of the remaining butter in the pan, add 15ml/1 tbsp water and fork in half of the rice.

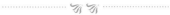

COOK'S TIP
Zereshk are very small dried berries that are delicious mixed with rice. They are available from most Persian and Middle Eastern food stores.

6 Sprinkle with half of the raisin and *zereshk* mixture, and top with all but 45ml/3 tbsp of the rice. Sprinkle the remaining raisin mixture evenly over the top.

7 Mix the reserved rice with the remaining cinnamon and cumin and scatter over the top of the rice mixture. Drizzle the remaining butter over and then cover the pan with a clean dish towel. Secure with a tight-fitting lid, lifting back the corners of the cloth over the lid. Steam the sweet and sour rice over a low heat for 30–40 minutes.

8 Just before serving, mix 45ml/3 tbsp of the rice with the saffron water. Spoon the rice on to a large flat serving dish and scatter the saffron rice over the top to decorate.

RICE WITH DILL AND BROAD BEANS

With its delicate colours and wonderful flavours, this dish is perfect for spring.

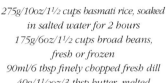

275g/10oz/1½ cups basmati rice, soaked
in salted water for 2 hours
175g/6oz/1½ cups broad beans,
fresh or frozen
90ml/6 tbsp finely chopped fresh dill
40g/1½oz/3 tbsp butter, melted
5ml/1 tsp ground cinnamon
5ml/1 tsp ground cumin
2–3 saffron strands, soaked in 15ml/
1 tbsp boiling water
salt

SERVES 4

1 Drain the rice and then boil in salted water for 5 minutes. Reduce the heat and simmer very gently for 10 minutes until partially cooked. Drain, rinse and drain again. Mix the broad beans and dill.

2 Put 15ml/1 tbsp of the melted butter in a non-stick saucepan, then add enough rice to cover the bottom of the pan. Add a quarter of the broad bean and dill mixture in an even layer.

3 Add another layer of rice, followed by a layer of broad beans and dill, and continue making layers until all the beans and dill are used, finishing with a layer of rice.

4 Cook over a gentle heat for 10 minutes. Pour the remaining melted butter over the rice.

5 Sprinkle the cinnamon and cumin evenly over the top of the rice. Cover the pan with a clean dish towel and secure with a tight-fitting lid, lifting back the corners of the cloth over the lid, and then steam over a low heat for 30–45 minutes.

6 Mix 45ml/3 tbsp of the rice with the saffron water. Spoon the remaining rice on to a large serving dish and scatter over the saffron rice to decorate. Serve with either a lamb or a chicken dish.

RISOTTO WITH SPRING VEGETABLES

This is one of the prettiest risotti, especially if you can manage to find yellow courgettes.

115g/4oz/1 cup shelled fresh peas
115g/4oz/1 cup French beans,
cut into short lengths
30ml/2 tbsp olive oil
75g/3oz/6 tbsp butter
2 small yellow courgettes,
cut into matchsticks
1 onion, finely chopped
275g/10oz/1½ cups risotto rice
120ml/4fl oz/½ cup Italian dry
white vermouth
about 1 litre/1¾ pints/4 cups
boiling chicken stock
75g/3oz/1 cup grated
Parmesan cheese
a small handful of fresh basil leaves,
finely shredded, plus a few whole
leaves, to garnish
salt and ground black pepper

SERVES 4

1 Blanch the peas and beans in a large saucepan of lightly salted boiling water for 2–3 minutes until just tender. Drain, refresh under cold running water, drain again and set aside for later.

2 Heat the oil and 25g/1oz/2 tbsp of the butter in a medium saucepan until foaming. Add the courgettes and cook gently for about 3 minutes until just softened. Remove with a slotted spoon and set aside. Add the onion to the pan and cook gently for about 3 minutes, stirring frequently, until softened.

3 Stir in the rice until the grains start to swell and burst, then add the vermouth. Stir until the vermouth stops sizzling and most of it has been absorbed by the rice, then ladle in a little of the stock, with salt and pepper to taste. Stir over low heat until the stock has been absorbed.

4 Continue cooking and stirring for 20–25 minutes, adding the remaining stock, a few ladles at a time. The rice should be *al dente* and the risotto should have a moist and creamy appearance.

5 Gently stir in the peas, beans, remaining butter and about half the grated Parmesan. Heat through, then stir in the shredded basil and taste for seasoning. Garnish with a few whole basil leaves and serve hot, with the remaining Parmesan.

RISOTTO WITH FOUR CHEESES

Risotto was originally a northern Italian dish but it is now found all over Italy. Serve this rich risotto for a dinner-party first course, with sparkling white wine.

40g/1½oz/3 tbsp butter
1 small onion, finely chopped
1 litre/1¾ pints/4 cups boiling
chicken stock
350g/12oz/1¾ cups risotto rice
200ml/7fl oz/scant 1 cup sparkling
dry white wine
50g/2oz/½ cup grated Gruyère cheese
50g/2oz/½ cup diced Fontina cheese
50g/2oz/½ cup crumbled
Gorgonzola cheese
50g/2oz/⅔ cup grated
Parmesan cheese
salt and ground black pepper
fresh flat leaf parsley, to garnish

SERVES 6

1 Melt the butter in a saucepan until foaming. Add the onion and cook gently, stirring frequently, for about 3 minutes, until softened. Have the hot stock ready in an adjacent pan.

2 Add the rice to the onions and stir until the grains start to swell and burst, then add the sparkling wine. Stir until it stops sizzling and most of it has been absorbed by the rice, then pour in a little of the hot stock. Add salt and pepper to taste.

3 Stir over a low heat until the stock has been absorbed. Add more stock, a little at a time, allowing the rice to absorb it before adding more. Stir constantly.

4 After 20–25 minutes the rice will be *al dente* and the risotto creamy. Turn off the heat under the pan, then add the Gruyère, Fontina, Gorgonzola and 30ml/2 tbsp of the Parmesan. Stir gently until the cheeses have melted, then taste for seasoning. Tip into a serving bowl and garnish with parsley. Spoon the remaining Parmesan into a bowl and serve it separately.

PORCINI AND PARMESAN RISOTTO

The success of a good risotto depends on the quality of the rice used and the technique. For this variation on the classic Risotto alla Milanese, saffron, porcini mushrooms and Parmesan cheese are stirred into the creamy cooked rice.

🌱 🌱

10g/¼ oz/2 tbsp dried porcini
mushrooms
300ml/½ pint/1¼ cups warm water
1.2 litres/2 pints/5 cups vegetable stock
a generous pinch of saffron strands
30ml/2 tbsp olive oil
1 onion, finely chopped
1 garlic clove, crushed
250g/9oz/1⅓ cups arborio or
carnaroli rice
150ml/¼ pint/⅔ cup dry white wine
or 45ml/3 tbsp dry vermouth
25g/1oz/2 tbsp butter
50g/2oz/⅔ cup freshly grated
Parmesan cheese
salt and ground black pepper

SERVES 4

🌱 🌱

1 Soak the dried mushrooms in the warm water for 20 minutes. Lift out with a slotted spoon. Filter the soaking water through a layer of kitchen paper in a sieve, then place it in a saucepan with the stock. Bring the liquid to a gentle simmer.

2 Put about 45ml/3 tbsp of the hot stock in a cup and stir in the saffron strands. Set aside.

3 Finely chop the mushrooms. Heat the oil in a separate pan and lightly sauté the onion, garlic and mushrooms for 5 minutes. Gradually add the rice, stirring. Cook for 2 minutes, stirring. Season generously.

🌱 🌱

VARIATIONS
There are endless variations on this delectable dish. The proportion of stock to rice, onions, garlic and butter must remain constant, but you can ring the changes with the flavourings and cheese. Try Pecorino with lightly blanched baby vegetables to make risotto primavera.

4 Pour in the wine or vermouth. Cook, stirring, until it has been absorbed, then ladle in a quarter of the stock. Bring to the boil, stirring. Cook, stirring constantly with a wooden spoon, until most of the liquid has been absorbed.

5 Continue to add the stock, a ladle at a time, stirring after each addition. The secret of a good risotto is to add the stock gradually and to stir frequently to encourage a creamy texture.

6 After about 20 minutes, when all the stock has been absorbed and the rice is cooked but still has a "bite", stir in the butter, saffron water and strands, and half of the Parmesan cheese. Serve, sprinkled with the remaining Parmesan.

PILAFF WITH SAFFRON AND PICKLED WALNUTS

Pickled walnuts have a warm, tangy flavour that is lovely in rice and bulgur wheat dishes. This Eastern Mediterranean pilaff is interesting enough to serve on its own or with grilled lamb or pork.

5ml/1 tsp saffron strands
40g/1½oz/½ cup pine nuts
45ml/3 tbsp olive oil
1 large onion, chopped
3 garlic cloves, crushed
1.5ml/¼ tsp ground allspice
4cm/1½in piece fresh root
ginger, grated
225g/8oz/generous 1 cup
long grain rice
300ml/½ pint/1¼ cups vegetable stock
50g/2oz/½ cup pickled walnuts,
drained and roughly chopped
40g/1½oz/¼ cup raisins
45ml/3 tbsp roughly chopped parsley
or fresh coriander
salt and ground black pepper
parsley or coriander, to garnish
natural yogurt, to serve

1 Put the saffron in a bowl with 15ml/1 tbsp boiling water and leave to stand. Heat a large frying pan and dry-fry the pine nuts until they turn golden. Set them aside.

2 Heat the oil in the pan and fry the onion, garlic and allspice for 3 minutes. Stir in the ginger and rice and cook for 1 minute more.

3 Add the stock and bring to the boil. Reduce the heat, cover and simmer gently for 15 minutes until the rice is just tender.

4 Stir in the saffron and liquid, the pine nuts, pickled walnuts, raisins and parsley or coriander. Season to taste with salt and pepper. Heat through gently for 2 minutes. Garnish with parsley or coriander leaves and serve with natural yogurt.

VARIATION
Use one small aubergine, chopped and fried in a little olive oil, instead of the pickled walnuts, if you prefer.

EGYPTIAN RICE WITH LENTILS

*Lentils are cooked with spices in many ways in the Middle East, and two important staples come together
in this dish, which can be served hot or cold.*

---

*350g/12oz/1½ cups large brown
lentils, soaked overnight in water
2 large onions
45ml/3 tbsp olive oil
15ml/1 tbsp ground cumin
2.5ml/½ tsp ground cinnamon
225g/8oz/generous 1 cup
long grain rice
salt and ground black pepper
flat leaf parsley, to garnish*

SERVES 6

1 Drain the lentils and put in a
large pan. Add enough water to
cover by 5cm/2in. Bring to the boil,
cover and simmer for 40 minutes to
1½ hours, or until tender. Drain
thoroughly.

2 Finely chop one onion, and
slice the other. Heat 15ml/1 tbsp
oil in a pan, add the chopped onion
and fry until soft. Add the lentils, salt,
pepper, cumin and cinnamon.

3 Measure the volume of rice and
add it, with the same volume of
water, to the lentil mixture. Cover and
simmer for about 20 minutes, until
both the rice and lentils are tender.
Heat the remaining oil in a frying pan,
and cook the sliced onion until very
dark brown. Tip the rice mixture into
a serving bowl, sprinkle with the
onion and serve hot or cold,
garnished with flat leaf parsley.

BROWN BEAN SALAD

Brown beans, sometimes called "ful medames", are widely used in Egyptian cookery, and are occasionally seen in health food shops here. Dried broad beans, black or red kidney beans make a good substitute.

350g/12oz/1½ cups dried brown
beans
3 thyme sprigs
2 bay leaves
1 onion, halved
4 garlic cloves, crushed
7.5ml/1½ tsp cumin seeds, crushed
3 spring onions, finely chopped
90ml/6 tbsp chopped fresh parsley
20ml/4 tsp lemon juice
90ml/6 tbsp olive oil
3 hard-boiled eggs, shelled and
roughly chopped
1 pickled cucumber, roughly chopped
salt and ground black pepper

SERVES 6

1 Put the beans in a bowl with plenty of cold water and leave to soak overnight. Drain, transfer to a saucepan and cover with fresh water. Bring to the boil and boil rapidly for 10 minutes.

2 Reduce the heat and add the thyme, bay leaves and onion. Simmer very gently for about 1 hour until tender. Drain and discard the herbs and onion.

3 Mix together the garlic, cumin, spring onions, parsley, lemon juice, oil and add a little salt and pepper. Pour over the beans and toss the ingredients lightly together.

4 Gently stir in the eggs and cucumber and serve at once.

COOK'S TIP
The cooking time for dried beans can vary considerably. They may need only 45 minutes, or a lot longer.

SPICED VEGETABLE COUSCOUS

Couscous, a cereal processed from semolina, is used throughout North Africa, mostly in Morocco,
where it is served with meat, poultry and Moroccan vegetable stews or tagines.

❧ ❧

45ml/3 tbsp vegetable oil
1 large onion, finely chopped
2 garlic cloves, crushed
15ml/1 tbsp tomato purée
2.5ml/½ tsp ground turmeric
2.5ml/½ tsp cayenne pepper
5ml/1 tsp ground coriander
5ml/1 tsp ground cumin
225g/8oz/1½ cups cauliflower florets
225g/8oz baby carrots, trimmed
1 red pepper, seeded and diced
4 beefsteak tomatoes
225g/8oz courgettes, thickly sliced
400g/14oz can chick-peas, drained
and rinsed
45ml/3 tbsp chopped fresh coriander
salt and ground black pepper
coriander sprigs, to garnish

FOR THE COUSCOUS
5ml/1 tsp salt
450g/1lb/2⅔ cups couscous
50g/2oz/2 tbsp butter

SERVES 6

❧ ❧

1 Heat 30ml/2 tbsp of the oil in a large pan, add the onion and garlic, and cook until soft. Stir in the tomato purée, turmeric, cayenne, ground coriander and cumin. Cook, stirring, for 2 minutes.

2 Add the cauliflower, carrots and pepper, with enough water to come halfway up the vegetables. Bring to the boil, then lower the heat, cover and simmer for 10 minutes.

❧ ❧

COOK'S TIP
Beefsteak tomatoes have excellent flavour and are ideal for this recipe, but you can substitute six ordinary tomatoes or two 400g/14oz cans chopped tomatoes.

❧ ❧

3 Plunge the tomatoes into boiling water for 30 seconds, then refresh in cold water. Peel away the skins and chop. Add the sliced courgettes, chick-peas and tomatoes to the other vegetables and cook for a further 10 minutes. Stir in the fresh coriander and season with salt and pepper. Keep hot.

4 To cook the couscous, bring 475ml/16fl oz/2 cups water to the boil in a large saucepan. Add the remaining oil and the salt. Remove from the heat, and add the couscous, stirring. Allow to swell for 2 minutes, then add the butter, and heat through gently, stirring to separate the grains.

5 Turn the couscous out on to a warm serving dish, and spoon the vegetables on top, pouring over any liquid. Garnish and serve.

SPICY CHICK-PEA AND AUBERGINE STEW

This is a Lebanese dish, but similar recipes are found all over the Mediterranean.

3 large aubergines, cubed
200g/7oz/1 cup chick-peas, soaked
overnight
60ml/4 tbsp olive oil
3 garlic cloves, chopped
2 large onions, chopped
2.5ml/½ tsp ground cumin
2.5ml/½ tsp ground cinnamon
2.5ml/½ tsp ground coriander
3 x 400g/14oz cans chopped tomatoes
salt and ground black pepper
cooked rice, to serve

FOR THE GARNISH
30ml/2 tbsp olive oil
1 onion, sliced
1 garlic clove, sliced
sprigs of coriander

SERVES 4

1 Place the aubergines in a colander and sprinkle them with salt. Sit the colander in a bowl and leave for 30 minutes, to allow the bitter juices to escape. Rinse with cold water and dry on kitchen paper.

2 Drain the chick-peas and put in a pan with enough water to cover. Bring to the boil and simmer for 30 minutes, or until tender. Drain.

3 Heat the oil in a large pan. Add the garlic and onion and cook gently, until soft. Add the spices and cook, stirring, for a few seconds. Add the aubergine and stir to coat with the spices and onion. Cook for 5 minutes. Add the tomatoes and chick-peas and season with salt and pepper. Cover and simmer for 20 minutes.

4 To make the garnish, heat the oil in a frying pan and, when very hot, add the sliced onion and garlic. Fry until golden and crisp. Serve the stew with rice, topped with the onion and garlic and garnished with coriander.

CHICK-PEA TAGINE

*One of the wonderful things about the tagine is its versatility. This vegetarian version
is delicious with a chunk of crusty bread.*

150g/5oz/³⁄₄ cup chick-peas, soaked
overnight, or 2 x 400g/14oz cans
chick-peas, drained
30ml/2 tbsp sunflower oil
1 large onion, chopped
1 garlic clove, crushed
400g/14oz can chopped tomatoes
5ml/1 tsp ground cumin
350ml/12fl oz/1¹⁄₂ cups
vegetable stock
¹⁄₄ preserved lemon
30ml/2 tbsp chopped fresh coriander

SERVES 4

1 If using dried, soaked chick-peas, cook in plenty of boiling
water for 1¹⁄₂–2 hours until tender.
Drain thoroughly.

2 Skin the chick-peas. Put them in a bowl of cold water and rub
them between your palms; the skins
will rise to the surface.

3 Heat the oil in a saucepan or flameproof casserole and fry the
onion and garlic for 8–10 minutes
until golden.

4 Add the chick-peas, tomatoes, cumin and stock, and stir well.
Bring to the boil, then simmer for
30–40 minutes, until the chick-peas
are soft and fairly dry.

5 Rinse the preserved lemon and cut away the flesh and pith. Cut
the peel into slivers and stir into the
chick-peas with the coriander. Serve.

SEMOLINA AND PESTO GNOCCHI

These gnocchi are cooked rounds of semolina paste, which are brushed with melted butter and then topped with cheese and baked. When they are carefully cooked, they taste wonderful, especially when served with a home-made tomato sauce.

750ml/1¼ pints/3 cups milk
200g/7oz/generous 1 cup semolina
45ml/3 tbsp pesto sauce
60ml/4 tbsp finely chopped sun-dried
tomatoes, patted dry if oily
50g/2oz/¼ cup butter
75g/3oz/1 cup freshly grated
Pecorino cheese
2 eggs, beaten
freshly grated nutmeg, to taste
salt and ground black pepper
tomato sauce, to serve
fresh basil sprigs, to garnish

SERVES 4

1 Heat the milk in a large non-stick saucepan. When it is on the point of boiling, sprinkle in the semolina, stirring constantly until the mixture is smooth and very thick. Lower the heat and simmer for 2 minutes until the paste starts to come away from the sides.

2 Remove from the heat and stir in the pesto and sun-dried tomatoes, with half of the butter and half of the Pecorino. Add the eggs, with nutmeg, salt and pepper to taste. Spoon on to a clean shallow baking dish or tin to a depth of 1cm/½in, and level the surface. Allow to cool, then chill.

3 Preheat the oven to 190°C/375°F/Gas 5. Lightly grease a shallow baking dish, then, using a 4cm/1½in scone cutter or a glass, stamp out as many rounds as possible from the semolina paste.

4 Place the leftover semolina paste on the bottom of the greased dish and arrange the rounds on top in overlapping circles.

5 Melt the remaining butter and brush it over the gnocchi. Sprinkle over the remaining Pecorino. Bake for 30–40 minutes until golden. Garnish with basil and serve with tomato sauce.

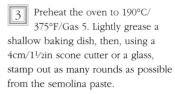

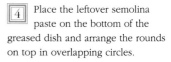

PUMPKIN GNOCCHI WITH A CHANTERELLE PARSLEY CREAM

Gnocchi is an Italian pasta dumpling, usually made from potatoes. In this special recipe, pumpkin is added, too. A chanterelle sauce provides both richness and flavour.

450g/1lb peeled floury potatoes
450g/1lb peeled pumpkin, chopped
2 egg yolks
200g/7oz/1¾ cups plain flour, plus more if necessary
pinch of ground allspice
1.5ml/¼ tsp ground cinnamon
pinch of grated nutmeg
finely grated rind of ½ orange
salt and ground black pepper
50g/2oz Parmesan cheese, shaved, to garnish

FOR THE SAUCE
30ml/2 tbsp olive oil
1 shallot, chopped
175g/6oz/2¼ cups fresh chanterelles, sliced, or 15g/½oz/¼ cup dried, soaked for 20 minutes in warm water
10ml/2 tsp almond butter
150ml/¼ pint/⅔ cup crème fraîche
a little milk or water
75ml/5 tbsp chopped fresh parsley

SERVES 4

1 Cover the potatoes with cold salted water, bring to the boil and cook for 20 minutes. Drain and set aside. Place the pumpkin in a bowl, cover and microwave on full power for 8 minutes. Alternatively, wrap the pumpkin in foil and bake at 180°C/350°F/Gas 4 for 30 minutes. Drain, add to the potato and pass through a vegetable mill into a bowl.

2 Add the egg yolks, flour, spices, orange rind and seasoning to the pumpkin and mix to a soft dough, adding more flour if needed. Spoon the mixture into a piping bag fitted with a 1cm/½in nozzle. Pipe on to a floured surface to make a 15cm/6in sausage. Roll in the flour and cut into 2.5cm/1in pieces. Repeat the process, making more sausage shapes.

3 Bring a large pan of salted water to the boil. Mark the gnocchi lightly with a fork and cook for 3–4 minutes in the boiling water.

4 Meanwhile, make the sauce. Heat the oil in a non-stick frying pan, add the shallot and fry until soft without colouring. Add the chanterelles and cook briefly, then add the almond butter. Stir to melt and stir in the crème fraîche. Simmer briefly and adjust the consistency with milk or water. Add the parsley and season to taste.

5 Lift the gnocchi out of the water with a slotted spoon, turn into bowls and spoon the sauce over the top. Scatter with the Parmesan.

SPINACH AND RICOTTA GNOCCHI

The success of this Italian dish lies in not overworking the mixture, to achieve delicious, light mouthfuls.

900g/2lb fresh spinach
350g/12oz/1½ cups ricotta cheese
60ml/4 tbsp freshly grated
Parmesan cheese
3 large eggs, beaten
1.5ml/¼ tsp grated nutmeg
45–60ml/3–4 tbsp plain flour
115g/4oz/½ cup butter, melted
salt and ground black pepper
freshly grated Parmesan cheese,
to serve

SERVES 4

1 Place the spinach in a large pan and cook for 5 minutes, until wilted. Leave to cool, then squeeze the spinach as dry as possible. Process in a blender or food processor, then transfer to a bowl.

2 Add the ricotta, Parmesan, eggs and nutmeg. Season with salt and pepper and mix together. Add enough flour to make the mixture into a soft dough. Using your hands, shape the mixture into 7.5cm/3in sausages, then dust lightly with flour.

3 Bring a large pan of salted water to the boil. Gently slide the gnocchi into the water and cook for 1–2 minutes, until they float to the surface. Remove the gnocchi with a slotted spoon and transfer to a warmed dish. Pour over the melted butter and sprinkle with Parmesan cheese. Serve at once.

POLENTA WITH MUSHROOM SAUCE

*In Italy, polenta often fulfils the same function as rice, bread or potatoes in providing the starchy base
for a meal. Here, it is cooked until it forms a soft dough, then flavoured with Parmesan.
Its subtle taste works well with this rich mushroom sauce.*

1.2 litres/2 pints/5 cups vegetable stock
350g/12oz/3 cups polenta
*50g/2oz/2/3 cup grated
Parmesan cheese*
salt and ground black pepper
fresh thyme sprigs, to garnish

FOR THE SAUCE
*15g/1/2oz/1 cup dried porcini
mushrooms*
15ml/1 tbsp olive oil
50g/2oz/1/4 cup butter
1 onion, finely chopped
1 carrot, finely chopped
1 celery stick, finely chopped
2 garlic cloves, crushed
*450g/1lb/6 cups mixed chestnut
and large flat mushrooms,
roughly chopped*
120ml/4fl oz/1/2 cup red wine
400g/14oz can chopped tomatoes
5ml/1 tsp tomato purée
*15ml/1 tbsp chopped fresh
thyme leaves*

SERVES 4

1 Make the sauce. Put the dried
mushrooms in a bowl, add
150ml/1/4 pint/2/3 cup hot water and
soak for 20 minutes. Drain the
mushrooms, reserving the liquid,
and chop them roughly.

2 Heat the oil and butter in a
saucepan. Fry the onion, carrot,
celery and garlic over a low heat until
the vegetables are beginning to
soften, then raise the heat and add the
fresh and soaked, dried mushrooms.
Cook for 8–10 minutes until the
mushrooms are soft and golden.

3 Pour in the wine and cook
rapidly for 2–3 minutes until
reduced, then tip in the tomatoes and
the reserved mushroom liquid. Stir in
the tomato purée, thyme and plenty
of salt and pepper. Lower the heat
and simmer for 20 minutes.

4 Meanwhile, heat the stock in a
large, heavy saucepan. Add a
generous pinch of salt. As soon as the
stock simmers, tip in the polenta in a
fine stream, whisking until the mixture
is smooth. Cook for 30 minutes,
stirring constantly, until the polenta
comes away from the pan. Remove
from the heat and stir in half of the
Parmesan and some black pepper.

5 Divide among four heated
bowls and top each with the
mushroom sauce. Sprinkle with the
remaining grated Parmesan cheese,
and garnish with thyme.

BAKED CHEESE POLENTA WITH TOMATO SAUCE

Polenta, or cornmeal, is a staple food in Italy. It is cooked like a sort of porridge, and eaten soft, or set, cut into shapes then baked or grilled.

5ml/1 tsp salt
250g/9oz/2¼ cups quick-cook polenta
5ml/1 tsp paprika
2.5ml/½ tsp ground nutmeg
30ml/2 tbsp olive oil
1 large onion, finely chopped
2 garlic cloves, crushed
2 x 400g/14oz cans chopped tomatoes
15ml/1 tbsp tomato purée
5ml/1 tsp sugar
75g/3oz Gruyère cheese, grated
salt and ground black pepper

SERVES 4

1 Preheat the oven to 200°C/ 400°F/Gas 6. Line a baking tin (28 x 18cm/11 x 7in) with clear film. Bring 1 litre/1¾ pints/4 cups water to the boil with the salt.

2 Pour in the polenta in a steady stream and cook, stirring continuously, for 5 minutes. Beat in the paprika and nutmeg, then pour into the prepared tin and smooth the surface. Leave to cool.

3 Heat the oil in a pan and cook the onion and garlic until soft. Add the tomatoes, purée and sugar. Season. Simmer for 20 minutes.

4 Turn out the polenta on to a chopping board, and cut into 5cm/2in squares. Place half the squares in a greased ovenproof dish. Spoon over half the tomato sauce, and sprinkle with half the cheese. Repeat the layers. Bake for about 25 minutes, until golden.

POLENTA ELISA

This dish comes from the valley around Lake Como, in Italy. Serve it solo as a starter, or with a mixed salad and some sliced salami or prosciutto for a midweek supper.

250ml/8fl oz/1 cup milk
225g/8oz/2 cups quick-cook polenta
115g/4oz/1 cup Gruyère cheese
115g/4oz/1 cup torta di Dolcelatte
cheese, crumbled
50g/2oz/¼ cup butter
2 garlic cloves, roughly chopped
a few fresh sage leaves, chopped
salt and freshly ground black pepper
prosciutto, to serve

SERVES 4

1 In a large pan, bring the milk and 750ml/1¼ pints/3 cups water to the boil, add 5ml/1 tsp salt, then tip in the polenta. Cook for about 8 minutes.

2 Preheat the oven to 200°C/400°F/Gas 6. Lightly grease a 20–25cm/8–10in baking dish.

3 Spoon half of the polenta into the baking dish and level. Cover with half of the grated Gruyère and crumbled Dolcelatte. Spoon the remaining polenta over the top and sprinkle with the remaining cheeses.

4 Melt the butter in a small pan until foaming, then fry the garlic and sage, stirring, until the butter turns golden brown.

5 Drizzle the butter mixture over the polenta and cheese and grind black pepper liberally over the top. Bake for 5 minutes. Serve hot, with slices of prosciutto.

COOK'S TIP
Pour the polenta into the boiling liquid in a continuous stream, stirring constantly. If using a whisk, change to a wooden spoon once the polenta starts to thicken, and keep stirring until it is very thick.

CALZONE

A calzone looks rather like a folded pizza, and consists of bread dough wrapped around a cheese and vegetable filling. The traditional tomato and garlic can be enlivened with chunks of sweet melting cheese, olives, crumbled grilled bacon, slices of pepperoni or anchovy fillets.

30ml/2 tbsp extra virgin olive oil
1 small red onion, thinly sliced
2 garlic cloves, crushed
400g/14oz can chopped tomatoes
50g/2oz sliced chorizo sausage
50g/2oz/1/2 cup pitted black olives
500g/1¼lb bread dough mix
200g/7oz mozzarella or other
semi-soft cheese, diced
5ml/1 tsp dried oregano
salt and freshly ground black pepper
oregano sprigs, to garnish

MAKES 4

[1] Heat the oil in a frying pan and sauté the onion and garlic for 5 minutes. Add the tomatoes and cook for 5 minutes more or until slightly reduced. Add the sliced chorizo and pitted black olives. Season with plenty of salt and pepper.

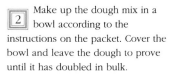

[2] Make up the dough mix in a bowl according to the instructions on the packet. Cover the bowl and leave the dough to prove until it has doubled in bulk.

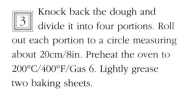

[3] Knock back the dough and divide it into four portions. Roll out each portion to a circle measuring about 20cm/8in. Preheat the oven to 200°C/400°F/Gas 6. Lightly grease two baking sheets.

[4] Spread the tomato filling on half of each dough circle, leaving a margin around the edge. Scatter the cheese on top. Sprinkle the filling with the dried oregano.

[5] Dampen the edges of the dough with cold water. Fold the dough in half and press the edges together to seal.

[6] Place two calzones on each baking sheet. Bake for 12–15 minutes until risen and golden. Cool for 2 minutes, then loosen with a palette knife and transfer to serving plates. Serve at once, garnished with oregano.

RADICCHIO PIZZA

This unusual pizza topping consists of chopped radicchio, leeks, tomatoes, and Parmesan and mozzarella cheeses. The base is a scone dough, making this a quick and easy supper dish to prepare. Serve with a crisp green salad.

FOR THE DOUGH
225g/8oz/2 cups self-raising flour
2.5ml/1/2 tsp salt
50g/2oz/1/4 cup butter
about 120ml/4fl oz/1/2 cup milk

FOR THE TOPPING
400ml/14fl oz/12/3 cups passata
pinch of dried basil
2 garlic cloves, crushed
25ml/11/2 tbsp olive oil, plus extra
for dipping
2 leeks, sliced
100g/31/2oz radicchio,
roughly chopped
20g/3/4oz Parmesan cheese, grated
115g/4oz mozzarella cheese, sliced
10–12 pitted black olives
fresh basil leaves, to garnish
salt and ground black pepper

SERVES 2

1   Preheat the oven to 220°C/
425°F/Gas 7 and grease a
baking sheet. Mix the flour and salt in
a bowl, rub in the butter, and stir in
enough milk to make a soft dough.
Roll it out on a lightly floured surface
to a 25–28cm/10–11in round. Place on
the baking sheet.

2   Mix the passata, basil and half
of the garlic in a small pan.
Season, then simmer over a moderate
heat until the mixture is thick and has
reduced by about half.

3   Heat the olive oil in a large
frying pan and fry the leeks and
remaining garlic for 4–5 minutes until
slightly softened. Add the radicchio
and cook, stirring continuously for a
few minutes, then cover and simmer
gently for about 5–10 minutes. Stir in
the Parmesan cheese and season with
salt and pepper.

4   Cover the dough base with the
passata mixture and then spoon
the leek and radicchio mixture on
top. Arrange the mozzarella slices
over this and scatter with the black
olives. Dip a few basil leaves in olive
oil, arrange on top and bake the pizza
for 15–20 minutes until the scone
base and top are golden brown.

RICOTTA AND FONTINA PIZZAS

The earthy flavours of the mixed mushrooms are delicious with the creamy cheeses.

2.5ml/½ tsp active dried yeast
pinch of sugar
450g/1lb/4 cups strong white flour
5ml/1 tsp salt
30ml/2 tbsp olive oil

FOR THE TOPPING
400g/14oz can chopped tomatoes
150ml/¼ pint/⅔ cup passata
5ml/1 tsp dried oregano
1 bay leaf
10ml/2 tsp malt vinegar
2 large garlic cloves, finely chopped
30ml/2 tbsp olive oil, plus extra
for brushing
350g/12oz/4 cups mixed mushrooms
(chestnut, flat or button), sliced
30ml/2 tbsp chopped fresh oregano,
plus whole leaves, to garnish
250g/9oz/generous 1 cup
ricotta cheese
225g/8oz Fontina cheese, sliced
salt and ground black pepper

SERVES 4

1 First, make the dough. Put 300ml/½ pint/1¼ cups warm water in a measuring jug. Add the yeast and sugar and leave for 5–10 minutes until frothy. Sift the flour and salt into a large bowl and make a well in the centre. Gradually pour in the yeast mixture and the olive oil. Mix to make a smooth dough. Knead on a lightly floured surface for about 10 minutes. Place the dough in a floured bowl, cover and leave to rise in a warm place for 1½ hours.

2 Make the tomato sauce. Place the tomatoes, passata, herbs, vinegar and half of the garlic in a pan, cover and bring to the boil. Lower the heat, remove the lid and simmer for 20 minutes, stirring occasionally, until reduced.

3 Make the topping. Heat the oil in a frying pan. Add the mushrooms and remaining garlic. Season to taste. Cook, stirring, for about 5 minutes or until the mushrooms are tender. Set aside.

4 Preheat the oven to 220°C/ 425°F/Gas 7. Knead the dough for 2 minutes, then divide into four equal pieces. Roll out each piece to a 25cm/10in round and place on to four lightly oiled baking sheets.

5 Spoon the tomato sauce over each dough round. Brush the edge with a little olive oil. Add the mushrooms, fresh oregano and cheeses. Bake for about 15 minutes until golden brown and crisp. Scatter the oregano leaves over the top.

MARRAKESH PIZZAS

In Morocco, cooks tend to place flavourings inside the pizza rather than on top of the bread.
The result is surprising – and quite delicious.

5ml/1 tsp sugar
10ml/2 tsp dried yeast
450g/1lb/4 cups white flour (or a
mixture of white and wholemeal
flour, according to preference)
salt
melted butter, for brushing
rocket salad and black olives, to serve

FOR THE FILLING
1 small onion, very finely chopped
2 tomatoes, peeled, seeded
and chopped
25ml/1½ tbsp chopped fresh parsley
25ml/1½ tbsp chopped
fresh coriander
5ml/1 tsp paprika
5ml/1 tsp ground cumin
50g/2oz vegetable suet, finely chopped
40g/1½ oz Cheddar cheese, grated

SERVES 4

1 First prepare the yeast. Place 150ml/¼ pint/⅔ cup warm water in a small bowl or jug, stir in the sugar and then sprinkle with the yeast. Stir once or twice, then set aside in a warm place for about 10 minutes until frothy.

2 Meanwhile, make the filling. Mix together the onion, tomatoes, parsley, coriander, paprika, cumin, suet and cheese, then season with salt and set aside.

3 In a large bowl, mix together the flour and 10ml/2 tsp salt. Add the yeast mixture and enough warm water (about 250ml/8fl oz/ 1 cup) to make a fairly soft dough.

4 Knead the mixture into a ball and then knead on a floured work surface for 10–12 minutes until the dough is firm and elastic.

5 Break the dough into four pieces. Shape each piece into a ball. On the floured surface, roll each into a rectangle, measuring 20 × 30cm/ 8 × 12in. Spread the filling down the centre of each rectangle, then fold into three, to make 20 × 10cm/ 8 × 4in rectangles.

6 Roll out the dough again, until it is the same size as before and again fold into three to make a smaller rectangle. (The filling will be squeezed out in places, but don't worry – just push it back inside.)

7 Place the pizzas on a buttered baking sheet, cover with oiled clear film and leave in a warm place for about 1 hour until slightly risen.

8 Heat a griddle and brush with butter. Prick the pizzas with a fork, five or six times on both sides, and then grill for about 8 minutes on each side until crisp and golden. Serve immediately, accompanied by rocket salad and black olives.

MUSHROOM AND PESTO PIZZA

—

Home-made Italian-style pizzas are a little time-consuming to make but the results are well worth the effort.

·········· 🌿 🌿 ··········

FOR THE PIZZA BASE

350g/12oz/3 cups strong plain flour
1.5ml/¼ tsp salt
15g/½oz easy-blend dried yeast
15ml/1 tbsp olive oil

FOR THE FILLING

50g/2oz dried porcini mushrooms
25g/1oz/¾ cup fresh basil
25g/1oz/⅓ cup pine nuts
40g/1½oz Parmesan cheese, thinly sliced
105ml/7 tbsp olive oil
2 onions, thinly sliced
225g/8oz chestnut mushrooms, sliced
salt and ground black pepper

SERVES 4

1 To make the pizza base, put the flour in a bowl with the salt, dried yeast and olive oil. Add 250ml/8fl oz/1 cup hand-hot water and mix to a dough using a round-bladed knife.

2 Turn on to a work surface and knead for 5 minutes until smooth. Place in a clean bowl, cover with clear film and leave in a warm place until doubled in bulk.

3 Meanwhile, make the filling. Soak the dried mushrooms in hot water for 20 minutes. Place the basil, pine nuts, Parmesan and 75ml/5 tbsp of the olive oil in a blender or food processor and process to make a smooth paste. Set the paste aside.

4 Fry the onions in the remaining olive oil for 3–4 minutes until beginning to colour. Add the chestnut mushrooms and fry for 2 minutes. Stir in the drained porcini mushrooms and season lightly.

5 Preheat the oven to 220°C/425°F/Gas 7. Lightly grease a large baking sheet. Turn the pizza dough on to a floured surface and roll out to a 30cm/12in round. Place on the baking sheet.

6 Spread the pesto mixture to within 1cm/½in of the edges. Spread the mushroom mixture on top.

7 Bake the pizza for 35–40 minutes until risen and golden.

BUTTERNUT SQUASH AND SAGE PIZZA

The combination of the sweet butternut squash, sage and sharp goat's cheese works wonderfully on this pizza. Pumpkin and winter squashes are popular vegetables in Italy.

15g/½oz/1 tbsp butter
30ml/2 tbsp olive oil
2 shallots, finely chopped
1 butternut squash, peeled, seeded and cubed
16 sage leaves
1 prepared pizza base, kneaded and proved
600ml/1 pint/2½ cups thick home-made or bottled tomato sauce
115g/4oz mozzarella cheese, sliced
115g/4oz firm goat's cheese
salt and ground black pepper

SERVES 4

1. Preheat the oven to 200°C/ 400°F/Gas 6. Oil four baking sheets. Put the butter and oil in a roasting tin and heat in the oven for a few minutes. Add the shallots, squash and half of the sage leaves. Toss to coat. Roast for 15–20 minutes until tender, turning the mixture several times.

2. Raise the oven temperature to 220°C/425°F/Gas 7. Divide the pizza dough into four equal pieces and roll out each piece on a lightly floured surface to a 25cm/10in round.

3. Transfer each round to a baking sheet and spread with the tomato sauce, leaving a 1cm/½in border all around. Spoon the squash and shallot mixture over the top.

4. Arrange the slices of mozzarella over the squash mixture and crumble the goat's cheese on top. Scatter the remaining sage leaves over that, and season with plenty of salt and pepper. Bake for 15–20 minutes until the cheese has melted and the crust on each pizza is golden.

SPINACH AND PEPPER PIZZA

The topping on this pizza is an unusual one, but no less delicious for that.

*25g/1oz fresh yeast or 15ml/1 tbsp dried
yeast and 5ml/1 tsp sugar
about 200ml/7fl oz/scant 1 cup
warm water
350g/12oz/3 cups strong white flour
5ml/1 tsp salt
30ml/2 tbsp olive oil*

FOR THE TOPPING
*450g/1lb fresh spinach
60ml/4 tbsp single cream
25g/1oz Parmesan cheese, grated
15ml/1 tbsp olive oil
1 large onion, chopped
1 garlic clove, crushed
1/2 green pepper, seeded and
thinly sliced
1/2 red pepper, seeded and
thinly sliced
175–250ml/6–8fl oz/3/4–1 cup passata
or puréed tomatoes
50g/2oz/1/2 cup pitted black
olives, chopped
15ml/1 tbsp chopped fresh basil
175g/6oz mozzarella, grated
175g/6oz Gruyère cheese, grated
salt*

SERVES 2–4

1   To make the dough, cream together the fresh yeast and 150ml/1/4 pint/2/3 cup of the water and set aside until frothy. If using dried yeast, stir the sugar into 150ml/1/4 pint/2/3 cup water, sprinkle over the yeast and leave until frothy.

2   Place the flour and salt in a large bowl, make a well in the centre and pour in the olive oil and the yeast mixture. Add the remaining water. Mix to make a stiff but pliable dough. Knead on a lightly floured surface for about 10 minutes.

3   Shape the dough into a ball and place in a lightly oiled bowl. Cover with clear film and leave in a warm place for about 1 hour until it has doubled in bulk.

4   To prepare the topping, cook the spinach over a moderate heat for 4–5 minutes until the leaves have wilted. Strain and press out the excess liquid. Place in a bowl and mix with the cream, Parmesan cheese and salt to taste.

5   Heat the oil in a frying pan and fry the onion and garlic over a medium heat for 3–4 minutes until the onion has softened slightly. Add the peppers and continue to cook until the onion is lightly golden.

6   Preheat the oven to 220°C/425°F/Gas 7. Knead the dough briefly on a lightly floured surface. Divide the dough and roll out into two 30cm/12in rounds.

7   Spread each base with passata or puréed tomatoes. Add the onions and peppers, then spread over the spinach mixture. Scatter the olives, basil, mozzarella and Gruyère on top. Bake for 15–20 minutes, or until the crust is lightly browned. Cool slightly before serving.

SPANISH ONION AND ANCHOVY PIZZA

This pizza has flavours and ingredients brought to Spain by the Moors and still used today in many classic Spanish recipes.

400g/14oz/2½ cups strong plain flour
2.5ml/½ tsp salt
15g/½oz easy-blend dried yeast
120ml/4fl oz/½ cup olive oil
150ml/¼ pint/⅔ cup milk and water,
in equal quantities, mixed together
3 large onions, thinly sliced
50g/2oz can anchovies, drained and
roughly chopped
30ml/2 tbsp pine nuts
30ml/2 tbsp sultanas
5ml/1 tsp dried chilli flakes or powder
salt and ground black pepper

SERVES 6–8

1 Sift the flour and salt together into a large bowl. Stir in the yeast. Make a well in the centre, and add 60ml/4 tbsp of the olive oil, and a little of the milk and water. Bring the flour mixture and liquid together, gradually adding the remaining milk and water, until a dough is formed. Knead on a floured surface for about 10 minutes. Return to the bowl, cover with a cloth, and leave in a warm place to rise for about 1 hour.

2 Heat the remaining oil in a large frying pan, add the onions, and cook until soft. Preheat the oven to 240°C/475°F/Gas 9.

3 Knock back the dough, and roll out to a rectangle about 30 x 38cm/12 x 15in. Place on an oiled baking sheet. Cover with the onions. Scatter over the anchovies, pine nuts, sultanas and chilli flakes. Season. Bake for 10–15 minutes, until the edges are beginning to brown. Serve hot.

GRILLED VEGETABLE PIZZA

Grilled vegetables are good at any time, but are particularly tasty when teamed with melted cheese.

1 courgette, sliced
2 baby aubergines or 1 small
aubergine, sliced
30ml/2 tbsp olive oil
1 yellow pepper, seeded and
thickly sliced
115g/4oz/1 cup cornmeal
50g/2oz/½ cup potato flour
50g/2oz/½ cup soya flour
5ml/1 tsp baking powder
2.5ml/½ tsp salt
50g/2oz/¼ cup butter or
soft margarine
about 105ml/7 tbsp milk
4 plum tomatoes, peeled and chopped
30ml/2 tbsp chopped fresh basil
115g/4oz mozzarella cheese, sliced
salt and ground black pepper
fresh basil leaves, to garnish

SERVES 4

1 Preheat the grill. Brush the courgette and aubergine slices with a little oil and place on a grill rack with the pepper slices. Cook under the grill until lightly browned, turning once.

2 Meanwhile, preheat the oven to 200°C/400°F/Gas 6. Place the cornmeal, potato flour, soya flour, baking powder and salt in a mixing bowl and stir to mix. Lightly rub in the butter or margarine until the mixture resembles coarse breadcrumbs, then stir in enough of the milk to make a soft but not sticky dough.

3 Place the dough on a sheet of non-stick baking paper on a baking sheet and roll or press it out to form a 25cm/10in round, pushing up the edges so that they are slightly thicker than the centre.

4 Brush the pizza dough with any remaining oil, then spread the chopped tomatoes over the dough.

5 Sprinkle with the chopped basil and season with salt and pepper. Arrange the grilled vegetables over the tomatoes and top with the sliced mozzarella cheese.

6 Bake for 25–30 minutes until crisp and golden brown. Garnish the pizza with fresh basil and serve, cut into slices.

ONION FOCACCIA

This pizza-like flat bread is characterized by its soft dimpled surface, sometimes dredged simply with coarse salt, or with onions, herbs or olives. It tastes delicious served warm with soups and stews.

675g/1½lb/6 cups strong plain flour
2.5ml/½ tsp salt
2.5ml/½ tsp caster sugar
15ml/1 tbsp easy-blend dried yeast
60ml/4 tbsp extra virgin olive oil
450ml/¾ pint/1⅞ cups hand-hot water

To finish
2 red onions, thinly sliced
45ml/3 tbsp extra virgin olive oil
15ml/1 tbsp coarse salt

Makes Two 25cm/10in Loaves

1. Sift the flour, salt and sugar into a large bowl. Stir in the yeast, oil and water and mix to a dough using a round-bladed knife. (Add a little extra water if the dough is dry.)

2. Turn out on to a lightly floured surface and knead for about 10 minutes until smooth and elastic.

3. Put the dough in a clean, lightly oiled bowl and cover with clear film. Leave to rise in a warm place until doubled in bulk.

4. Place two 25cm/10in plain metal flan rings on baking sheets. Oil the insides of the rings and the baking sheets.

5. Preheat the oven to 200°C/400°F/Gas 6. Halve the dough and roll each piece to a 25cm/10in round. Press into the tins, cover with a dampened dish cloth and leave for 30 minutes to rise.

6. Make deep holes, about 2.5cm/1in apart, in the dough. Cover and leave for a further 20 minutes.

7. Scatter with the onions and drizzle over the oil. Sprinkle with the salt. then a little cold water, to stop a crust from forming.

8. Bake for about 25 minutes, sprinkling with water again during cooking. Cool on a wire rack.

FOCACCIA

This is a flattish bread, originating from Genoa in Italy, made with flour, olive oil and salt.
There are many variations, from many regions, including stuffed varieties, and versions topped
with onions, olives or herbs.

🌾 🌾

25g/1oz fresh yeast
400g/14oz/3½ cups strong plain flour
10ml/2 tsp salt
75ml/5 tbsp olive oil
10ml/2 tsp coarse sea salt

MAKES 1 ROUND 25CM/10IN LOAF

🌾 🌾

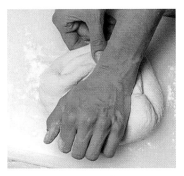

1   Dissolve the yeast in 120ml/ 4fl oz/½ cup warm water. Allow to stand for 10 minutes. Sift the flour into a large bowl, make a well in the centre, and add the yeast, salt and 30ml/2 tbsp oil. Mix in the flour and add more water to make a dough.

2   Turn out on to a floured surface and knead the dough for about 10 minutes, until smooth and elastic. Return to the bowl, cover with a cloth, and leave to rise in a warm place for 2–2½ hours until the dough has doubled in bulk.

3   Knock back the dough and knead again for a few minutes. Press into an oiled 25cm/10in tart tin, and cover with a damp cloth. Leave to rise for 30 minutes.

4   Preheat the oven to 200°C/ 400°F/Gas 6. Poke the dough all over with your fingers, to make little dimples in the surface. Pour the remaining oil over the dough, using a pastry brush to take it to the edges. Sprinkle with the salt.

5   Bake for 20–25 minutes, until the bread is a pale gold. Carefully remove from the tin and leave to cool on a rack. The bread is best eaten on the same day, but it also freezes very well.

SUN-DRIED TOMATO BREAD

In the south of Italy, tomatoes are often dried off in the hot sun. They are then preserved in oil, or hung up in strings in the kitchen, to use in the winter. This recipe uses the former.

675g/1½lb/6 cups strong plain flour
10ml/2 tsp salt
25g/1oz/2 tbsp caster sugar
25g/1oz fresh yeast
400–475ml/14–16fl oz/1⅔–2 cups
warm milk
15ml/1 tbsp tomato purée
75ml/5 tbsp oil from the jar of
sun-dried tomatoes
75ml/5 tbsp extra virgin olive oil
75g/3oz/¾ cup drained sun-dried
tomatoes, chopped
1 large onion, chopped

MAKES 4 SMALL LOAVES

1 Sift the flour, salt and sugar into a bowl, and make a well in the centre. Crumble the yeast, mix with 150ml/¼ pint/⅔ cup of the warm milk and add to the flour.

2 Mix the tomato purée into the remaining milk, until evenly blended, then add to the flour with the tomato oil and olive oil.

3 Gradually mix the flour into the liquid ingredients, until you have a dough. Turn out on to a floured surface, and knead for about 10 minutes, until smooth and elastic. Return to the clean bowl, cover with a cloth, and leave to rise in a warm place for about 2 hours.

4 Knock the dough back, and add the tomatoes and onion. Knead until evenly distributed through the dough. Shape into four rounds and place on a greased baking sheet. Cover with a dish towel and leave to rise again for about 45 minutes.

5 Preheat the oven to 190°C/ 375°F/Gas 5. Bake the bread for 45 minutes, or until the loaves sound hollow when you tap them underneath with your fingers. Leave to cool on a wire rack. Eat warm, or toasted with grated mozzarella cheese on top.

COOK'S TIP
Use a pair of sharp kitchen scissors to cut up the sun-dried tomatoes.

OLIVE BREAD

*Olive breads are popular all over the Mediterranean. For this Greek recipe
use rich oily olives or those marinated in herbs rather than canned ones.*

- - - - - - - - - - ❧ ❧ - - - - - - - - - -

2 red onions, thinly sliced
30ml/2 tbsp olive oil
225g/8oz/1⅓ cups pitted black or
green olives
750g/1¾lb/7 cups strong plain flour
7.5ml/1½ tsp salt
20ml/4 tsp easy-blend dried yeast
45ml/3 tbsp each roughly chopped
parsley, coriander or mint

MAKES TWO 675G/1½LB LOAVES

- - - - - - - - - - ❧ ❧ - - - - - - - - - -

1 Fry the onions in the oil until
soft. Roughly chop the olives.

2 Put the flour, salt, yeast and
parsley, coriander or mint in a
large bowl with the olives and fried
onions and pour in 475ml/16fl oz/
2 cups hand-hot water.

- - - - - - - - - - ❧ ❧ - - - - - - - - - -

VARIATION
Shape the dough into 16 small rolls.
Slash the tops as above and reduce
the cooking time to 25 minutes.

- - - - - - - - - - ❧ ❧ - - - - - - - - - -

3 Mix to a dough using a round-
bladed knife, adding a little
more water if the mixture feels dry.

4 Turn out on to a lightly floured
surface and knead for about
10 minutes. Put in a clean bowl,
cover with clear film and leave in a
warm place until doubled in bulk.

5 Preheat the oven to 220°C/
425°F/Gas 7. Lightly grease two
baking sheets. Turn the dough on to a
floured surface and cut in half. Shape
into two rounds and place on the
baking sheets. Cover loosely with
lightly oiled clear film and leave until
doubled in size.

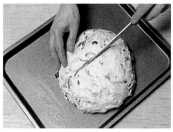

6 Slash the tops of the loaves with
a knife then bake for about
40 minutes or until the loaves sound
hollow when tapped on the bottom.
Transfer to a wire rack to cool.

MOROCCAN BREAD

Warm this bread in the oven and cut it into thick slices to serve with any classic Moroccan savoury dish.
It is just the thing for mopping up a really good sauce.

275g/10oz/2½ cups strong white flour
175g/6oz/1½ cups wholemeal flour
10ml/2 tsp salt
about 250ml/8fl oz/1 cup warm milk
and water, mixed
10ml/2 tsp sesame seeds

FOR THE YEAST STARTER
150ml/¼ pint/⅔ cup warm milk and
water, mixed
5ml/1 tsp sugar
10ml/2 tsp dried yeast

MAKES 2 LOAVES

1 First prepare the yeast. Place the warm milk mixture in a small bowl or jug, stir in the sugar and then sprinkle the yeast on top. Stir, then set aside in a warm place for about 10 minutes until frothy.

2 In a large bowl, mix together the two flours and salt. Add the yeast mixture and enough diluted warm milk to make a fairly soft dough. Knead the mixture into a ball and then knead on a floured surface for 10–12 minutes until firm and elastic.

3 Break the dough into two pieces and shape into flattened ball shapes. Place on floured baking sheets and press down with your hand to make round breads about 13–15cm/5–6in in diameter.

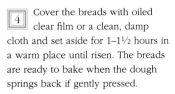

4 Cover the breads with oiled clear film or a clean, damp cloth and set aside for 1–1½ hours in a warm place until risen. The breads are ready to bake when the dough springs back if gently pressed.

5 Preheat the oven to 200°C/ 400°F/Gas 6. Sprinkle the risen loaves with the sesame seeds and bake for 12 minutes. Reduce the oven temperature to 150°C/300°F/Gas 2 and bake for 20–30 minutes more until the loaves sound hollow when tapped on the base.

SEED BREAD

This bread is quite delicious – just the thing to make for special occasions.

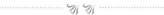

375g/12oz/3 cups strong white flour
115g/4oz/1 cup cornmeal
10ml/2 tsp salt
150ml/¼ pint/⅔ cup warm milk and
water, mixed
25ml/1½ tbsp pumpkin seeds
25ml/1½ tbsp sunflower seeds
15ml/1 tbsp sesame seeds

FOR THE YEAST STARTER
150ml/¼ pint/⅔ cup warm water
5ml/1 tsp sugar
10ml/2 tsp dried yeast

MAKES 2 LOAVES

1 First prepare the yeast. Place the warm water in a small bowl or jug, stir in the sugar and then sprinkle the yeast over the top. Stir, then set aside in a warm place for about 10 minutes until frothy.

2 In a large bowl, mix together the flour, cornmeal and salt. Add the yeast mixture and enough of the diluted warm milk to make a fairly soft dough. Knead the mixture into a ball and then knead on a floured surface for 5 minutes.

3 Add the pumpkin, sunflower and sesame seeds, and knead them into the dough. Continue kneading for about 5–6 minutes until the dough is firm and elastic.

4 Break the dough into two pieces and shape into balls, flattening them to make two round frisbee shapes. Place on floured baking sheets and press down with your hand to make round breads measuring about 13–15cm/5–6in in diameter.

5 Cover with oiled clear film or a damp dish towel and set aside for 1–1½ hours in a warm place until risen. The bread is ready to bake when it springs back if gently pressed.

6 Preheat the oven to 200°C/ 400°F/Gas 6 and bake the breads in the oven for 12 minutes. Reduce the oven temperature to 150°C/300°F/Gas 2 and continue cooking for 20–30 minutes until the loaves are golden and sound hollow when tapped on the bottom.

SESAME BREADSTICKS

Breadsticks are one of the most versatile snack foods. Try serving them with aubergine dip,
or with prawns and a bowl of garlic mayonnaise and a glass of red wine.

225g/8oz/2 cups strong white flour
5ml/1 tsp salt
7g/¼oz easy-blend dried yeast
30ml/2 tbsp sesame seeds
30ml/2 tbsp olive oil

MAKES 30

 Preheat the oven to 230°C/
450°F/Gas 8. Sift the flour
into a bowl. Stir in the salt, yeast
and sesame seeds and make a well
in the centre.

2 Add the olive oil to the flour
mixture and enough warm
water to make a firm dough. Tip out
the dough on to a lightly floured
surface and knead for 5–10 minutes
until smooth and elastic.

3 Rub a little oil on to the surface
of the dough. Return it to the
clean bowl and cover with a clean
dish towel or oiled plastic bag. Leave
the dough to rise in a warm place for
about 40 minutes, until it has doubled
in bulk.

COOK'S TIP
Breadsticks can be made with many
different flavourings – try using fennel
seeds, poppy seeds or finely grated
Parmesan cheese instead of sesame
seeds. They are best eaten fresh, so
don't make them more than a day or
two in advance. Store them in an
airtight container until ready to eat.

4 Punch down the dough, then
knead lightly until smooth. Pull
off small balls of dough, then, using
your hands, roll out each ball on a
lightly floured surface to a thin
sausage about 25cm/10in long.

 Place the breadsticks on baking
sheets and bake for 15 minutes,
until crisp and golden. Cool the
breadsticks on a wire rack, then store
them in an airtight container until
ready to serve.

VARIATION
Try using wholemeal flour for a rich
nutty flavour. You may find that a
little water, or more oil, is required
to achieve the same consistency as
the white-flour breadsticks.

FRIED DOUGH BALLS WITH FIERY SALSA

These crunchy dough balls are accompanied by a hot and spicy tomato salsa. You may prefer to serve them with a juicy tomato salad.

⁂

450g/1lb/4 cups strong white flour
5ml/1 tsp easy-blend dried yeast
5ml/1 tsp salt
30ml/2 tbsp chopped fresh parsley
2 garlic cloves, finely chopped
30ml/2 tbsp olive oil, plus extra
for greasing
vegetable oil, for frying

FOR THE SALSA
6 hot red chillies, seeded and roughly
chopped
1 onion, roughly chopped
2 garlic cloves, quartered
2.5cm/1in piece of fresh root ginger,
roughly chopped
450g/1lb tomatoes, roughly chopped
30ml/2 tbsp olive oil
a pinch of sugar
salt and ground black pepper

MAKES 40 DOUGH BALLS

⁂

1 Sift the flour into a large bowl. Stir in the yeast and salt and make a well in the centre. Add the parsley, garlic, olive oil and enough warm water to make a firm dough.

2 Gather the dough together then tip out on to a lightly floured surface or board. Knead for about 10 minutes, until the dough feels very smooth and elastic.

3 Rub a little oil into the surface of the dough. Return it to the clean bowl, cover with clear film or a clean dish towel and leave in a warm place to rise for about 1 hour, or until doubled in bulk.

⁂

COOK'S TIP
These dough balls can be deep-fried for 3–4 minutes or baked at 200°C/400°F/Gas 6 for 15–20 minutes.

⁂

4 Meanwhile, make the salsa. Combine the chillies, onion, garlic and ginger in a food processor and whizz together until very finely chopped. Add the tomatoes and olive oil, and process until smooth.

5 Sieve the mixture into a saucepan. Add the sugar, salt and pepper to taste, and simmer gently for 15 minutes. Do not allow the salsa to boil.

6 Roll the dough into 40 balls. Shallow-fry them in batches in hot vegetable oil for 4–5 minutes until crisp and golden. Drain on kitchen paper and serve hot, with the fiery salsa in a separate bowl for dipping.

SULTANA AND WALNUT BREAD

This bread is delicious with soup for a first course, or with salami, cheese and salad for lunch.
It also tastes good with jam, and toasts extremely well when it is a day or two old.

300g/11oz/2¾ cups strong plain flour
2.5ml/½ tsp salt
15g/½oz/1 tbsp butter
7.5ml/1½ tsp easy-blend dried yeast
115g/4oz/⅔ cup sultanas
75g/3oz/¾ cup walnuts,
roughly chopped
melted butter, for brushing

MAKES 1 LOAF

1 Sift the flour and salt into a bowl, cut in the butter with a knife, then stir in the yeast.

2 Gradually add 175ml/6fl oz/ ¾ cup tepid water to the flour mixture, stirring with a spoon at first, then gathering the dough together with your hands.

3 Turn the dough out on to a floured surface and knead for about 10 minutes until elastic.

4 Knead the sultanas and walnuts into the dough until they are evenly distributed. Shape into a rough oval, place on a lightly oiled baking sheet and cover with oiled clear film. Leave to rise in a warm place for 1–2 hours until doubled in bulk. Preheat the oven to 220°C/425°F/Gas 7.

5 Remove the clear film from the loaf. Bake for 10 minutes, then reduce the oven temperature to 190°C/375°F/Gas 5 and bake for a further 20–25 minutes.

6 Transfer to a wire rack, brush with melted butter and cover with a dish towel. Allow to cool before slicing and serving.

LITTLE SPICED BREADS

These rich breads are delicious served with butter and honey.

4 Add the yeast and half of the butter and water mixture to the flour, and process so that they combine slowly. Continue processing, adding the remaining butter and water, to make a smooth and glossy dough. (You may need to add extra flour or warm water.)

5 Continue to process the dough for 1–2 minutes, then transfer it to a floured board and knead by hand for a few minutes until it is smooth and elastic.

6 Place in a clean, lightly oiled bowl, cover with clear film and leave in a warm place for 1–1½ hours until doubled in bulk. Knead again for a few minutes and then break into 12 small balls and flatten slightly with oiled hands. Place on a greased baking sheet, cover with oiled clear film and leave to rise for 1 hour.

5ml/1 tsp sugar
10ml/2 tsp dried yeast
75g/3oz/6 tbsp butter, melted,
plus extra for greasing
15ml/1 tbsp orange flower water or
almond essence (optional)
400g/14oz/3½ cups strong white flour
75g/3oz/¾ cup icing sugar
5ml/1 tsp salt
30ml/2 tbsp sesame seeds
15ml/1 tbsp fennel seeds
1 egg, beaten with 15ml/1 tbsp water

MAKES 12

1 First start the yeast. Place 120ml/4fl oz/½ cup warm water in a jug, stir in the sugar and sprinkle the yeast on top. Stir and then set aside for about 10 minutes until frothy.

2 Place the butter, orange flower water or almond essence, if using, in a separate jug. Stir in 175ml/ 6fl oz/¾ cup warm water.

3 Put the flour, icing sugar, salt, sesame seeds and fennel seeds in the bowl of a food processor fitted with the dough blade.

7 Preheat the oven to 190°C/ 375°F/Gas 5. Brush the breads with the beaten egg and water, then bake in the oven for 12–15 minutes or until golden brown. Serve warm or cold.

GREEK EASTER BREAD

In Greece, Easter celebrations are very important, and involve much preparation in the kitchen. This bread is sold in all the bakers' shops, and also made at home. It is traditionally decorated with red dyed eggs.

25g/1oz fresh yeast
120ml/4fl oz/½ cup warm milk
675g/1½lb /6 cups strong plain flour
2 eggs, beaten
2.5ml/½ tsp caraway seeds
15ml/1 tbsp caster sugar
15ml/1 tbsp brandy
50g/2oz/4 tbsp butter, melted
1 egg white, beaten
2–3 hard-boiled eggs, dyed red
50g/2oz/½ cup split almonds

MAKES 1 LOAF

1 Crumble the yeast into a bowl. Mix with one or two tablespoons of warm water, until softened. Add the milk and 115g/4oz/1 cup of the flour and mix to a creamy consistency. Cover with a cloth, and leave in a warm place to rise for 1 hour.

COOK'S TIP
You can often buy fresh yeast from bakers' shops. It should be pale cream in colour with a firm but crumbly texture.

2 Sift the remaining flour into a large bowl and make a well in the centre. Pour the risen yeast into the well, and draw in a little of the flour from the sides. Add the eggs, caraway seeds, sugar, and brandy. Incorporate the remaining flour, until the mixture begins to form a dough.

3 Mix in the melted butter. Turn on to a floured surface, and knead for about 10 minutes, until the dough becomes smooth. Return to the bowl, and cover with a cloth. Leave in a warm place for 3 hours.

4 Preheat the oven to 180°C/ 350°F/Gas 4. Knock back the dough, turn on to a floured surface and knead for a minute or two. Divide the dough into three, and roll each piece into a long sausage. Make a plait as shown above, and place the loaf on a greased baking sheet.

5 Tuck the ends under, brush with the egg white and decorate with the eggs and split almonds. Bake for about 1 hour, until the loaf sounds hollow when tapped on the bottom. Cool on a wire rack.

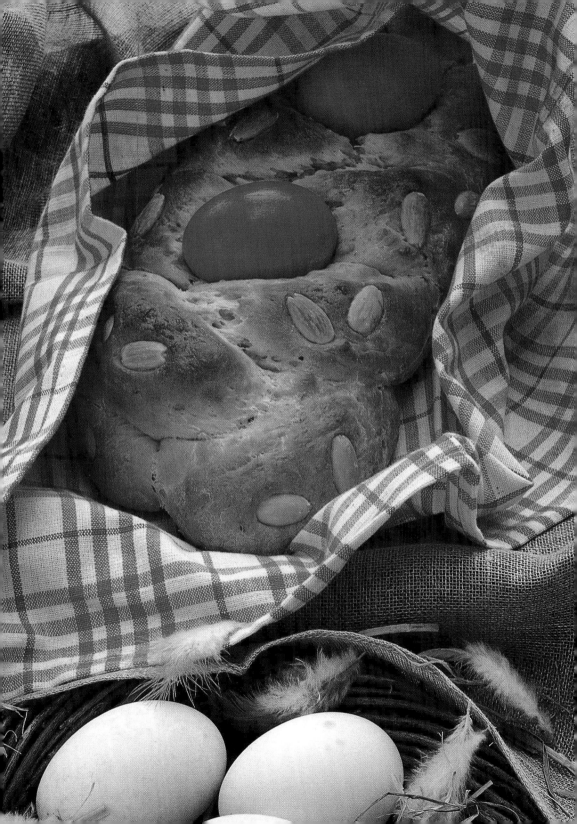

DESSERTS
AND PASTRIES

Mediterranean meals are often finished simply with
fresh fruit. Sweet pastries, ices and sweetmeats are
usually served separately, with black coffee.

The rich variety of produce and ingredients available in Mediterranean countries is particularly in evidence in the diversity of sweet dishes. From the most refreshing ices and fragrant fruit desserts to luscious creams, fabulous gâteaux and heavily spiced, honey-dressed pastries – there is truly a sweet experience to suit all tastes.

At home, for everyday desserts the abundance of fresh fruits is enough. For a special occasion a colourful selection of figs, plums, apricots, peaches, melons and cherries make a stunning finale. Arranged on a platter lined with vine, orange or even fig leaves, crushed ice is scattered over the fruit, some of which may be cut open decoratively. The flesh of juicy fruits, such as pomegranates or oranges, is often arranged in pretty bowls, then sprinkled with sugar and rose water or orange flower water and served chilled and iced.

Fresh fruit is also lightly poached in syrup, sometimes with honey and the warm spices, such as cinnamon. Pears, quinces, apricots and figs are often prepared in this way and they keep well as the syrup protects and flavours them. Simple classics, like peaches filled with a little sweet almond stuffing and laced with liqueur are appreciated well outside their countries of origin.

BELOW: Orange groves abound in this fertile valley near Jaén in Spain.

ABOVE: Pyramids of perfect fruit await the shopper at the covered market in Florence.

ABOVE: Plump, rosy and ready for picking, peaches make a perfect dessert, alone or with a delicious amaretto stuffing.

The smooth sorbets of France and crunchy granitas of Italy are also enjoyed all over the world. Fruit-flavoured ice-creams that make perfect summer snacks are ideal light desserts, particularly piled into decorative glasses or served in scooped-out fruit shells, such as oranges or melons. Italy is renowned for the elaborate multi-flavoured ice-cream gâteaux that are the pride of every dessert chef.

Other prominent Mediterranean desserts include sweet milk-based puddings and satin-smooth creams. In North Africa and the Middle East, ground or short-grain rice is used in milk puddings spiced with cinnamon, cloves, aniseed or fennel. They are usually served cold, sometimes drizzled with a honey and orange-flavoured syrup. One of Spain's classic puddings is the irresistible Crema Catalana, a creamy custard topped with caramel, served on its own or accompanied by fruit. One of the most famous creams is the Italian "pick-me-up", tiramisu, which is laced with liqueur or wine and often dredged with cocoa.

It is in the display cabinets of any pâtisserie, confectioner or coffee house that the skill of the Mediterranean pastry chefs is truly revealed. From gâteaux and torte, lavishly finished with sugared decorations, to stuffed and glazed or candied fruits, the choice is wide and there is an abundance of fabulous, complex flavours to be discovered. In Turkey, Greece, Lebanon and Egypt, small sweet pastries and sweetmeats are enjoyed with good strong coffee. Rich pastries, doughnuts or semolina and nut cakes are drenched in lightly-spiced syrup. Honey, almonds, pistachios, sesame seeds, pine nuts, rose water and orange flower water are all used with skill to create divine flavours in these unusual specialities.

RUBY ORANGE SHERBET IN GINGER BASKETS

This superb frozen dessert is perfect for people who do not have ice-cream makers and who cannot be bothered with the freezing and stirring that home-made ices normally require. It is also ideal for serving at a special dinner party, as both the sherbet and the ginger baskets can be made in advance.

grated rind and juice of
2 blood oranges
175g/6oz/1½ cups icing sugar
300ml/½ pint/1¼ cups double cream
200g/7oz/scant 1 cup Greek-style
natural yogurt
blood orange segments, to
decorate (optional)

FOR THE GINGER BASKETS
25g/1oz/2 tbsp unsalted butter, plus
extra for greasing
15ml/1 tbsp golden syrup
30ml/2 tbsp caster sugar
1.5ml/¼ tsp ground ginger
15ml/1 tbsp finely chopped mixed
citrus peel
15ml/1 tbsp plain flour

SERVES 6

[1] Place the orange rind and juice in a bowl. Sift the icing sugar over the top and set aside for about 30 minutes, then stir until smooth.

[2] Whisk the double cream in a large bowl until the mixture forms soft peaks, then fold in the yogurt with a metal spoon.

[3] Gently stir in the orange juice mixture, and pour into a freezerproof container. Cover and freeze until firm.

[4] Make the baskets. Preheat the oven to 180°C/350°F/Gas 4. Place the butter, syrup and sugar in a heavy-based saucepan and heat gently until melted.

COOK'S TIP
When making the ginger baskets, it is essential to work quickly. Have the greased moulds ready before you start.

[5] Add the ground ginger, mixed citrus peel and flour, and stir until the mixture is smooth.

[6] Lightly grease two baking sheets. Using about 10ml/2 tsp of the mixture at a time, drop three portions of the ginger dough on to each baking sheet, spacing them well apart. Spread out each one to make a 5cm/2in circle, then bake for 12–14 minutes or until the biscuits are a dark golden colour.

[7] Remove the biscuits from the oven and allow to stand on the baking sheets for 1 minute to firm slightly. Lift off with a fish slice and drape over six greased upturned mini pudding basins or upturned cups. Flatten the top (which will become the base), and quickly flute the edge of each to form a basket shape.

[8] When cool, lift the baskets off the basins or cups and place on individual dessert plates. Arrange small scoops of the frozen orange sherbet in each basket. Decorate each portion with a few blood orange segments, if you like.

FRESH ORANGE GRANITA

A granita is like a water ice, but coarser and grainier in texture — hence its name. It makes a refreshing dessert after a rich main course, or a cooling treat on a hot summer's day.

4 large oranges
1 large lemon
150g/5oz/⅔ cup granulated sugar
475ml/16fl oz/2 cups water
dessert biscuits, to serve

SERVES 6

1 Thinly pare the rind from the oranges and lemon, taking care to avoid the bitter white pith, and set aside. Cut the fruit in half and squeeze the orange and lemon juice into a jug. Set aside.

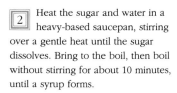

2 Heat the sugar and water in a heavy-based saucepan, stirring over a gentle heat until the sugar dissolves. Bring to the boil, then boil without stirring for about 10 minutes, until a syrup forms.

3 Remove the syrup from the heat, add most of the reserved pieces of orange and lemon rind but keep a few for decoration. Shake the pan. Cover and allow to cool.

4 Strain the sugar syrup into a shallow freezer container and add the fruit juice. Stir well to mix, then freeze, uncovered, for about 4 hours until slushy.

5 Remove the half-frozen mixture from the freezer and mix with a fork, then return to the freezer and freeze again for another 4 hours or until frozen hard.

6 To serve, turn into a bowl and allow to soften for about 10 minutes, then break up into small pieces with a fork again and pile the granita into long-stemmed glasses. Blanch the reserved strips of orange and lemon rind, and serve with dessert biscuits.

COFFEE GRANITA

*Served in Italian cafés, Granitas are very refreshing, particularly in the summer.
Some are made with fruit, but the coffee version is perhaps the most popular and is often served
with a spoonful of whipped cream on top.*

350ml/12fl oz/1½ cups hot strong
espresso coffee
30ml/2 tbsp sugar
250ml/8fl oz/1 cup double cream
10ml/2 tsp caster sugar

SERVES 6–8

1 Stir the sugar into the hot coffee until dissolved. Leave to cool, then chill. Pour into a shallow plastic or metal freezer container, cover and freeze for about 1 hour.

2 The coffee should have formed a frozen crust around the rim of the container. Scrape this away with a spoon and mix with the rest of the coffee. Repeat this process every 30 minutes, using the spoon to break up the clumps of ice.

3 After about 2½ hours, the granita should be ready. It will have the appearance of small, fairly uniform ice crystals. Whip the cream with the caster sugar until stiff. Serve the granita in tall glasses, each topped with a spoonful of cream.

ICED ORANGES

These little sorbets served in the fruit shell were originally sold in the beach cafés in the south of France.
They are pretty and easy to eat – a good picnic treat to store in the cold box.

150g/5oz/⅔ cup granulated sugar
juice of 1 lemon
14 medium oranges
8 fresh bay leaves, to decorate

SERVES 8

1   Put the sugar in a heavy-based pan. Add half the lemon juice, and 120ml/4fl oz/½ cup water. Cook over a low heat until the sugar has dissolved. Bring to the boil, and boil for 2–3 minutes, until the syrup is clear. Leave to cool.

2   Slice the tops off eight of the oranges, to make "hats". Scoop out the flesh of the oranges, and reserve. Put the empty orange shells and "hats" on a tray and place in the freezer until needed.

3   Grate the rind of the remaining oranges and add to the syrup. Squeeze the juice from the oranges, and from the reserved flesh. There should be 750ml/1¼ pints/3 cups. Squeeze another orange or add bought orange juice, if necessary.

4   Stir the orange juice and remaining lemon juice, with 90ml/6 tbsp water into the syrup. Taste, adding more lemon juice or sugar, as desired. Pour the mixture into a shallow freezer container and freeze for 3 hours.

5   Turn the mixture into a bowl, and whisk to break down the ice crystals. Freeze for 4 hours more, until firm, but not solid.

6   Pack the mixture into the orange shells, mounding it up, and set the "hats" on top. Freeze until ready to serve. Just before serving, push a skewer into the tops of the "hats" and push in a bay leaf.

COOK'S TIP
Use crumpled kitchen paper to keep the shells upright.

PISTACHIO HALVA ICE CREAM

Halva is made from sesame seeds and is available in several flavours. This ice cream, studded with chunks of pistachio-flavoured halva, is as unusual as it is irresistible.

3 egg yolks
115g/4oz/¹/₂ cup caster sugar
300ml/¹/₂ pint/1¹/₄ cups single cream
300ml/¹/₂ pint/1¹/₄ cups double cream
115g/4oz pistachio halva
chopped pistachio nuts, to decorate

SERVES 6

[3] Whisk the double cream lightly, then whisk in the cooled custard. Crumble the halva into the mixture and stir in gently.

[4] Pour the mixture into a freezerproof container. Cover and freeze for 3 hours or until half set. Stir well, breaking up any ice crystals, then return to the freezer until frozen solid.

[5] About 15 minutes before serving, remove the ice cream from the freezer so that it softens enough for scooping and to allow the full flavour to develop. Decorate with chopped pistachio nuts.

[1] Turn the freezer to its lowest setting. Whisk the egg yolks with the caster sugar in a bowl until the mixture is thick and pale. Pour the single cream into a small saucepan and bring to the boil, then remove from the heat. Stir the hot cream into the egg yolk mixture.

[2] Transfer the mixture to a double boiler or a heatproof bowl placed over a pan of boiling water. Cook, stirring continuously, until the custard is thick enough to coat the back of a spoon. Strain into a bowl and leave to cool.

TURKISH DELIGHT ICE CREAM

Turkish delight is delicious whichever way you serve it, but this ice cream is particularly good.
Serve it scattered with rose petals, if you have them.

4 egg yolks
115g/4oz/½ cup caster sugar
300ml/½ pint/1¼ cups milk
300ml/½ pint/1¼ cups double cream
15ml/1 tbsp rose water
175g/6oz rose-flavoured Turkish
delight, chopped

SERVES 6

1 Beat the egg yolks and sugar until light. In a pan, bring the milk to the boil. Add to the egg and sugar, stirring, then return to the pan.

2 Continue stirring over a low heat until the mixture coats the back of a spoon. Do not boil, or it will curdle. Leave to cool, then stir in the cream and rose water.

3 Put the Turkish delight in a pan with 30–45ml/2–3 tbsp water. Heat gently, until almost completely melted, with just a few small lumps. Remove from the heat and stir into the cool custard mixture.

4 Leave the mixture to cool completely, then pour into a shallow freezer container. Freeze for 3 hours until just frozen all over. Spoon the mixture into a bowl.

5 Using a whisk, beat the mixture well, and return to the freezer container and freeze for 2 hours more. Repeat the beating process, then return to the freezer for about 3 hours, or until firm. Remove the ice cream from the freezer 20–25 minutes before serving. Serve with thin almond biscuits or meringues.

COFFEE AND CHOCOLATE BOMBE

In Italy, the commercial ice cream is so good that no one would dream of making their own for this dessert. Assembling the bombe is impressive enough in itself.

*15–18 savoiardi (Italian
sponge fingers)
about 175ml/6fl oz/³/4 cup
sweet Marsala
75g/3oz amaretti biscuits
about 475ml/16fl oz/2 cups coffee
ice cream, softened
about 475ml/16fl oz/2 cups vanilla
ice cream, softened
50g/2oz bittersweet or plain
chocolate, grated
chocolate curls and cocoa powder or
icing sugar, to decorate*

SERVES 6–8

1 Line a 1 litre/1³/4 pint/4 cup pudding basin with a large piece of damp muslin, letting it hang over the top edge. Trim the sponge fingers to fit the basin, if necessary. Pour the Marsala into a shallow dish. Dip a sponge finger in the Marsala, turning it quickly so that it becomes saturated but does not disintegrate. Stand it against the side of the basin, sugared-side out. Repeat with the remaining sponge fingers until the basin is fully lined.

2 Fill in the base and any gaps around the side with any trimmings of sponge finger, cut to fit. Chill for about 30 minutes.

3 Put the amaretti biscuits in a stout bowl and crush them with a rolling pin. Then transfer the crushed biscuits to a larger bowl, add the coffee ice cream and any remaining Marsala, and beat until thoroughly mixed. Spoon into the sponge-finger-lined basin.

4 Press the ice cream against the sponge to form an even layer with a hollow in the centre. Freeze for 2 hours.

5 Put the vanilla ice cream and grated chocolate in a bowl and beat together until evenly mixed. Spoon into the hollow in the centre of the mould. Smooth the top, then cover with the overhanging muslin. Place in the freezer overnight.

6 To serve, run a palette knife between the muslin and the basin, then unfold the top of the muslin. Invert a chilled serving plate on top of the pudding basin, then invert the two and lift off the bowl. Decorate with the chocolate curls, then sift the cocoa powder or icing sugar over the top. Serve at once.

CHOCOLATE SALAMI

This after-dinner sweetmeat resembles a salami in shape, hence its intriguing name. It is very rich and will serve a lot of people. Slice it thinly and serve with espresso coffee and amaretto liqueur.

24 Petit Beurre biscuits, broken
350g/12oz bittersweet or plain chocolate,
broken into squares
225g/8oz/1 cup unsalted
butter, softened
60ml/4 tbsp amaretto liqueur
2 egg yolks
50g/2oz/1/2 cup flaked almonds,
lightly toasted and thinly
shredded lengthways
25g/1oz/1/4 cup ground almonds

SERVES 8–12

1 Place the biscuits in a food processor or blender fitted with a metal blade and process until coarsely chopped.

2 Place the chocolate in a large heatproof bowl. Place the bowl over a saucepan of barely simmering water, add a small chunk of the butter and all of the liqueur, and heat until the chocolate melts, stirring the mixture occasionally.

3 Remove the bowl from the heat, allow the chocolate to cool for a minute or two, then stir in the egg yolks followed by the remaining butter, a little at a time. Tip in most of the crushed biscuits, reserving a good handful, and stir well to mix. Stir in the flaked almonds. Leave the mixture in a cold place for about 1 hour until it begins to stiffen.

4 Process the reserved crushed biscuits in the food processor until they are very finely ground. Tip into a bowl and mix with the ground almonds. Cover and set aside until you are ready to serve.

5 Turn the chocolate and biscuit mixture on to a sheet of lightly oiled greaseproof paper. Shape into a 35cm/14in sausage using a palette knife, tapering the ends slightly so that the roll looks like a salami. Wrap in the paper and freeze for at least 4 hours until solid.

6 To serve, unwrap the "salami". Spread out the finely ground biscuits and almonds on a clean sheet of greaseproof paper, and roll the salami in them until evenly coated. Transfer to a board and leave to stand for about 1 hour before cutting into thin slices to serve.

COOK'S TIP
Take care when melting chocolate that it does not overheat or it will form a hard lump. The base of the bowl containing the chocolate must not touch the water, and the chocolate must be melted very slowly. If you think the mixture is getting too hot, remove the pan from the heat.

APPLE FROTH

This simple dessert is easy to make and perfect after a rich meal.

4 eating apples
30ml/2 tbsp lemon juice
30ml/2 tbsp rose water
45–60ml/3–4 tbsp icing sugar
crushed ice, to serve

SERVES 4

COOK'S TIP
Pears can also be used to make this delicious dessert. Choose ripe pears, which yield when pressed gently.

1 Carefully and thinly peel the apples, using a swivel peeler. Discard the peel. Work quickly, otherwise the apples will begin to brown. If necessary, place the peeled apples in a bowl of acidulated water while you peel the others.

2 Grate the apples coarsely into a bowl, discarding the cores. Stir in the lemon juice and rose water, and add icing sugar to taste. Chill for at least 30 minutes. Mount on a platter and serve with crushed ice.

PINEAPPLE ICE CREAM

Light, refreshing and slightly tangy, pineapple ice cream is always an excellent choice.

8 eggs, separated
115g/4oz/½ cup caster sugar
2.5ml/½ tsp vanilla essence
600ml/1 pint/2½ cups
whipping cream
60ml/4 tbsp icing sugar
425g/15oz can pineapple chunks
75g/3oz/¾ cup pistachio
nuts, chopped
wafer biscuits, to serve

SERVES 8–10

2 In a separate bowl, whip the cream and icing sugar to soft peaks, then add to the egg-yolk mixture and mix well.

4 Cut the pineapple into very small pieces, add the pistachio nuts and stir into the cream mixture. Mix well with a spoon.

3 Whisk the egg whites in a separate large bowl until they are firm and hold stiff peaks. Gently fold the whipped egg whites into the cream mixture and mix gently so that the ingredients are combined with no loss of volume.

5 Pour the mixture into an ice-cream container and place in the freezer for a few hours until it is set and firm, stirring it occasionally.

1 Place the egg yolks in a bowl, add the sugar and vanilla essence and beat until thick and pale.

6 Serve in scoops or slices, with wafer biscuits.

RICOTTA PUDDING

This rich, creamy dessert is easy to make and, as it can be made up to 24 hours ahead, it is ideal for a dinner party. The combination of ricotta cheese and candied fruits is a popular one in Sicily, where this recipe originated.

225g/8oz/1 cup ricotta cheese
50g/2oz/⅓ cup candied fruits
60ml/4 tbsp sweet Marsala
250ml/8fl oz/1 cup double cream
50g/2oz/¼ cup caster sugar, plus extra, for dusting
finely grated rind of 1 orange
350g/12oz/2 cups fresh raspberries
strips of thinly pared orange rind, to decorate

SERVES 4–6

1 Press the ricotta through a sieve into a bowl to remove any lumps. Finely chop the candied fruits and stir into the sieved ricotta with half of the Marsala. Put the cream, sugar and grated orange rind in another bowl and whip until the cream is standing in soft peaks.

2 Fold the whipped cream into the ricotta mixture. Spoon into individual glass serving bowls and top with the raspberries. Chill until serving time. Sprinkle with the remaining Marsala and dust the top of each bowl liberally with caster sugar just before serving. Decorate with the pared orange rind.

442

TIRAMISU

The name of this popular dessert translates as "pick me up", which is said to derive from the fact that it is so good that it literally makes you swoon when you eat it. There are many, many versions, and the recipe can be adapted to suit your own taste — you can vary the amounts of mascarpone, eggs, sponge fingers, coffee and liqueur.

3 eggs, separated
450g/1lb/2 cups mascarpone cheese,
at room temperature
1 sachet of vanilla sugar
175ml/6fl oz/3/4 cup cold, very strong,
black coffee
120ml/4fl oz/1/2 cup Kahlúa or other
coffee-flavoured liqueur
18 savoiardi (Italian sponge fingers)
sifted cocoa powder and grated bittersweet chocolate, to decorate

SERVES 6–8

1 Put the egg whites in a grease-free bowl and whisk with an electric mixer until stiff and standing in peaks. You should be able to tilt the bowl without losing any of the mixture.

2 Mix the mascarpone, vanilla sugar and egg yolks in a separate large bowl, and whisk with the electric mixer until evenly combined. Fold in the egg whites, then put a few spoonfuls of the mixture in the bottom of a large serving bowl and spread out evenly.

3 Mix together the coffee and liqueur in a shallow dish. Dip one of the sponge fingers in the mixture, turn it quickly so that it becomes saturated but does not disintegrate, and place it on top of the mascarpone mixture in the bowl. Add five more dipped sponge fingers in this way, placing them side-by-side.

4 Spoon in about one-third of the remaining mixture and spread out. Make more layers in the same way, ending with mascarpone. Level the surface, then sift the cocoa powder over the top. Cover and chill overnight. Before serving, sprinkle grated chocolate on top, to decorate.

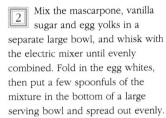

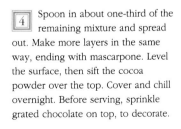

LEMON COEUR A LA CREME WITH COINTREAU ORANGES

This zesty dessert is the ideal choice to follow a rich main course.

225g/8oz/1 cup cottage cheese
250g/9oz/generous 1 cup
mascarpone cheese
50g/2oz/¼ cup caster sugar
grated rind and juice of 1 lemon
spirals of pared orange rind,
to decorate

FOR THE COINTREAU ORANGES
4 oranges
10ml/2 tsp cornflour
15ml/1 tbsp icing sugar
60ml/4 tbsp Cointreau

SERVES 4

1 Put the cottage cheese in a food processor or blender and whizz until the mixture is smooth and of one consistency.

2 Add the mascarpone cheese, caster sugar, lemon rind and juice, and process briefly to mix all the ingredients together.

3 Line four coeur à la crème moulds with damp muslin, then divide the mixture among them. Level the surface of each, then place the moulds on a plate to catch any liquid that drains from the cheese. Cover all the moulds and chill overnight.

4 Meanwhile, make the Cointreau oranges. Squeeze the juice from two of the oranges; pour into a measuring jug. Make the juice up to 250ml/8fl oz/1 cup with water, then pour into a small saucepan. Blend a little of the juice mixture with the cornflour and add to the pan with the icing sugar. Heat the sauce, stirring until thickened.

5 Using a sharp knife, peel and segment the remaining oranges. Add the segments to the pan, stir to coat, then set aside. When cool, stir in the Cointreau. Pour into a bowl, cover and chill overnight.

6 Turn the coeur à la crème moulds out on to plates and lift off the muslin. Surround with the oranges and sauce. Decorate with spirals of orange rind and serve at once.

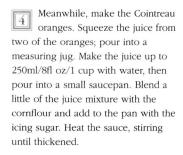

CREMA CATALANA

This delicious Spanish pudding is a cross between a crème caramel and a crème brûlée.
It is not as rich as a crème brûlée, but has a similar caramelized sugar topping.

475ml/16fl oz/2 cups milk
pared rind of ½ lemon
1 cinnamon stick
4 egg yolks
105ml/7 tbsp caster sugar
25ml/1½ tbsp cornflour
ground nutmeg

SERVES 4

1 Put the milk in a pan with the lemon rind and cinnamon stick. Bring to the boil, then simmer for 10 minutes. Remove the lemon peel and cinnamon. Place the egg yolks and 45ml/3 tbsp of the sugar in a bowl, and whisk until pale yellow. Add the cornflour and mix well.

2 Stir in a few tablespoons of the hot milk, then add this mixture to the remaining milk. Return to the heat and cook gently, stirring, for about 5 minutes, until thickened and smooth. Do not let it boil. There should be no cornflour taste.

3 Pour into 4 shallow ovenproof dishes, about 13cm/5in in diameter. Leave to cool, then chill for a few hours, overnight if possible, until firm. Before serving, sprinkle each pudding with a tablespoon of sugar and a little of the ground nutmeg. Preheat the grill to high.

4 Place the puddings under the grill, on the highest shelf, and cook until the sugar caramelizes. This will only take a few seconds. Leave to cool for a few minutes before serving. (The caramel will only stay hard for about 30 minutes.)

445

BANANA AND MASCARPONE CREAMS

If you like cold banana custard, you will love this recipe. It is a grown-up version of an old favourite. No one will guess that the secret is ready-made custard sauce.

250g/9oz generous 1 cup
mascarpone cheese
300ml/1/2 pint/11/4 cups fresh ready-
made custard sauce
150ml/1/4 pint/2/3 cup Greek yogurt
4 bananas
juice of 1 lime
50g/2oz/1/2 cup pecan nuts,
coarsely chopped
120ml/4fl oz/1/2 cup maple syrup

SERVES 4–6

1 Combine the mascarpone, custard sauce and yogurt in a large bowl, and beat together until smooth. Make this mixture several hours ahead, if you like. Cover and chill, then stir before using.

2 Peel the bananas, slice diagonally and place in a separate bowl. Pour the lime juice over the top, and toss together until the bananas are coated in the juice.

3 Divide half of the custard mixture among four to six dessert glasses and top each portion with some of the banana slices, until you have used half of them.

4 Spoon the remaining custard mixture into the glasses and top with the remaining bananas. Scatter the nuts over the top. Drizzle maple syrup over each portion and chill for 30 minutes before serving.

BANANAS WITH LIME AND CARDAMOM SAUCE

Serve these bananas solo, with vanilla ice cream, or spoon them over folded crêpes.

6 small bananas
50g/2oz/1/4 cup butter
seeds from 4 cardamom pods, crushed
50g/2oz/1/2 cup flaked almonds
thinly pared rind and juice of 2 limes
50g/2oz/1/3 cup light muscovado sugar
30ml/2 tbsp dark rum
vanilla ice cream, to serve (optional)

SERVES 4

1 Peel the bananas and cut them in half lengthways. Heat half the butter in a large frying pan. Add half the bananas, and cook until the undersides are golden. Turn carefully, using a spatula. Cook until golden.

2 As they cook, transfer the bananas to a heatproof serving dish. Cook the remaining bananas in the same way.

3 Melt the remaining butter, then add the cardamom and almonds. Cook, stirring until golden.

4 Stir in the lime rind and juice, then the sugar. Cook, stirring, until the mixture is smooth, bubbling and slightly reduced. Stir in the rum. Pour the sauce over the bananas and serve immediately, with vanilla ice cream, if you like.

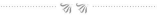

COOK'S TIP
If you prefer not to use alcohol in your cooking, replace the rum with orange juice or even pineapple juice.

STUFFED PEACHES WITH MASCARPONE CREAM

Mascarpone is a thick velvety Italian cream cheese, made from cow's milk.
It is often used in desserts, or eaten with fresh fruit.

⁓ 🌿 🌿 ⁓

4 large peaches, halved and stoned
40g/1½oz amaretti biscuits, crumbled
30ml/2 tbsp ground almonds
45ml/3 tbsp sugar
15ml/1 tbsp cocoa powder
150ml/¼ pint/⅔ cup sweet wine
25g/1oz/2 tbsp butter

FOR THE MASCARPONE CREAM
30ml/2 tbsp caster sugar
3 egg yolks
15ml/1 tbsp sweet wine
225g/8oz/1 cup mascarpone cheese
150ml/¼ pint/⅔ cup double cream

SERVES 4

⁓ 🌿 🌿 ⁓

3 Place the peaches in a buttered ovenproof dish and fill them with the stuffing. Dot with the butter, then pour the remaining wine into the dish. Bake for 35 minutes.

4 To make the mascarpone cream, beat the sugar and egg yolks until thick and pale. Stir in the wine, then fold in the mascarpone. Whip the double cream to soft peaks and fold into the mixture. Remove the peaches from the oven and leave to cool. Serve at room temperature, with the mascarpone cream.

1 Preheat the oven to 200°C/ 400°F/Gas 6. Using a teaspoon, scoop some of the flesh from the cavities in the peaches, to make a reasonable space for stuffing. Chop the scooped-out flesh.

2 Mix together the amaretti, ground almonds, sugar, cocoa and peach flesh. Add enough wine to make the mixture into a thick paste.

FRESH FRUIT SALAD

When peaches and strawberries are out of season, use other fruits, such as bananas and grapes.

2 eating apples
2 oranges
16–20 strawberries
2 peaches
30ml/2 tbsp lemon juice
15–30ml/1–2 tbsp orange flower water
icing sugar, to taste (optional)
a few fresh mint leaves, to decorate

SERVES 4

1 Peel and core the apples and slice finely. Peel the oranges with a sharp knife, removing all the pith, and segment them, catching any juice in a bowl.

2 Hull half the strawberries and halve or quarter them, depending on size. Keep the remaining strawberries with their hulls intact for a pretty effect. Blanch the peaches for about 1 minute in boiling water, then using a knife, peel away the skin and cut the flesh into thick slices. Discard the stones. Place all the fruit in a large serving bowl. Toss lightly to mix.

3 Mix together the lemon juice, orange flower water and any leftover orange juice. Taste and add a little icing sugar to sweeten, if liked. Pour the fruit juice mixture over the salad and serve, decorated with fresh mint leaves.

VARIATION
There are no rules with this fruit salad, and you can use almost any fruit that you like. Oranges, however, should form the base and are available all year round. Apples give a welcome contrast in texture.

DRIED FRUIT SALAD

This is a wonderful combination of fresh and dried fruit, and makes an excellent dessert throughout the year. Use frozen raspberries or blackberries in winter.

115g/4oz/1/2 cup dried apricots
115g/4oz/1/2 cup dried peaches
1 fresh pear
1 fresh apple
1 fresh orange
115g/4oz/2/3 cup mixed raspberries
and blackberries
1 cinnamon stick
50g/2oz/1/4 cup caster sugar
15ml/1 tbsp clear honey
30ml/2 tbsp lemon juice

SERVES 4

1 Soak the apricots and peaches in water for 1–2 hours until plump, then drain. Cut into halves, quarters or thin slices.

2 Peel and core the pear and apple and cut them into cubes. Peel the orange with a sharp knife, removing all the pith, and cut into wedges.

3 Place all the fruit in a large saucepan with the raspberries and the blackberries.

4 Add 600ml/1 pint/2 cups water, the cinnamon, sugar and honey and bring to the boil. Cover and simmer very gently for 10–12 minutes, then remove the pan from the heat. Stir in the lemon juice. Allow to cool, then pour into a bowl and chill for 1–2 hours before serving.

VARIATION
To vary the flavour of the fruit salad, try using cloves or root ginger.

CHAROSET

This is an unusual Israeli recipe. Variations of it go back at least two thousand years.

1 large cooking apple
75g/3oz/¾ cup blanched almonds
10ml/2 tsp ground cinnamon
30ml/2 tbsp kosher sweet red wine

MAKES ENOUGH TO FILL A
350G/12OZ JAR

1 Peel, quarter and chop the apple. Chop it finely with the blanched almonds. If using a food processor, make sure that you don't process the mixture too finely – it should still be crunchy.

2 Stir in the cinnamon and sweet wine, and spoon the mixture into a jar. Cover and set aside. The colour and flavour will develop after 1–2 hours. Serve the mixture as a topping for Israeli unleavened bread.

RED FRUIT SALAD

Cut fruit usually deteriorates quickly, but the juices from lightly-cooked mixed berries make a brilliant red coating, so this salad can be made the day before. It is also one of the quickest ways of making fruit salad for a crowd.

225g/8oz/1⅓ cup raspberries
or blackberries
50g/2oz/½ cup redcurrants
or blackcurrants
30–60ml/2–4 tbsp sugar
8 ripe plums
8 ripe apricots
225g/8oz/2 cups seedless grapes
115g/4oz/1 cup strawberries

SERVES 8

VARIATION
Use dried apricots instead of fresh, if you prefer, or even dried mango.

3 Leave to cool slightly and then add the reserved plums and apricots, and the grapes. Taste for sweetness and add more sugar if the fruit is too tart. Leave the fruit salad to cool, then cover and chill.

1 Mix the berries and currants with 30ml/2 tbsp sugar. Stone the plums and apricots, cut them into pieces and put half of them into a pan with all of the berries.

2 Cook over very low heat with about 45ml/3 tbsp water until the fruit is just beginning to soften and the juices are starting to run.

4 Just before serving, transfer the fruit to a serving bowl. Hull and slice the strawberries, and arrange them over the fruit in the bowl.

FRESH FIGS WITH HONEY AND WINE

Any variety of figs can be used in this recipe, their ripeness determining the cooking time. Choose ones that are plump and firm, and use them quickly as they do not store well.

450ml/¾ pint/1⅞ cups dry white wine
75g/3oz/⅓ cup clear honey
50g/2oz/¼ cup caster sugar
1 small orange
8 whole cloves
450g/1lb fresh figs
1 cinnamon stick
mint sprigs, or bay leaves, to decorate

FOR THE CREAM
300ml/½ pint/1¼ cups double cream
1 vanilla pod
5ml/1 tsp caster sugar

SERVES 6

1. Put the wine, honey and sugar in a heavy-based saucepan and heat gently until the sugar dissolves.

2. Stud the orange with the cloves and add to the syrup with the figs and cinnamon. Cover and simmer very gently for 5–10 minutes until the figs are softened. Transfer to a serving dish and leave to cool.

3. Put 150ml/¼ pint/⅔ cup of the cream in a small saucepan with the vanilla pod. Bring almost to the boil, then leave to cool and infuse for 30 minutes. Remove the vanilla pod and mix with the remaining cream and sugar in a bowl. Whip lightly. Transfer to a serving dish. Decorate the figs, then serve with the cream.

APRICOTS STUFFED WITH ALMOND PASTE

*Almonds, whether whole, flaked or ground, are a favourite Moroccan ingredient. They have a
delightful affinity with apricots, making this a popular — and delicious — dessert.*

75g/3oz/scant ½ cup caster sugar
30ml/2 tbsp lemon juice
115g/4oz/1 cup ground almonds
50g/2oz/½ cup icing sugar or
caster sugar
a little orange flower water (optional)
25g/1oz/2 tbsp melted butter
2.5ml/½ tsp almond essence
900g/2lb fresh apricots
fresh sprigs of mint, to decorate

SERVES 6

1 Preheat the oven to 180°C/
350°F/Gas 4. Place the caster
sugar, lemon juice and 300ml/½ pint/
1¼ cups water in a small pan and
bring to the boil, stirring until the
sugar has dissolved. Simmer gently for
5–10 minutes.

2 In a bowl, mix together the
ground almonds, icing sugar (or
caster sugar, if preferred), orange flower
water, if using, butter and almond
essence to make a smooth paste.

3 Wash the apricots, then make
a slit in the flesh and ease out
the stone. Take small pieces of the
almond paste, roll into balls and press
one into each of the apricots.

4 Arrange the stuffed apricots in a
shallow ovenproof dish and
carefully pour the sugar syrup around
them. Cover with foil and bake in the
oven for 25–30 minutes.

5 Serve the apricots with a little of
the syrup, if liked, and decorate
with sprigs of mint.

TOFFEE BANANAS

Although the method for this recipe sounds simple, it can, in fact, be a bit tricky to master. You need to work fast, especially when dipping the fruit in the caramel, as it will cool and set quite quickly. The luscious results, however, are worth the effort.

4 firm bananas
75g/3oz/¾ cup plain flour
50g/2oz/½ cup cornflour
10ml/2 tsp baking powder
175ml/6fl oz/¾ cup water
5ml/1 tsp sesame oil
oil, for deep frying
iced water

FOR THE CARAMEL
225g/8oz/1 cup sugar
30ml/2 tbsp sesame seeds
60ml/4 tbsp water

SERVES 4

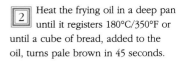

2 Heat the frying oil in a deep pan until it registers 180°C/350°F or until a cube of bread, added to the oil, turns pale brown in 45 seconds.

1 Peel the bananas, then slice them thickly, at an angle, into a bowl. Sift the flour, cornflour and baking powder into a separate large bowl. Quickly beat in the water and sesame oil, taking care not to overmix. Stir in the bananas until evenly coated.

3 Using a fork, remove a piece of banana from the batter, allowing the excess batter to drain back into the bowl. Gently lower the piece of banana into the hot oil. Add more pieces of battered banana in the same way, but do not overcrowd the pan. Fry for about 2 minutes or until the coating is golden brown.

4 As they are cooked, remove the banana fritters from the oil with a slotted spoon and place on kitchen paper to drain. Cook the remaining battered bananas in the same way.

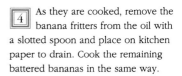

5 When all the banana pieces have been fried, make the caramel. Mix together the sugar, sesame seeds and water in a pan. Heat gently, stirring occasionally, until the sugar has dissolved. Raise the heat slightly and continue cooking, without stirring, until the syrup becomes a light caramel. Remove from the heat.

6 Have ready a bowl of iced water. Working quickly, drop one fritter at a time into the hot caramel. Flip over with a fork, remove immediately and plunge the piece into the iced water, taking care not to burn yourself. Quickly remove from the water and drain on a wire rack while you coat the rest. Serve.

CITRUS FRUIT FLAMBE WITH PISTACHIO PRALINE

A fruit flambé makes a dramatic finale for a dinner party. Top this refreshing citrus fruit dessert with crunchy pistachio praline to make it extra-special.

4 oranges
2 ruby grapefruit
2 limes
50g/2oz/¼ cup butter
50g/2oz/⅓ cup light
muscovado sugar
45ml/3 tbsp Cointreau
fresh mint sprigs, to decorate

FOR THE PRALINE
oil, for greasing
115g/4oz/½ cup caster sugar
50g/2oz/½ cup pistachio nuts

SERVES 4

1 First, make the pistachio praline. Brush a baking sheet lightly with oil. Place the caster sugar and pistachio nuts in a small heavy-based saucepan and swirl over a gentle heat until the sugar has melted.

2 Continue to cook over a fairly low heat until the nuts start to pop and the sugar turns a dark golden colour. Pour on to the oiled baking sheet and set aside to harden. Chop the praline into rough chunks.

3 Cut off all the rind and pith from all the citrus fruit. Holding each fruit in turn over a large bowl, cut between the membranes so that the segments fall into the bowl, with any juice.

4 Heat the butter and muscovado sugar together in a heavy-based frying pan until the sugar has melted and the mixture is golden. Strain the citrus juices into the pan and continue to cook, stirring occasionally, until the juice has reduced and is syrupy.

5 Add the fruit segments and warm through without stirring. Pour over the Cointreau and set it alight. As soon as the flames die down, spoon the fruit flambé into serving dishes. Scatter some praline over each portion and decorate with mint. Serve at once.

BERRY BRULEE TARTS

This quantity of pastry is enough to make 8 tartlets, so freeze half of it for another day.
The brûlée topping is best added no more than 2 hours before serving the tarts.

250g/9oz/2¼ cups plain flour
a pinch of salt
25g/1oz/¼ cup ground almonds
15ml/1 tbsp icing sugar
150g/5oz/⅔ cup unsalted butter,
chilled and diced
1 egg yolk
about 45ml/3 tbsp cold water

FOR THE FILLING
4 egg yolks
15ml/1 tbsp cornflour
50g/2oz/¼ cup caster sugar
a few drops of pure vanilla essence
300ml/½ pint/1¼ cups creamy milk
225g/8oz/2 cups mixed berry fruits,
such as small strawberries,
raspberries, blackcurrants
and redcurrants
50g/2oz/½ cup icing sugar

MAKES 4

3 Use the pastry rounds to line four individual tartlet tins, letting the excess pastry hang over the edges. Chill for 30 minutes.

4 Preheat the oven to 200°C/ 400°F/Gas 6. Line the pastry with non-stick baking paper and baking beans. Bake blind for 10 minutes. Remove the paper and beans and return the tartlet cases to the oven for 5 minutes until golden. Allow the pastry to cool, then carefully trim off the excess pastry.

5 Beat the egg yolks, cornflour, sugar and vanilla in a bowl.

1 Mix the flour, salt, ground almonds and icing sugar in a bowl. Rub in the butter by hand or in a food processor until the mixture resembles fine breadcrumbs. Add the egg yolk and enough cold water to form a dough. Knead the dough gently, then cut it in half and freeze half for use later.

2 Cut the remaining pastry into four equal pieces and roll out thinly on a lightly floured surface.

COOK'S TIP
A culinary blow torch can be used to melt and caramelize the brûlée topping.

6 Warm the milk in a heavy-based pan, pour it on to the egg yolks, whisking constantly, then return the mixture to the clean pan.

7 Heat, stirring, until the custard thickens, but do not let it boil. Remove from the heat. Press a piece of clear film directly on the surface of the custard and allow to cool.

8 Scatter the berries in the tartlet cases and spoon over the custard. Chill the tarts on a baking sheet for 2 hours.

9 To serve, sift icing sugar generously over the tops of the tartlets. Preheat the grill to the highest setting. Place the tartlets under the hot grill until the sugar melts and caramelizes. Allow the topping to cool and harden for about 10 minutes before serving the tarts.

BAKED LATTICE PEACHES

If you would rather use nectarines for the recipe, there is no need to peel them first.

3 peaches
juice of 1/2 lemon
75g/3oz/scant 1/2 cup white marzipan
375g/13oz ready-rolled puff pastry,
thawed if frozen
a large pinch of ground cinnamon
beaten egg, to glaze
caster sugar, for sprinkling

FOR THE CARAMEL SAUCE
50g/2oz/1/4 cup caster sugar
30ml/2 tbsp cold water
150ml/1/4 pint/2/3 cup double cream

MAKES 6

1 Preheat the oven to 190°C/
375°F/Gas 5. Place the peaches
in a large bowl and pour over boiling
water to cover. Leave for 60 seconds,
then drain the peaches and peel off
the skins. Toss the skinned fruit in
the lemon juice to stop them from
going brown.

2 Divide the marzipan into six
pieces and shape each to form
a small round. Cut the peaches in half
and remove their stones. Fill the stone
cavity in each with a marzipan round.

3 Unroll the puff pastry and cut it
in half. Set one half aside, then
cut out six rounds from the rest,
making each round slightly larger
than a peach half. Sprinkle a little
cinnamon on each pastry round, then
place a peach half, marzipan side
down, on the pastry.

4 Cut the remaining pastry into
lattice pastry, using a special
cutter if you have one. If not, simply
cut small slits in rows all over the
pastry, starting each row slightly
lower than the last. Cut the lattice
pastry into six equal squares.

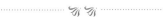

COOK'S TIP
Take care when adding the cream to
the hot caramel as the mixture is
liable to spit. Pour it from a jug,
protecting your hand with an
oven glove.

5 Dampen the edges of the pastry
rounds with a little water, then
drape a lattice pastry square over
each peach half. Press around the
edge to seal, then trim off the excess
pastry and decorate with small peach
leaves made from the trimmings.

6 Transfer the peach pastries to a
baking sheet. Brush with the
beaten egg and sprinkle with the
caster sugar. Bake for 20 minutes or
until the pastries are golden.

7 Meanwhile, make the caramel
sauce. Heat the sugar with the
water in a small pan until it dissolves.
Bring to the boil and continue to boil
until the syrup turns a dark golden
brown. Stand back and add the cream
carefully. Heat gently, stirring until
smooth. Serve the peach pastries with
the sauce.

APRICOT PARCELS

Apricots, mincemeat and marzipan layered with filo pastry make a delicious end to a meal.

350g/12oz filo pastry, thawed
if frozen
50g/2oz/¼ cup butter, melted
8 apricots, halved and stoned
60ml/4 tbsp luxury mincemeat
12 ratafias, crushed
30ml/2 tbsp grated marzipan
icing sugar, for dusting

MAKES 8

1 Preheat the oven to 200°C/
400°F/Gas 6. Spread the filo
pastry on to a flat surface. Cut into
32 × 18cm/7in squares. Brush four of
the squares with a little melted butter
and stack them one on top of the
other, giving each layer a quarter
turn so that the stack acquires a star
shape. Repeat the process to make
eight stars.

2 Place an apricot half, hollow
up, in the centre of each pastry
star. Mix together the mincemeat,
crushed ratafias and marzipan, and
spoon a little of the mixture into the
hollow in each apricot.

3 Top with another apricot half,
then bring the corners of each
pastry together and squeeze to make
a gathered purse. Place the purses
on a baking sheet and brush each
with a little melted butter. Bake for
15–20 minutes or until the pastry is
golden and crisp.

4 Lightly dust with icing sugar to
serve. Whipped cream,
flavoured with a little brandy, makes
an ideal accompaniment.

COOK'S TIP
Filo pastry dries out quickly, so keep
any squares that are not currently
being used covered under a clean
damp dish towel, and work as quickly
as possible. If the filo should turn dry
and brittle, simply brush it with
melted butter to moisten.

OMM ALI

This is an Egyptian version of a traditional bread and butter pudding.

10–12 sheets filo pastry
600ml/1 pint/2½ cups milk
250ml/8fl oz/1 cup double cream
1 egg, beaten
30ml/2 tbsp rose water
50g/2oz/½ cup each chopped pistachio
nuts, almonds and hazelnuts
115g/4oz/⅔ cup raisins
15ml/1 tbsp ground cinnamon,
for dusting
single cream, to serve

SERVES 4

1   Preheat the oven to 160°C/
325°F/Gas 3. Bake the filo
pastry, on one or two baking sheets,
for 15–20 minutes until crisp. Remove
from the oven and raise the
temperature to 200°C/400°F/Gas 6.

2   Scald the milk and cream by
pouring into a pan and heating
very gently until hot but not boiling.
Slowly add the beaten egg and the
rose water. Cook over a low heat until
the mixture begins to thicken, stirring.

3   Crumble the pastry, using your
hands, and then spread in
layers with the nuts and raisins in a
shallow baking dish.

4   Pour the custard mixture over the
nut and pastry base and bake
for 20 minutes until golden. Dust with
cinnamon and serve with cream.

YELLOW PLUM TART

In this tart, glazed yellow plums are arranged on a delectable almond filling in a crisp pastry shell.
When they are in season, greengages make an excellent alternative to the plums.

❦ ❦

175g/6oz/1½ cups plain flour
pinch of salt
75g/3oz/6 tbsp butter, chilled
30ml/2 tbsp caster sugar
a few drops of pure vanilla essence
45ml/3 tbsp iced water
cream or custard, to serve

FOR THE FILLING
75g/3oz/6 tbsp caster sugar
75g/3oz/6 tbsp butter, softened
75g/3oz/¾ cup ground almonds
1 egg, beaten
30ml/2 tbsp plain flour
450g/1lb yellow plums or greengages,
halved and stoned

FOR THE GLAZE
45ml/3 tbsp apricot jam, sieved
15ml/1 tbsp water

SERVES 8

❦ ❦

1 Sift the flour and salt into a bowl, then rub in the chilled butter until the mixture resembles fine breadcrumbs. Stir in the caster sugar, vanilla essence and enough of the iced water to form a soft dough.

2 Knead the dough gently on a lightly floured surface until smooth, then wrap in clear film and chill for 10 minutes.

3 Preheat the oven to 200°C/400°F/Gas 6. Roll out the pastry and line a 23cm/9in fluted flan tin, allowing any excess pastry to overhang the top. Prick the base with a fork and line with non-stick baking paper and baking beans.

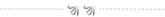

COOK'S TIP
Ceramic baking beans are ideal for baking blind, but any dried beans will do. You can use them over and over again, but make sure you keep them in a special jar, separate from the rest of your dried beans, as they cannot be used for conventional cooking after being used for baking blind.

4 Bake blind for 10 minutes, remove the paper and beans, then return the pastry case to the oven for 10 minutes. Remove and allow to cool. Trim off any excess pastry with a sharp knife.

5 To make the filling, whisk or beat together all the ingredients except the plums or greengages. Spread on the base of the pastry case. Arrange the plums or greengages on top, placing them cut side down. Make a glaze by heating the jam with the water. Stir well, then brush a little of the glaze over the top of the fruit.

6 Bake the plum tart for about 50 minutes, until the almond filling is cooked and the plums or greengages are tender. Warm any remaining jam glaze and brush it over the top. Cut into slices and serve with cream or custard.

DATE AND ALMOND TART

Fresh dates make an unusual but delicious filling for a tart. The influences here are French and Middle Eastern – a true Mediterranean fusion!

FOR THE PASTRY
175g/6oz/1½ cups plain flour
75g/3oz/6 tbsp butter
1 egg

FOR THE FILLING
90g/3½oz/scant ½ cup butter
90g/3½oz/7 tbsp caster sugar
1 egg, beaten
90g/3½oz/scant 1 cup ground almonds
30ml/2 tbsp plain flour
30ml/2 tbsp orange flower water
12–13 fresh dates, halved and stoned
60ml/4 tbsp apricot jam

SERVES 6

[1] Preheat the oven to 200°C/400°F/Gas 6. Place a baking sheet in the oven. Sift the flour into a bowl, add the butter and work with your fingertips until the mixture resembles fine breadcrumbs. Add the egg and a tablespoon of cold water, then work to a smooth dough.

[4] Spread the mixture evenly over the base of the pastry case. Arrange the dates, cut side down, on the almond mixture. Bake on the hot baking sheet for 10–15 minutes, then reduce the heat to 180°C/350°F/Gas 4. Bake for a further 15–20 minutes until light golden and set.

[2] Roll out the pastry on a lightly floured surface and use to line a 20cm/8in tart tin. Prick the base with a fork, then chill until needed.

[5] Transfer the tart to a rack to cool. Gently heat the apricot jam, then press through a sieve. Add the remaining orange flower water.

[3] To make the filling, cream the butter and sugar until light, then beat in the egg. Stir in the ground almonds, flour and 15ml/1 tbsp of the orange flower water, mixing well.

Brush the tart with the jam and serve at room temperature.

HONEY AND PINE NUT TART

Delicious tarts of all descriptions are to be found throughout France, and this recipe recalls the flavours of the south.

FOR THE PASTRY
225g/8oz/2 cups plain flour
115g/4oz/½ cup butter
30ml/2 tbsp icing sugar
1 egg

FOR THE FILLING
115g/4oz/½ cup unsalted butter, diced
115g/4oz/½ cup caster sugar
3 eggs, beaten
175g/6oz/⅔ cup sunflower or other flower honey
grated rind and juice of 1 lemon
225g/8oz/2⅔ cups pine nuts
pinch of salt
icing sugar for dusting

SERVES 6

1 Preheat the oven to 180°C/ 350°F/Gas 4. Sift the flour into a bowl, add the butter and work with your fingertips until the mixture resembles fine breadcrumbs. Stir in the icing sugar. Add the egg and 15ml/1 tbsp of water and work to a firm dough that leaves the bowl clean.

3 Cream together the butter and caster sugar until light. Beat in the eggs one by one. Gently heat the honey in a small saucepan until runny, then add to the butter mixture with the lemon rind and juice. Stir in the pine nuts and salt, then pour the filling into the pastry case.

2 Roll out the pastry on a floured surface and use to line a 23cm/9in tart tin. Prick the base with a fork, and chill for 10 minutes. Line with foil or greaseproof paper and fill with dried beans or rice, or baking beans if you have them. Bake the tart shell for 10 minutes.

4 Bake for about 45 minutes, until the filling is lightly browned and set. Leave to cool slightly in the tin, then dust generously with icing sugar. Serve warm, or at room temperature, with crème fraîche or vanilla ice cream.

GLAZED PRUNE TART

Generously glazed, creamy custard tarts are a pâtisserie favourite all over France. Plump prunes, heavily laced with brandy or kirsch, add a wonderful taste and texture to this deliciously sweet and creamy filling.

225g/8oz/1 cup ready-to-eat prunes
60ml/4 tbsp brandy or kirsch

FOR THE SWEET PASTRY
175g/6oz/1½ cups plain flour
pinch of salt
115g/4oz/½ cup unsalted butter
25g/1oz/2 tbsp caster sugar
2 egg yolks

FOR THE FILLING
150ml/¼ pint/⅔ cup double cream
150ml/¼ pint/⅔ cup milk
1 vanilla pod
3 eggs
50g/2oz/¼ cup caster sugar

TO FINISH
60ml/4 tbsp apricot jam
15ml/1 tbsp brandy or kirsch
icing sugar for dusting

SERVES 8

---

1 Put the prunes in a bowl with the brandy or kirsch and leave for about 4 hours until most of the liqueur has been absorbed.

2 To make the pastry, sift the flour and salt into a bowl. Add the butter, cut into small pieces, and rub in with the fingertips. Stir in the sugar and egg yolks and mix to a dough using a round-bladed knife.

3 Turn the dough out onto a lightly floured surface and knead to a smooth ball. Wrap closely and chill for 30 minutes.

4 Preheat the oven to 200°C/400°F/ Gas 6. Roll out the pastry on a lightly floured surface and use to line a 24–25cm/9½–10in loose-based flan tin.

5 Line with greaseproof paper and fill with dried beans or rice, or baking beans if you have them. Bake for 15 minutes. Remove the beans and paper and bake for a further 5 minutes.

6 Arrange the prunes, evenly spaced, in the pastry case, reserving any liqueur left in the bowl.

7 For the filling, put the cream and milk in a saucepan with the vanilla pod and bring to the boil. Turn off the heat and leave the mixture to infuse for 15 minutes.

8 Whisk together the eggs and sugar in a bowl. Remove the vanilla pod from the cream and return the cream to the boil. Pour over the eggs and sugar, whisking to make a smooth custard.

9 Cool slightly then pour the custard over the prunes. Bake the tart for about 25 minutes until the filling is lightly set and turning golden around the edges.

10 Press the apricot jam through a sieve into a small pan. Add the liqueur and heat through gently. Use to glaze the tart. Serve warm or cold, dusted with icing sugar.

COOK'S TIP
The vanilla pod can be washed and dried, ready for using another time. Alternatively, use 5ml/1 tsp vanilla or almond essence.

LEMON TART

*This is one of the classic French desserts, and it is difficult to beat. A rich lemon curd is
encased in crisp pastry. Crème fraîche is an optional accompaniment.*

3 Roll the pastry out on a floured
surface, and use to line a
23cm/9in tart tin. Line with foil or
greaseproof paper and fill with dried
beans or rice, or baking beans if you
have them. Bake for 10 minutes.

FOR THE PASTRY
225g/8oz/2 cups plain flour
115g/4oz/½ cup butter
30ml/2 tbsp icing sugar
1 egg
5ml/1 tsp vanilla essence

FOR THE FILLING
6 eggs, beaten
350g/12oz/1½ cups caster sugar
115g/4oz/½ cup unsalted butter
grated rind and juice of 4 lemons
icing sugar for dusting

SERVES 6

1 Preheat the oven to 200°C/
400°F/Gas 6. Sift the flour into
a large bowl, add the butter, cut into
small pieces, and work with your
fingertips until the mixture resembles
breadcrumbs. Stir in the icing sugar.

4 To make the filling, put the eggs,
sugar and butter into a pan, and
stir over a low heat until the sugar has
dissolved completely. Add the lemon
rind and juice, and continue cooking,
stirring all of the time, until the lemon
curd has thickened slightly.

2 Add the egg, vanilla essence
and a scant tablespoon of cold
water, then work to a dough.

5 Pour the mixture into the pastry
case. Bake for 20 minutes, until
just set. Transfer the tart to a wire
rack to cool. Dust with icing sugar
just before serving.

RICOTTA AND MARSALA TARTS

These sweet, melt-in-the-mouth tarts have a crisp puff-pastry base. The light cheese filling is flavoured in the Italian way with Marsala.

375g/13oz packet ready-rolled puff
    pastry, thawed if frozen
250g/9oz/generous 1 cup
    ricotta cheese
1 egg, plus 2 egg yolks
45–60ml/3–4 tbsp caster sugar
30ml/2 tbsp Marsala
grated rind of 1 lemon
50g/2oz/⅓ cup sultanas

MAKES 12

1 Cut out 12 × 9cm/3½in rounds of pastry and line a tray of deep muffin cups. Set the tray aside to rest the pastry for 20 minutes. Meanwhile preheat the oven to 190°C/375°F/ Gas 5.

2 Put the ricotta cheese in a bowl and add the egg, extra yolks, sugar, Marsala and lemon rind. Whisk until smooth, then stir in the sultanas.

3 Spoon the mixture into the lined tins. Bake the tarts for about 20 minutes or until the filling has risen in each and the pastry is crisp and golden.

4 Cool the tarts slightly before easing each one out with a small spatula. Serve warm.

FRESH FIG FILO TART

Figs cook wonderfully well and taste superb in this tart – the riper the figs, the better.

25g/1oz/2 tbsp butter, melted, plus
extra for greasing
5 sheets of filo pastry, each 35 × 25cm/
14 × 10in, thawed if frozen
6 fresh figs, cut into wedges
75g/3oz/3⁄4 cup plain flour
75g/3oz/1⁄2 cup caster sugar
4 eggs
450ml/3⁄4 pint/13⁄4 cups creamy milk
2.5ml/1⁄2 tsp almond essence
15ml/1 tbsp icing sugar, for dusting
whipped cream or Greek yogurt,
to serve

SERVES 6–8

1 Preheat the oven to 190°C/
375°F/Gas 5. Grease a 25 × 16cm/
10 × 6¼in baking tin with butter.
Brush each filo sheet in turn with
melted butter and use to line the
prepared tin.

2 Using scissors, cut off any
excess pastry, leaving a little
overhanging the edge. Arrange the
figs in the filo case.

3 Sift the flour into a bowl and
stir in the caster sugar. Add the
eggs and a little of the milk, then
whisk until smooth. Slowly whisk in
the remaining milk and the almond
essence. Pour the mixture over the
figs and bake for 1 hour.

4 Remove the tart from the oven
and allow it to cool in the tin
on a wire rack for 10 minutes. Dust
with the icing sugar and serve with
whipped cream or Greek yogurt.

RICOTTA CHEESECAKE

Ricotta cheese is excellent for cheesecake fillings because it has a firm texture. Here it is enriched with eggs and cream and enlivened with tangy orange and lemon rind to make a Sicilian-style dessert which would make an impressive finale for a dinner party.

450g/1lb/2 cups ricotta cheese
120ml/4fl oz/½ cup double cream
2 eggs
1 egg yolk
75g/3oz/6 tbsp caster sugar
finely grated rind of 1 orange
finely grated rind of 1 lemon
pared orange and lemon rind,
to decorate

FOR THE PASTRY
175g/6oz/1½ cups plain flour
45ml/3 tbsp caster sugar
pinch of salt
115g/4oz/½ cup chilled butter, diced
1 egg yolk

SERVES 8

2 Gather the dough together, reserving about a quarter for the lattice, then press the rest into a 23cm/9in fluted tart tin with a removable base. Chill the pastry case for 30 minutes.

4 Prick the bottom of the pastry case, then line with foil and fill with baking beans. Bake blind for 15 minutes, then transfer to a wire rack, remove the foil and beans and allow the tart shell to cool in the tin.

3 Meanwhile, preheat the oven to 190°C/375°F/Gas 5 and make the filling. Put the ricotta, cream, eggs, egg yolk, sugar and orange and lemon rinds in a large bowl, and beat together until evenly mixed.

5 Spoon the cheese and cream filling into the pastry case and level the surface. Roll out the reserved dough and cut into strips. Arrange the strips on the top of the filling in a lattice pattern, sticking them in place with water.

6 Bake for 30–35 minutes until golden and set. Transfer to a wire rack and leave to cool, then carefully remove the side of the tin, leaving the cheesecake on the tin base. Serve in slices, decorated with pared orange and lemon rind.

1 Make the pastry. Sift the flour, sugar and salt on to a cold work surface. Make a well in the centre and add the diced butter and egg yolk. Gradually work the flour into the diced butter and egg yolk, using your fingertips.

VARIATIONS

Add 50–115g/2–4oz/⅓–⅔ cup finely chopped candied peel to the filling in Step 3, or 50g/2oz/⅓ cup plain chocolate chips. For a really rich dessert, you can add both candied peel and some grated plain chocolate.

CHERRY CLAFOUTIS

When fresh cherries are in season this makes a deliciously simple dessert for any occasion.
Serve warm with a little pouring cream.

675g/1½lb fresh cherries
50g/2oz/½ cup plain flour
pinch of salt
4 eggs, plus 2 egg yolks
115g/4oz/½ cup caster sugar
600ml/1 pint/2½ cups milk
50g/2oz/¼ cup melted butter
caster sugar, for dusting

SERVES 6

1 Preheat the oven to 190°C/
375°F/Gas 5. Lightly butter the
base and sides of a shallow
ovenproof dish. Stone the cherries
and place in the dish.

2 Sift the flour and salt into a
bowl. Add the eggs, egg yolks,
sugar and a little of the milk and
whisk to a smooth batter.

3 Gradually whisk in the rest of
the milk and the rest of the
butter, then strain the batter over the
cherries. Bake for 40–50 minutes until
golden and just set. Serve warm,
dusted with caster sugar, if you like.

VARIATION
Use 2 x 425g/15oz cans stoned black
cherries, thoroughly drained, if fresh
cherries are not available. For a
special dessert, add 45ml/3 tbsp
kirsch to the batter.

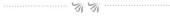

MOROCCAN RICE PUDDING

This is a simple and delicious alternative to a traditional rice pudding. The rice is cooked in almond-flavoured milk and delicately flavoured with cinnamon and orange flower water.

25g/1oz/¼ cup blanched almonds,
chopped
450g/1lb/2¼ cups pudding rice
25g/1oz/¼ cup icing sugar
7.5cm/3in cinnamon stick
50g/2oz/¼ cup butter
pinch of salt
1.5ml/¼ tsp almond essence
175ml/6fl oz /¾ cup milk
175ml/6fl oz/¾ cup condensed milk
30ml/2 tbsp orange flower water
toasted flaked almonds and ground
cinnamon, to decorate

SERVES 6

1 Put the almonds in a food processor or blender with 60ml/4 tbsp of very hot water. Process, then push through a sieve into a bowl. Return to the food processor or blender, add a further 60ml/4 tbsp very hot water, and process again. Push through the sieve into a saucepan.

2 Add 300ml/½ pint/1¼ cups water to the almond "milk" and bring to the boil. Add the rice, sugar, cinnamon and half the butter, the salt, the almond essence, and half the milk. (Mix the milks together.)

3 Bring to the boil, then simmer, covered, for about 30 minutes, adding more milk if necessary. Continue to cook the rice, stirring, and adding the remaining milk, until it becomes thick and creamy. Stir in the orange flower water, then taste the rice pudding for sweetness, adding extra sugar, if necessary.

4 Pour the rice pudding into a serving bowl, and sprinkle with the flaked almonds. Dot with the remaining butter and dust with ground cinnamon. Serve hot.

HAZELNUT SPONGE CAKE

This is an interesting cake, which does not contain any flour. The fruit coulis and the vanilla sauce make a delicious combination or they can be served separately.

---

6 large eggs, separated
175g/6oz/³⁄₄ cup caster sugar
juice and grated rind of 1 lemon
175g/6oz/1¹⁄₂ cups ground hazelnuts
25g/1oz polenta
oil, for greasing

FOR THE FRUIT COULIS
225g/8oz/2 cups blackberries
or strawberries
30ml/2 tbsp caster sugar
15–30ml/1–2 tbsp water

FOR THE VANILLA SAUCE
10ml/2 tsp potato flour
30ml/2 tbsp vanilla sugar
3 egg yolks (or 2 small eggs)
300ml/¹⁄₂ pint/1¹⁄₄ cups milk

SERVES 6–8

1 Preheat the oven to 180°C/ 350°F/Gas 4. Whisk the egg yolks with the sugar until the mixture is pale, thick and mousse-like. Add the lemon juice and grated rind, and fold these into the mixture.

2 Whisk the egg whites until stiff. Add a quarter of the whisked whites to the yolk mixture and then fold in the hazelnuts, polenta and remaining whites. Take care to fold these in gently so as not to deflate the mixture.

3 Pour the mixture into a greased 25cm/10in cake tin and bake for 30–40 minutes. The centre should be dry when tested with a cocktail stick or thin skewer.

4 Meanwhile, make the fruit coulis and vanilla sauce. To make the coulis, put the berries in a pan with the sugar and water. Cook over a low heat until the berries collapse. Then strain the fruit and juice through a nylon sieve into a jug.

5 To make the vanilla sauce, mix the potato flour, vanilla sugar and egg yolks until they form a smooth paste. Add the milk a little at a time and stir thoroughly. Put the mixture in a pan over a low heat and bring slowly to the boil, stirring constantly. It will thicken after about 5 minutes. Take it off the heat, strain and cool.

6 When the cake is cool, take it out of the tin and sift icing sugar over the top. Cut the cake into six or eight wedges, depending on the number of servings required. Spoon the vanilla sauce on to dessert plates, and swirl a little fruit coulis through each portion and top with a slice of cake.

COOK'S TIP
To make your own vanilla sugar, store a cut vanilla pod in a jar of sugar. The sugar will absorb the vanilla flavour.

WALNUT AND RICOTTA CAKE

Soft, tangy ricotta cheese is widely used in Italian sweets. Here, it is included along with walnuts and orange to flavour a whisked egg sponge. Don't worry if it sinks slightly after baking – this gives it an authentic appearance.

115g/4oz/1 cup walnut pieces
150g/5oz/⅔ cup unsalted butter, softened
150g/5oz/⅔ cup caster sugar
5 eggs, separated
finely grated rind of 1 orange
150g/5oz/⅔ cup ricotta cheese
40g/1½oz/6 tbsp plain flour

TO FINISH
60ml/4 tbsp apricot jam
30ml/2 tbsp brandy
50g/2oz bitter or plain chocolate, coarsely grated

MAKES 10 SLICES

1 Preheat the oven to 190°C/ 375°F/Gas 5. Grease and line the base of a deep 23cm/9in round, loose-based cake tin. Roughly chop and lightly toast the walnuts.

2 Cream together the butter and 115g/4oz/½ cup of the sugar until light and fluffy. Add the egg yolks, orange rind, ricotta cheese, flour and walnuts and mix together.

3 Whisk the egg whites in a large bowl until stiff. Gradually whisk in the remaining sugar. Using a large metal spoon, fold a quarter of the whisked whites into the ricotta mixture. Carefully fold in the rest of the whisked whites.

4 Turn the mixture into the prepared tin and level the surface. Bake for about 30 minutes until risen and firm. Leave the cake to cool in the tin.

5 Transfer the cake to a serving plate. Heat the apricot jam in a small saucepan with 15ml/1 tbsp water. Press through a sieve and stir in the brandy. Use to coat the top and sides of the cake. Scatter the cake generously with grated chocolate.

VARIATION
Use toasted and chopped almonds in place of the walnuts.

SICILIAN RICOTTA CAKE

In most of Italy, the word cassata is often used to describe a layered ice-cream cake. In Sicily, however, it is a traditional cake made of layers of sponge, ricotta cheese and candied peel, imbibed with alcohol. It both looks and tastes truly delicious.

675g/1½ lb/3 cups ricotta cheese
finely grated rind of 1 orange
2 sachets vanilla sugar
75ml/5 tbsp orange-flavoured liqueur
115g/4oz/⅔ cup candied peel
8 trifle sponges
60ml/4 tbsp freshly squeezed
orange juice
extra candied peel, to decorate

SERVES 8–10

2 | Finely chop the candied peel and beat into the remaining ricotta cheese mixture until evenly mixed. Set aside while you prepare the loaf tin.

1 | Push the ricotta cheese through a sieve into a bowl, add the orange rind, vanilla sugar and 15ml/1 tbsp of liqueur, and beat well. Transfer one-third of the mixture to another bowl and chill until needed.

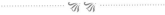

COOK'S TIP
If the cake has become an uneven shape, this can be disguised by the covering of chilled ricotta.

3 | Carefully line the base of a 1.2 litre/2 pint/5 cup loaf tin with non-stick baking paper. Cut the trifle sponges in half through their thickness. Arrange four pieces of sponge side by side in the bottom of the loaf tin and sprinkle with 15ml/1 tbsp of the remaining liqueur and 15ml/1 tbsp orange juice.

4 | Put one-third of the ricotta and fruit mixture in the tin and spread it out evenly. Cover with four more pieces of sponge and sprinkle with another 15ml/1 tbsp each liqueur and orange juice, as before.

5 | Repeat the alternate layers of ricotta mixture and sponge until all the ingredients have been used, soaking the sponge pieces with liqueur and orange juice each time, and ending with soaked sponge. Cover with a piece of non-stick baking paper.

6 | Cut a piece of card to fit inside the tin, place on top of the non-stick baking paper and weight down evenly. Chill for 24 hours.

7 | To serve, remove the weights, card and paper, and run a palette knife between the sides of the filling and the tin. Invert a serving plate on top of the tin, then invert the two so that the cake is on the plate. Lift off the tin and peel away the lining paper.

8 | Spread the chilled ricotta mixture over the cake to cover it completely, then decorate the top with the extra candied peel. Serve chilled.

GREEK YOGURT AND FIG CAKE

Baked fresh figs, thickly sliced, make a delectable base for a featherlight sponge.
Figs that are a bit on the firm side work best for this particular recipe.

2 In a large mixing bowl, cream together the butter and caster sugar with the lemon and orange rinds until the mixture is pale and fluffy, then beat in the egg yolks, a little at a time.

3 Sift together the flour, baking powder and bicarbonate of soda. Add a little to the creamed mixture, beat well, then beat in a spoonful of Greek yogurt. Repeat this process until all the dry ingredients and Greek yogurt have been incorporated.

4 Whisk all the egg whites in a grease-free bowl until they form stiff peaks. Stir half of the whites into the cake mixture to slacken it slightly, then fold in the rest. Pour the mixture over the figs in the tin, then bake for 1¼ hours until golden and a skewer inserted in the centre of the cake comes out clean.

6 firm fresh figs, thickly sliced
45ml/3 tbsp clear honey, plus extra for glazing the cooked figs
200g/7oz/scant 1 cup butter, softened
175g/6oz/¾ cup caster sugar
grated rind of 1 lemon
grated rind of 1 orange
4 eggs, separated
225g/8oz/2 cups plain flour
5ml/1 tsp baking powder
5ml/1 tsp bicarbonate of soda
250ml/8fl oz/1 cup Greek yogurt

SERVES 6–8

1 Preheat the oven to 180°C/ 350°F/Gas 4. Lightly grease a 23cm/9in cake tin and line the base with non-stick baking paper. Arrange the figs over the base of the tin and drizzle over the honey.

5 Turn out the cake on to a wire rack, peel off the lining paper and cool. Drizzle the figs with extra honey before serving.

MOROCCAN SERPENT CAKE

This is perhaps the most famous of all Moroccan pastries, filled with lightly fragrant almond paste.

8 sheets of filo pastry
50g/2oz/¼ cup butter, melted
1 egg, beaten
5ml/1 tsp ground cinnamon
icing sugar, for dusting

FOR THE ALMOND PASTE
about 50g/2oz/¼ cup butter, melted
225g/8oz/2 cups ground almonds
2.5ml/½ tsp almond essence
50g/2oz/½ cup icing sugar
egg yolk, beaten
15ml/1 tbsp rose water or orange
flower water (optional)

SERVES 8

1. First make the almond paste. Blend the melted butter with the ground almonds and almond essence. Add the icing sugar, egg yolk and rose or orange flower water, if using, mix well and knead until soft and pliable. Chill the paste for about 10 minutes.

2. Break the almond paste into 10 balls. Roll them into 10cm/4in "sausages". Chill again.

3. Preheat the oven to 180°C/350°F/Gas 4, then place two sheets of filo pastry on a work surface so that they overlap to form an 18 × 56cm/7 × 22in rectangle. Brush the overlapping pastry to secure and then brush all over with butter. Cover with another two sheets of filo and brush again with butter.

4. Place five "sausages" of almond paste along the lower edge of the filo sheet and roll up the pastry tightly, tucking in the ends. Shape the roll into a loose coil. Repeat with the remaining filo and almond paste, so that you have two coils.

5. Brush a large baking sheet with butter and place the coils together to make a coiled "serpent".

6. Beat together the egg and half of the cinnamon. Brush over the pastry snake and then bake in the oven for 20–25 minutes until golden brown. Carefully invert the snake on to another baking sheet and return to the oven for 5–10 minutes until the side now uppermost is golden.

7. Place on a serving plate. Dust with icing sugar and then sprinkle with the remaining cinnamon. Serve warm.

CASSATA

*Another version of a world-famous dessert. Unlike Sicilian Ricotta Cake,
this one flavours the ricotta with chocolate and uses coffee and rum for soaking the sponge biscuit layer.
Try to track down authentic Savoiardi biscuits.*

500g/1¼lb/2½ cups ricotta cheese
75g/3oz/¾ cup icing sugar, plus extra
for dusting
2.5ml/½ tsp pure vanilla essence
grated rind and juice of
1 small orange
50g/2oz dark chocolate, grated
250g/9oz/1½ cups mixed candied
fruits, such as orange, pineapple,
citron, cherries and angelica
250ml/8fl oz/1 cup freshly brewed
strong black coffee
120ml/4fl oz/½ cup rum
24 Savoiardi biscuits
geranium leaves, to decorate

SERVES 8

1 Line the base and sides of a
20cm/8in round cake tin with
clear film. Put the ricotta in a bowl.
Sift in the icing sugar, then add the
vanilla essence with the orange rind
and juice. Beat until smooth, then stir
in the chocolate.

2 Cut the candied fruits into small
pieces and stir into the ricotta.

3 Mix the coffee and rum. Line
the bottom of the tin with
biscuits, dipping each biscuit in the
coffee mixture first. Cut the remaining
biscuits in half, dip them in the liquid
and arrange around the sides.

4 Spoon the cassata mixture into
the centre and level the top.
Cover with more clear film, then
place a plate on top that fits exactly
inside the rim of the tin. Weight this
with a bag of dried beans or sugar,
then chill overnight until firm.

5 Turn out to serve, shaking the
tin firmly if necessary and
tugging the clear film gently. Lift the
clear film off. Dust the top of the
cassata with a little sifted icing sugar
and serve in wedges, decorated with
geranium leaves.

SPICY FRUIT CAKE FROM SIENA

*This is a delicious flat cake, known as panforte, with a wonderful spicy flavour. It is very rich,
so it should be cut into small wedges. Offer a glass of sparkling wine to go with it.*

butter, for greasing
175g/6oz/1 cup hazelnuts,
roughly chopped
75g/3oz/⅓ cup whole almonds,
roughly chopped
225g/8oz/1⅓ cups mixed candied
fruits, diced
1.5ml/¼ tsp ground coriander
4ml/¾ tsp ground cinnamon
1.5ml/¼ tsp ground cloves
1.5ml/¼ tsp grated nutmeg
50g/2oz/½ cup plain flour
115g/4oz/⅓ cup honey
115g/4oz/generous 1 cup
granulated sugar
icing sugar, for dusting

SERVES 12–14

 Preheat the oven to 180°C/
350°F/Gas 4. Grease a 20cm/8in
round cake tin. Line the base with
non-stick baking paper.

 Spread the nuts on a baking
sheet and lightly toast in the
oven for about 10 minutes. Remove
and set aside. Lower the oven
temperature to 150°C/300°F/Gas 2.

3 In a large mixing bowl, mix the
candied fruits with all the spices
and the flour, and stir together with a
wooden spoon. Add the nuts and stir
in thoroughly.

4 In a small heavy saucepan, stir
together the honey and sugar,
and bring to the boil. Cook the
mixture until it reaches 138°C/280°F
on a sugar thermometer or when a
small amount spooned into iced water
forms a hard ball when pressed
between the fingertips. Take care
when doing this.

5 At this stage, immediately pour
the sugar syrup into the dry
ingredients and stir in well until
evenly coated. Pour into the prepared
cake tin. Dip a spoon into water and
use the back of the spoon to press
the mixture firmly into the tin. Bake
in the oven for 1 hour.

6 When ready, the cake will still
feel quite soft, but will harden
as it cools. Cool completely in the tin
and then turn out on to a serving
plate. Cut into wedges and dust with
icing sugar before serving.

BISCOTTI

These lovely Italian biscuits are part-baked, sliced to reveal a feast of mixed nuts and then baked again until crisp and golden. Traditionally they're served dipped in Vin Santo, a sweet dessert wine - perfect for rounding off a Mediterranean meal.

50g/2oz/¼ cup unsalted butter, softened
115g/4oz/½ cup caster sugar
175g/6oz/1½ cups self-raising flour
1.5ml/¼ tsp salt
10ml/2 tsp baking powder
5ml/1 tsp ground coriander
finely grated rind of 1 lemon
50g/2oz/½ cup polenta
1 egg, lightly beaten
10ml/2 tsp brandy or orange-flavoured liqueur
50g/2oz/½ cup unblanched almonds
50g/2oz/½ cup pistachio nuts

MAKES 24

1 Preheat the oven to 160°C/325°F/Gas 3. Lightly grease a baking sheet. Cream together the butter and sugar.

2 Sift all the flour, salt, baking powder and coriander into the bowl. Add the lemon rind, polenta, egg and brandy or liqueur and mix together to make a soft dough.

3 Stir in the nuts until evenly combined. Halve the mixture. Shape each half into a flat sausage about 23cm/9in long and 6cm/2½in wide. Bake for about 30 minutes until risen and just firm. Remove from oven.

4 When cool, cut each sausage diagonally into 12 thin slices. Return to the baking sheet and cook for a further 10 minutes until crisp.

5 Transfer to a wire rack to cool completely. Store in an airtight tin for up to 1 week.

COOK'S TIP
Use a sharp, serrated knife to slice the cooled biscuits, otherwise they will crumble.

CINNAMON ROLLS

These delicately spicy rolls are delicious served fresh for breakfast or tea, spread with butter.

FOR THE DOUGH
400g/14oz/3½ cups strong white flour
2.5ml/½ tsp salt
30ml/2 tbsp caster sugar
5ml/1 tsp easy-blend dried yeast
45ml/3 tbsp oil
1 egg
120ml/4fl oz/½ cup warm milk
120ml/4fl oz/½ cup warm water

FOR THE FILLING
40g/1½oz/3 tbsp butter, softened
25g/1oz/2–3 tbsp dark brown sugar
2.5–5ml/½–1 tsp ground cinnamon
15ml/1 tbsp raisins or sultanas

MAKES 24 SMALL ROLLS

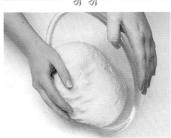

1 Preheat the oven to 200°C/ 400°F/Gas 6. Sift together the flour, salt and sugar, and sprinkle over the yeast. Mix the oil, egg, milk and water, and add to the flour. Mix to a dough, then knead until smooth. Leave to rise in a covered bowl until doubled in bulk, then knock back again.

2 Roll out the dough into a large rectangle and cut in half vertically. Spread over the softened butter, reserving 15ml/1 tbsp for brushing. Mix together the brown sugar and cinnamon, and sprinkle this over the top. Dot the surface with the raisins or sultanas.

3 Roll each piece into a long Swiss roll shape, to enclose the filling. Cut into 2.5cm/1in slices, arrange flat on a greased baking sheet and brush with the remaining butter. Leave to rise again for 30 minutes.

4 Bake the cinnamon rolls in the preheated oven for about 20 minutes. Leave to cool on a wire rack.

FLAKED ALMOND BISCUITS

These well-travelled biscuits have their origins in Greece and are now enjoyed in several Eastern Mediterranean countries, including Israel.

175g/6oz/³/4 cup butter or margarine
225g/8oz/2 cups self-raising flour, plus
extra for dusting
150g/5oz/¹/2 cup caster sugar
2.5ml/¹/2 tsp ground cinnamon
1 egg, separated
30ml/2 tbsp cold water
50g/2oz/¹/2 cup flaked almonds

MAKES ABOUT 30

1 Preheat the oven to 180°C/350°F/Gas 4. Rub the butter or margarine into the flour. Reserve 15ml/1 tbsp sugar and mix the rest with the cinnamon. Stir into the flour and then add the egg yolk and cold water and mix to a dough.

2 Roll the dough out on a lightly floured board. When 1cm/¹/2in thick, sprinkle over the almonds. Continue rolling, pressing all the almonds into the dough until it is about 5mm/¹/4in thick.

3 Using a fluted round cutter, cut the dough into rounds. Use a palette knife to lift them on to an ungreased baking sheet. Re-form the dough and cut more rounds to use it all up. Whisk the white of the egg lightly, brush it over the biscuits, and sprinkle over the reserved sugar.

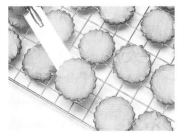

4 Bake in the centre of the oven for about 10–15 minutes or until golden. To remove, slide a palette knife under the biscuits. They will still seem a bit soft, but will harden as they cool. Leave on a wire rack until quite cold.

SEMOLINA AND NUT HALVA

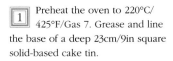

Semolina is a popular ingredient in many desserts and pastries in the Eastern Mediterranean. Here it provides a spongy base for soaking up a deliciously fragrant spicy syrup.

1 Preheat the oven to 220°C/ 425°F/Gas 7. Grease and line the base of a deep 23cm/9in square solid-based cake tin.

2 Lightly cream the butter in a bowl. Add the sugar, orange rind and juice, eggs, semolina, baking powder and hazelnuts and beat the ingredients together until smooth.

3 Turn into the prepared tin and level the surface. Bake for 20–25 minutes until just firm and golden. Leave to cool in the tin.

4 To make the syrup, put the sugar in a small heavy-based saucepan with 575ml/18fl oz/2¼ cups water and the half cinnamon sticks. Heat gently, stirring, until the sugar has dissolved completely.

5 Bring to the boil and boil fast, without stirring, for 5 minutes. Measure half the boiling syrup and add the lemon juice and orange flower water to it. Pour over the halva. Reserve the remainder of the syrup in the pan.

6 Leave the halva in the tin until the syrup is absorbed then turn it out on to a plate and cut diagonally into diamond-shaped portions. Scatter with the nuts.

7 Boil the remaining syrup until slightly thickened then pour it over the halva. Scatter the shredded orange rind over the cake and serve with lightly whipped or clotted cream.

FOR THE HALVA
*115g/4oz/½ cup unsalted butter,
softened
115g/4oz/½ cup caster sugar
finely grated rind of 1 orange, plus
30ml/2 tbsp juice
3 eggs
175g/6oz/1 cup semolina
10ml/2 tsp baking powder
115g/4oz/1 cup ground hazelnuts*

TO FINISH
*350g/12oz/1½ cups caster sugar
2 cinnamon sticks, halved
juice of 1 lemon
60ml/4 tbsp orange flower water
50g/2oz/½ cup unblanched hazelnuts,
toasted and chopped
50g/2oz/½ cup blanched almonds,
toasted and chopped
shredded rind of 1 orange*

SERVES 10

COOK'S TIP
Be sure to use a deep solid-based cake tin, rather than one with a loose base, otherwise the syrup might seep out.

GAZELLES' HORNS

Kaab el Ghzal is one of Morocco's favourite and best known pastries — so popular, in fact, that the French have honoured it with their own name, Cornes de Gazelles. The horn-shaped, filled pastries are commonly served at wedding celebrations.

200g/7oz/1¾ cups plain flour
pinch of salt
25g/1oz/2 tbsp butter, melted
30ml/2 tbsp orange flower water
1 large egg yolk, beaten
icing sugar, to serve

FOR THE ALMOND PASTE
200g/7oz/scant 2 cups
ground almonds
115g/4oz/1 cup icing sugar
30ml/2 tbsp orange flower water
25g/1oz/2 tbsp butter, melted
2 egg yolks, beaten
2.5ml/½ tsp ground cinnamon

MAKES ABOUT 16

1 First make the almond paste. Mix together all the ingredients to make a smooth paste.

2 Make the pastry. Mix the flour with the salt. Stir in the melted butter, orange flower water and about three-quarters of the egg yolk. Stir in enough cold water to make a fairly soft dough.

3 Knead the dough for about 10 minutes until smooth and elastic, then place on a floured surface and roll out as thinly as possible. Cut the dough into long strips about 7.5cm/3in wide.

4 Preheat the oven to 180°C/ 350°F/Gas 4. Pinch off small pieces of the almond paste and roll them between your hands into thin "sausages" about 7.5cm/3in long with tapering ends.

5 Place these in a line along one side of the strips of pastry, about 3cm/1¼in apart. Dampen the pastry edges with water and then fold the other half of the strip over the filling and press the edges together.

6 Using a pastry wheel, cut around each "sausage" to make a crescent. Make sure that the edges are firmly pinched together.

7 Prick the crescents with a fork and place on a buttered baking sheet. Brush with the remaining egg yolk and bake for 12–16 minutes until lightly coloured. Cool and then dust with icing sugar.

CHURROS

These Spanish doughnuts are commercially deep-fried in huge coils and broken off into smaller lengths for selling. Serve this home-made version freshly cooked, with hot chocolate or strong coffee.

200g/7oz/1¾ cups plain flour
1.5ml/¼ tsp salt
30ml/2 tbsp caster sugar
60ml/4 tbsp olive or sunflower oil
1 egg, beaten
caster sugar and ground cinnamon,
for dusting
oil for deep frying

MAKES 12–15

1 Sift the flour, salt and sugar on to a plate or piece of paper. Heat 250ml/8fl oz/1 cup water in a saucepan with the oil until it boils.

2 Tip in the flour mixture and beat with a wooden spoon until the mixture forms a stiff paste. Leave to cool for 2 minutes.

3 Gradually beat in the egg until smooth. Oil a large baking sheet. Sprinkle plenty of sugar on to a plate and stir in a little cinnamon.

4 Put the dough in a large piping bag fitted with a 1cm/½in plain piping nozzle. Pipe little coils or "s" shapes on to the baking sheet.

5 Heat 5cm/2in of oil in a large pan to 168°C/336°F or until a little dough sizzles on the surface.

6 Using an oiled fish slice, lower several of the piped shapes into the oil and cook for about 2 minutes until light golden.

7 Drain on kitchen paper then coat with the sugar and cinnamon mixture. Cook the remaining churros in the same way and serve immediately.

ALMOND FINGERS

———

This is a very simple sweetmeat, which is especially popular in the countries that border the Eastern Mediterranean. In Arab countries it is known as Zeinab's Fingers.

200g/7oz/1¾ cups ground almonds
50g/2oz/½ cup ground pistachio nuts
50g/2oz/¼ cup sugar
15ml/1 tbsp rose water
2.5ml/½ tsp ground cinnamon
12 sheets of filo pastry
115g/4oz/½ cup butter, melted
icing sugar, to decorate

MAKES UP TO 48

1 Preheat the oven to 160°C/ 325°F/Gas 3. Mix together the almonds, pistachio nuts, sugar, rose water and ground cinnamon for the filling.

2 Cut each sheet of filo pastry into four rectangles. Work with one rectangle at a time, covering the rest with a damp dish towel to prevent them from drying out.

3 Brush one of the rectangles of filo pastry with a little melted butter and place a heaped teaspoon of the nut filling in the centre.

4 Fold in the sides and roll into a cigar shape. Continue making "cigars" until all the filling has been used. Place the fingers on a greased baking sheet. Bake for 30 minutes, until lightly golden. Cool, dust with icing sugar and serve.

COCONUT HALVA

———

This delicious coconut cake can be served either hot as a dessert or cold with tea or strong black coffee.

115g/4oz/½ cup unsalted butter
175g/6oz/¾ cup sugar
50g/2oz/½ cup plain flour
150g/5oz/scant 1 cup semolina
75g/3oz/1 cup shredded coconut
175ml/6fl oz/¾ cup milk
5ml/1 tsp baking powder
5ml/1 tsp pure vanilla essence
almonds, to decorate

FOR THE SYRUP
115g/4oz/½ cup caster sugar
150ml/¼ pint/⅔ cup water
15ml/1 tbsp lemon juice

SERVES 4–6

1 First make the syrup. Place the sugar, water and lemon juice in a saucepan, stir to mix, then bring to the boil. Simmer for 6–8 minutes, until the syrup has thickened. Allow to cool and chill.

2 Preheat the oven to 180°C/ 350°F/Gas 4. Melt the butter in a pan. Add the sugar, flour, semolina, shredded coconut, milk, baking powder and vanilla essence, and mix thoroughly.

3 Pour the cake mixture into a shallow baking tin, flatten the top and bake for 30–45 minutes, until the top is golden.

4 Remove the halva from the oven and cut into diamond-shaped lozenges. Pour the cold syrup evenly over the top and decorate each lozenge with an almond placed in the centre.

DATE MA-AMOUL

From Gibraltar to Baghdad, women used to get together to make hundreds of these labour-intensive, date-filled pastries. Making a small quantity is not nearly so laborious. These make a delicious sweet snack which will be particularly welcome to children.

75g/3oz/6 tbsp butter or margarine, softened
175g/6oz/1½ cups plain flour, sifted
5ml/1 tsp rose water
5ml/1 tsp orange flower water
45ml/3 tbsp water
20ml/4 tsp sifted icing sugar, for sprinkling

FOR THE FILLING
115g/4oz/²⁄₃ cup stoned dates
2.5ml/½ tsp orange flower water

MAKES ABOUT 25

1 To make the filling, separate the dates from each other. Chop the dates finely with a very sharp, smooth-edged knife. Add 60ml/4 tbsp boiling water and the orange flower water, beat the mixture vigorously until it almost becomes a purée. Put the mixture to one side and leave it until it is cool.

2 To make the pastries, rub the butter or margarine into the flour. If the butter is hard, it may be helpful to chop it into small pieces first. Add the rose and orange flower waters and the water, and mix to make a firm dough.

3 Shape the dough into about 25 small balls, by rolling about a teaspoonful of mixture between your hands. Keep your hands cool.

4 Preheat the oven to 180°C/350°F/Gas 4. Press your finger into each ball so that it forms a small container in which to put the date mixture. Press the sides round and round to make the walls quite thin. Put about 1.5ml/¼ tsp of the date mixture carefully into each one. Then seal each ball by pressing the edges of the pastry together.

5 Arrange the date pastries, seam side down, on a lightly greased baking sheet and prick each one with a fork or, if you prefer to use the traditional method, use tweezers. Bake for 15–20 minutes, then remove the pastries from the oven and allow them to cool.

6 When the pastries are cool, put them on to a plate and sprinkle generously with sifted icing sugar. Shake the plate lightly and make sure that the date ma-amoul are all well-covered with the icing sugar.

COOK'S TIP
The secret of good Ma-amoul is to get as much date filling into the pastry as possible, but you must be sure to seal the opening well. The traditional way to decorate them was to make a pattern using tweezers, but it is quicker to use a fork. Orange flower water is now readily available in most supermarkets; it is usually found in the baking section.

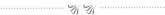

BAKLAVA

This is the queen of all pastries, with its exotic flavours. It is served in Greece, Turkey and further east, often with a cup of strong black coffee.

350g/12oz/3 cups ground
pistachio nuts
150g/5oz/1¼ cups icing sugar
15ml/1 tbsp ground cardamom
150g/5oz/⅔ cup unsalted
butter, melted
18 sheets filo pastry

FOR THE SYRUP
450g/1lb/2 cups granulated sugar
300ml/½ pint/1¼ cups water
30ml/2 tbsp rose water

SERVES 6–8

1. First make the syrup. Place the sugar and water in a saucepan, bring to the boil and then simmer for 10 minutes until syrupy. Stir in the rose water and leave to cool.

2. Mix together the nuts, icing sugar and cardamom. Preheat the oven to 160°C/325°F/Gas 3.

3. Brush a large rectangular baking tin with melted butter. Taking one sheet of filo pastry at a time, and keeping the remainder covered with a damp dish towel, brush the sheets with melted butter and lay on the bottom of the tin. Continue until you have six buttered layers in the tin. Spread half of the nut mixture over, pressing down with a spoon.

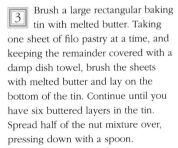

4. Take another six sheets of filo pastry, brush with butter and lay over the nut mixture. Sprinkle over the remaining nuts and top with a final layer of six filo sheets, brushed again with butter. Cut the pastry diagonally into small lozenge shapes using a sharp knife. Pour the remaining melted butter over the top.

5. Bake for 20 minutes and then increase the heat to 200°C/400°F/Gas 6. Bake for 15 minutes more, until light golden in colour.

6. Remove from the oven and drizzle about three-quarters of the syrup over the pastry, reserving the remainder for serving. Arrange the baklava lozenges on a large dish and serve with extra syrup.

CINNAMON BALLS

Ground almonds or hazelnuts form the basis of most Passover cakes and biscuits. These balls should be soft inside, with a very strong cinnamon flavour. They harden with keeping, so it is a good idea to freeze some and only use them when required.

3 Wet your hands with cold water and roll small spoonfuls of the mixture into balls. Place these at intervals on the baking sheet.

4 Bake for about 15 minutes in the centre of the oven. They should be slightly soft inside – too much cooking will make them hard and tough.

5 Slide a palette knife under the balls to release them from the baking sheet, and leave to cool. Sift a few tablespoons of icing sugar on to a plate and when the cinnamon balls are cold, slide them on to the plate. Shake gently to completely cover the cinnamon balls in sugar. Store in an airtight container or in the freezer.

oil, for greasing
175g/6oz/1½ cups ground almonds
75g/3oz/6 tbsp caster sugar
15ml/1 tbsp ground cinnamon
2 egg whites
icing sugar, for dredging

MAKES ABOUT 15

1 Preheat the oven to 180°C/ 350°F/Gas 4. Grease a large baking sheet with oil.

2 In a bowl, mix the ground almonds, sugar and cinnamon. Whisk the egg whites until they begin to stiffen; fold enough into the almonds to make a fairly firm mixture.